LIGHT FOR THE NEW MILLENNIUM

Seele gesprochen oder geschrieben hätte.
Allein es giebt jetzt wirklich keinen
Mitteilungsweg. Jeder indirecte könnte
Unheil bringen.

Im Ganzen mußte der Weg zur Seele
so weiter gesucht werden wie ich Ihnen
im vorigen Jahre in Berlin gesagt
habe. Es verlaufen ja die Dinge dort
langsamer als hier. „Warum konnten
die Dinge nicht auch anders verlaufen?"
das wird oft gefragt. Dann aber
tritt die Frucht der Brief-Rücklesen
in ihre Wirkung und davon geht
dann aus ein Zusammenhang mit
den Gedanken der Geisteswissenschaft
ein großes Verständnis, daß alles,
was geschehen ist, eine geistige Not-
wendigkeit war und ist. „Man
muß ja nur sehen, was jetzt ist,
und man erkennt, warum es damals

Facsimile from a letter from Rudolf Steiner to Eliza von Moltke dated June 1920 (see page 257).

LIGHT FOR THE NEW MILLENNIUM

Rudolf Steiner's association with Helmuth and Eliza von Moltke

Letters, Documents and After-Death Communications

Edited by T.H. Meyer

RUDOLF STEINER PRESS
LONDON

Translated by Heidi Herrmann-Davey, William Forward and
Martin Askew

Rudolf Steiner Press
51 Queen Caroline Street
London W6 9QL

Published by Rudolf Steiner Press 1997

Originally published in German in two volumes under the title *Helmuth von
Moltke, Dokumente zu seinem Leben und Wirken* by Perseus Verlag, Basel 1993

A catalogue record for this book is available from the British Library

ISBN 1 85584 051 0

Cover by Andrew Morgan
Typeset by DP Photosetting, Aylesbury, Bucks
Printed and bound in Great Britain by Cromwell Press Limited,
Broughton Gifford, Wiltshire

Contents

PART TWO

List of Illustrations

Foreword to the English Edition

This single-volume edition for English-speaking readers originally appeared in two separate German-language volumes in 1993. Volume I covers Moltke's life up to his death in 1916 and includes key documents about the outbreak of the war. It represents the exoteric side of Moltke's life and work. Volume II contains all the after-death messages. The two parts of the present book roughly retain this basic structure of the German edition. But it was found appropriate to shorten the contents of the first German volume considerably as some of its documents—e.g., some letters by Moltke to his wife—are of a more special character and might be less interesting to English readers.* Part Two has only been shortened very slightly. Any shortening within a document is indicated by an ellipsis within two brackets—(...).

Part One now almost exclusively contains those letters and documents to whose contents there is a reference somewhere in the after-death messages in Part Two. Thus readers who are especially interested in finding and comparing the exoteric description of some events with their corresponding after-death esoteric messages or comments will find this easier than in the more extensive German edition. In this respect the present English edition has an advantage over the German.

The essay by Johannes Tautz was originally written as an introduction to Part Two. For technical reasons it was put after the Introduction before all the documents in this book. As it deals extensively with Moltke's relationship with Rudolf Steiner, the reader might well come back to it after having read through Part One or even the whole book.

*

The second part of this book, in particular, requires some familiarity with, or at least a degree of serious interest in, the spiritual

---

*Among the omitted documents are a biographical sketch on Moltke by Jens Heisterkamp, two detailed studies on the Battle of the Marne by Jürgen von Grone, as well as some letters by Moltke to his wife of a more personal character.

science of Rudolf Steiner. It cannot be our task here to give a general outline of this science, which is by no means a negation of natural science but rather its natural-organic complement. For a more detailed study of spiritual science the reader is referred to the numerous English publications of Steiner's works from the Rudolf Steiner Press. But a few remarks may be of some help. *The Philosophy of Freedom*, *Occult Science* and some lectures on the Folk Souls are fundamental to the background of Part Two. In *Occult Science* and other works Steiner describes the method of developing higher forms of cognition. Only through these could the messages contained in Part Two be received. Steiner speaks of the faculties of Imagination, Inspiration and Intuition and shows 1) how they can be developed and 2) that they lead to a knowledge of supersensible facts and beings that is just as exact and objective as any really scientific knowledge on the level of natural science. Many people believe that the results of spiritual science cannot be verified but must be taken on authority. This is in itself an unscientific prejudice for it is not based on facts. Generally speaking, any results of spiritual scientific research may be verified in basically three ways: 1) As to the inner logic prevailing in the research presented; 2) By relating the results of spiritual scientific research to ordinary life and asking whether the latter becomes more comprehensible by taking them into account; 3) By adopting the methods given by Rudolf Steiner to develop the spiritual faculties of Imagination, Inspiration and Intuition for oneself. Of course, the third way of verifying is in itself a (spiritually) scientific one and therefore the highest of the three. But nobody is likely to arrive at this level who refrains from checking in the first two ways. And this can be done by everyone. Any blanket rejection of spiritual scientific results, however, without verifying them at all, cannot, of course, claim to be scientific.

The messages in Part Two of this book are a perfect example of the exercise of both Intuition and Inspiration. For it is by no means Inspiration alone which would be enough to be sure about the actual source of these messages. Only combined with Intuition, in the technical sense of the term, could Steiner know from which spiritual entity they were proceeding. Herein lies the fundamental difference to so-called 'channelling'. In most cases Intuition plays no part in the process of receiving 'channelled' material, with the consequence that no certainty about the source of the messages can be attained, with a concomitantly high risk of deception and illusion. To refer to 'channelling' in the context of Rudolf Steiner's communications with the Moltke soul is tantamount to abrogating the initiate's ability to communicate with the dead in full waking consciousness. Hence objections of this nature can only spring from a total misapprehension and ignorance of the methods of spiritual cognition introduced by Rudolf Steiner to modern humanity.

Furthermore, Part Two of this book also provides a wonderful example of a fundamental feature of the basic aim of all science in general, and of spiritual science in particular: not to develop any subjective opinions about the world and its phenomena, but to let the world speak its own truth. In such a way Steiner enabled the deceased Moltke soul to speak the truth he was experiencing within the spiritual world.

Of course, Steiner could have commented on these extraordinary messages. As far as I know, he never did, at least not in writing, but seems to have left it to Eliza von Moltke, Helmuth von Moltke's widow, to interpret and understand them. This, as the reader will soon discover for himself, is by no means always an easy task. There are riddles in this book, especially in its second part. But riddles are a healthy means of developing a process of spiritual understanding. It may be conducive to such an understanding to structure the messages of Part Two from the point of view of the various 'themes' being introduced, followed up for some time and sometimes suddenly dropped again. In such a way we can distinguish some main thematic threads running through Part Two: the German Folk Spirit, karmic causes of the war, the ninth century, St Odilie, demonic beings, the Christ, Europe, future relations between East and West and the end of the century. Anyone who confines himself in a second, close reading to one or the other of these or other threads will have a remarkable experience. These 'subjects' seem to grow organically, they seem to breathe, and what is *not* being said appears to be a necessary fertilizer of this growth and breath. One should learn to listen also to the silence between the lines to get into the right mood and disposition for a fruitful reading of Part Two in particular.

In such a way Part Two could also serve as a kind of text book for a basic understanding of some key questions of supersensible realities, such as reincarnation and karma or the relationship between the living and the dead.

But the biographical basis in earthly life for the unique spiritual unfolding of the after-death experiences is presented in Part One of this book. It is the foundation without which these experiences would, so to speak, 'hang in the air'. And only after experiencing this foundation can there be a thorough understanding of the heavenly perspectives in the second part.

*

With regard to the genesis of this publication some personalities should be mentioned here without whom it would not exist. Jürgen von Grone (1887–1978), an air force officer during the First World War, and later a pupil of Rudolf Steiner, was an untiring defender of the true character of Moltke's exoteric life and work. He was a specialist in German war strategy and one of his essays met with the approval of the Military Archive of the German Federal Defence Forces. Grone was appointed by Astrid Bethusy-Huc (1882–1961), the elder daughter of Helmuth and Eliza von Moltke, to be the trustee of the manuscripts published in Part Two. Following Grone it was Johannes Tautz and the editor of the present volume who were authorized to publish these documents. A first typescript version was made by Emil Bock (1895–1959), a founding priest of the Christian Community. Bock was especially interested in Moltke's karmic background and the First World War.

During the war it was quite risky for Rudolf Steiner to send the after-death messages by mail to Berlin where Eliza von Moltke was living. They could have been regarded as meddling with political affairs, which might have endangered Steiner's neutral position in Switzerland. Thus, while he stayed in Dornach (Switzerland), he sometimes used a messenger who copied his notes, took them over the border and mailed them in Mannheim. This task was fulfilled by Helene Röchling (1866–1945), one of the great sponsors of the first Goetheanum building. Helene Röchling saw herself as a real Grail messenger with a holy task. That is why she sometimes signs her letters to Eliza von Moltke 'Kundry' (in the Wagnerian sense).

In the original manuscripts references to the individual Moltke family members (here in Part Two) were always abbreviated or coded in the following way: 'She' refers to Eliza von Moltke, 'it' to Astrid Bethusy and 'El' to the second daughter Else (see Introduction, page xvi).

The editor wishes to thank Heidi Herrmann-Davey, William

Forward and Martin Askew for the English translation. Heidi Herrmann translated almost all the documents in Part Two which, due to the unique nature of the messages, was a particular challenge. Finally, I wish to thank Sevak Gulbekian for his decision and courage to publish this book. May it be met with unbiased critical understanding. And by 'critical' is meant: may it be verified—in the threefold sense outlined above.

Thomas Meyer
Basel, 1 August 1997

Introduction
by Thomas H. Meyer

People on earth must learn from events that thoughts are facts.
Helmuth von Moltke, 24 May 1918

Twelve questions, or why this book was published

This book provides an opportunity to gain a deeper understanding of some key questions with which humanity was and still is confronted in the twentieth century.

These questions can be summarized as follows: 1) What were the origins of the First World War? 2) What was the share or 'guilt' of Germany in its unfolding, and what was the share of other European nations? 3) What is the true task of the German nation in the world and why did Germany—during the darkest hour of its history—degenerate into Hitlerism? 4) Is there also a spiritual evolution of individual man as well as of nations and humanity as a whole? 5) What is the destiny of the individual human soul after death? 6) Does reincarnation exist and, if so, in what way does it bear on historical events? 7) What is the function of evil in evolution? 8) What, after the demolition of all old social patterns and the structure of the classical nation state, is the future shape Europe should give itself? 9) How can a better understanding between the peoples of the world be attained for the third millennium? 10) Or is there an inevitably increasing 'clash of civilizations' awaiting humanity in the future? 11) Can man become able to really 'learn' from history? 12) Is there a science of the spirit and, if so, what can it contribute to solving those questions?

All these questions are intimately linked with the life and, in a very literal sense, also with the death of Helmuth von Moltke who, in the last two years of his life, became a friend and pupil of Rudolf Steiner (1861–1925), the Austrian-born philosopher and founder of spiritual science, later called 'Anthroposophy'. But let us first turn to some biographical facts from the life of von Moltke, as he is often confused with certain other personalities of the same name.

Which Moltke?

The name of Helmuth von Moltke is usually identified with the Prussian Field Marshal who won the war against the Austrians in 1866 and against the French in 1870/71, and who died in 1891. In other words, it is linked with the foundation and rise of the German Reich. Or else one thinks of Helmuth James von Moltke who was a leading figure in organizing the opposition to Hitler and who was executed in January 1945.

This book contains primarily documents from and about a third Moltke, who was the nephew of the Field Marshal and who led the German army into the First World War. Although his two name-sakes are widely known and appreciated today, little is known or rightly understood about this third important son of the Moltke family. A history of the Moltke family focusing on these three bearers of the name has been available in English since 1995: Otto Friedrich's book *Blood and Iron—from Bismarck to Hitler—The von Moltke Family's Impact on German History*.[1] The headings of the main parts of the book are 'The Field Marshal', 'The Martyr' and 'The Nervous Nephew', and they clearly reflect the factual recognition of the first, a high appreciation of the second and a prejudice against the third Moltke which still prevails today. In her widely-read book *The Guns of August*, Barbara Tuchman[2] provides a similarly biased picture of this Moltke, and within most German-language publications on the history of the First World War the general is by no means treated in a more balanced manner.[3] Another source on Moltke for the English-speaking public is *The Spear of Destiny* by Trevor Ravenscroft.[4] This book, however, which enjoys a certain popularity among some people with uncritical occult interests, is full of inadequacies and wild fantasies.[5] To sum up: Moltke is either unknown or depicted in a very distorted way. One of the chief aims of the present publication, therefore, has to be to set this record straight. And one of the key issues in this record is Moltke's association with Rudolf Steiner (1861–1925), the founder of spiritual science, later called 'Anthroposophy'. This is not an easy task as both Moltke and Steiner, as well as their close association, have been the subject of gross speculation and much slander.

Who was Helmuth von Moltke?

Helmuth von Moltke was born on 23 May 1848 on the estate of Gerstorff in Mecklenburg (Northern Germany). The Moltke family had been deprived of much of its wealth during the Napoleonic wars. The regional mood was that of old and noble Protestant families, landowners and officers of the more conservative kind with no inclination whatever to join in the choir of revolutionary voices that resounded throughout Europe in that year. Helmuth (Johannes Ludwig) was the second son of Augusta (née von Krohn) and Adolph von Moltke, the brother of the later Field Marshal Helmuth von Moltke. He spent his early childhood on the idyllic river island of Rantzau to the North of Hamburg. Four years before his death Moltke took a pleasure trip in a Zeppelin airship, flying over this very spot where he had spent the happiest years of his childhood. And this little scene is like a foreshadowing of what was going to happen *after* his death, but this is for later...

The young Moltke was highly interested in literature, history and music. He learned to play the cello with great skill and was to cultivate the arts throughout his whole life. After visiting the high school of Hamburg Altona, Moltke decided on a military career, having nearly opted for a training as a merchant or a seaman; in his youth he had wished to become a forester. Going into the military was a normal choice for a member of the impoverished nobility, but in his case it was also motivated by the high regard Moltke had always felt for his uncle. Thus at the age of 22 he participated in the Franco-Prussian war. Here he had his first serious encounter with the reality and mystery of death; while he himself barely escaped it, his lieutenant told him just before the first battle that he was going to die and presented him with a photograph on which he put a little cross instead of his signature. The whole company was killed in this battle—except Moltke.

When the German Reich was proclaimed in Versailles in January 1871, this was a significant 'event' in Moltke's life. For this Reich, he felt, he was going to live and work with all his strength—for as the vessel of the impulses of Goethe, Bach and Beethoven and innumerable other spirits, it seemed to him very worthy of consolidation and protection. That this vessel was increasingly to adopt quite another kind of impulse that involved empty power struggles and nationalism was one of the most painful disappointments Moltke had to encounter and overcome during his lifetime.

In 1876 he entered the 'Prussian Garde' and soon afterwards the Office of the Chief of the General Staff and the Berlin Military Academy. Moltke's appreciation of his uncle, whose personal adjutant he had become, was by no means confined to the Field Marshal's strategic abilities. For it was particularly in the house of the older Moltke that his nephew enjoyed many excellent music performances and met highly renowned singers and musicians. Joseph Joachim, the violinist and composer, performed regularly. And Joachim was a close friend of Herman Grimm, the Goethe scholar and author of the outstanding biography of Michelangelo. Grimm himself was the discoverer and friend of Ralph Waldo Emerson whom he introduced to Germany. Joachim's son, Herman, later became a colleague of the younger Moltke on the General Staff; he had a deep interest in spiritual questions and had become a devoted Freemason and a pupil of Rudolf Steiner. He died about a year after Moltke in 1917. Thus there was a sort of cosmopolitan cultural and artistic atmosphere in the house of the older Moltke, frequently visited by the younger. Almost all the letters in Part One of this book reflect something of this artistic side of Moltke: they are written in a prose which shows a kind of natural excellence. The same atmosphere prevailed in Kreisau (Silesia), the Field Marshal's retreat, with which the Kaiser had rewarded him for his victory in 1866. And it was only in the logic of things that Kreisau, which thus harboured the highest appreciation of true Germanic cultural achievements, later became through Helmuth James von Moltke the symbol of unrelenting opposition to Hitler.

Helmuth von Moltke was in his late twenties when he met the first of the three personalities who were—besides his uncle—to become the three pillars of his mature life: Eliza, Countess of Moltke-Hutfeldt from a Danish offshoot of the family. After her, only Wilhelm II and Rudolf Steiner played a similarly significant part in Moltke's life—of course, in quite different respects. Eliza was born in 1859 in Quesarum (Sweden), had herself deep artistic and spiritual interests and was—after a materialistic phase—confronted at an early age with some spiritualistic phenomena which convinced her of the reality of a living spiritual world. On the other hand she was a woman with both feet on the ground and with a keen sense of appreciation for other people in a very realistic way. The letters in Part One are almost exclusively addressed to her and show the deep bond of mutual understanding between the two lovers who married in 1878. Four children were born: Wilhelm (called Bill, 1881), Astrid (later countess Bethusy-Huc, 1882), Else (later Koennecke, 1885) and Adam (1887). Astrid shared most of her parents' interests. She had many far-reaching spiritual experiences herself and it was she who looked after the documents published in Part Two for many decades.

In 1888 Wilhelm II became the German emperor. And with this event the second 'pillar' in Moltke's life was pompously erected before his gaze.

In the nineties Moltke had to travel quite frequently and exten- sively, sometimes as Wilhelm II's emissary. And it is evident from his letters that he had a special love for Russia. But despite this love something mysterious and almost uncanny can be felt in the way he describes his first encounter with Tsar Nicholas II. In October 1895, when leaving the Tsar's room, one of his gloves fell to the ground as if pointing to a future disharmony between Germany and Russia ... (see page 41ff.). Moltke was always determined not to become one-sided in his outlook on the world and he therefore kept up with the historical, philosophical and theological literature of his day. He studied Chamberlain, Bebel, Eduard von Hartmann and the early works of Rudolf Steiner. Steiner had met Eliza von Moltke in 1903 in Berlin, and it was Eliza who told her husband about the spiritual science which Steiner was building up on the foundations of what Goethe had inaugurated. Thus Moltke studied Steiner's books on Nietzsche and Haeckel as well as his *Theosophy*, and on 8 March 1904 he writes to his wife: 'No other philosophizing author has so far been more comprehensible to me than he.' But he is no rash 'believer'. He submits everything he reads to the severe test of common sense and to the process of a kind of slow and thorough mental digestion. And, contrary to what has been told and retold many times, it was never he who invited Steiner to his Berlin home, but Eliza. And it was never matters belonging to Moltke's pro- fessional sphere which were discussed on those occasions but spiritual or cultural questions. There was one exception to this rule, and this was shortly before Moltke died. It is important to keep this in mind, for the theory has been invented that Moltke lost the Battle of the Marne *under Steiner's influence!*[3]

One year after having encountered Rudolf Steiner, Moltke was offered by Wilhelm II the post of the Chief of the General Staff, as Count Schlieffen, his predecessor, was getting too old. It was Schlieffen who—with regard to the complicated European system of alliances—had begun to prepare Germany for the eventuality of a war on two fronts and the younger Moltke was to take over and refine this strategy. But at first he declined the Kaiser's offer. He hoped 'that this cup would pass me by'. And in a conversation with the Kaiser he asked him whether he hoped to win twice in the same lottery—the younger Moltke's modesty did not permit him to bank on the victories and successes of his great uncle. As the Kaiser persisted, Moltke insisted on having a very frank conversation with him. In this conversation, which took place in January 1905, Moltke set out the stipulation under which he might be ready to accept the post: Wilhelm had to keep himself out of any military operations. For the Kaiser used to take an active part in the manoeuvres and it was clear to all involved that his side always had to win. This weakened the Army's confidence and cohesion considerably. The Kaiser accepted Moltke's condition and appointed him to the post in January 1906. It is in the letter of 29 January 1905, included in Part One of this book, that Moltke tells us this important story which shows his admirable lack of personal ambition, his sense of moral responsibility and his unusual straightforwardness in matters of truth.

Despite the new burden on Moltke's shoulders the letters written to his wife between 1906 and the outbreak of the war still reflect his interest in religious and cultural affairs or in visiting old sites like the famous Odilie's Mount in the Vosges (in June 1911). But as his life was now so closely linked to the destiny of Germany, it became more and more a mirror of the destiny of his own people.

Though Moltke was certainly not personally interested in leading Germany into war, he was realistic enough to see that events in Europe were increasingly tending towards one. On the one hand there was the growing rivalry between Germany and England in trade and commerce. As early as 1905 (3 August) Moltke writes to his wife: 'There is no need at present to fear the worst but there is enough inflammable matter around (...) The worst part for us is England's jealousy about our expanding commerce and industrial development.'

On the other hand Moltke was very aware of the disadvantages to the Slav people within the allied Austrian-Hungarian monarchy that led to the assassination of the Archduke Franz Ferdinand which, in turn, triggered the Serbian-Austrian conflict. We deliberately say Serbian-Austrian conflict, for there was no immediate necessity for Russia ever to involve itself in the conflict by mobilizing all its armies.

Illusions and expectations on 1 August 1914

For Moltke the outbreak of war coincided with the sudden and totally unexpected breakdown of confidence between the Kaiser and himself. This was by no means a purely personal or private affair for it had an impact on the whole future course of events. What brought about this tragic event in Germany which stood at the very beginning of the war? Let us briefly look at what happened in Berlin and London on 1 August.

At 5 p.m. the Kaiser proclaimed general mobilization. Russia had already effected its general mobilization the day before which was a threat not only to the Austrians, but to Germany as well. France had, like Germany, ordered general mobilization on 1 August. Shortly after 5 p.m. a telegram from Karl Max von Lichnowsky, the German ambassador in London, arrived in Berlin. Lord Edward Grey, the head of the British Foreign Office, had allegedly declared to Lichnowsky that 'England would pledge herself to prevent France from joining a war against Germany if Germany in turn were to pledge herself not to commit any hostile action against France'. On the basis of this telegram the Kaiser believed that England would adopt a neutral stance and would itself influence France towards neutrality if Germany refrained from marching through Belgium as provided for in the Schlieffen plan. The Kaiser sent for Moltke, explained the 'new' situation and joyfully declared: 'Now we simply post our entire army to the East!' With this action he broke his own pledge given to Moltke as the condition for his acceptance of the post of Chief of Staff. In this way the Kaiser, who was an absolute dilettante in matters of war strategy, destroyed the confidence between him and Moltke and was about to destroy years of the minutest planning. Moltke refused to obey the new 'order' from His Majesty. What followed were without any doubt the most painful hours in

Helmuth von Moltke's life. He just sat in his room, 'in sombre mood'.

In the late evening a second telegram arrived, this time from George V. It destroyed the illusion of any serious intention on the part of the British and the French to remain neutral. The Kaiser, already in his bedroom, again sent for Moltke and said: 'Now you may do as you wish!' Barbara Tuchman's comment on this scene is: 'Moltke, who clung to the pre-arranged plan, lacked the necessary courage for such a change'.[6] It was, however, not a question of courage at all but of a realistic assessment of the European situation. And the second telegram would have required even more of this strange sort of 'courage'—to change the whole strategy once more! To Moltke's keen eye for political realities the first telegram had seemed illusory from the outset.

Some deeper causes for the outbreak of the War

The movement of German troops into Belgium on 3 August caused Britain, as is well known, to declare war. If, as has always been emphasized, the key political powers in Great Britain had indeed wished for nothing more than to keep out of the war, it is difficult to reconcile the actual conduct of the British Government between 1 and 3 August 1914 with this desire. This is a point to which historians have given too little or no attention so far. Nevertheless, it was documented long ago, though this is by no means widely enough known, that in certain circles in England, to which Edward VII also belonged, there had already in the 1880s been talk of the necessity of the next great European War. C.G. Harrison very openly spoke about such views in his lectures *The Transcendental Universe* held in 1893 in a London club.[7] Such views were linked with definite plans for a radical restructuring of all future social conditions in Europe and in the Slav East. In place of the old monarchies there were to be republics everywhere—indeed, in Germany there was to be more than one! And Russia had been selected as *terra nova* for 'experiments in socialism' unsuited for the western populations. An apparently harmless echo of such far-sighted international planning in the West—of which there has hitherto been no evidence in Central Europe—may be found in the 1890 Christmas edition of the satirical magazine *Truth* which illustrates such intentions in a remarkable way on a map of Europe (see page xxxiv). The map is entitled 'The Kaiser's Dream' and shows Wilhelm II revealing his worst fears for the future under the influence of hypnosis. What does he see? He sees a completely post-monarchic Europe! Everywhere republics, and over Russia the enigmatic words 'Russian desert', which means territory for experimenting with new forms of social conditions.

Was not the Kaiser, with his sabre-rattling superficiality and pomposity, indeed an idle dreamer, compared to the skilled statesmen of the West, such as Disraeli, Lord Salisbury, Lord Rosebery or Gladstone—as may be seen by his behaviour on 1 August 1914? And were not Lord Rosebery or Cecil Rhodes and others much more realistic in their 'dreams' than Wilhelm had ever been in his ordinary waking life? And did they not 'dream' of the universal power that should be given to the English-speaking nations in the modern industrialized era? And did some of these statesmen, like Rhodes, not think in terms of long-range spiritual laws governing the rise and decline of nations and people?

Was it not so that German export figures had risen to alarming heights in the years preceding the war? Did they not represent unwanted competition for Great Britain? And how could one become the teacher and thus the ruler of the young Slav peoples in the 'Russian desert', if an economically and politically strong Central Europe remained independent between the East and the West?

Certainly the British *people* did not want war, as it is rarely ever the people which wants any war. Neither did many leading Members of Parliament. The deciding influence on Britain's diplomatic moves in the first days of August must therefore have issued from quite other circles in Great Britain. The time may not be too far off when such questions may be taken more seriously in connection with the outbreak of the First World War and possibly also in relation to the immediate future of Europe.

A document that could have changed world history

It cannot be denied that it would still have been possible to confine the war to the East if an official British declaration of neutrality had been given. And Germany made an attempt to get such an English guarantee. On the very same day (1 August) Lichnowsky had put the question to the British Foreign Minister Grey, 'whether Britain would agree to remain neutral if the Germans respected Belgium's neutrality. Sir Edward Grey would not give this assurance, wishing to keep his options open.'[8] Thus it would only have needed a firm commitment on the part of Sir Edward Grey for the war in the West to have been avoided. There are three facts which historians till now have not dealt with in appropriate objectivity: 1) There was no need for Russia to order general mobilization at that stage of events; 2) England had the choice of giving an assurance of neutrality in the West; 3) On the night of 30 July Helmuth von Moltke decided to wait for a third confirmation of the mobilization in Russia (which was also directed against Germany) before he was going to advise the Kaiser to order general mobilization.[9] It was and is unjust and utterly absurd to accuse a nation with such a chaotic leadership as that provided by Wilhelm II, and such a highly conscientious military leadership as that represented by Helmuth von Moltke, of having willingly and consciously led Europe into the abyss of war. This, however, was stated in the Versailles treaty of 1919 where Germany was held 'solely guilty' for the war, and has been re-stated again and again, by German historians, too, up to the present day. (With regard to this question see also notes 55–57 of Part One and note 66 of Part Two.)

It was precisely in this direction that Rudolf Steiner took action after Moltke's death in 1916 and before the final proclamation of the so-called Peace Treaty of Versailles. Steiner's efforts in this direction were based on Moltke's 'Reflections and Memories' which he wrote down in November 1914 immediately after his dismissal by the Kaiser from the post of Chief of the General Staff (see next sub-heading). Moltke wrote these memories for his wife without any intention of ever publishing them. In 1919 Eliza von Moltke consented to a publication by Steiner. Steiner wrote a foreword and published the memories under the title 'Who was to blame for the War? Thoughts and recollections of the Chief of Staff H. v. Moltke on the events of July 1914 to November 1914.'

First of all Steiner wanted the Germans to have clear ideas about the outbreak of the war. He begins his foreword with the words: 'The German people must confront the truth about the outbreak of the war.' He considered Moltke's memoirs as 'the most important document to be found in Germany on the beginnings of the war'. Moltke's memoirs show that in the years leading up to the war, and quite particularly on 1 August 1914, Germany's political leadership had reached an absolute 'nadir', as Steiner puts it. Had this little publication appeared in time it would undoubtedly have had a very significant influence on the progress of the peace negotiations in Versailles. It would, above all, have been of cardinal importance in forming a judgement on the question of who was to blame for the war's outbreak. One has only to think of the extent to which the fatal paragraph 231 of the Versailles treaty, which attributed sole blame to Germany, provoked and contributed to the rise of right-wing forces in post-war Germany to realize the impact the prevention of its publication had on the history of the twentieth century.

As soon as the brochure was printed an impatient anthroposophist handed it on prematurely (see document No. 66 on page 250f and the notes to it). Thus it immediately came into the hands of Germany's military leadership. Its publication was then prevented, primarily by General Wilhelm von Dommes, who intervened at the end of May 1919 on behalf of the Supreme Command and the German Foreign Office with Moltke's widow and then with Rudolf Steiner as the publisher of Moltke's notes. In the course of an interview with Steiner in Stuttgart, which lasted several hours, von Dommes made the point that there were three factual errors in Moltke's notes, and that they could not therefore be published. Dommes declared that he was prepared to testify on oath to the erroneousness of these three points. If Steiner had gone on and published the brochure anyway and had sent it to Versailles he would have exposed himself to public ridicule—by trying to defend Germany without the backing of its own military and political leadership. Thus he was forced to give in.

In reality those around the Kaiser were anxious to avoid exposing to the whole world the pathetic house of cards which German politics had become—in contrast to its British counterpart which rested on incomparably firmer foundations! Thus a false national pride stood in the way of preventing a genuine disaster, and one which was to prove so ominous for the development of Central Europe: the fatal paragraph 231.

Only recently have von Dommes' diaries come to light in which he sets out in detail the conversation which he had with Steiner in the spring of 1919. The relevant passages are to be found on page 114ff. of this book.

Moltke, Steiner and the true German Folk Spirit

There is perhaps no clearer example of Steiner's attitude to the essential quality of the German spirit than the position he took on the question of war guilt. Yet even this has frequently been subject to dire misrepresentation. Steiner had energetically opposed the policy of attributing sole blame to Germany but in doing so he had, of course, never wished to present Germany as being 'completely innocent' as has been maintained even among those in sympathy with him.[10] For him Moltke's notes are 'a terrible indictment of [German] politics'; they prove that there was no German policy capable of preventing decisions being made on the basis of purely military considerations. Only by means of clearly defined policies could the events of the year 1914 have taken a different course to the one they did.

The true nature of Germany's 'guilt' lies in its failure to develop such policies. Thus Steiner's struggle to oppose the acceptance of the policy of the Entente in attributing sole blame to the Germans is at the same time the strongest possible rejection of Germany's political stance. How, in his eyes, should such a political stance have been conceived? In his own words: 'The German Reich had been placed into the context of world politics without having substantial aims to justify its existence. These aims should not have been such that they could be furthered only by military might, should, indeed, not in any sense have been directed towards the *exercise of power*. They should, on the contrary, have been directed towards the *inner* development of its culture. Such aims would never have made it necessary for Germany to concern itself with things which needs must place it in competition with, and then in open conflict with, other powers to which it must inevitably succumb in the exercise of *military power*. Far from developing power politics, a German Reich should have developed genuine cultural policies. The idea should never have arisen, in Germany of all places, that anyone who saw these cultural policies as the only possible ones would be an "unpractical idealist".' (See page 96.)

Inner development of culture, of faculties of the soul and the spirit and of a cosmopolitan attitude—these were what Steiner (and Moltke) saw as the principal mission of the German people. And Moltke, who used to carry Goethe's *Faust* in his pocket during maneouvres, had wished to place himself at the service of a Germany with such aims. An impulse of this kind towards inner development lay behind the words that Steiner wrote to Moltke in November 1915: 'This destiny of the German people is bound up with the deepest and most noble aims of human development.' Among these aims one can count the full emergence of the human being as a truly free spirit. But just because of this inner spiritual freedom, 'inner development' also bears within it the risk of illusion and untruth. Both aspects are reflected in the history of the German people: the ascent to the peaks of spiritual achievement but also the fall into the abysmal illusion of false, external power play and fictitious notions of racial supremacy. The latter tendency, of course, is identical with a *break* with the true German Folk Spirit. Steiner had already warned in 1888 that the increasing superficiality of German politics could lead to such a break—to the detriment of Germany and the whole world. And during the time of the holocaust brought about by Germany this break was complete.[11] National Socialism, therefore, has nothing whatsoever to do with the true German spirit, but is, on the contrary, only the expression of this break in its most radical form.

Moltke, at any rate, was well aware of the dangers threatening a further real ascent of the German people, when he wrote to his wife in 1904: 'The German people as a whole is a pathetic society. Full of politicians in ivory towers, lacking any trace of magnanimity, petty, mean, full of envy and resentment, hateful and myopic—one can only feel sorry for it. Everywhere things are torn down, soiled, there is slander and lies, and all in the guise of virtuous moral outrage. Hypocrisy wherever you look, mean-minded egotism and crass materialism. Ideals no longer have any validity, everything is outer semblance. Whatever still stands is torn down, everyone seeks to raise only himself, and when the great heap of ruins is complete, the judgement will fall upon us.'

And Steiner once said: 'If the German individual manages to truly grasp the spirit, he is a blessing for the world: if he does not, he is the world's scourge.'[12]

Moltke of all people was the man to feel deeply the truth of such words.

Where will the German people turn in the future—after all that has happened since the First World War, including the external union of the German Republics in 1989 which featured as early as 1890 on the political map referred to above? Will the individual

members of this people now turn with renewed strength to the
spiritual roots of its deeper mission? This would mean the fulfilment of the most earnest hopes of both Moltke and Steiner.

Retreat on the Marne, martyrdom and fantasies about the after-death messages

It was Moltke's destiny to himself become the target of the kind of
'slanders and lies' that he found at work among his compatriots.
And this in the most hideous manner and to the highest degree. For
it will be difficult to find another personality within German culture
of this century who has been similarly misrepresented in public
opinion—except for Rudolf Steiner. These slanders and lies, which
are endlessly repeated even now, usually focus on the part Moltke
played during the first weeks of the war.

Let us therefore briefly turn back to our General while he had the
task of leading German armies into war. Though the first weeks of
fighting in the West were successful for the Germans, after six
weeks the German armies suddenly retreated—undefeated. It was a
turning point in the whole war. The French spoke of the 'Miracle on
the Marne'.

As Jürgen von Grone points out in his contribution on page 127,
there were several factors which were decisive for the final loss of
the Battle of the Marne by the Germans despite the fact that they
were in a far better position than the enemy. Among the chief
factors are the following: after the break in confidence between
Moltke and the Kaiser, Moltke's instructions were ignored, particularly by the Headquarters of the 1st Army on the right wing
which advanced much too quickly. Moltke despatched a Lieutenant-Colonel to the front who spread false information with the
consequence that on 12 September he had to undertake what he
calls 'the hardest decision of my life which cost me my life-blood'—
he had to pull the army back. The Kaiser did not like the news of
this decision and broke his promise for a second time by requesting
Moltke to resign! General Falkenhayn was to replace him. But in
order to ameliorate the bad impression this rash change in leadership would have on the troops, Moltke agreed to cover Falkenhayn's decisions for the time being with his own name! And
Falkenhayn's decisions led only to the prolongation of the (mobile)
war (by turning it into a positional trench war) and to innumerable

victims on both sides. 'I was left like a bystander without any influence whatsoever,' Moltke writes in his memoirs. 'I took this martyrdom upon myself and covered all further operations with my name, for the sake of the country and to spare the Kaiser from any speculation that he had sent away his Chief of the General Staff at the very first setback.' 'Sparing' the Kaiser—this was more than martyrdom; it was actual heroism rising far above any considerations of personal sorrow and disappointment.

After his formal dismissal in November 1914 Moltke wrote down his memoirs, assisted in the occupation of Antwerp and later started to organize the chaotic production and circulation of food within the country. Still serving Germany!

It was after these painful events in the autumn of 1914 that Helmuth von Moltke moved for the first time into closer contact with Rudolf Steiner. Steiner wanted to help Moltke by trying to widen his soul's horizon beyond the boundaries of the physical world and of life between birth and death.

At this point a few words about Rudolf Steiner as a scientist of the spirit are necessary.[13] Steiner's spiritual science holds fast to the ideals of observation and exact thinking that have to reign in ordinary science. Its observations are not made in the physical world, however, but in spheres only perceivable after a certain 'inner development' has taken place. This is based on a special cultivation of the faculty of human thinking combined with certain moral exercises. 'For every step forward that you take in seeking knowledge of occult truths take three steps forward in the improvement of your own character.'[14] This was his 'Golden Rule' for any inner development leading to the faculty of spiritual observation. The assertion that spiritual science is just a new form of dogmatic belief would in itself be an expression of a (negative) dogmatic belief. (This is, of course, not to deny that a movement which in itself is in no way sectarian or dogmatic may have sectarian followers.) Thus in its methods spiritual science is just as exact and objective as any science which really deserves this name. Any open-minded study of the philosophical and scientific basis of Steiner's spiritual science can easily persuade any thinking person of the essentially scientific character of this supersensible field of research. But among those who have a dogmatic prejudice about the 'dogmatic' character of spiritual science or Anthroposophy, thinking is notably absent where it would be most needed, namely, in the formation of such a prejudice which is nowadays so wide-spread that it is even often considered to be scientific! It is necessary to make the above remarks since it may be seen from Tuchman's and Friedrich's and others' comments on Moltke and his achievements that the false or distorted conception of them is intimately bound up with a false conception of the true character of anthroposophically oriented spiritual science. Thus the former can only be corrected to the extent that the latter is.

In his personal letters to Moltke, Steiner pointed to the entity of the true German Folk Spirit then being deserted by most German people. Then, in the summer of 1915, he revealed to Moltke something of his past life as Pope Nicholas I (died 867) in the ninth century. In August 1915 Moltke made excerpts from what Gregorovius had written about this significant pope. Nicholas was paving the way for the separation of the East and the West from Central Europe in order to enable Europe to develop the capacity for material observation and a free thought life. Out of a still highly spiritual consciousness, and advised by his counsellor Anastasius Bibliothecarius, he took the hard decision to inaugurate the West-East separation that was to become the vital destiny of Europe for a whole millennium. When in 1054 the Orthodox and the Roman Catholic churches were formally separated from one another this was just the outward fulfilment of Nicholas's deeds.

In such a way Moltke, through Steiner's help, was afforded the opportunity to feel and understand the world historic background of his being placed in the very centre of a conflict between East and West which he himself had initiated a millennium before. At that time Central Europe needed to be closed off for a while against Western and Eastern influences in order to develop its own special mission. When Moltke died unexpectedly in June 1916 of a broken heart, as his wife put it, his soul and spirit had been nourished on such far–reaching insights into the connection of his own destiny with that of Europe.

Steiner, who was so deeply interested in the individuality and the destiny of this man, followed his path even after he had passed through the portal of death. This Steiner did in innumerable other cases. But in no other case has he left such an extensive bulk of written notes on the spiritual destiny of a human individuality.

Eliza von Moltke, who herself was not clairvoyant and who received all these messages, supported Steiner's research by keeping a meditative link to the deceased and by reading to him the letters he had once sent her. The immense value of this kind of working for the dead is affirmed many times by the discarnate soul, and the reader will find many examples of this in Part Two of this book. It is also remarkable that Rudolf Steiner's own indications about the most effective methods of establishing fruitful links with the dead are particularly concentrated and detailed in the intense period of his own communication with the Moltke soul. Furthermore, the initiate seemed to have gained considerable inspiration for his own work from the regular intercourse with the discarnate soul of Moltke. Some of his lectures reflect remarkable parallels to certain motifs in the after-death communications from about the same time. It would certainly be worthwhile to investigate this connection further.

*

The reader of Otto Friedrich's book on the Moltke family gets quite another picture of these subtle processes of spiritual understanding in the last two years of Moltke's life. This is mainly due to the fact that Friedrich, instead of going to the primary source of this extraordinary material, quotes Ravenscroft's book *The Spear of Destiny* and in so doing contributes to spreading some ridiculous nonsense even more widely over the English-speaking world. Here are some examples: 'There are also some very strange stories,' says Friedrich, 'that he lost the Battle of the Marne because he fell into trances and had visions.' According to Ravenscroft, Moltke, both during the Marne battle and before his dismissal, had a kind of visionary state of mind in which he saw himself as Pope Nicholas, Schlieffen as Pope Benedict II and his uncle as Pope Leo IV. Moltke had allegedly stood in front of the Holy Spear at the Hofburg in Vienna together with his Austrian colleague General Conrad von Hötzendorf—the same spear in front of which Hitler later stood, according to Ravenscroft. Friedrich reports that it was Eliza von Moltke who in spiritualist séances became by 'inspiration' the mouthpiece for the messages of her late husband! He calls this 'a peculiar technique of conjugal glossolalia'.[15]

Furthermore, according to him, the deceased supposedly even spoke in his after-death messages of a certain Adolf Hitler: 'A little stranger was the late general's naming of the obscure Adolf Hitler as the Führer of a Third Reich, but that, of course, may have been the basic reason why these séances were held in the first place.' No such statement can be found anywhere in the real after-death messages! Friedrich's 'explanation' for it is especially frivolous, for it associates Moltke with Hitler, as if somehow they were moving on the same line. At this point I ask the reader to remember well the distinction made between the true German Folk Spirit to which Steiner and Moltke were deeply linked and its demonic caricature to which Hitler delivered himself. There are hardly any greater spiritual opposites than these two spirits!

The only thing that has *some* truth in it so far is that Moltke from 1915 onwards (!) slowly (!) came to consider a karmic relationship between himself and Pope Nicholas. All the other quotes from Ravenscroft which Friedrich states are objectively untrue and pure invention, as the reader can easily check in Part Two of this book.

Friedrich himself states: 'This all sounds bizarre even if one recalls that Moltke and many of his contemporaries believed in the doctrines of anthroposophy.' But instead of seriously checking what sounds 'bizarre' he actually concludes his long chapter on the General with the following statements: ' "The Moltke 'Mitteilungen' [messages] are very extensive," Ravenscroft writes, "and amount to several hundred pages of typescript, photostats of which are still circulating secretly among hidden Grail groups in Germany today." Freya von Moltke, who probably knows more than anyone else about the Moltke family history, says she knows nothing about these transcripts or about the séances that led to their existence.'

Thus Friedrich in the end leaves it open whether all the things he quotes from Ravenscroft are fictitious or true, despite the fact that in his bibliography the two-volume German Moltke edition which includes the 'Mitteilungen' is correctly listed. Thus works some 'scientific' modern scholarship! True or not the quoted stories seem to fit and nourish the prejudices against both Steiner and Moltke. For what sounds 'bizarre' is directly associated with 'the doctrines of anthroposophy'. How could such an 'anthroposophy' therefore be anything serious or even scientific? Such insinuations and prejudices are generally nothing but the dogmatic expression of an utterly unscientific antipathy against the reality of the spirit with which both Moltke and Steiner, though in very different ways, established a very earnest, serious link.

In other words: At the basis of the distorted picture of Helmuth von Moltke there seems to lie a certain antipathy or fear of the spirit in its reality. And a sort of very hideous trick to 'disguise' this fear is to try to associate directly or indirectly both Moltke and Steiner's spiritual science with Hitler...

After these remarks on Friedrich's most 'bizarre' treatment of the after-death messages the reader may well wish to embark on his own journey of discovery of this new 'ocean' of knowledge and wisdom. And he may do so in full public view and without having to be a member of any hidden Grail group.

From a higher vantage point

Four years before his death Moltke looked at the landscape within which he spent his childhood from a higher vantage point, flying over it in an aircraft. After his death he starts looking back at the dramatic scenery of his earthly life from the higher vantage point of after-death life. Every human soul looks at his past life and incarnations from this higher point of view whenever he has passed through the gate of death. But usually little or nothing is known about the spiritual experiences of the deceased by those left behind. But here is a man whose life developed at the focus of world-historic events and for whose after-death panorama there was a unique witness who could also act as a messenger: Rudolf Steiner.

The stream of spiritual vision unfolding after Moltke's death can be seen to be developing in four main time-steps: 1) Present spiritual experiences; 2) Flashbacks into the time still 'near'—in other words the past immediately before death stretching backwards to the last birth; 3) The view widens and includes experiences in the time before the last birth and goes back to the second to last incarnation in the ninth century; 4) Previews to the time at the end of the century—that is our present historical moment—and beyond it into the third millennium. Let us briefly consider some examples of each of these steps. 1) One of the most characteristic present experiences interwoven with the whole variety of all the other after-death experiences is put by Moltke in the following words: 'Out of the body, one must direct the gaze of the soul across centuries' (1 March 1918). Just as in physical space one is able to look over a wide space in all spatial directions, similarly in the spiritual world the same happens within time-space and its time-directions. What is just farther in the distance, is farther back in the past or farther away in the future. 2) Naturally it is events and facts during the preparation for and then the actual war itself that repeatedly become the focus for the spiritual eye of the deceased. And looking back at all his own efforts to safeguard the existence of Germany through his military office and service, the soul reveals a shattering truth without any of the embellishment with which we so often surround truths found in earthly consciousness. 'Whoever is able to see that materialism has ruined noble forces in the inner nature of Germany will also see that all that happened was bound to happen (…) German militarism had to become an empty vessel, without spiritual content. And as such it could not but destroy itself because it had not been called upon to defend something of value which it cannot give itself but which it ought to serve. German militarism wanted to fight for Germany; but what was Germany fighting for in the shape of the people who led its politics? No word of significance was ever heard from any quarters that should have acted in the place of the military. *German militarism fought for Germany, but Germany fought for—nothing.* That is why the spirit of Bismarck and the older Moltke stood apart through those years.' (27 January 1919.) 3) There are many flashbacks into the ninth century and 4) significant previews towards the end of the century and the soul's renewed mission in the East. As these elements of the messages have so much to do with certain efforts in our own present time to reshape European as well as world politics after the breakdown of socialism in 1989, we should like to give it some special attention here.

Two maps fighting for a new shape of Europe and the World

The soul often looks back into the ninth century where the shaping of the future Europe was initiated through Pope Nicholas I. Nicholas, aided by his wise counsellor, was actually drawing a new map of Europe for the second millennium. It was his mission to prepare the world-historical separation of the West from the East to bring about an independent Central European culture. The 'soul' now recognizes the karmic consequences of this mission in the ninth century. One of these (dated 28 July 1918) is expressed as follows: 'It was my task then to conceive of ways to separate the East from the West. Many people were involved in this separation (…) In those days there was still a closeness to the spiritual world (…) Yet the inhabitants of Central and Western Europe were striving away from the spiritual beings. Already at that time they needed to prepare for materialism.' For only through looking at the world solely as matter for a while could man become a really free being, merely relying on sense perception and clear thoughts which, being themselves only dead images of living reality, form the basis of freedom. For the dead thought-images contain no immediate driving forces, as emotions and instincts do. Therefore, in any action based on thought this driving force is nothing other than man's own free will. This is where the deeper meaning of developing the faculty of looking at mere material processes, at dead matter to which dead thoughts are the corresponding counterpart, lies. This was Europe's mission, and this mission has been achieved. This is why modern Europe should take a new step—and use free thinking now for gaining knowledge of supersensible realities, as is done in spiritual science.

'The counsellor would often say then: The spirits will withdraw from Europe; but later on the Europeans will long for them. Without the spirits the Europeans will make their machines and their institutions. They will excel at that. But in doing so they will breed in their midst the western people who will drive ahrimanic culture to its highest peak and take their place.' Now, according to a number of other messages, it becomes quite clear to the soul that the separation-task had been completely fulfilled with the end of the last incarnation on earth. From the message of 22 June we learn: 'In the ninth century we pushed back to the East what was of no use for the West and Central Europe (...) *Our task* (...) *will be the opposite task from the one we had in the ninth century.*' The task now will be to erect a bridge between what had to be separated a millennium ago. From this point of view the still prevailing borderline between Roman and Orthodox Christianity, which was the result of the church policy of Nicholas and which again runs across Europe with renewed strength in our own days, is totally outdated. As early as in the message of 19 October 1916 we read: 'It is the clearest mission of my "I" to work on the European relationship between the Germans and the Slavs.' And the soul experiences it as a blessing that he did not have to wage war against the East in the last incarnation. The bridging mission, which is his task at the end of the century and the beginning of the next, can unfold itself on unspoiled ground. Thus the Moltke individuality, so to speak, draws a *new map of Europe and the world* which obliterates the old borders between the East and the West and abolishes the frontiers between Orthodox and Roman Christendom. Within the framework of this 'Moltke map' it is also clear from the message of 23 March that 'we may not approach the East with purely economic thinking; we have to think in such a way that the East can reach a spiritual understanding of the Middle European. Otherwise, "the Beast" will be unable to spiritualize itself. We need to bear the thought within us: in the East many people are waiting who must be found, for they would be able to understand, if one spoke to them in the right way. Any attempt to reach an understanding with those people of the East who have become western is futile. The West corrupts these people (...)'[16]

Not only is there a true German element and its horrible counterpart, which became active in Hitlerism, there is a healthy layer as well in the Eastern Slav people which must be clearly distinguished from that other layer which was gradually corrupted by purely materialistic and economic western thinking and by the Roman Catholic church.[17]

This spiritual map, with the realization of which the individuality sees himself deeply connected for the present and near future, stands in the sharpest possible contrast to the main forces now shaping European and world politics. We should like to remind our readers of a map published in the British magazine *The Economist* in September 1990 (see page xxxiv), just 100 years after 'The Kaiser's Dream' was published in the magazine *Truth*. On this map, which is accompanied by a very serious commentary, we see a huge continent called Euro-America, another huge continent called Euro-Asia and some huge islands called Islamistan, Confuciana and Hinduland. On the earth of Euro-America we see a kind of kneeling pilgrim father, on the soil of Euro-Asia an Orthodox Pope. If we look closely enough we see that the two halves of Europe are exactly divided along the borderline of Roman Catholicism and the Orthodox belief! This map is in perfect tune with the new political philosophy of Samuel Huntington which outlined the coming clashes between the different types of world civilizations based on different religions and confessions.[18] And both this map and Huntington's philosophy are actually being translated into external historical reality. All the countries now admitted to the European Union belong, according to this criterion, to Euro-America. And the Nato expansion towards the East functions according to the same principle of division. On

'The Kaiser's Dream' from The Truth, *26 December 1890.*

'A Survey of Defence and the Democracies' from The Economist, *1 September 1990.*

the one hand we have old religious beliefs that are strengthened again, and on the other 'purely economic thinking', the false 'bliss' of the so-called free market for the East.

In reality, the map from *The Economist*, the corresponding philosophy of clashes of civilizations and both their realization in European and world politics today are nothing other than a renewal of the impulses of Nicholas in the ninth century. According to the insight of the Nicholas-Moltke individuality, however, they are— viewed from a higher vantage point—totally anachronistic, in other words anything but 'new'.

This means that on the level of international politics *the real conflict at the end of this century is by no means between different civilizations, as Huntington suggests, but the somewhat more hidden conflict between the renewal of impulses which were adapted to the needs of the second millennium, and those needed by humanity for the third millennium.* And whereas *The Economist*'s map is an expression of the former impulses, the 'Moltke map' implicitly contained in some of the after-death messages of this book is the only really new map for Europe and the world that has so far been designed. And because the old one is no longer appropriate any more to modern humanity it can only create chaos. We need only glance at the state of affairs in the former Yugoslavia after the Dayton plan had been imposed to see that no true peace can ever come of it. Besides, American foreign policy in general and the architect of Dayton, Richard Holbrooke, in particular, are perfectly representative of what is called 'the western people' in one of the messages (28 July 1918), 'who will take their [the Europeans'] place'. But no true European should blame the US foreign policy or certain American individuals for doing what is being done in Europe. It is the Europeans themselves who have nothing to oppose to such 'new' western maps and their political aims. They could only do so if they cared about a fundamentally new West-East map and its spiritual implications as outlined in these documents.

The European Union—new 'clothes' for Europe?

It is hardly possible to consider the present European Union to be a really new and European answer to the needs of the time. As a brief glance at its origins can easily demonstrate, the EU was founded to serve the desire for western economic predominance in the world on the one hand, and, spiritually, it is guided by the old Roman Catholic spirituality on the other. Brussels is little more than a crossroads between Washington and the Vatican. Furthermore, the exclusion of the Orthodox countries of Eastern Europe from both EU and NATO clearly shows the continuation of the cultural separation impulse which on a world-historical level became outdated long ago, as shown above.

Helmuth von Moltke witnessed the beginning of the demolition of old social structures. After his death in 1916 he was gradually awakening to a full comprehension of his 'Kaiser's Dream'. But the crash of monarchies is representative of the crash of all old systems in an all-powerful nation state. In the nation state cultural, political and economic matters are chaotically handled out of one and the same source. It is of no fundamental importance whether this source is a sovereign king (monarchy) or a sovereign people (democracy) or anything between these two extremes. But humanity was, and is, more and more in need of a social structure that is adapted to what unfolds increasingly within each human individuality itself: a separation of the inner faculties of thinking, feeling and willing.[19] Because of this fact in the inner development of each individual the social structure has to become threefold as well. A cultural domain has to be created within which the thinking or spiritual activity of man finds a possibility of expression within a free spiritual life, unhampered by any national or political differences. The economic activities on the other hand should be taken out of the political domain of the individual nation state and work on a worldwide level. This they do today to a high degree already, but unfortunately the international globalization serves the ends of a few mighty trusts or individual persons and prepares the way for a two-geared world society without a middle class—the increasingly rich on one side and the increasingly poor on the other. Only by basing worldwide economic life on what Steiner called 'associations' where producers, distributors and consumers express their needs and share their insights into the actual economic processes can an international economy serving the needs of every human being slowly evolve.

Each of the above-mentioned soul faculties thus finds its own field of unfoldment. The old nation state cannot satisfy this modern development within human nature any more. Its demolition was ripe. This was well known in some western circles and therefore preparation was made for an experiment in socialism in the East. This experiment was actually launched in 1917 in Russia and ceased in 1989. But instead of producing anything basically new it was nothing but a new form of the all-powerful nation state. In the same year, 1917, however, a really new model for the social organism was created by Rudolf Steiner's idea of the threefold social order—as outlined in his book *Die Kernpunkte der Sozialen Frage* and in some memoranda—as the answer to the inner threefoldness of human soul life.[20]

In the after-death message of 16 February 1921 we learn: 'Europe had to cast off its old garments'. That refers to the natural decay or artificial demolition of the old nation state, no matter whether in the form of monarchies, democracies, republics or state socialism. 'Now it will wander naked through human evolution for a while.' Is the present European Union about to provide such new garments? Only short-sightedness, superficiality or simply *naïveté* could induce one to think so. And what would be the remedy? The threefold social order. But this can only develop if in Europe, after a millennium of materialist outlook, a new spirituality spreads and is cultivated. We read in the message of 2 February 1922: 'Central Europe cannot progress through unspirituality but only by the power of the spirit (...) In Central Europe science, too, will have to become spiritual. Central Europe has yet to pass this test.' All the components for passing this test successfully are already there. They have only to be taken seriously as something really new in the twentieth century. They are to be found in Rudolf Steiner's spiritual science.

A new, individual Spirit of Truth for Europe

Only if Europe breaks through to a new spirituality can the future bridge between East and West be built. If, however, Europe prefers to remain buried under the spiritual debris and ruins of what has been destroyed at the beginning of this century this would have dire consequences. 'The lie of the age has led to ruin. Truth must lead to the building of the new. The spirit can only work in truth,' we read in the message of 3 May 1919. 'Truth must hold sway. Otherwise not only German culture will perish; the entire European world would perish, too, and Eastern Europe would have to be rebuilt from Asia. That must not happen. Europe must come to its senses and find its way to the spirit.'

There are numerous indications about the prerequisites needed to find this way to the spirit. One is linked to a certain awakening process in the human mind. Rudolf Steiner often talked in the war years about the fact that ordinary human consciousness is no more awake with regard to the actual historical processes within which it lives than it is awake about its own ordinary dream life. In this context the Moltke soul says (on 22 April 1918): 'Down below, it is quite rightly being said to people: history is being dreamed, indeed, to some extent, even being slept through. But this dream must not go on being dreamed on the earth.'

Another fundamental insight refers to the different attitude to truth and to the spirit in western, European and the future eastern man. How in the West and the Centre truth is often really featured is expressed in the message of June 1921 as follows: 'In Central Europe many people are afraid of the truth because they have lived a lie for so long; in the West people fear the truth because they would have to change their whole life if they admitted to the truth. Only a humanity that understands what it is to live in the spirit will be able to bear the truth.' About certain tendencies in the West the Moltke soul says (on 15 July 1918): 'Anglo-American nature will misapprehend this spirit and fight against it. It will be given materialistic forms. That will be the part of the world that will become more and more soulless.' And about eastern man and his relation to the spirit we hear in the message of 14 May 1918: 'In this East there will be people one day who will speak a very particular language (...) They will be speaking of spiritual matters. And one ought to understand them in the rest of Europe (...) The time is coming in which one will have to learn to distinguish whether it is someone from the East or someone from the West who says something. Though they may be saying the same thing, it will in fact be quite different.'

Above all, the new spirituality that *Europe* requires must be centred within each individual, if there is to be a free spiritual life in Europe as the foundation for a threefold social organism. Rudolf Steiner termed this spirituality 'ethical individualism', which of course includes the individualism of true knowledge. Such an individualism, anchored in every individual's concrete relation to the world of truth, is also the true basis of all social life and should not be confused with anti-social egotism. The latter can, however, be rightly determined as that part or sphere of the individual which

really lacks any relevant relation to truth. We find a message of the
Moltke soul (of 27 March 1919) which shows him to be a true
representative of such a spiritual or ethical individualism: 'People
who want to accomplish things on earth have to become builders of
bridges (pontifices).' Now, what is really remarkable here is that a
Latin expression is added—it is the only place in all the messages—
the plural form of the Latin word for bridgebuilder: 'pontifices'.
'Pontifex' was the technical term for the Roman pope who had the
task to build the bridge between the earthly and the spiritual realm.
By force of a spiritual appointment he was privileged in this function and acted on behalf of all other believers, in their place. From
this privileged spiritual position all spiritual authority within the
Church was derived. This authority was justified up to the time that
the spiritual freedom of the individual began. If we now bear in
mind that the Moltke soul had himself previously been incarnated
as Pope Nicholas I, we might come to an even more profound view
of this statement. Nicholas may be considered to be the last pope
who was still aware of the individual spirit and of the world of the
hierarchies. And he was the last pope who, based on this true
individual experience, justly acted as a spiritual authority and as a
representative for others. But just two years after Nicholas' death
the world-historical attempt was made to wipe out any consciousness of the individual spirit in mankind. This was tried at the
Council of Constantinople in 869. At about the same time we see on
the other hand the emerging fight for a new individual spirituality as
reflected in the various legends of the Quest for the Holy Grail. For
it is precisely the individual spiritual activity to be found by Parsifal
which enables him, by asking a truly individual question, to become
a healing factor in his social surroundings. If a thousand years later
the soul who lived in Nicholas spiritually pronounces the word
'pontifices', he is actually saying: *While up to the time of Nicholas
one pontifex had to act for many people, now each individual has to
become an independent pontifex for himself.* In addition, it is
important in this case not only to pay attention to *what* is being said
in this sentence, but to *who* is saying it. If this former true pontifex
soul now points to the need to have 'pontifices' all over the world,
he thereby *pronounces the world-historical end of the old pontifex
principle with its spiritual authority.* From now on each individual
must become his own spiritual authority through his own relation to
truth! This means that any traditional authority-based spirituality in

any church can play no true part whatsoever in the development of
the new individual spirituality needed in Europe.

Such a *vertical* individual bridging between the earthly and the
spiritual world, only briefly outlined here, is also the fundamental
prerequisite for the *horizontal* bridge-building between East and
West to be undertaken by all true Europeans—unless a spiritually
ruined Europe is to be built up from Asia...

Light for the new millennium

In Part Two of this book there are about 30 references to the end of
this century and to the renewed task of the individuality that lived
in the earthly personality of Helmuth von Moltke. In this respect
the after-death messages were like a secret prelude to what Rudolf
Steiner openly revealed in 1924 to his pupils. Many of them, he said,
would reincarnate at the end of this century, thereby breaking the
rules governing the ordinary span of time between two incarnations. There is no doubt that one of the highlights of this book is to
see the gradual emergence of this end-of-the-century perspective.
At the same time we can again learn with amazement how different
the spiritual outlook of the deceased is from the earthly way of
looking at the future. To the spiritual gaze events of the future are
like definite places in spiritual space to which one might decide to
go. Whereas the earthly Moltke—like everyone else—was sometimes struggling with doubts about the steps to be undertaken the
next day or week, the heavenly individuality speaks with unwa-
vering firmness about a task lying 80 years ahead in the future. And
as this future has now become our present it may be worthwhile to
take a short look at the nature of the task the soul foresaw for his
present incarnation in the East, probably Russia. First of all it has to
do, as already stated, with a new bridging of East and West. This
calls for Europe to want and find a new spirituality. But the Moltke
soul will make no outward political effort in this present incarnation: 'In the East my task can only be a spiritual one (...) Earthly
institutions must then be founded which will be an image of spiritual ones. "She" and others who are linked with us are to work
together on this,' we read in the message of 8 February 1918. And in
the same message: 'A spiritual wilderness is now spreading over the
earth (...) In the twentieth century there will be a great deal of
materialism which will be even more powerful in the twenty-first

century. But everywhere there will be centres of spiritual will and deed.' Such centres will also have the function of cultivating 'a spiritual understanding of the world situation on earth' (8 January 1917).

It is of fundamental importance for such an understanding that mankind learns to take thoughts and thinking activity as seriously as outwardly visible acts are regarded. For it is only our normal waking consciousness that considers thoughts to be lifeless—no more than mere images. In reality they have a hidden relation to the living world of the spirit. It is therefore no less harmful for the world as a whole if I live in lies and keep untruth alive than if I were to hit or even kill a human being. Steiner often called a lie an astral murder. If the disastrous events of the twentieth century have anything to teach us perhaps the most basic lesson might be to learn to treat human thinking as a reality with quite definite effects. This is expressed in the following statement by the Moltke individuality (24 May 1918): 'People on earth must learn from events that thoughts are facts.'

Wrong thoughts create wrong facts, i.e. are hindrances to the evolution of man and the world. One of the hopes linked to the publication of this book is precisely this: that the mass of wrong thought-facts about the life and work of Helmuth von Moltke, whom Otto Friedrich simply calls 'the nervous nephew', are replaced by thoughts with real and truthful substance.

*

Of course, both the editor as well as the publisher of this book are under no illusion that its second part, in particular, is open to misrepresentation—if it is merely studied superficially. They are also aware that many a representative of the anthroposophical movement may raise perhaps very justified objections against the publication of the after-death communications it contains. Nevertheless they are fully convinced of the need for its publication at the present time. For only by risking it may the mass of half truths and lies about Helmuth von Moltke and his association with Rudolf Steiner be gradually outweighed. Thus the publication of Part Two was undertaken in the sense of the following words of the Moltke soul from January 1918: 'What is decisive in the world is not just what is right but what is of heavier weight.'

Furthermore, there are so many positive and constructive

thought-facts about the course of man's evolution over and beyond the manifold dramatic crossroads awaiting us at the end of this century, that this book could contribute to the growth of a certain spiritual courage which more and more people today increasingly lack—a courage that can organically arise in the mind and heart of every reader who, step by step, becomes a witness to the grandeur and immutability of the spiritual laws governing evolution.

'Many adversities are yet to come to pass. But the light at the end of the twentieth century shines brightly before my soul.' Thus we read in the message of 22 February 1922. And three years earlier: 'Fruit will ripen before the end of the century (...) Europe's materialistic era will be like an interlude when the new Spirit Sun begins to shine for humanity.' (3 May 1919.)

This Spirit Sun will be the true light for the new millennium.

Helmuth von Moltke and Rudolf Steiner
by *Johannes Tautz*

On 18 June 1916 the funeral service for Field Marshal von der Goltz was held in the Reichstag in Berlin. Helmuth von Moltke, the Chief of the General Staff, who had been dismissed after the Battle of the Marne, gave the memorial address and called out the following words about his friend with whom he felt a closeness in destiny: 'History has shown repeatedly how heroism and tragedy can stand side by side.' After he had finished—the service was still going on— he died of heart failure.

Two days later Rudolf Steiner pointed to the significance of the deceased before giving his lecture on 'The Twelve Senses of Man'. It was, he said, a symptom of eminent importance that this man, who had been the bearer of historical decisions in 1914, had 'found the bridge to the life of the spirit which is sought by this [anthroposophical] spiritual science'.[1] Such words indicate the essential quality of the Moltke individuality whose task it is to work as a 'builder of bridges' in the succession of earthly lives. In his last incarnation he succeeded in bridging the gap between his outer deeds and the spiritual-scientific orientation of consciousness, in accordance with the necessities of the time. This bestowed upon the discarnate soul a 'deeply significant and effective power in the spiritual world'.[2]

But what was it that made Steiner say: 'that which flows and pulses through our spiritual-scientific movement has received as much from this soul as we were able to give it'?[3] What was at the basis of such giving and receiving?

*

In 1904 Moltke, a man of considerable military expertise, was awarded the most senior post under the Chief of the General Staff Schlieffen, whom he was to succeed in office. However, Moltke made certain conditions before he accepted the highest post in the army: he was not prepared to participate in the 'operetta wars' the Kaiser liked to stage during the annual manoeuvres, which always had to end with the glorious victory of the army led by him. This is how that memorable conversation of 7 January 1905 came about, during which Moltke demanded of his 'Supreme Commander' that he would refrain from any interference in the imperial manoeuvres devised by the General Staff. Although Kaiser Wilhelm was not accustomed to honest and open talk in his immediate environment, he agreed to Moltke's request and appointed Moltke, the nephew of the identically named Field Marshal, Chief of the General Staff.

In those days society was still bound to the rules of the monarchy and its structure of social classes. The members of the upper classes—land-owning nobility, officers and diplomats—represented an élite and enjoyed many privileges. They were committed to the absolutist idea of statehood which to them was embodied by the Royal Family; their attitude towards the monarch was one of total loyalty and faith, even if they saw through this monarch's vain love of pageantry, as Moltke did. So truly there was a relationship of trust between Moltke and the Kaiser; but this was destroyed at the outbreak of war.

*

In 1904, a biographical turning point in his life, Moltke made the acquaintance of Rudolf Steiner through his wife Eliza. Eliza von Moltke was a friend of Marie von Sivers who had introduced her to the Theosophical Society; she met Rudolf Steiner there and immediately recognized him, the younger of the two, as her teacher. She was open to all things spiritual and occult and had an interest in spiritualism and mediums; this inclination was by no means unusual among the nobility of the time. Her sober powers of discrimination, however, caused her to search for a conscious way of accessing the world of the supersensible, and for this the spiritual researcher provided the key. Thus a closeness in destiny to Rudolf Steiner developed in the years following the turn of the century; at that time he was an unknown private scholar who lectured at an institute offering higher education to the working classes while she, as a member of courtly society, moved in the circles around the Kaiser. She invited Rudolf Steiner to converse with her husband who was astounded at the political far-sightedness and perspicacity of his visitor's observations. Eliza von Moltke was among the first people Rudolf Steiner invited to join the

Esoteric School founded in 1904. His letter of invitation of 12 August 1904 ends with the comment: 'I often recall the delightful hours I was able to spend at your house. I have indeed come to feel great affection for your husband and I have great hopes for his spiritual future. Sometimes people walk along special paths but many different paths lead to knowledge.'

The two Moltkes were exceedingly close, with a familiarity and trust that spanned more than this life; but in soul disposition they could hardly have been more different. Helmuth von Moltke, still imbued with the spiritually refined concept of man and the world of Goethe's era, was very well-read and lived out of the forces of a sentient-soul religiousness; he was a man of impeccable conscience and had a fine sense of justice. While he was sceptical of his wife's inclinations to the mediumistic and did not approve, his attitude was one of tolerance.

*

1 August 1914 was the day of German mobilization and declaration of war against Russia—and at the same time the most fateful day in Moltke's life: the beginning of his 'time of suffering' which culminated in his death two years later. The automatism of alliance commitments came into full play; within one week a European war flared up that developed into a world war which fundamentally changed political structures in Europe. The rivalries between the great powers, which had been growing in intensity since the last decades of the nineteenth century, culminated in the July crisis and erupted in the utter catastrophe of the war. Moltke had seen it coming a long time before. On 5 March 1904 he wrote: 'No one has any idea what thunderstorms are forming above us; instead of preparing in solemn earnestness for the serious times ahead the nation is tearing itself to pieces.'[4] In his capacity as Chief of the General Staff responsible for guaranteeing the military security of the Reich he did 'prepare in solemn earnestness for the serious times ahead': namely, for the possibility of war on two fronts against Russia and France. German appraisal of the political situation made such a war seem unavoidable. The political world-view was dominated by a social-Darwinist fatalism *vis-à-vis* history; unceasing conflict was held to be a normal form of existence among the states of the world and armament the supreme dictate of politics.

The debate concerning the events leading to war and the outbreak of the First World War is not yet over, and in many cases the
view of historical reality is lop-sided and partisan in nature. In
November 1914—two months after his dismissal—Moltke wrote his
'Reflections and Memories', an immediate and personal account of
the course of events and the part he played in them. Faced with the
threat posed by the Alliance between France and Russia, the Chief
of Staff pressed for speedy strategic decisions. Such action was in
line with Schlieffen's operational plan which aimed at the defeat of
France after first marching through neutral Belgium, followed by
offensive action against Russia. On the first of August, the day of
German mobilization and declaration of war against Russia, the
utterly helpless political leadership, which relied on England's
neutrality, believed, as a result of an erroneous telegram, that
England would guarantee French neutrality and that therefore the
war had to be waged solely against Russia. When this illusory hope
flashed up the Kaiser carelessly and amateurishly stepped into
Moltke's sphere of responsibility and demanded that all the
mobilized forces be redirected towards the East. This would have
led to chaos. A few hours later the illusion collapsed and the
'Supreme Commander' restored Moltke's authority to act. 'This
was my first experience in this war,' Moltke writes. 'I have never
been able to get over the impression of this experience. Something
within me was destroyed that could never be restored. My confidence and trust were shattered.'[5] This traumatic experience left its
permanent mark on Moltke.

As early as 1915 Rudolf Steiner set out what he considered
essential background information about the war's outbreak in his
essay 'Gedanken während der Zeit des Krieges'.[6] In times of high
tension in history, when the present moment condenses and an all-
engulfing darkness threatens to descend, powers of a higher order
work into the dynamics of events; they do this through the consciousness of the leading players. Rudolf Steiner writes: 'When the
realities of the summer of 1914 unfolded they hit Europe in a world-
historical situation in which the powers that work in a nation's life
interfere in the course of events in such a way that the decision
about what is to happen is taken away from the realm of ordinary
human judgement and placed at a higher level—that level at which
world-historical necessity works in the whole of mankind's evolution. Anyone who senses the essence of such moments in world

history will also raise his judgement far beyond the level where questions such as this creep in: What would have happened if in this fateful hour this or that proposal of this or that personality had carried more weight than it actually did? In times of world-historical change human beings are apt to feel that their decisions are empowered by certain forces, and these can only be judged properly if there is genuine striving—let us recall Emerson's words here—to not just "consider the detail" but to conceive of humanity "as a whole that is subject to higher laws". Why should it be possible to judge the decisions of human beings by the laws of ordinary life when these decisions cannot be made by such laws for they are the work of the spirit that can only be perceived in *world-historical necessities!*' This is summarized as follows in the final sentence: 'Natural laws are part of the natural order; above them are the laws governing the order of ordinary [human] coexistence; and above these are the spiritual laws of *world-historical evolution* which belong to yet another order, namely the one by which individuals and nations fulfil their tasks and pass through developments which lie outside the realm of ordinary human coexistence.'[6]

*

August 1914 marked the beginning of a turn in Moltke's destiny. The inner distance from the Kaiser brought with it increasing closeness to Rudolf Steiner. Their first meeting after the outbreak of war took place on 27 August at the headquarters near Koblenz. Eliza von Moltke was also present. We know from Jürgen von Grone's descriptions that the conversation centred on the 'preservation of the national individuality of the German people in the context of the great and lasting culture of the spirit it had given birth to'.[7]

Moltke believed in a universal task of the Central European spirit arising out of the cultural heritage of philosophers and idealists. In the fatal power politics of Kaiser Wilhelm's Reich he recognized the seeds of self-destruction and moral decay. He considered the war a great misfortune; to him it was a fight for the preservation of his people, but a people destined for the creation of culture rather than the attainment of power. This inner attitude is reflected in the verse Rudolf Steiner gave him at the end of their conversation:

That strength will conquer
which the destiny of time

has ordained for the people
which guided by the Spirit
bears light out of battle
into the heart of Europe
for the healing of mankind

This conversation took place during the advance of the German armies in the West, at a time when reports of success were accumulating fast—ten days before the decisive events of the Marne Battle began to take shape.

The situation was very different in November 1914 when Rudolf Steiner, again responding to an invitation, met Moltke in Homburg von der Höhe (near Frankfurt am Main). After the Battle of the Marne and the German retreat, Moltke had been replaced by Falkenhayn who pursued a totally opposite strategy. Moltke suffered a great deal from the loss of influence and responsibility and his worsening health, as well as from the increasing military difficulties. It was in this state of soul that he spoke openly for the first time about military and political affairs; thus Rudolf Steiner learned first-hand from him what had taken place at the outbreak of war in Berlin. This marked the beginning of the mutual trust which continued and deepened right until Moltke's death.

After Moltke's dismissal the emphasis of these conversations with Rudolf Steiner shifted; now the question of how Moltke's own dramatic destiny related to the course of historical events became the focus of inquiry; the question of the 'spiritual law of the evolution of world history'. What the sorely afflicted soul of Moltke learned in these conversations led to far-reaching spiritual perceptions after his death in which karmic connections were revealed.

A memorable constellation: the spiritual researcher in conversation with the General! Having been forced to let go, Moltke was beset by questions about the deeper meaning of existence and destiny: What are the reasons for a sudden drastic change in one's life? How can one become aware of the forces of karma? Using the example of Moltke's own experience of suffering Rudolf Steiner encouraged him to look at the question of destiny from a spiritual-scientific perspective, and directed his attention to the spiritual background of the individuality who carries the results of a previous earthly life into the succeeding one.[8]

The letters, messages and verses Rudolf Steiner sent to Moltke in the ensuing period are all based on what was established in relation to karma during this conversation in Homburg. Thus the researcher of spirit and destiny was able to take the next step; probably in August 1914 he revealed to Moltke his karmic connection with Pope Nicholas I as well as the relationship of particular events and people around Moltke with those from the ninth century; i.e. such historical facts as became known later through Albert Steffen's play *Der Chef des Generalstabs* and Emil Bock's lectures on the ninth century.[9]

Apparently Moltke found it difficult at first to accept an understanding of karma which 'traces history right into the innermost wisdom of man'.[10] However, he did note the most important facts relating to the pontificate of Nicholas I (858–67) on five sheets of paper; he extracted these from *Klassische Chronik der Stadt Rom im Mittelalter* by Ferdinand Gregorovius.

*

In the last two years of his life, which from the outside appeared so full of suffering, Moltke enjoyed Rudolf Steiner's support and friendly encouragement. Rudolf Steiner's long letters—in themselves testimony to a method of soul guidance that truly leaves the other free—as well as the helpful indications he gave in private conversation, helped Moltke recognize the benefit of his suffering and enabled him to trust in a newly emerging strength.

This correspondence began in December 1914 and ended in November 1915. In the first six months of 1916 Rudolf Steiner spent most of his time in Berlin, so there were opportunities for meeting in person; such meetings were always initiated by Eliza von Moltke, with the exception of the last conversation, which Moltke had asked for himself, 14 days before his death.

The themes of Rudolf Steiner's letters and the lectures he held during the same period are related. The spiritual researcher confronts the challenges of contemporary history. The content of his lectures was inspired by his 'historical conscience'; he paints a picture of the supersensible processes which cast their shadows on to outer events.

'About a Time of Serious Destiny' is the title of his public lectures; 'The Destinies of Individuals and of Nations' the title of lectures to members. The destiny of a nation can be reflected in the destiny of an individual: this is what Rudolf Steiner can read in the tragic life of Moltke, whom he addresses as the representative of the German Folk Spirit in his letters.

The first letter of 20 December 1914—written three months after Moltke's dismissal and the setbacks in the western arena of the war—begins with the momentous statement: 'It remains an irrefutable fact before this spiritual vision that the Genius of the German people stands with his torch held high, hopeful and confident, and that the forces coming from this side are with your thoughts about the course of events. Your thoughts, Excellency, have been the instrument needed by this side of the spiritual world for many years now. Even if the physical course of events appears to contradict this it is not the case *in reality*. In the spiritual realm it is still the thread of your thoughts, Excellency, which shapes the course of events.' The heavy repercussions of the war and the military defeat Moltke and the German people had to suffer 'are the ground from which the powers of the spirit must weave the salvation of the earth'. 'The task which lies ahead of this people is so significant that it may only be accomplished through solemn working.'

Rudolf Steiner rounds off these thoughts as follows: 'Individual people can *appear* to have been removed from a particular incarnation before they have achieved what was predestined; this is because they come back in future incarnations; a people, however, does not lose the conditions of its mission before this mission is fulfilled.'[11]

This final comment challenges our understanding and our will: What exactly is the task of the Folk Spirit and how can it be fulfilled? The conversations with Rudolf Steiner must have encompassed this double-sided question. The Berlin lectures to which Moltke had access may provide us with clues to the topics of these conversations. The lecturer explains that in the fifteenth century spiritual powers worked through the maid Joan of Arc to bring about the structure of nations in Europe that was right for that time, whereas, in the twentieth century, man must recognize and fulfil the intentions of the spirit out of his own 'I'-forces. Only then can a connection with the impulses of the Folk Spirit be made. Rudolf Steiner says: 'What needs to arise for a future civilization can only arise if the German Folk Spirit finds souls which plant the Christ impulse into their astral bodies and their egos in full waking consciousness.'[12] So the task of the Germans must be understood to be a purely human one: the humanization of man, the spiritualization of the consciousness soul on the ascent to the Spirit-Self, that spiritual power of the future from which the Slav culture of brotherliness is to arise.

Rudolf Steiner has left no doubts about the fact that the task of the German people can only be a spiritual-cultural one, and is in no way related to power politics or economic endeavour. If one clearly perceives the centrality of Germany's position in relation to geography, soul disposition and the spiritual life, this becomes plausible. The German-speaking people together with the Slav border people and the Hungarians all settled in the centre of Europe. Central Europe is a 'conglomerate of people', an ethnic diversity, which for Rudolf Steiner comprises Czechs, Slovaks, Ruthenians, Hungarians and Poles as well as Germans.[13] Their territory was a self-contained spiritual-cultural landscape between East and West which disintegrated after the First World War and has been almost destroyed following the misguided developments since 1933. The question of the retarded development of Central European culture has only re-emerged in the 'Central Europe debate' of the Eighties.

The Central European element, at the core of which there is a 'striving for individuality'—not nationality—is reflected in the image of the staff of Mercury. Thus it was characterized by Steiner in the sculptural language of the first Goetheanum building.[14]

The future task becomes visible in the image of the serpents winding their way up the vertical with their heads raised up high from the ground: for the forces of the 'I' to raise the earthly intellect to encompass supersensible reality through thinking. This is how the peoples of Central Europe can take hold of their task: as mediators between one-sided spiritual and materialistic orientation. The strength needed for the fulfilment of this task can grow out of the scientific and social impulses of Anthroposophy, whose seeds were planted in the cultural renaissance of the Goethean era.

As far as the soul aspect is concerned, Rudolf Steiner characterizes the German Folk Spirit's way of working as a phenomenon of breathing: a rhythmic 'swinging to and fro' of the Spirit who unites himself with the evolutionary stream at different levels of intensity.[15] This spirit only responds to the activities of individuals who want to work together in fulfilling the specific mission of that people. This makes clear what Rudolf Steiner means by this comment: 'If the German individual manages to truly grasp the Spirit he is a blessing for the world; if he does not, he is the world's scourge.'[16] The classical Staufen period around 1200, the time of

Walther von der Vogelweide and Wolfram von Eschenbach, and
the classical Weimar era of Goethe around 1800, were the pinnacles
of the Folk Spirit's working.

The period of National Socialism marked the 'breaking away
from the Folk Spirit', the 'turning away' from the spiritual task of
the middle: a development foreseen by the 27-year-old Rudolf
Steiner in his analysis of the materialistic trends of the time.[17] What
had been theory in the nineteenth century became practical reality
in the twentieth. This resulted in Germany's self-destruction and
the unspeakable crimes against humanity committed in concentration and death camps.

In his last and longest letter to Moltke on 23 November 1915[18]
Rudolf Steiner points to the riddle posed by the destiny of the
German nation which can only be understood in the light of 'world-
historical necessities'. 'Excellency is now living through the time
where the paths of destiny shape themselves into the riddle of life.
The powers whose mission is the spirit guidance of man hold sway in
the paths of destiny. Through your spiritual guidance your own inner
life destiny has been interwoven with the guidance of the German
people for this era. The destiny of the German people is connected
with the deepest and loftiest aims of humanity's evolvement in the
world. The threads of such a folk destiny, in particular, are not
straightforward. They must often become entangled. The path of
destiny leads through trials. Trials which lead to the brink of World
Mysteries. To that abyss where the great question 'to be or not to be'
comes before the soul. Where apparent darkness spreads before
one's gaze. But at the abyss there stands the Genius of the German
people, and his torch is not lowered but raised up high.'

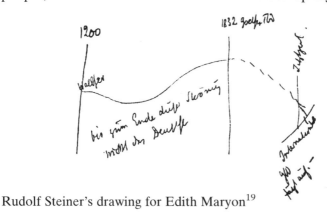

Rudolf Steiner's drawing for Edith Maryon[19]

Rudolf Steiner points to that which is difficult to fathom in German history. Its darkest phase was then still to come. The megalomanic dictatorship of the Nazis began 17 years later and ended in the abyss of total defeat. Had the universal mission of the Central European Spirit failed? Is the depth of the fall related to the greatness of the task? The German misfortune began with the foundation of the empire which, as Rudolf Steiner says, lacked 'a task which really emanated from the essential being of the German people'.[20] The facts of history show Bismarck, Wilhelm II and Hitler to have been the 'greatest enemies of the Central European Spirit'.[21] They were the originators of that Central European self-alienation and self-destruction that brought the spiritual vulgarization of Europe in its wake. The global crisis now emerging at the end of the century is a waking call to the conscience of every single individual intent on joining forces in rebuilding a European culture from out of a spirit of mediation between East and West.

Rudolf Steiner ends this significant letter with a personal remark: 'I am writing these lines to you, Excellency, on the morning of 23 November between six and eight o'clock in the morning, after my soul has dwelled with you a great deal.'

After Moltke's sudden death on 18 June 1916, Steiner perseveres with this soul exercise of beholding the spiritual form in calmness of soul. Sharing Moltke's destiny in this way gave him further insights into the guidance of nations. Now he accompanies the Moltke individuality on the succeeding stages of his life after death, in adherence to *Memento Mori* which he rewords in a spiritual sense to say 'Share in the destinies of the Dead!'[22] As early as the next day he appeared beside the bier of the deceased who was laid out in his home and spoke three great mantric verses. This, too, was done to continue and build on what had been practised earlier: the communication of verses to Moltke. On the following day Rudolf Steiner repeated this simple ceremony, but now the answer of the departed was already reflected in the verses.

He also gave Eliza von Moltke a message from her deceased husband about their karmic connection in past and future incarnations. This unusual event was just the beginning of a series of communications continuing over many years which Rudolf Steiner translated from the language of the occult into physical language and entrusted to Moltke's widow.

Eliza von Moltke participated in this spiritual conversation

inasmuch as she had acquired some knowledge about the conditions of life after death and was able to establish a connection with
the deceased through meditative concentration. She read him letters which he had once written to her and took him into her
thoughts during her anthroposophical work or when listening to
Rudolf Steiner's lectures. As a personal pupil of Rudolf Steiner she
had received written answers to questions about her schooling—
such as the message of 11 December 1909 which relates to the
quality of consciousness after death. When the physical and the
etheric bodies have been cast off and the paralysis of the spiritual
senses lifts, the 'I' starts to perceive astrally. Rudolf Steiner writes:
'This is indeed like a slow awakening in the spiritual world. One
feels free of the physical body and the "I" begins to perceive. This
applies to *everyone*. With respect to *this* there is no difference at all
between the initiate and the uninitiated after death. The only difference between the two is that the initiate has better orientation as
well as a deeper understanding of what is happening in the spiritual
world. But this is already true to a very high degree when a person
has absorbed knowledge of the spiritual world during his physical
life merely in the form of logical (as opposed to actually perceived)
truths ... The clairvoyant encounters the dead in the spiritual world
and he finds them really awake and fully conscious of their environment. They also gain awareness of what is happening on the earth
(in the physical world) insofar as this is imbued with soul and spirit.
However, for the perception of the purely physical in the physical
world they avail themselves of the sense organs of incarnated
individuals; this is always possible. However, even that is not an
absolute necessity because every physical process has a spiritual
counter-image (a kind of negative exposure) and this is always
perceptible to the dead without any mediation whatsoever.'

Prepared in this way Eliza von Moltke received the messages of
the discarnate soul and accompanied the stages of looking back, of
living through the consequences of the preceding earth life in
reverse order.

In his *Anthroposophical Leading Thoughts* Rudolf Steiner gave a
concise account of the results of his research into destiny, describing
the stages of life after death with a view to the formation of
karma.[23] A few days after death the life-review, in the course of
which individual pictures merge into one panoramic view, recedes,
and the cathartic phase, which spans about one third of the earth

life, begins; this is also referred to as kamaloca. Now the night biography is experienced in reverse order; the soul beholds the effects of the past life in the sense of a moral world order. From this the intention is formed to make good in the next earthly life what has been 'committed' in the preceding one. The actual foundations for the new earth destiny are worked on in the third phase which is purely spiritual.

In the retrospective phase the discarnate soul beholds the deeds and omissions of the previous life on earth from a totally different perspective: not from a personal point of view but in the light of an all-encompassing world justice. What had remained unconscious during life now enters consciousness; but 'the Unconscious' is the sphere of the true 'I' and its supersensible helpers. Their work is revealed to the soul through spiritual experiences. Rudolf Steiner has translated the experiences of the Moltke individuality during this retrospective phase into the language of concept and idea. Now the curtain lifts and a mystery drama begins to unfold: the eternal being of the deceased enters centre-stage.

The course of that life becomes transparent and is perceived as a picture of interweaving forces, seeking and forming destiny. Their repercussions show in the relationships with karmically connected souls as well as with personal opponents in the immediate environments of family and work. The key events and turning points of one's life emerge clearly, the previously hidden leitmotiv of one's destiny becomes visible. The view expands to encompass the incarnation before the last one as well as the immediately preceding one, and these interweave into one picture, in accordance with the individuality's rhythm of maturing.

Two personalities occupy a prominent position on account of their karmic closeness to Moltke: the woman who shared his life with him and the Kaiser. These connections derive from past karma; but their effects were totally opposite: helpful and hindering. This showed as early as the ninth century when both were in the service of the *Curia* and had decisive influence on Pope Nicholas.

Eliza was the person in whose strength of soul Moltke had complete faith. A letter which he wrote to his bride on 1 November 1877,[24] shortly after he had 'discovered' her in Sweden, is a declaration of his innermost certainty and at the same time a testimony to a soul disposition which would ultimately lead him to

Anthroposophy. Both experienced their togetherness as inviolable and absolute.

The Kaiser drew Moltke into his closest circle, conferred numerous distinctions on him and appointed him Chief of the General Staff. Out of this grew tragic calamity. When the political leadership in Germany collapsed in 1914 the military leadership had to operate in its place. And Moltke acted out of a military way of thinking. The General Staff had devised an operational plan for the envisaged war on two fronts which was based on the concept of Moltke's predecessor Schlieffen. This so-called Schlieffen plan was the outcome of military-historical analysis and provided for the destruction of the main enemy, France, through a 'guaranteed victory'. Moltke, an artist in strategy rather than a military technician like Schlieffen, adapted the 1905 plan to the prevailing situation. Nevertheless it failed because the forces and technical resources that the mobile warfare of 1914 required were insufficient.

Steiner's assessment of the situation in which Moltke found himself was that 'military thinking in Germany could arrive at no other conclusion. And this conclusion *condemned* Germany to be in conflict with the whole of the rest of the world. The German people will have to learn from this disaster that *its* way of thinking must be a different one in the future. From a military point of view the war could only appear necessary. Politically, it was unjustifiable, indefensible and futile.'[25]

It was Moltke's tragic destiny to be obliged to wage a war which was considered necessary but doomed to fail. This is Rudolf Steiner's conclusion in his commentary on the intended publication of Moltke's 'Reflections and Memories' in May 1919. This documentation was intended to make a decisive contribution to the debate over Germany's responsibility for the war during the peace negotiations in Versailles. However, its publication was foiled by the intervention of General von Dommes who claimed that the General Staff objected to its contents.[26]

Other events in Moltke's life appear like echoes from the Nicholas incarnation. During an official trip he visited the convent on the Mount of Odilie in the Vosges mountains; he writes about this in a letter to his wife.[27] This convent was founded by St Odilie who lived 150 years before Nicholas; Rudolf Steiner told Eliza von Moltke that it was a spiritual centre: 'from here originated that

Christian stream which Pope Nicholas strove to propagate especially; this stream was to be completely opposite to the Byzantian stream; later on there was a continuous exchange of letters between the Mount of Odilie and Pope Nicholas.'[28] (There is no written evidence of this connection.) In the retrospective journey of the soul after death this soul also recognizes the mirror image character of that memorable encounter with the Russian Tsar Nicholas II. In 1895, the year in which Europe intervened against Japan which had just won the Chinese-Japanese War, Moltke was asked to present a letter from the Kaiser to the Tsar, as well as a painting which had been executed to a design of the Kaiser. It shows a group of Valkyrie-like figures in theatrical attitudes, allegories of the European powers, led by the genius with the flaming sword, standing firm and united against the devastating onslaught of the Mongols with the Christian cross floating above. The Kaiser's handwritten legend 'Nations of Europe, guard what you hold most sacred' points to the meaning of it all, as Moltke explains to the Tsar: the future 'struggle for survival between the white and the yellow race'.[29] Moltke mentions another detail in his report of this visit. While taking leave of the Tsar one of his gloves dropped to the floor. After death the destiny-shaping forces which work through succeeding earth lives rise into consciousness as spirit perception: Rudolf Steiner communicated to Eliza von Moltke on 24 May 1918 what the discarnate soul beheld in connection with the scene described above: 'There is always something like a veil between the human being and the truth: many an apparently insignificant outer event in life is symbolic of this. I stood before the Tsar. Before the representative of the power which after the ninth century had to be confined to the East. I was placed there in the physical body with the painting which has me speak words to do with the opposition of West and East. Words whose origin in thought went back hundreds of years before my birth this time; I spoke. The words which I spoke were a veil. For there was a feud between me and the Tsar. I had to throw down "the gauntlet". The soul can learn so much when it can see the truth through the veils! I have a great deal still to do in order to place the truth of Europe before my soul.'

*

For historical research to attain a level of reality the facts of reincarnation and karma must be considered. 'It is of the utmost importance,' Rudolf Steiner writes in his *Anthroposophical Leading Thoughts*, 'to point out that the observation of the historical evolution of humanity is much enlivened when it is shown that it is the human souls themselves who carry the results of one historical epoch into another as they wander from epoch to epoch in repeated lives on earth.' He adds: 'What is needed is a heartfelt sense for the living human soul, into which one gains deepest insights as a consequence.'[30]

What Rudolf Steiner tells us about Pope Nicholas is in fact inspired by such a sense of karmic insight. Seven years after revealing to Moltke his karmic connection with this personality Rudolf Steiner describes the historical significance of the Pope in a lecture to members (naturally enough, without mentioning the karmic connection). He had received this out of 'anthroposophical esotericism', he said at the end, in order to 'awaken, by means of these "crucial deliberations", a sense [which can become certain knowledge at the end of the century] of the tremendous importance of the present time in history, the importance of seeking to take part in the spiritual worlds.'[31]

When the final words of the last lecture of the cycle *Die Grundimpulse des weltgeschichtlichen Werdens der Menschheit*[31] had been spoken, Rudolf Steiner ended with an appeal to his listeners to become spiritually active. Albert Steffen, who was among them, wrote a summary of this lecture entitled 'Papst Nikolaus I und das europäische Geistesleben' for the weekly journal *Das Goetheanum* (8 April 1923) which he edited at that time. Rudolf Steiner's descriptions, together with the Moltke documentation published by Eliza von Moltke during the same period, inspired him to create a memorial to Moltke's destiny in his play *Der Chef des Generalstabs*.

The Roman Catholic Nicholas was one of the most important and energetic popes in history. Historical sources paint a picture of an imposing ruler and indomitable defender of papal prerogative. 'A second Elias, in spirit and strength,' wrote one chronicler. During his pontificate (858–67) he was confronted with the East-West problem as a result of entanglements with Greece and Franconia. He had to stem the influence of the Byzantine Church in the East and fend off the claims of Franconian bishops and rulers in the West. These facts have been substantiated by historical research. Rudolf Steiner revealed an even deeper layer of reality in his description of the great trials of soul Nicholas had to endure in the severe conflict between East and West.

An eminent personality among the Byzantine church leaders was the patriarch Photius who represented the eastern stream. Its adherents felt superior to the Roman clergy as they considered themselves the heirs of ancient Mystery wisdom. Theirs was a rich and complex cultus which appealed to a more dreamlike soul consciousness and encouraged atavistic vision. Their gaze was directed at the grave of the Redeemer, the pilgrim's haven, Jerusalem, where the Spirit of the Resurrected was sought.

Nicholas encountered a different mentality among the followers of the western stream. There, the Franconian rulers felt themselves connected to the Teutonic priest kings and their Druidic Mystery heritage. This is where the foundations for a culture of the ego were laid. Leaders and followers tested their courage in battle and adventure, continually exercising the virtue of bravery. We find an echo, a higher manifestation of this way of life, in the Arthurian knighthood to which Parzival is connected. He is the embodiment of a stage of evolution where man takes hold of his autonomous self. In his search for the ultimate truth he finds the Grail community which cultivated the esoteric knowledge of the Mystery of Golgotha.

From the vantage point of the Roman pontifex Nicholas experienced the cataclysmic events of his century that was to become one of the nodal points of history. The dissolution of the Carolingian Empire, the Norman invasions and the advance of the Arabs made for constant unrest. In these chaotic conditions there grew an openness for spiritual impulses as well as a desire for far-reaching change. Nicholas was aware of the dangers threatening the emerging consciousness of the Occident from the East and the West; for in the ninth century the Folk Souls began to awaken and respective languages began to form.

The Roman church was now faced with an extraordinary pedagogical task *vis-à-vis* the whole of humanity: to establish the ordering spirit of formalized Christendom within the emerging Occident. With a view to a future of this kind the Pope became the originator of a third stream which fulfilled its historic mission between East and West for the next thousand years. Nicholas, who knew himself to be inspired by the spirit of St Peter, recognized the historic necessity of developing a middle way. Through building on its own foundations and rejecting the influences from both West and East this middle stream acquired a distinct character of its own. In the eastern ritual the soul was held back in a hazy dreamlike state which prevented the ascent to an awakened 'I'-consciousness—this was an echo of a far distant realm of magic. The western Grail stream led the soul to cosmic heights before those thinking forces were developed which are needed to attain to the spiritual in a conscious way and to act out of freedom—prelude of a future which can only turn into the present when materialism has run its course.

The middle and western European parts of humanity were on the path towards a culture of the intellect and of the 'I' and therefore required a different 'evolutionary concept': the modification of the cultus and the intellectualization of the esoteric. The Latin ritual became mere symbol, a demonstration of faith, something that could no longer work into man's etheric being. What had been extracted from the esotericism of the Grail (which did encompass the living experience of the etheric) was merely that which served the intellect to formulate the Christian doctrine of salvation as dogma, and absolved the faithful from finding their own path to supersensible knowledge. The evolutionary impulses engendered by Nicholas in the ninth century carried on working for hundreds of years—with added impetus provided by the Counter-Reformation. This particular orientation of faith has retained its strength and power right into the present, aided by the mummification of spiritual content in the form of dogma as well as by a strict ecclesiastical discipline which obliges the faithful to attend Mass. Since the beginning of the twentieth century, however, this Roman impulse has been waning—as was clearly symbolized by the Vatican II Council (11 October 1962 to 8 December 1965).

Pope Nicholas had to take momentous decisions, decisions of great historical significance. They were rooted in the spirit-related depths of will of certain eminent personalities connected with the 'laws of the evolution of world history'.

In the after-death letters which Rudolf Steiner sent to Eliza von Moltke two key scenes are described which show Pope Nicholas in consultation with his adviser:

In the ninth century 'she' stood by my side ... with the map of Europe in her mind. It was my task then to conceive of ways to separate the East from the West. Many people were involved in this separation. 'She' formed a view of all of these in 'her' mind. But then one was still close to the spiritual world. One was aware of the comings and goings of spiritual beings. Yet the inhabitants of Middle and Western Europe were turning away from the spiritual beings. Already at that time they had to prepare for materialism. But for us in the ninth century there was a lot of directly perceptible spiritual influence. The 'counsellor' would often say then: 'The spirits will withdraw from Europe but, later on, the Europeans will long for them. Without the spirits the Europeans will create their machines and institutions. They will excel at that. But in doing so they will breed in their midst the western people who will drive ahrimanic culture to its highest peak and then take their place.[32]

However, the decision to separate the western and eastern streams of Christianity in order to initiate a culture of the personality from the centre of Europe results in the loss of spiritual reality:

I [the Pope]: Must we lose what spirituality has brought us through the descent from heaven to earth in the tidings of the Crucified One?
'She', the cardinal: What is outmoded must fade; death is but renewed life. I see the life of Europe rising out of Asia's decline.
I: It will be a hard decision.
'She': Nevertheless, it is willed by higher powers so that Ahriman is given proper direction into the life of soul which shall shine forth from Franconia to the East. It was told me by the Northern Lights, which also possess a soul, as I lay in my own country one bright summer evening and listened to the voice of Gabriel, who wishes to bring a New Europe to birth.
I: Are you sure?
'She': There can only be certainty where higher powers are speaking, and I am certain that their message is clear.
I: Maybe they speak clearly enough, but I also know that the centuries to come will weigh heavily upon our souls.

The schism which had been looming ever since the ninth century finally led to the drawing of borders in the Balkans and in eastern Europe which have once again become the source of bloody conflicts in our time.

Moltke's destiny led him through his 'counsellor' to Rudolf Steiner, who has recovered for modern consciousness what was lost from Grail and cultus in the early Middle Ages. The wisdom of the Grail, the esoteric knowledge of the being and the working of the Christ, appears in the language of anthroposophical knowledge and idea; and the reality of the cultus can be gained anew through the spiritual consciousness of inner communion.

In the encounter with the forms of knowledge and experience provided by modern spiritual science the Moltke individuality awakened to its true being; and in looking over his life after death the individuality became aware of what had remained unconscious during earthly life—the direction of working and willing on the eternal path. On 19 October 1916 Rudolf Steiner communicates the following spiritual insight of the deceased to Eliza von Moltke: 'It is the clearest mission of my "I" to work on the European relationship between the Germans and the Slavs. For that it was necessary, during the Nicholas incarnation, to bring about a separation from Europe for the future eastern Slavs. The Greek-Catholic church, as herald of what was to happen later on with the eastern Slavs, was brought about by the church policy of my "I".'

The messages from the Moltke individuality reach particular intensity and frequency in the year 1918. The communication of 22 June 1918 is something of a culmination to its spiritual experience up to that point:

The events of the ninth century are now passing in their own peculiar way into the sphere of existence in which they express their effects on the earth as if in reverse. In the ninth century we pushed back to the East what was of no use for the West and Central Europe. But it continued to live in the East. Since then, it has lived in the souls of the people of the East, but now it is disengaging from the people and is becoming like an auric cloud rolling from East to West. What is thus rolling like an auric cloud across Europe from the East during the course of the twentieth century will take shape at the end of the century in such a way that it will be our task to take hold of it. Humanity is being prepared more and more for the realization that one cannnot be happy with what is to be found solely on the physical plane, though everyone is seeking for it there. People will have to cease looking for *this* happiness and will have to realize that what comes from the spiritual world must flow into everything that the human being experiences on the earth. It is only the combination of earthly and spiritual experience which will produce what is desirable for humanity. But this cannot be made clear to the human being of today. And our task will be concerned with acquiring the forces by means of which the interrelationship of spirit and body can be made clear in social and political life as well. It will be the opposite task from the one we had in the ninth century.

While the Bolsheviks were starting to turn their 'socialist experiment' into reality in Russia, the spiritual and social changes due in the course of the twentieth century entered the vision of the deceased. Meta-history emerges on the spiritual horizon; the view is opened to the end of the century when the seeds of a social order interlinking material and spiritual culture will be planted. This historical turn-around in the twentieth century is now pieced together—like picture and counter-picture—with the events and personalities of the ninth century. At that time the soul disposition of the East, where people were still inspired by the spirit-led forces of the sentient soul, was pushed back while the people of the West and the Middle were already in the process of evolving a world view which resulted in the era of materialism and the social theory of Marxism. But since the beginning of the twentieth century new soul forces have been emerging which build a bridge to the spiritual world. Out of these arise the new centres of spiritual thought and deed in a purely materially-orientated civilization characterized by a one-sided consciousness-soul development: the milieu in which the Moltke individuality can fulfil its intentions.

During the war years Moltke's soul, accompanied by Rudolf Steiner, gained insight into the karma of humanity, into the inter-relationships of human 'I' and world history. Now it is beholding the past of the ninth and the present of the twentieth centuries merged into one picture. Broad perspectives are opening up through a synoptic view of the two centuries. The political-economic polarity of the world powers of East and West reflect the schism of Eastern and Western Christendom. In the ninth century these polarities effected separation—at the end of the twentieth century they disappear. The Roman Church, too, has been seeking a closer relationship to the eastern churches after the Vatican II Council which ended in 1965. In the ninth century national differentiations become apparent in Europe. In the twentieth century there is a clear move towards greater integration—irrespective of nationalist counter-forces. In 869/70 the Eighth Ecumenical Council condemned the concept of trichotomy—the threefoldness of man as body, soul and spirit—as a dual soul doctrine and thus decreed the duality of body and soul. In our time the denied autonomy of the human spirit may be rediscovered on the individual path of schooling shown by Anthroposophy. In the ninth century, approximately, a change in the form of intelligence sets in. What was previously received as intuition from spiritual beings in intelligent behaviour is now taken to be personal achievement. Thus the ninth century appears to be the prelude to the consciousness soul. Through modern spiritual science the consciousness soul is encouraged to attain to a spiritual world content and to form relationships with specific spiritual beings. When that which has been received spiritually finally becomes a formative force in life and begins to work as 'I' or 'Self', the seeds of the so-called Spirit-Self are born. In this way the twentieth century becomes the prelude to the culture of the Spirit-Self, the beginnings of which will be found in a culture of broth-erliness in the Slav East. The co-operation of Central European and Slav elements will pave the way for this stage of evolution.

The Moltke individuality has acquired the ability to perform such work after passing through the necessary preparatory stages during its incarnations in the ninth and twentieth centuries, the nodal points in the evolution of the European people.

*

The historian is tempted to speculate on the history which might have been: What direction might events have taken had Moltke still been alive in 1917? After all there had been an increasingly close co-operation with Rudolf Steiner since the outbreak of war, inter-rupted by Moltke's death in the early summer of 1916. What might have arisen out of such co-operation in the realm of outer cir-cumstances?

From 1916 on developments in the warring states called for urgent decisions. Military strength was waning, and the longing for peace grew. December 1916 marked the beginning of the first fruitless attempts to find a peaceful solution. Then things happened thick and fast. In March 1917, the Tsar was forced to abdicate. In April, America entered the war. In the same month Lenin returned to

Russia from his exile in Switzerland with the approval of the (German) Supreme Army Command to prepare for the revolution with the support of the German Government. The concentration of power in the West, the vacuum in the East, the growing helplessness in the leadership of the Central powers: these were the circumstances that led certain anthroposophists who were familiar with the political scene to ask Rudolf Steiner's advice on the starting of peace negotiations. His answer consisted in describing a method of cognition and creativity in the social sphere which has become known as the 'threefold social order'. Following that, Rudolf Steiner was given the opportunity to present his insights to the politicians in charge and to summarize its central points in two memoranda intended for the German and Austrian governments. Their core message was: 'National liberation is possible, but it can only be the result, not the *foundation*, of man's liberation. When individual people are liberated, national liberation will follow suit.' Rudolf Steiner substituted the right of national self-determination with the individual's right of self-determination. In accordance with the principle of nationality— the programme of the American President Wilson—the peace treaties resulted in the creation of 'nation states' whose ethnic heterogenity has, as a rule, led to terrible conflicts. In the context of the formative principle of social 'threefolding', the power of the state is limited to the legislative field so that cultural autonomy and a self-administering co-operative economy can develop. This principle of social order is derived from the perception of a historical 'settlement date'; because in the twentieth century evolution has reached a stage where the centralization of state power can be replaced by a free system of contracts with mature citizens. That is why political structures must be created which correspond to the actual degree of freedom attained by modern man. The politicians, however, failed to recognize this world-historical challenge and considered it sufficient to revise what already existed. The 'waking call of the spirit', which could be heard in the social willing and feeling of the people, died away in the chaos of the post-war era.

*

From the point of view of the century's end the perspectives widen. Events have taken place which are generally referred to as the 'Great Change': the collapse of the eastern bloc and the settlement of the East-West conflict. The cataclysmic events which for the most part have come to pass in a peaceful manner defy the conventional analyses of political scientists and sociologists. 'Moments of world-historical changes', as Rudolf Steiner characterized them, have become part of our contemporary experience. What seemed at first to be beyond anyone's imagination has now become reality. Since the 'Great Change' a variety of anthroposophical activities have taken root in Eastern Europe, mostly in the fields of education, curative work and agriculture. This work has led to a new stage in the process of history; for the combining of Central European and Slav elements in fruitful co-operation helps lay the foundations for the coming age of civilization.

This new situation invites us to embark on an inner path that may lead us from the formative way of thinking more characteristic of the Central European to the devotional way of thinking of the East, thus opening our soul to the realities of the spirit. In that readiness to receive, the 'I' can open up to the guiding powers of spiritual beings whose impulses are waiting to stream in from the spheres of the Folk Spirit, the Time Spirit and the Spirit of Mankind. In this way the 'interrelationship of spirit and body in social and political life', as envisaged by the Moltke individuality, can become our individual experience.

It is astonishing how readily people in the East accept the way in which Anthroposophy is brought to them by Central Europeans: it is as if the German self-estrangement at the time of National-Socialist rule and the decades of European division and westernization of the Federal Republic had never happened. This shows that a factor of reality which is needed for the future of humanity is coming to prevail in changed form and independent of its original territory. What is to be encouraged by the impulses of the threefold social order—in agriculture as operating structure, as land rights and system of revenue; in education as pedagogy oriented by the true needs of the child in self-administered schools—is inherently convincing because it speaks to a deeply-rooted longing for a Christian order in the Slav soul; the yearning for a 'revolution of brotherliness', of which Bolshevism was a mere caricature.

Rudolf Steiner was counting on this openness of Eastern Europe to the cultural mission of Central Europe, as we perceive it today, when he developed the key elements of the threefold social order in 1917. For one historic moment the possibility shone out that the spiritual researcher's proposal with regard to the social restructuring in Central and Eastern Europe—even before the beginning of the 'socialist experiment'—might be openly received by those in power.

With hindsight it is clear that there was an opportunity in the crucial year of 1917 to fundamentally redirect the course of events. What came to pass instead of a new social order in Middle and Eastern Europe, where thrones were toppling, was the misguided development of Bolshevist and Fascist dictatorships with the resultant threat to humanity. Following the dissolution of the Soviet Union and the anachronistic People's Democracies it is obvious that the present difficulties and conflicts are related to the failure to take up the modern social impulse. Neither nationalistic struggles nor ecologically destructive activities can be remedied without breaking up the interdependence of political, economic and cultural systems.

Now that the division of Europe, signed and sealed in Yalta in 1945, has outlived its destiny the facts of history point towards a common European home. The economic giant in the middle of Europe—the Federal Republic of Germany—is investing financially in the desolated areas left behind by the Communist regimes in the South-East and East of the continent. But this kind of commitment, which is driven by economic power considerations, has proved, in the past, to be inimical to life. The establishment of true culture in Eastern Europe does, however, require the spark of ideas to release truly creative forces. This is the field of activity the Moltke-'I' has set its sights on. 'Now my willing is connected with the resurgent weaving of the spirit. We must sow seeds in the ruins of the past. The untruth of the time has led into wreckage and ruin. Truth must lead to the building of the new.'[34]

Building bridges has always been the hallmark of the Moltke individuality's task. As Roman Pope he carried the title of Pontifex, the bridge builder. As Prussian Chief of the General Staff he found the connection to the German Folk Spirit. At the turn of the century he perceives his task as 'working on the relationship between the German and the Slav people'. In this way he serves the progress of evolution, the preparation of the next cultural epoch.

PART ONE

Certainly we should strive for ever greater spiritualization but, in my view, not by negating and despising what is material but by always emphasizing more clearly the ideal elements within it, by transfiguring and lighting up with the spiritual that is there: love, compassion for others, sensitivity, forbearance towards others' mistakes. In this way we will create a spiritual world in material clothing for ourselves, we will not despise what is earthly but ennoble it. We will not want to tear the world in which we live from its hinges but will recognize our material existence for what it should be—an intermediate step to a better existence. If we were to want to break this rung out of the ladder of world development our foot would step into the void and since we haven't got any wings we should fall. In my opinion we should stand firmly and safely on this rung with our gaze directed upwards, conscious that there are further rungs to come, but very clear, too, that we cannot step on to the next one until we have found our balance on this one.

(Helmuth von Moltke in a letter to his wife of 15 April 1903)

1. Letters from Helmuth von Moltke to Eliza von Moltke 1877–1914

Creisau, 1 September 1877

Today is the first of September. Seven years ago I stood on the battlefield and listened with trepidation to the roar of the artillery ahead of us in the hills surrounding Sedan.[1] At the same hour at which I now write, the iron dice were still hurtling to and fro and nobody knew whose throw would be successful. Now, seven years later, church bells are ringing out throughout all the German Reich and thousands of hearts bow to him who directs the fate of nations with a firm hand; and from thousands upon thousands of German hearts there rises a prayer of thanks that the dream which the German people had dreamed for centuries had come true—a prayer of thanks, too, that we have experienced the radiant, full rise of the sun of union even if it did come after a bloody and dark night; that sun for which our fathers and ancestors had already given their blood and of which they had glimpsed but the first glow in the morning sky.

GHQ, Berlin, 4 October 1877

I am glad that you liked the *Faust* performance. I am continually drawn back irresistibly to this book that I have read so many countless times that I know it nearly all by heart. It is a work which combines all the music of poetry within itself, from the archangels' song of praise to the derisive laughter of hell—from the powerful thoughts of a man's wrestling with titans to the chatter of an innocent girl's heart. The greatest work that our German literature has ever created.

GHQ, Berlin, 13 October 1877

I think I have done enough work for today. My thoughts, which I have focused for long enough on my own papers, wish to have their own way, and are tearing themselves away—reaching far into the distance towards the North. I wish I could go there with them! It is now late at night. I have been so steeped in my work that I have not noticed how the hours have passed by, and the hands of the clock advanced further and further. Around me there is only the silence of the night. Sleep has enveloped the town, descending with softly beating wings and silencing the noise of the day. The friend of the poor and the needy, it is probably gracing already many a face which only hours ago was furrowed by stress and anxiety with a quiet peaceful smile, bringing sweet dreams to the tormented in which the toil of the day may be forgotten—there is no sign of movement in the quiet rooms adjoining mine. There is only the clock ticking away in its busy monotone, and my lamp sheds its yellow light on the sheet of paper on which I am now writing in black letters. It really is the time when I love to work. When the carriages no longer clatter through the streets, and there is no loud noise to distract my attention, that is when the powers of my spirit awaken; everything can be so quickly and easily understood, that it is a sheer delight, and I can really feel what it is to work with relish, and to wage a campaign against the books, as if they were an enemy who must be defeated if one is to experience the joy of victory. However I am not alone in these hours devoted to work. Your spirit and your image are with me, my faithful companion. You join me in my work, and endure with me until I push back the books and say, 'Enough for today'. The feeling grows stronger in me every day that I have the power to make something of myself, and it is the thought of you which is the living spring at which I gather strength to go onwards, onwards ever onwards, as is my duty both to you and to my name.

GHQ, Berlin, 1 November 1877[2]

I have often thought that a human spirit's thoughts are a model of how he will later develop. That is how I imagine the soul after death. The body is then discarded and, as foreordained, turns to dust and ashes returning to the earth out of which it was formed and to which it belongs; whereas consciousness remains alive and just as now we can transfer ourselves in thought in a moment from one place to another, so then we can travel in reality through the unending spaces of creation; just as now, in thought, we can look ahead in time or backwards into the days of early childhood and even back into the dimmest recesses of the oldest history known to man so, after death, we are in reality able to shift ourselves backwards and forwards—time has then ceased to carry us along with it without our willing it; we stand above time, that is time no longer exists, and that is Eternity. I find the idea beautiful—to be able to wander from world to world through the infinite pillars of heaven, to see that which is now only an inkling, and to enjoy in it the bliss that has been promised in perceiving God's glory which reveals itself, as we may understand it, in the tremendous works of the almighty Creator. This thought gives me more pleasure than the rigid peace of death in which it is said that we sleep until the Trumpets of the Day of Judgement frighten us out of our slumber. We sleep a lot down here on earth already without needing to get down to it properly after death! But don't think that I share the views of the spiritualists. In my opinion when we die we have finished with this earth and do not return to it. I think you will understand me and not take me for a mystical visionary.

GHQ, Berlin, 7 November 1877

You must not believe the silly rumours of war. France still has too many wounds to lick to wish for any more. But if we really do have to go to war then you too must grit your teeth and let me go to do my duty like everyone alse. My blood and my body belong to the King and to the Fatherland, but my heart is my own.

GHQ, Berlin, 28 November 1877

You ask me in your last letter whether I don't find social conversation awful. I can't say that I do. One can't discuss everything with everybody and before one finds somebody who interests himself in something other than what directly affects him, the search can take a long time. You are quite right in thinking that there are very few really bright people: but it is really a blessing that this kind of conversation, which you find dreadful, has been invented. How should one carry on in society and with a person who, hearing something he does not encounter every day, can only respond with a 'yes' or a 'no' and sometimes not even that, if we did not have this kind of social intercourse which we can pull on like a pair of well-worn slippers into which the whole world knows how to slip? What could one talk to such a person about? If I am quite indifferent to the person I prefer to choose a quite indifferent subject of conversation—like is attracted to like. So one speaks words for half an hour and afterwards each party considers himself to have participated in an excellent conversation. Everything is pleasing and satisfying and each one thinks about himself 'You really are much more important than the other person'. And, because both think this way, they are very kind and charming, for human beings are never more kind and charming than when they are pleased with themselves. Not that I would go so far as to maintain that one gains anything from this kind of conversation but it is nevertheless the great roadway on which everybody can get together and find their way and which is sufficiently broad and well-worn that no one can miss it. This intercourse is conventional and laid down like all rules connected with decency and good manners which, at times admittedly, are stupid and amazing and yet, if they were not adopted, we should revert to an age where we would live on acorns like our ancestors, attacking one another with clubs.

GHQ, Berlin, 24 January 1878

When you encounter a person with petty thoughts, someone who crawls in the dust and feels at home in filth, let all the pride in your soul burst out like a hurricane; turn away in contempt from everything that is petty and vulgar and hold fast to the ideal, the true and the beautiful and then feel pride in your belief in truth and right, pride against petty people, pride against lies and slander. Always turn your gaze upwards; never downwards. Open wide your heart wherever you come across truth and beauty but close it firmly against everything that is wrong.

GHQ, Berlin, 10 February 1878

A knot and a piece of national colour is what I now have from your activities. Shall I send you something from mine as well? What shall it be? The odd thought about fortifications or some piece of war history from which it can be seen that human beings have fought wars against each other since time began, that they have shed their blood for phantoms which disappeared in their hands like soap bubbles! I could also send you war history in black and white and then we would both have our work in two colours!

GHQ, Berlin, 3 April 1878

Now I have really had enough of everything known by the name of society, and I am drawing a line under it and checking the balance. What is the outcome? Not much profit as far as I am concerned. The same people as before, the same interests, the same kind of thoughts that I got to know last winter present themselves to me once again. How petty these people are whose only thoughts concern their own dear selves, the god to whom all sacrifices are made. I do not know whether this year I judge them more harshly than previously or whether, perhaps, my observations are more objective than last year, but I have never before noticed the triviality of society people to the same extent as this winter; and if I am honest I have never before seemed to myself so foolish as in recent months, acting a polite figure in society without my heart being in it. I don't want to have anything to do with this society, I find nothing of value in it worth stooping for if it lay at my feet; it offers nothing uplifting, it is just a pale imitation of ordinary people with all their faults, petty interests, egotism, hidebound and irresponsible. Now all this has come to an end, all these pleasures and vanities have lost their value, I have found life's true value. You once wrote to me 'Life in high society has no lasting value'. You really were right. I think that you are very often right but you must always say it to me as well.

Wittenberg, 14 September 1879

Here I sit in the old town of the Elbe which was home to Luther. Today is another day of rest. We're quartered in a village called Dabrun near the town, and have gone in today to see the sights. Actually very interesting. I stood for a long time before the door of the old *Schlosskirche* where Dr Martin Luther once nailed up his 95 Theses, and in doing so sparked off a fire in the excitable minds of his time which, within a few years, flared into the huge torch of the Thirty Years' War, which blazed its way across Germany's flowery meadows, and set culture back by centuries. At the same time, this European conflagration cleansed the corrupt religion of old, leaving it with new and purer ideals. Now there is a door of bronze there in which Luther's Theses are engraved in old, cumbersome Latin. In those days the German language was not used by the belligerents within the Church. The Church militant fought with the sword of Rome. Today it is different, and our common German language, perhaps the only thing we really have in common, is something we owe to a very large extent, to that monk from Wittenberg, who fearlessly took up the struggle against Pope and Emperor, and fought on to eventual victory. Then we went to Luther's rooms in the old University. His living room is still preserved as it was then. The wooden benches against the walls, the big table, the stove. Pictures of Luther, painted by Cranach. At that window, with its dull leaded panes, sat Katharina Bora, his wife and looked out for the Doctor as he made his way back from the College to his home. In the main hall of the University building, one can still see the tall old lectern from which he gave his lectures, and at which, while still almost a boy, he gave his doctoral dissertation and received his degree. One feels almost enveloped by the old spirit of the Reformation when one walks through these rooms. Ancient, powerful, sturdy and blunt. But healthy and lasting. Those were great and important times, and Luther was a man to be reckoned with.

Vichel, 11 July 1880

I have my *Faust* again as a constant companion. You should see me bending over my surveyor's table alone in the middle of the waving grass declaiming monologues from *Faust* while simultaneously measuring the distances with my dividers. Every now and again I have to laugh at myself and it sounds quite solitary and lost in the quiet air. A person who laughs at himself on his own is quite remarkable; just as well that it isn't the cutting laughter of mockery or despair, but a comfortable inner laugh at a fantasist, who, in the middle of the most practical and prosaic work, has to satisfy his spiritual thirst for beauty with a draught from the crystal spring of Goethe's poetry. In this way hours pass like minutes and again and again I discover new gems which I had not previously noticed. A working day like this lasting twelve to thirteen hours always makes me contented. When I go home in the evening I have a certain joyful feeling of satisfaction.

Nackel, 21 July 1880

Look, how beautiful the world is! What would man be if he couldn't hope? A stunted character wallowing in dark, obscure pains and tormenting himself with secret horrors. Mourning and weeping over the past, over what has been lost and what has not been achieved, reproaching himself in unspeakable anguish. No, Hope, this true daughter of heaven, according to the lovely old saga, was a gift to humans when all the sorrows flew around them from out of Pandora's box: hope alone balanced out all the sorrows. Men's eyes are directed forwards and this is the right direction to look—towards the light that the morning brings us. Anyone who looks round or back turns into a pillar of salt like Lot's wife. Open eyes and open hearts, you know, is my outlook and attitude.

Charlottenburg, 10 July 1881

If only I could be with you and so be able to take delight in the wonderful, gigantic, natural surroundings whose quite unimagined magic must already have taken you captive. What feelings will take you by storm at your first sight of these rigid snow crests which rear up in eternal silence into the blue sky, the clouds weaving a crown around their foreheads, gazing down in icy calm on the restlessness of human crowds below with their quarrels and wrangling, their tears and joys, and their hates and loves. Does one not feel to have got closer to nature when one enters into these gigantic shapes which it has created? Does one not believe that one can still sense the almighty Creator's breath blowing about these mountain tops, does one not feel tiny when one gazes up at the rock faces which stood there long before the first helpless human being began to learn how to live on earth? How wonderful it is to look at Nature in its richness. Certainly it is not flowing pleasantly or gently. There it confronts us, rough and jagged but full of strength and backbone, full of the mysterious beholding of an almighty World Spirit and powerful Creator that strengthens and steels heart and senses. You will see how the nerves become strong at the sight of greatness and how the chest expands and the pulse quickens on breathing the tangy mountain air. I take it that you crossed Lake Constance and then went up to the Rhine Valley? Now you are close to the source of this ancient German river along whose vineyard-covered banks so much German and French blood has flowed. Later you will see this aristocrat of rivers in its lower reaches and be overcome by their charming beauty. 'To the Rhine, to the Rhine, do not wander to the Rhine' sings the poet, because once you have seen it, and its charms have captured your heart, you will fall sick with a permanent longing for its green banks. How great are the events in world history connected with this stream whose weak, trickling spring you will have seen. You are now enthroned so many thousands of feet above us other mortals who have to get on with our existence below on a deep, sandy plain.

Berlin, 15 July 1881

You write so charmingly and so interestingly that I can savour once more with you everything that you have seen. I can really see from your letter how much your inner life has awakened, and strives towards the light, towards self-knowledge, and towards the world around you. Only continue in this way to let everything that you see work upon you, open yourself to all that is magnificent and beautiful in the world, and you yourself will feel how your delight in these joys becomes purer each day, how every day you will learn how better to take unsullied delight in the beauties of life. When you experience this joy within you, you will make others happy, and then, in consciousness of being in harmony with your fellow human beings, you will find an ever new source of joy. That is why I, too, attach such importance to this journey, since I know that nothing is more likely to distract one's spirit from its own preoccupations and to direct it to the world around us than a journey, with its new impressions attracting our attention each day, with the interest it awakens for things one has never seen before, and its appeal to the yearning for travel that lies within each of us, to be awakened as soon as we hear the sound of the posthorn, and the clatter of the carriage wheels on cobbles. All this forces one out of oneself and as new impressions come towards one each day, one has no time to relax into one's musings, no time to speculate or brood, for the beauties of the world out there are simply too attractive. The springs leaping from the crags, the larks singing aloud for joy— which of us would not wish to sing with them with untroubled mind and open heart.

Ragaz, 25 August 1884

I have experienced another couple of delightful incidents with Uncle Helmuth of which I shall give you a brief account, since I have neither the time nor the peace of mind for a long letter. Firstly: a few days ago we were sitting in the garden in the morning when he said to me he would like to walk up to the Wartenstein ruin. Since it was rather a steep climb, we could walk slowly up the footpath which crosses the road, and catch the mail coach on its way up which would leave at ten o'clock. Then he gave me some money, and asked me to change it for him. So I go to the office and he remains sitting on the bench. When I return after ten minutes, he is no longer there. This wasn't altogether surprising since, knowing him as I do, I hadn't expected to find him where I left him. So I resign myself to searching for him, walk through the garden, the reading room, look for him in his room, nowhere is there a trace of him to be found. So then I think he may have gone on ahead, and I set off briskly up the steep footpath, don't find him, reckon he cannot possibly have gone as far as that, turn back, search the whole area once more, make enquiries at the reception, ask the waiter, no one has seen him.

In the meantime, it is almost ten o'clock, and I think to myself—if he had wanted to catch the mail coach, he must already be quite a long way up the hill. So I run up like a stag—straight up the hill, cutting the corners of the path while far above me the mail coach is already setting off. In 15 minutes I reach the top of the Wartenstein. I have never sweated so much in all my life! Rivers of sweat were running off me, but I had reached the top a little ahead of the mail coach. However, Uncle Helmuth is not on board! So I give up all hope of finding him, run back, and on my return have a complete change of clothes. At one o'clock a beaming Uncle Helmuth turns up. Where has he been? Straight across the garden towards Magenfeld in the very opposite direction to Wartenstein. There he had had a look at an old castle, after which, he reported gleefully, he had wanted to give a tip to the owner who had shown him everything, and whom he had mistaken for the gardener. He had only recognized his mistake when the latter had indignantly turned down his tip!

Secondly: yesterday at eight o'clock, while I was still getting dressed, Uncle Helmuth knocks at my door with his stick as he goes past in the way he always does when he wants to go for a coffee. I set off after him about five minutes later, and find he has already finished his coffee. I say 'Good Morning', he says 'Good Morning', remains seated while I drink my coffee, and then goes into the garden. I calmly finish my coffee, and follow him into the garden. No Uncle Helmuth to be found. I scour the whole garden, no trace of him. I happen to return to the entrance hall of the hotel, and the receptionist says there is a message from His Excellency that he has gone to the station hoping to be there in time to catch the train to Glarus. So I set off after him and catch up with him. He is furious: 'Of course, we'll be too late, you might have got up earlier.' I say, 'Well, if I had only had the faintest inkling that we were going to Glarus!' A few steps later he said, 'You might at least have taken your *Baedeker* with you to check whether we have a connection back.' I declare I will make good both these omissions, turn back, run to the hotel, fetch the *Baedeker*, and run back after him. I am astonished that I can't find him until at last I see him far in the distance, on a wrong path! So I calmly walk down to the station and wait for him there. He eventually arrives five minutes before the departure of the train, half dead with asthma, and still cross at me for being so unprepared for this journey, of which I had not the faintest inkling. I did not voice the thought that occurred to me: 'Why did you not mention it when you knocked at my door?'

Otherwise he is always delightfully amiable, and once we were sitting in the train with our first class return tickets, certain of a convenient connection for our return journey, his good mood was quickly restored.

GHQ, Berlin, 16 June 1888

At ten o'clock Uncle Helmuth and I will be leaving for Potsdam, where Uncle Helmuth will visit the young Kaiser. Now we are back again from Potsdam, and I have also seen this dead Kaiser,[3] as the one before him.[4] How different was that impression! In the case of the latter peace and calm, the end of a life that has run its course and trickled away quietly, but here all the traces of dreadful suffering that has stripped a man of his vitality and torn him from life, a man who seemed destined by nature to carry on for a long time yet. I would have never recognized those sunken features as belonging to a man whom I had last seen in blooming health and strength. His nose was sharp and protruding, his eye-sockets deeply sunken, his cheekbones protruding. Around his mouth, visible in spite of the beard, and between the drawn-together eyebrows, a trait of deepest woe, of unspeakable pain. Something totally strange in the yellowy pale emaciated face with its almost stubbly moustache. The hair on the broad forehead had thinned, the beard on his chin was shaded in grey. Out of this whole appearance there spoke uncannily, almost devilishly triumphant, the demon of that gruesome illness. The dead face told a shocking story of unspeakably painful wrestling with the Angel of Death. It was as if it had trodden the resisting human strength under its feet until it collapsed, moaning woefully, heart-rendingly. His great strong hands were emaciated to the bone, almost transparently pale, crossed over the chest, holding his heavy cuirassier's dagger that lay across the bed—long and shining. It looked as if he was pressing his own executioner's sword to his chest! Under the cover one could make out the contours of his long rigid body. I cannot express how painfully all this imprinted itself within me, what unspeakable misery spoke out of it all. How dreadful are the lies that have been spread about the state of the poor Kaiser, for his death did not arrive suddenly and unexpectedly, that can be seen all too clearly, but slowly and gradually, step by step, he was tortured to death; and when he had to fulfil representative duties and when it was said of him: he enjoyed a good night, in fact he sleeplessly counted the strikes of the clock, each of which as it faded away brought him a step closer to his end, an end of unspeakable torture, which he, God alone knows how, must have fervently longed for and prayed for. Poor Kaiser, his heart filled with plans for the exercising of a power for which he had to wait over many years beyond the prime of his life, devoted to the utmost to the well-being of the people with whom he has fought and argued in difficult, yet heroically fresh and beautiful times, how cruel has been his destiny! Is it not as if he has paid heavily for all the sins of his people, he, the pure and idealistic Prince!

Can the relatively short suffering on the stem of the cross have been more terrible than this protracted dying over many months, than this cruelly enforced renunciation of everything that fills heart and soul, of the preparation of an entire lifetime? Poor Kaiser, shaken to the uttermost depth of our being we are turning away, as if painfully numbed in head and senses. I hardly know how we got back, but I had to tell you about the impression I received and I know that you will feel it with me.

Weimar, 10 October 1892

I spent the few hours that remained to me looking round the Goethehaus, and the library that he kept. The room in which he died, a small one facing the garden, containing a bed with coarse sheets, the armchair before it in which Goethe died, his little washstand with the simplest wash basin, and a brown earthenware water jar has been preserved exactly how it was. A solemn mood comes over one when one steps into this little chamber, which does not even contain a stove, and contemplates this unadorned, almost poor room in which one of the greatest of spirits relinquished his earthly sheath. The adjoining study is just as simply furnished. Hard, straight limbed furniture, entirely without ornament, or provision for comfort. The rich and vital spiritual world in which Goethe lived probably meant that he did not concern himself with externals. I could have spent many hours in these rooms in which are preserved all the collections he made and ordered. But time was short, and I had to be content with a cursory stroll through the house.

Berlin, 15 December 1892

I know that you too have a sense for the beautiful and ancient memories which are so abundant in Weimar, and I can imagine the uncanny feeling of holy awe that comes over you when you visit the places which still bear the mark of the great spirits who lived and, as you say, suffered there. Certainly they will have suffered there. How else could they have achieved such greatness. Just as the human being is born in pain, so too his best spiritual creations come through great suffering and pain. The pain that he has gone through becomes a blessing for his fellow human beings. The surroundings in which these spiritual heroes lived were plain and simple. They built their temples within themselves. One cannot imagine the man who could conceive and express *Faust* in the midst of the comforts of modern life.

St Petersburg, 17 November 1894

This was all so rushed and unexpected, the news of the death of your father[5] and our departure which could not be delayed at that point. Now I stood by the bier of another dead,[6] by a bier around which all the pomp and glamour of the earthly is unfolding once more before the quiet man resting upon it will be placed in the tomb, and at the same time there lies in Sweden that other quiet man, probably still on his simple bed, and what difference has now remained between the two? They have become equal before the Almighty equalizer, they are removed from human activity and Our Lord will weigh them up irrespective of what was the difference between them in earthly life.

St Petersburg, 2 October 1895[7]

I arrived here on 29 September and, as the mission was a complete surprise and I had no things with me, I ordered my uniform and passport from Berlin by telegram. They arrived on the same train on which I continued my journey and were handed over to me at Trakehnen. At the Russian frontier at Wirballen my arrival had been notified and I was very politely received by the Chief of

Customs and I was admitted without difficulty. The same gentleman had reserved a sleeping compartment for me which, as he said, had already been sold, but from which the occupant had been ejected without further ceremony, a procedure which for the one who profits from it is very pleasant but which for the one who has to accept it must be equally unpleasant. As the expellee was not known to me and remained so I slept with a pretty clear conscience on the comfortable sleeping sofa in the wide coach which, travelling at the very slow speed of the Russian trains, provided an excellent resting place. I left Rominten at 9 a.m. and Trakehnen at 11.30 a.m. and the train arrived in Petersburg at midday the next day—an hour late by the timetable. Our Ambassador, Count Radolin, and the Military Attaché, Captain Lauenstein, were on the platform and had been waiting for a full hour. The former told me that the Imperial Russian Lord Chamberlain's office had arranged for me to stay in the Hotel de l'Europe as the Tsar's guest and that a palace carriage and manservant had been placed at my disposal. I drove to my hotel where I found that a lovely suite had been prepared for me consisting of an anteroom, sitting room and bedroom; then to our Embassy in order to pay my call there and to stay to luncheon. In the evening I went to the Opera with Lauenstein.

At 11 a.m. next day, 30 September, an audience with the Tsar had been arranged in Zarskoje Selo. I travelled out there by the 10 a.m. train from here. It takes about 30 minutes like the journey from Berlin to Potsdam. From the station I drove for about ten minutes to the small Alexander Palace where the Tsar lives, leaving the great baroque-style palace built by Catherine the Great unoccupied. I was received immediately by the Lord Chamberlain, Count Benckendorf, and led straight away through a series of rooms, halls and corridors into the Tsar's ante-room. As we were passing along a narrow corridor, the entrance to which was guarded by two huge pitch-black Moors dressed in oriental costume and armed to the teeth, a door opened at our side and the Tsar appeared in a white piqué jacket in the act of crossing to a door opposite. As soon as he saw us he quickly shut the door and we were left making deep bows to the closed door. Then we arrived at the ante-room in the middle of which stood a billiard-table, just as in the *aide-de-camp*'s room in Berlin, and a short stout man with a large roll of drawings under his arm who was waiting for the moment when he would be admitted to make his presentation. He was introduced to me as the Minister for Naval Affairs.

After a few minutes' wait a footman, duly instructed by Count Benckendorf, announced my arrival to the Tsar. There was no sign of either a general or an *aide-de-camp*. The Tsar is said to live most of the time in non-military surroundings; as I understood it the only other persons present at the palace are the Equerry to the Imperial Stud and the Commander of the Bodyguard. I now entered—pretty heavily burdened—His Majesty's study. I was naturally wearing full-dress uniform and carried in one hand my helmet and sabre, and in the other our Emperor's letter, and under my arm a rolled-up picture. The latter had been designed by our Emperor, drawn by Professor Knackfuß and duplicated in lithograph. I was to hand over this picture at the same time as the letter. The Tsar immediately came towards me with outstretched hand and said 'I am glad to see you here. We know one another already.' It was only after I had concentrated in my left hand—not without difficulty—all my things, plus the glove taken off my right hand, that I was able to take the hand so kindly offered to me. I then handed over the letter and an explanation of the picture which I unrolled with His Majesty's help on a table. The picture shows a group of female figures dressed in ancient costumes of the kind worn by the Valkyries, standing on a rocky spur, gazing out over prosperous towns, rivers carrying shipping, and a plain of cultivated fields. They represent the European states; in the foreground is Germany, pressed close up against Russia, and to one side is France; behind France, Austria, Italy, England, etc. In front of them pointing into the distance with one hand and holding a flaming sword in the other, the Cherub of War, and above them, radiant, the Cross. Beyond the blooming landscape, trade and commerce, representing European culture and civilization, can be seen dense clouds of smoke rising from a burning city. The choking fumes advance threateningly in thick clouds which as they thicken take on the shape of a dragon. Out of the smoke the picture of Buddha rises up gazing at the destruction with cold and staring eyes. What this is all about is the coming struggle for existence, already discernible, between the white and yellow races. The idea for this picture occurred to His Majesty as the first steps towards peace between China and Japan were taken; these presented a danger that the huge mass of the Chinese empire, on whose development Japan was trying to gain significant influence, might be brought into ferment to further Japan's expansionist aims. The consequence of this would be a wave of destruction across Europe caused by the yellow race. Below the picture, written by the Kaiser himself, are the words 'Peoples of Europe, guard all that you hold most holy'. I did not miss the opportunity to add to my explanation that this danger had been averted for the time being by the wise policies and joint actions of Russia, Germany and France. The Tsar took a keen interest in the picture and I had to explain all the details to him. I pointed out how in the silhouette of the towns one could see the cupolas of the Orthodox Church alongside the spires of the Protestant Cathedral and when the Tsar asked whether one city at which he pointed represented Moscow I replied that although I did not actually know whether my Most Gracious Master had had this particular city in mind Moscow would certainly be just as threatened as every other European city. After viewing the picture the Tsar was kind enough to carry on quite a long conversation with me and he charged me with the task of conveying his letter of reply back to our Kaiser. After he had said goodbye to me in a most gracious manner he went on to say, 'You will certainly wish to see the Empress. Do send in your name to her.' As I retired backwards, bowing low as I went, I lost a glove which was brought out to me by a footman. A superstitious person would perhaps have seen an omen in this which, hopefully, God and all the Saints will wish to avert.

I then had myself announced to the Empress who after a short delay received me on her own. Here, too, there was no sign of a lady-in-waiting and I was announced by a footman. The Empress looked exquisite. She had a fresh complexion, the radiant eyes of a Madonna and really looked like an Empress in her braided mourning dress. She carried on a very friendly conversation with me; I had to tell her about the Kaiser at Rominten and about the Kaiserin and their children. As she offered her hand to me on my departure I raised it to my lips with the feeling that the Russians ought to be really grateful to their Orthodox God that he had summoned such an Angel of Light to sit on the throne of their empire.

Later I received a telegram from the Lord Chamberlain, Benckendorf: 'L'Empereur vous recevra demain jeudi a onze heures. Train a dix heures.' So, tomorrow I shall receive my written reply and will be able to set out on my return journey at midnight tomorrow.

(...)

The oldest railway in Russia runs from Pavlovsk via Zarskoje Selo to Petersburg. It is the fourth railway ever to be constructed in Europe and is unique in that the width of its track is even wider than the rest of the Russian rail network. The wooden station buildings, wooden platforms, the extraordinarily wide coaches with rattling windows and dirty, threadbare upholstery give the impression that nothing has been changed or repaired since the railway was built. Yet, in spite of this, it is most heavily used since in summer half of the population of St Petersburg streams out every afternoon in order to stroll along the dry paths under the damp old trees or to sit in front of the huge wooden music pavilion in which concerts are given every day by the best band-masters.

This morning I went to the Peter and Paul Cathedral and laid a wreath on the sarcophagus of the deceased Tsar Alexander III. I had a wreath made entirely from laurel leaves with a large black and silver bow, on one side of which was a large W and on the other side a crown, both made from laurel leaves. 'De la part de sa Majesté l'Empereur d'Allemagne' as I told the Fortress Commander. The church was full of people who stared in amazement at me in my Prussian uniform.

Moscow, 27 May 1896

Yesterday the coronation took place in the most perfect weather. The Russians really do have luck with these functions. Just as on the day of moving in, the weather yesterday for the coronation was marvellous. The sun burned down with almost southern warmth from a cloudless sky. If it had been rainy the coronation could not actually have taken place as the whole procession with all its pomp moves along mostly in the open. We had to drive off to the Kremlin as early as 7.30 a.m. to take our places on a stand set up in a wide castle courtyard. At 8.30 the ceremonies began with the Tsar's Empress mother going to church. Under a golden baldachin with ostrich feathers and with a diamond crown on her head and an ermine cloak around her shoulders, supported by ten gentlemen, she walked out of the palace to the Uspensky cathedral where the coronation is to take place. We had very good seats from which we could see the whole of the courtyard in which two intersecting board paths for the procession had been set up, covered with red cloth. One led from the great staircase of the palace to the cathedral a few hundred paces away while the other crossed the courtyard transversely. A third path led along the side of the coronation cathedral to the Ivan Weliky, then to the Archangel cathedral, on to the church of Mary's Annunciation and then back to the open-air stairs. This is the path that the Tsar has to take when his coronation has been completed and in each of the churches named above, which surround the courtyard, he has to pray. The huge courtyard was crammed with deputations from the whole population—all the peoples united under the Russian sceptre were represented here— from Uzbeks in turbans to Finns dressed in furs. The Horse Guards in helmets and cuirasses formed a guard of honour on one side of the courtyard and the Members of the Imperial Caucasian Body-guard in their scarlet tunics on the other. Towards nine o'clock trumpet fanfares announced that the procession had moved off. Everyone removed his headdress. A rolling cheer swelled up from the multilingual throats of the masses who in their excitement milled around among themselves. The whole of the huge courtyard, lined with numerous stands on which the bright dresses of the ladies glimmered, in between them the glittering uniforms of the troops forming the guard of honour, and the whole surrounded by the gold-covered towers and churches and by the high facade of the old Tsarist castle and flooded overall with bright sunshine, was in itself sufficient to create an enchanting impression. And now upon the red boarded path through the middle of all the confusion the cor-onation procession, in all its oriental and fairy-tale splendour, passed before us to the cathedral, at the entrance of which stood the Metropolitan of St Petersburg, surrounded by high-ranking clergy with the holy picture of the Mother of God, ready to bless the entrance of the Imperial pair. It took almost a quarter of an hour for the whole procession to pass. First came a detachment of knights, then the pages, the Masters of Ceremonies, the syndicates from the whole Empire, the municipalities, delegates of the nobles, the bourgeoisie, commerce, and of the artists, then countless Gentle-men of the Bedchamber in uniforms covered excessively with gold braid, representatives of the universities, of the ministries, the delegates from the different Cossack branches, the marshals of the nobility, the General Synod, the Senators, the State Council, the Heralds, the castle guard, and then in great ceremonial pomp, the Imperial Insignia, the Imperial Standard and Sword, Crown,

Sceptre, Apple, Cloak, etc., a platoon of the Tsarina's Gentlemen of the Guard, the Higher Court and Lower Court Marshals and, finally, the Tsar and Tsarina beneath a golden baldachin with ostrich feathers which was carried by 20 generals. Following ancient ceremonial the Tsarina walked under the same baldachin behind the Tsar. Now followed the long procession of all the Russian Grand Dukes and of all the princes who are assembled here for the coronation, then a long procession of ladies belonging to the Court and Palace dressed in Russian court dress, the red silk outer garment and the *kokoschnik* on the head, another detachment of Gentlemen-at-Arms and then a whole group of generals, *aides-de-camp*, representatives of the hereditary nobility, etc. All this passed before us like a fairy-tale, and disappeared into the cathedral. And accompanying all this the ringing of bells, the thunder of artillery and the roar of cheering, indeed an indescribable impression. The ceremony in the church lasted from 9.00 a.m. until 1.30 p.m. When it was over the procession came out to circulate again. The Tsar was now wearing the heavy diamond crown and the Cloak, and holding in his hand the Sceptre at the tip of which the largest diamond in the world, the Orloff, sparkled, and the Imperial Apple, a sight which one otherwise would only see in a picture book. He had crowned himself and then the Tsarina, had received the Holy anointing and, as the highest dignitary of the Church, had partaken of communion in both forms. And now he stepped forward before his people as the legal Tsar in all the splendour of his enormous power. There is something great in these ceremonies, reports of which will be carried away by all the delegations present into the endless steppes of the Empire; they will recount how they saw the White Tsar in the total splendour of his power followed by hundreds of subject princes, blessed by God, who let the sun shine for him, and blessed by the clergy, cheered by all the people, decorated with the treasures of the earth, a Higher Being, in whose hands rested the weal and woe of countless millions. This people and empire need such an external display and it is a good thing that all this is carried out in all respects according to the ancient blessed ritual where religion and worldly power are so deeply fused together that neither can be separated from the other without both of them bleeding to death. One has to have seen all this in order to understand why in Russia the Orthodox Church often takes draconian steps, in order to comprehend how it is possible to bring and hold together this enormous empire, stretching from the permanent ice in the North to the unchanging summer in the South, in one single thought. Only absolute power, supported by the general Orthodox Church, can rule Russia, and any split between these two cornerstones would cause the enormous structure to collapse.

After the coronation procession has gone past all the churches, the Tsar and Tsarina climb the red-carpeted, open-air steps to the castle. Arrived at the top both turn around and salute the people with three bows. Both their Majesties looked marvellous, the precious stones on their heads flashed in the sunshine and their bodies were enveloped in the wide folds of the ermine cloaks; it seemed as if the heavens breathed a kiss of blessing over them and all the thousands, who had remained on their knees in the open during the anointing of the Tsar in the church, shouted up to the ruling pair with joy. One felt oneself surrounded by a tide of benediction, enthusiasm and loyalty which came from the whole people.

On this day almost 3000 people were fed in the Kremlin, innumerable tables had been set up in marquees, salons and halls. We extricated ourselves from the crush and drove home, arriving there towards five o'clock. The whole ceremony had taken nine hours!

The Tsarina looked charming. Her fine face was pale with excitement and strain. She wore a dress of silver brocade. The Imperial crown, worked entirely of diamonds, which the Tsar had placed on her head in the church after he had crowned himself and touched the heads of those kneeling before him with his crown, sat on her abundant hair like a beam of heavenly light. The Tsar, too, carried his heavy crown in a royal manner. It must be extremely heavy as it, too, consists entirely of diamonds. Its tip is formed by a ruby the size of a hen's egg in which the sunlight was refracted in a blood-red glow.

In the evening, Moscow was lit up. What that means is difficult to describe. The whole Kremlin was glittering with electric light. The towers and gates were built up from top to bottom of millions of light bulbs. They stood there like representatives from another world. The whole eight kilometres of the surrounding wall was covered with lamps in its battlements. This huge ocean of fire was lit up by the hands of the Tsarina. She took hold of a bouquet and at the very same instant everything flared up. From the terrace of the Kremlin we looked down on to a city of fire. The houses, bridges and towers shone in blue, red and green with flashing sparks. Garlands of light dotted the Moskva river as far as the eye could see. It was all of such indescribable splendour that we were quite overcome. It is also quite impossible to describe the impression. Let your imagination know no bounds and you will still be a long way from reaching the reality. Here all thought ceases. Even when one sees these illuminations one considers them impossible. We clutch our heads and ask ourselves whether we are normal or suffering from hallucinations. And this performance is supposed to go on for three consecutive evenings!

Norway, Digarmulen (Lofoten), 20 July 1898

At midday we passed the polar circle, sitting out on deck, caressed by the warm sun which was burning down so intensely on the sundeck that one might have thought oneself deep in the South. We saw whales spraying up their great jets of water, skuas and eiders gliding by, and spreading out to our right the mountainous strands of Norway in their thousandfold variation of form and colour; between the violet mountain shapes the glimmering back of the world's greatest snowfield, the Svart Jisen, extending for miles. It is indescribably beautiful up here when the sky is clear. The far distances of the views draw the spirit into the infinite, the magnificence of nature which appears to have been made for its own rather than human beings' sake engendering a mood of solemnness. Equally indescribable is the ever-changing play of colour, from the deepest tones through countless tender variations to the very lightest of hues. One can never grow tired of gazing at this panorama. Wherever one rests one's gaze there are new beauties to be seen, and drunk from the lustrous sunshine and the clearness of the air it rushes over the infinite sea which melts together with the sky in the endlessly far-off distance.

Norway, Lofoten, 23 July 1898

It was very beautiful, the midnight sun which was sinking down over the horizon under a cloud of banks up to roughly 30 minutes of arc, then stayed for about ten minutes, flooding the ship and the distant mountain tops of the Lofoten with a purple light, and then slowly rose again. The Prince of Monaco joined us on board to show us the catch he had made with his trawl net. He brought with him several big glass vessels which also contained a number of horrid animals preserved in alcohol. There were sea-spiders, with legs as long as this sheet, sea-cucumbers that look like horrendous fat leeches, with an opening at the front and at the back so that the sludge of the sea can flow through them, etc., etc. In short, a collection of horrors which was, however, most interesting. One wonders to what end all these beasts exist. What is Creation intending for them? Might one be changed into a sea-cucumber as punishment for a bad life, condemned to swallow sludge in deepest darkness?

Potsdam, 9 August 1900

This morning I was in Berlin where a High Mass was celebrated for King Humbert[8] at the Hedwig Church. The entire ritual with the incomprehensible manipulations of the priests before the altar, the clouds of incense and the nasal chanting made an almost repellent impression on me. It is, after all, like a form of idolatry. I cannot imagine that the Christ can be in agreement with this kind of service, He, who held His sermons under God's free sky and who rejected everything that was reminiscent of the ritual customs of the Old Law and who said Himself when you pray you shall not blab like the heathens.

Neu-Ruppin, 19 September 1901

It would look terrible tomorrow if it carries on pouring with rain, for tomorrow is the first day of the corps manoeuvres, when all troops have to bivouac. As I gather from the newspaper the Kaiser has interrupted the great manoeuvres for one day because of the rain. A layman will hardly be able to imagine what this means for those in charge of the manoeuvres. All the dispositions made are messed up. The railway transports, which have long since been agreed with the rail administrations, have to be stopped, everything is in turmoil, and quite apart from all these difficulties an impression is created within the army that the soldiers can no longer tolerate rain. Imagine the consequences if such violent interference should take place when things really matter.[9]

Berlin, 31 March 1903

Believe me, nothing is further from my thoughts than to deprive you of your belief or even to want to trespass on it. Simply as a matter of prudence I want to remind you that your good nature is only too easily abused and that in the transfiguration of the common shared outlook of your circle you do not see people as they really are. I will willingly share with you that which is beautiful and comforting in this belief and I am sure that we will always be as one in this striving towards the ideal—it is just that I cannot go along with all these nasty formalities. You idealize them for yourself. I see the plain and often repellent reality and am unable to incorporate them into my concepts of spirit and its essential nature. These concepts are admittedly vague and I must try to give them a clearer foundation, something that is to be found above our earth existence and not descending into gloomy earthly depths. A person who possesses a precious stone should not pin it to his chest and enter the market place; if he does, dirty hands will stretch out for it and it can fall into the mud and be trampled upon.

Berlin, 10 April 1903

Today E. and I were in the Kaiser-Friedrich Church where we heard a very beautiful sermon. Seldom has a sermon so touched my heart and seldom have I become so conscious within myself of the sublimity of pure Christian faith in its indefinable power. How, indeed, those people are to be envied who from complete inner conviction have this belief in a peace-bringing Redeemer, a belief which guarantees full satisfaction for the deep inner needs of the striving, seeking human soul if it really does raise itself to the lofty heights of unshakeable certainty. You know that this belief has not been granted to me, that I have struggled, and still struggle in vain to achieve it. If I were able to switch off my so-called understanding it might be possible for me to acquire the peace which passes all understanding. But the dogma of redemption with which I am faced

I cannot understand or grasp. I cannot comprehend why a god, who is supposed to be Love itself, found it necessary to demand the blood of an innocent in order to be reconciled with those who were guilty, and how it could be possible for my guilt to be pardoned because another has suffered. I cannot find the way out of this conflict and so, in consequence, cannot comprehend redemption. I cannot move on to the bedrock of belief and continue to wade about in the quicksands of brooding doubt. I hope, however, that God will help me and, if not in this life, then perhaps in another he may give me a ray of light which I can follow.

At two o'clock we had your Mama here for a meal. E. had arranged a small birthday table for her; a picture she had bought, of blind people walking through poppy flowers, seemed to me a likeness of my soul. It, too, walks blindly and gropingly along its path, darkness covers its eyes and yet it knows that the sun is shining and that the poppies are flowering in all their red splendour. The poppy, symbol of sleep—that sleep that will open the eyes of the blind as well.

Berlin, 15 April 1903

Certainly we should strive for ever greater spiritualization but, in my view, not by negating and despising what is material but by always emphasizing more clearly the ideal elements within it, by transfiguring and lighting up with the spiritual that is there: love, compassion for others, sensitivity, forbearance towards other's mistakes. In this way we will create a spiritual world in material clothing for ourselves, we will not despise what is earthly but ennoble it. We will not want to tear the world in which we live from its hinges but will recognize our material existence for what it should be—an intermediate step to a better existence. If we were to want to break this rung out of the ladder of world development our foot would step into the void and since we haven't yet got any wings we should fall. In my opinion we should stand firmly and safely on this rung with our gaze directed upwards, conscious that there are further rungs to come, but very clear, too, that we cannot step on to the next one until we have found our balance on this one.

Berlin, 16 April 1903

In the last few days I have read a really interesting book by Chamberlain, it is called *Dilettantism—Babel and Bible—Rome*. Get hold of a copy. Among other things I found in it, as evidence of Luther's unsatisfactory translation of the Bible and as a result the conclusions to be drawn from a literalistic belief, proof that the first verse of Genesis which in Luther's rendering reads 'In the beginning God created heaven and earth—full stop—and the earth was without form and void' is incorrect. The first sentence is only the prefix to the following sentence, i.e. there should be no full stop between the two. Secondly, if translated literally from the Hebrew it should read 'As the demons began to separate the air and the firm land the earth was still empty and uninhabited'. In the text that word 'Elohim' is used which is plural and means 'the demons'. In the singular it would be 'ël' which means God. In consequence the very first verse has been faked in favour of monotheism. Whether Chamberlain is right I cannot, of course, judge but I would like to believe he is.

Island of Flor, Norway, 4 August 1903

It has just occurred to me that it is today that the new Pope has been elected, as expected, an outsider, a compromise Pope.[10] The cardinals were unable to agree which of the outstanding candidates should be chosen and, in the end, chose the one who was least likely to upset them. When one thinks about it, what monstrosities flow from this decision. The man chosen for these reasons is now infallible![11] The sovereign ruler of the spiritual health of millions of people for whom he can either open the door to paradise or slam it in their faces. It is incomprehensible that a thinking person should believe that this is how God has arranged for his representation on earth. And what power is nevertheless incorporated in this faith which is founded on the broad basis of the incapability of the mass of mankind to think!

Odde, Norway, 8 August 1903

We continue to live our lives calmly as if there were no such thing as death and do not know how near ours is. How delicate and transitory a human life is if one measures it against the thousands of years that these granite mountains have existed. And yet at some time they will pass away; the difference lies in the time-span and what is time measured against eternity?

That's the kind of life that I would like to lead, to end the day, which has had its burdens, with a lecture of serious content and then perhaps followed by a discussion to clarify opinions, in which everybody for once descends into his own thought-world and seeks for the pearl of truth.

Berlin, 5 March 1904

How nice it would have been if we could all have been together. If only one were free! It is not just that my uncertain position and future weighs heavily on me but I feel depressed by the whole untruthfulness and intolerability of the state of affairs in our country. The German nation, taken as whole, really is a pitiful society. Parish-pump politicians, without a trace of generosity, petty, malicious, full of envy and resentment, spiteful and short-sighted—really to be pitied. Everywhere things are torn down, covered with filth, insulted, lied about and all this is done under a cloak of righteous indignation. Hypocrisy, wherever one looks, mean-hearted egotism and crass materialism. Ideals are no longer valid, everything is external appearance. Anything which still has substance is torn down, everybody wants to climb upwards and when the building of the great heap of rubble has been completed the day of judgement will follow. Does it not sound like a statement from a lunatic asylum when an MP in the Reichstag says that we should not build any more ships but await the experiences of the naval war in South-East Asia? And that is said by men who consider themselves to be wise. They want to wait and see which cover would be best for the well into which the child will fall. No one has any idea what thunderstorms are forming above us; instead of preparing in solemn earnestness for the serious times ahead the nation is tearing itself to pieces. How long will it be before the pillars of the proud edifice of the Empire, built of blood and iron, and now undermined by petty quarrelling, crash to the ground?

Berlin, 6 March 1904

Waldersee's death has come as a great surprise. Although I have not lost a friend or patron in him I do regret his departure; at any rate he was one of the Army's old standards. In the General Staff the opinion is that Count Schlieffen will now be nominated Army Inspector in place of Waldersee and that a successor for him will be announced shortly. I hope his Majesty will at least have a word with me beforehand and not simply send a blue letter to my house again. I had hoped that the decision would have been drawn out until I had arrived at Corps and until then God knows how many years will have passed, for there is no more promotion and the high positions are fixed as if they have been rammed.

I am presently reading a very interesting book by Dr Steiner[12] about Nietzsche whom I have never been able to understand in the slightest. His development and line of thought are so clearly and understandably presented that it is a real pleasure. Whereas Schopenhauer bases all human actions and thought on the transcendental will for life, Nietzsche maintains that the basic motive for all actions is the real will to power. Those who are weak and are afraid to follow this will to power create for themselves a foreign (divine) will to which they submit themselves. Hence the concepts of Good and Evil, whereas in reality it cannot be proved what Good and Evil are. Over and beyond Good and Evil. You must read the book some time. One really begins to have an idea what the man wanted to say.

Berlin, 8 March 1904

Yesterday evening I read a further book by Steiner on Haeckel[13] which, like all his writings, interested me. In this book he declares himself wholeheartedly in favour of Haeckel's monistic philosophy of nature (not to be confused with monotheistic) and it is quite incomprehensible to me how he made the jump from this to Theosophy. I am quite keen to see him again some time in order to ask him about it. On the basis of this work one could confidently place him in the middle of the phalanx of materialists, moreover this is one of his more recent books. But he is always clear and gripping. No other philosophizing author has so far been more comprehensible to me than he.

Berlin, 29 June 1904

The fourteen-day ride through the territory of the Reich has been very interesting. Alsace and the Vosges are a beautiful country. In Lorraine the population is going to the dogs in dirt and indolence. I saw with concern that 35 years of belonging to the German Reich has had hardly any effect; the devil take the local mayors or, as they are called locally, the District Directors! Absolutely nothing has taken place, not even an efficient administrative authority has been set up and everything goes on along a rut. It is hard to imagine how slovenly the agricultural cultivation is; mostly one cannot tell whether they are growing wheat or weeds and yet it is wonderful, fertile soil in which everything grows by itself and the vine and walnut trees thrive. Half the villages consist of dung heaps which all lie on the street in front of the run-down houses and in between them stand the draw wells for water. Consequently, typhus is rampant. It really is a lamentable state of affairs in this beautiful landscape. The people have very fine cattle rather like the Simmentaler, though somewhat smaller, but nevertheless one only gets rancid butter. In the gardens cabbages grow just as they do in the Osdorfer fields, heavily fruiting cherry and apricot trees, but the inns face one with filth, peeling wallpaper in all the rooms, dreadful food except for the good fresh potatoes. It is wretched to see how this blessed countryside is going to the dogs and being squandered without anything being done about it.

Molde, Norway, 17 July 1904

I am reading Carlyle's[14] *History of the French Revolution*. The book is intelligently written even if somewhat affectedly. In addition, I am occupied with Steiner's *Theosophy*.[15] Quite by accident yesterday conversation turned to the theosophical conception of the world. There were four or five of us sitting together and as I was the only one who knew anything about these matters it fell to me to lead the discussion. At first some of them laughed, then they became increasingly serious and in the end they were listening to me as if I was a pastor in church. It is remarkable how this theme interests everybody even if they behave as if they were far too superior to concern themselves with it.

We have a prince here on board whose brother is an ardent spiritualist and in the end pretty well everybody has experienced this or that, either themselves or from someone close to them. But hardly anyone had tried to account to themselves for these things or reflected on them. People are such lazy thinkers and set aside anything that might worry them and does not fit into their accustomed scheme of life.

Trondheim, Norway, 23 July 1904

The Kaiser harangued me on the way about the manoeuvres, etc. I must give my support to Count Schlieffen. I see more and more how difficult the inheritance is going to be for whoever succeeds him. That this is the case is certainly to a large extent Schlieffen's fault.

Reaching the point when mankind is spiritualized enough to control the forces of nature is going to take a good long time. Thousands of years will certainly be needed. You live in your own world among books and many human beings who share your views, and so lose sight of the great mass of humanity; you have no true picture of the tremendous backwardness of this mass and think you already glimpse light where there is nothing but the thickest darkness. Your light burns within yourself; in the heavily burdened masses it is dark and will stay dark for inconceivable times to come. However, all beginnings are small. Even the highest human spirit must develop from its mother's egg and slowly ripen and it is certain that truth will conquer in the end even if it is after lengthy and hard battles. It really did please me that you wrote to me once again in a philosophical vein.

Trondheim, Norway, 25 July 1904

The main social activity here is provided by the Americans. All the financial bosses from the New World lie in wait for the Kaiser here and know very well that he will join them on board. And the All-Highest really believes that through this concession towards a few American money-bags he can exercise an influence on the political relationship between the two countries; believes that if he visits a Mr Vanderbilt, Drexel or Goelette on board or lunches with them, if he receives and entertains them with exceptional courtesy on board the *Hohenzollern*, he will be able to settle the conflicting economic interests of a hundred million people—all of whom are locked in a struggle for existence, who all live and want to become rich at the expense of others, who fight for their existence in agriculture, trade and industry, who are all hungry and thirsty and don't give a damn for anything but the most favourable living conditions.

Yesterday's sermon, which was better than its threadbare predecessor, was on the theme 'If life has been valuable it has also been trouble and toil'. How true that rings is something we all feel in our enforced idleness. All of us except one, unfortunately.

I have now finished Carlyle's *History of the French Revolution*—all three volumes. It is intelligently and dramatically written from the standpoint of a philosopher who seeks for the driving impulses amid the multicoloured confusion of appearances and finds them deep beneath the foaming and bloody surface in human hearts. That is the trouble with most monarchs and ruling classes—they forget that in everyone's breast, even in that of the most humble of their subjects, there beats a heart full of a desire for happiness and joy in existence, that they are all human beings with human feelings and a lust for life. And here we lie and eat and drink as if there were nothing else in the world while up there in Silesia the land is parched. Even the earth fails to provide what it usually furnishes for free—water! Those who are not financially strong have to sell their cattle, perhaps lose their home and farm. How many destroyed existences, how many embittered hearts, how much wretchedness and misery whose cry of despair, however, certainly does not force its way on to the elegant American promenade decks where we drink tea and smoke cigarettes. In such surroundings it is good to read a book like Carlyle's!

Molde, Norway, 31 July 1904

All our church services begin with one of the woe cries of the old Jehovah—'woe to you that you do this, woe to you that you do that!' Then the Gospel is read but again an Old Testament verse is the basis for the sermon. Today we heard the Gospel about the unjust householder, one of the most involved of parables in the whole Bible which was evidently completely misunderstood and mutilated by those who copied the old writings, leaving, very wisely, its interpretation to the astuteness of the listeners. A few days ago I read a book which you really ought to read and which will interest you. It is called *Die Quellen des Lebens Jesu* ('The Sources of Jesus' Life') by Professor Dr Paul Wernle of Basle. It is the best thing I have read up till now about the genesis of the Gospels and is completely convincing due to the clarity of its thought and its logical conclusions. It was interesting for me to find my own opinion confirmed—which I had formed as the result of reading the Gospels—that the Gospel according to St Mark is, in its naïve portrayal, the first of the four.

Another tract of the same kind that I have also read is *Was Wissen wir von Jesus* ('What do we know about Jesus?') by Bossuet. But it is not on the same level as the first book, and is more a polemic against something Kalthoff has written who maintained that the story of Jesus is nothing more than a posthumous clothing of the history of the Christian Church with the role of the person of Christ. Kalthoff actually wants to get rid of the historical Christ, which in my opinion is entirely wrong.

Berlin, 5 September 1904

I read a lot of Chamberlain's *Die Grundlagen des neunzehnten Jahrhunderts* ('The Foundations of the Nineteenth Century') yesterday and found that I could understand and judge many of the matters he discusses better than previously. One sentence struck me as very striking. He writes of the duality of appearances, for instance, as one could say of the material and spiritual worlds, and says that one could best define these two aspects of existence as those that are mechanically explicable and those that are not mechanically explicable. I find that very well expressed. I read *The Four Religions*[16] by A. Besant with great interest. It surprises me that she confines herself to these four, Hinduism, Zoroastrianism, Buddhism and Christianity and makes no mention of the religion which, after Buddhism, has the most believers on earth, Islam. Many of her statements about Christianity correspond with Chamberlain's. When one reads these things it becomes more and more incomprehensible that people should have been content for so long with the distorted picture of religion that humanity has made of Christ's teachings. It proves how thoughtlessly the masses cling to the external form and how powerful the spiritual life of these teachings must be not to have completely suffocated within this external form.

Berlin, 20 December 1904

I can well imagine that the old suckling Madonnas don't particularly appeal to you. Most of them are really not beautiful but they are interesting as evidence of how art gradually developed in conjunction with religious feeling until, finally having outgrown this teacher, it became independent and directed its increasingly firm steps into the great region of Nature—just like a child, when it has learned to walk by itself, runs into the garden in order to pick flowers. In this early period in the awakening of art there was an active urge within it to give visible expression to the deepest feelings of which mankind was capable at that time and these were religious—they were what moved people most deeply. That is why all the old painters stuck to religious themes and this is why Madonna painting was the mother of present-day art and Christian architecture fathered that of our present day. When these old painters were at work nothing was known about the master-works of Greek art which had long been lost from sight, and the growing desire among the Central European peoples for artistic expression had to be met by artists groping their way and overcoming only very gradually a good deal of rawness and childlikeness.

Berlin, 26 January 1905

I think it would be interesting to read some Roman history which one could then immediately experience at the actual sites. Much more interesting than any novel. If, perhaps, you could get hold of

Mommsen's *Römanische Geschichte* ('Roman History') for example. Perhaps somebody in the Embassy has one.

Berlin, 29 January 1905[17]

One morning about four weeks ago I had a ride in the Tiergarten with the Reich Chancellor. The conversation came round to the political situation which was very tense at the time. On parting he asked me if I would not shortly be taking Count Schlieffen's place, with whom he apparently did not see eye to eye, to which I replied that I hoped that this cup would pass me by. Some days later ... came to me to tell me that in conversation with His Majesty the Reich Chancellor had told him that I would not be inclined to take on the post of Chief of the General Staff. At this His Majesty was extremely astonished and worried and thereupon sent ... to me to say that he had absolute confidence in me. He had been hurt, if I did not want to take it on, that I had not told him so myself and he had had to hear it from the Reich Chancellor. I then had a fairly long talk with ... during which I gave him my reasons for finding it difficult to take on this appointment. He agreed with me and asked if he should pass this on to His Majesty, to which I replied that I would prefer it if I could discuss it with His Majesty myself and that I would be grateful to His Majesty if he would receive me and hear what I had to say.

Two days later I received an invitation to dinner at the Castle together with a message calling on me to arrive half an hour earlier and to ask to see His Majesty. You can well imagine with what strange feelings I journeyed to the Castle. I was quite determined to be completely frank with His Majesty about everything and had no idea how matters would turn out. I told myself, however, that this had nothing to do with me as a person but that it was my duty, should things so develop, to sacrifice myself for the sake of this matter; that I could really only be of use to His Majesty if I told him once and for all what was talked about among the officers, as well as secretly rumoured, without anyone finding the courage to come out with it to His Majesty. His *aide-de-camp* ushered me into His Majesty's study and I stood—I don't know for how long—and waited. At last the Kaiser came in and greeted me in a very friendly manner. He leaned against his desk as if he wanted to say: 'Now let's hear what it is you want to put forward'.

I started by saying that what I had told the Reich Chancellor had been said privately and that it had never crossed my mind that he would repeat it to His Majesty. I got no further because the Kaiser interrupted me with great animation and said: 'Now I want to tell you how that came about. When the Reich Chancellor was with me a few evenings ago we discussed the serious political situation in which we find ourselves in relation to England and how we must be prepared to be attacked by England one fine day. It was clear that this war could not be localized but would lead to further European embroilments. The Reich Chancellor then remarked that he considered Count Schlieffen to be getting pretty old to which I replied "When he can no longer cope, Moltke is there". To this he said "Your Majesty, he will not take on the post." You can imagine that I was completely amazed at this statement. I posted you to the General Staff a year ago so that you could orientate yourself and I certainly had in mind that you would be there to stand in for him if for any reason Count Schlieffen had to retire. He is old and anything could happen to him, he could become ill or something like that, and there must be someone there who can take his place. Now General v. der Goltz has been suggested to me, whom I do not want, and then General v. Beseler whom I do not know. I do know you and I have confidence in you. I know very well that you are too modest to believe that you could meet the requirements of the post. Count Schlieffen, whose opinion I sought, told me that he had observed you for a year and could not propose to me a better successor than yourself. Your deceased uncle said once that, in selecting someone for this post, it was less important for the choice to be a genius than that he should be somebody on whom one could rely in all circumstances—it was the character that was the main thing and it was this that would be put to the test in war. I can only say to you that it is you in whom I have complete confidence. You are a well-known personality in the Army, everybody regards you highly and, like me, will have confidence in you. When as a young man I came to the throne I, too, told myself that the task was beyond my capabilities. I was entirely on my own, nobody could help me and when I had to accomplish something extremely difficult—parting from the old Reich Chancellor—I said to myself it must be done and I went on to do what I had to do. If you take on the task you will find the strength within yourself.'

This is a shortened version of what His Majesty said. In his animated state he spoke at length and in much greater detail than I have repeated here. I saw it coming that he would give me no opportunity on my side to say what I had to say but I was quite determined not to go before I had done it. So I listened respectfully until he had finished his speech. Then I said: 'May Your Majesty please accept my deeply felt gratitude for the honour shown by his expression of confidence in me; this obliges me even more strongly to speak openly and honestly to Your Majesty. What matters is not only that your Majesty has confidence in me but also whether I deserve this confidence or not. Your Majesty will only be able to assess this when Your Majesty knows my views better and I therefore humbly request Your Majesty's permission to put forward my worries as openly as if to my own conscience. Should I say something which perhaps displeases Your Majesty this will at least have as a consequence that Your Majesty will be able to form a complete judgement and assessment of me. Your Majesty has contemplated making me a possible Chief of the General Staff later on ... How I would prove in the case of war I do not know. I judge myself very critically. In my opinion it is extremely difficult at this stage to picture how a modern European war would turn out. We have had peace for a period of over 30 years and I believe that our views have in many respects taken on a peace-time quality. I believe that no one can know in advance how, or even if, it will be possible to direct centrally the mass armies which we will create. Our enemy, too, is now different, we shall not be dealing, as last time, with a hostile army, which we confront with superiority, but with a nation in arms. It will become a People's War that will not be ended by one decisive battle, but it will be a long, arduous struggle with a country which will not admit defeat until all its power has been shattered and which, even if we should be victorious, will exhaust us in the extreme. And when I now look at the strategic war game plans which are put before Your Majesty year after year, regularly ending with the taking prisoner of enemy armies consisting of five or six hundred thousand men, and that, too, after only a few days of operations, I cannot avoid the feeling that this in no way meets the conditions of war. I cannot engage in such war games. Your Majesty knows yourself that the armies led by you regularly encircle the enemy and in this way allegedly end the war with one blow. In my opinion these results can only be brought about by forcefully distorting circumstances in such a way that the basic principle that the war games should be a study for real war, and should take into account all the friction and obstacles that arise in war, is not met. This kind of war game in which, to a certain extent, Your Majesty's enemy is at your mercy, with his hands tied from the outset, must give rise to false ideas which can only be pernicious when war comes. But in my view this is not the worst part of it. I hold it to be even more disturbing that the distorted war games have the effect of destroying their interest for the wide circle of officers involved. Everybody has the feeling that it doesn't matter what you do, a higher destiny controls the business and brings it one way or another to the desired conclusion. Your Majesty will have noticed that it becomes increasingly difficult to find officers who want to exercise command against you. That is because, everyone says, I'll only be wiped off the map. However, what I complain about most and what I must say to Your Majesty, is that because of all this the officers' confidence in their Supreme Commander is severely shaken. The officers say among themselves that the Kaiser is much too clever not to notice how everything is arranged that he shall turn out to win, so that must be the way he wants it.'

At this point the Kaiser interrupted me and said that he had had no idea that both sides were not fighting on equal terms. He had acted in good faith. I should tell Schlieffen that he should not treat him any better in the next war games than his opponent.

I replied: 'Count Schlieffen says that when the Kaiser plays he must win; as Kaiser he cannot be beaten by one of his generals. That is quite right, too. For this reason Your Majesty ought not to command at all. Let Your Majesty call for a war game in which Your Majesty has the overall direction and thus stands above the parties instead of being a party himself.'

The Kaiser agreed with me on this. Then I added: 'If Your Majesty would like to sound out the gentlemen I believe all of them would confirm what I have just told you if they have the courage to tell Your Majesty the truth. And what I have said about the war games applies equally to the manoeuvres. The value of large-scale manoeuvres as a preparation for war is in the practice it gives senior commanders of opposing an enemy who has freedom of decision. The troops, as such, learn less in the large-scale manoeuvres than in detached exercises where one can pay attention to all the details. If, however, the generals' decisions are constantly influenced by Your

Majesty's interventions they are robbed of their pleasure in taking initiative and are made listless and uncertain.'

There the Kaiser interrupted me again and said that he had always allowed the generals in command freedom of decision. I replied: 'In the last Kaiser manoeuvres my role was that of an umpire so I was not myself present but I was told that on one day Your Majesty gave the Corps Commander of the ... Corps orders, literally dictated, which were contrary to his intentions.' His Majesty had to admit this. He said: 'Yes, that was when he wanted to put his Corps back so that it would not have come to a battle that day.' I said: 'Then Your Majesty could simply have had him told that you wanted to see a battle on the next morning and then left the arranging of this to him, or Your Majesty could have given him some supposition which would have caused him to stay where he was. As it is, the whole Army knows that Your Majesty simply dictated orders for his Corps to the Corps Commander and that does not help to raise the General's standing with his Corps and must have a depressing effect on him. During the whole time he occupies his post a Commanding General has one opportunity only, and that during the Kaiser manoeuvres, of leading his Corps against an enemy and usually that amounts to only three days. If now Your Majesty directs a Corps during the manoeuvres he loses one of these three days. In war Your Majesty will not be leading a Corps.' His Majesty: 'No, that is correct.' I responded: 'That is the job of the Corps Commander and he must exploit every hour in which he can practise it.' His Majesty: 'I lead in order to show the Commanding General how I want it to be done.' I replied: 'Your Majesty could express that at the discussion. In my opinion the manoeuvres can only be warlike and useful when they are conducted without forcible intervention from above. If mistakes are made that does not matter since it is from mistakes that one learns most. But if Your Majesty commands everyone knows that he must win and the hostile side considers itself foredoomed to be sacrificed in battle and becomes disgruntled. The manoeuvres are discussed throughout the whole of the army, the whole officer corps judges them, and the criticism gets constantly sharper. And there is a further point. The soldiers do not get to see Your Majesty and that is extremely important because a soldier who has seen Your Majesty on manoeuvres will not forget it as long as he lives. I hope Your Majesty will not take offence that I have spoken more freely in a way that

Your Majesty is not used to hearing. I would not have dared to do so had not the matter concerned what I consider to be, above all else, the welfare of Your Majesty and of the Army.' The Kaiser then asked: 'Why didn't you tell me all this much earlier?' I replied: 'Because I did not feel justified in imposing my views on Your Majesty. It would not do if everyone came to Your Majesty and said, "I don't find that this and that that you do is right."' His Majesty: 'But you are the Adjutant-General and you know that you can always come.' I said: 'Whenever Your Majesty asks for my views I will always give them frankly.'

At this the Kaiser shook my hand and said: 'I thank you'. I then said: 'If Your Majesty really wants to try out things with me then give me an opportunity to put myself to the test. Permit me for once to set up the Kaiser manoeuvres this year. Should things go well, Your Majesty can keep me on; if it transpires that things don't go well, or the difficulties prove too great, then Your Majesty can simply dispense with me and choose someone else. Here it is not a question of personalities, what really matters is that what is needed should be done.' The Kaiser was in full agreement with this and said: 'I will speak to Count Schlieffen.' I replied: 'If Your Majesty will permit me I will myself report this to Count Schlieffen and seek his consent.' His Majesty then shook my hand again and preceded me into the reception salon where the Kaiserin and those taking part in the dinner had been waiting for quite a time. For the rest of the evening the Kaiser was very silent and thoughtful. I really felt very sorry for him but God knows I had to do it.

I was very curious how he would behave towards me when next we met after some time had elapsed and he had recovered from his initial surprise. But when we did he continued to behave in the same friendly way. How all this will work out eventually I do not know. Perhaps it will have a lasting effect, perhaps it will become blurred with the passage of time.

When I reported to Count Schlieffen about the manoeuvres he looked taken aback. It was clearly extremely unpleasant for him and he tried to dodge the issue and said, when I asked him directly whether he agreed to my arranging the manoeuvres this year: 'We can talk about that some time'. If he doesn't agree I shall fight. I have His Majesty's approval and shall not let myself be deprived of that.

Well, now you know all about it. Please let me know immediately this letter reaches you as I don't want anyone else to learn about this and I am actually nervous about sending it through the post. Put it somewhere safe where it cannot come into the wrong hands.

Berlin, 6 February 1905

I have just read a very interesting book, *Paulus, die Anfänge des Christentums und des Dogmas* ('Paul, the Beginnings of Christianity, and of Christian Dogma'), by Professor Weinel. There is just a tiny whiff of orthodoxy about it even if the professor would be horrified if one were to tell him so, for he is known to be the most liberal of all liberal theologians. But no one can completely shake off the dust of their origins, and even if he thinks he has completely brushed off the Christian dogma that he grew up with, a little of it still adheres to him. Not enough to be seen, but just enough to be felt when one probes the structure of his work with one's mental fingers.

Berlin, 9 February 1905

Yesterday's court ball did not particularly capture my imagination. It always leaves a peculiar impression on me when I watch the entry of the court into the White Hall, the Kaiser always brings with him something of the Middle Ages.[18] S. wigged, also the old Süß, the Officer of the Kaiserin's bodyguard; it is as if the dead rise up again in wig and powder.

Sweden, Visby, 26 July 1905

We arrived here at seven o'clock, direct from Björkö in the Finnish Gulf where we had the rendezvous with the Emperor of Russia. When we departed from Hernosand all we knew was that we were heading for Gotland. However, when we awoke in the morning, we were on the open sea and soon noticed, as we were going due East, that we were not on course to Gotland. But deepest silence was observed about the destination of our journey. Hour after hour went by, and we were still going eastward at a speed of 18 knots. Then it finally dawned on us that we must be going into the Finnish

Gulf, or else we would have long reached a coast. Our tension mounted steadily throughout the day. All sorts of possibilities were suggested but we were not put in the picture. Afternoon came, still no land in sight, and still heading eastwards. Suddenly a ship came into view, a warship which saluted, it was flying the Russian ensign. Now our conjectures turned into certainty but none of us had an inkling of where we were going. The Kaiser was impenetrably secretive. The naval officers were under strict orders not to pass on any information. At six o'clock when we were all sitting in the saloon, going back and forth over whether Reval, Riga or Kronstadt, the Kaiser entered and said: 'Now then, chaps, get your parade uniforms in order; in two hours' time you will stand before the Emperor of Russia.' No one said a word, we were as if beaten, deathly silence pervaded the room. Not one of us had an inkling of the motive for this sudden and so secretly initiated visit, but we all sensed the tremendous political significance of the hours ahead whose consequences no one was able to anticipate. At nine o'clock we sailed into a bay, flat and lonely banks on which meagre fir trees grew, stony elevations behind, no human habitation as far as the eyes could reach, no living being, only a grey sky and the infinite solitude. Before us in the descending dark a mighty dark vessel, the *Polar Star* with the Tsar on board. We cast anchor at a small distance away from it, the boats were lowered into the water, and the Kaiser went across. Soon after we were sent for, we were all to come over. A few minutes later we stood on the deck of the *Polar Star* and were presented to the Tsar by the Kaiser. He looked serious, but not broken, as he has so often been described. He addressed us all in German and to me he said: 'It is a great joy to me to see you again'. As soon as the introductions were completed we returned to the *Hohenzollern*, followed shortly after by the two monarchs with the Russian entourage. Then dinner was served on the *Hohenzollern*. I was quite astonished by the Tsar. The longer we sat at table the more he opened up. At the end he was quite cheerful, laughing and talking animatedly, and it was quite evident that he felt comfortable in an environment where he was safe. He as well as all the gentlemen in his entourage were exceptionally amiable. (...)

On the next morning, during breakfast, I sat next to Dr Hirsch who spoke very candidly. He said that it had been a great joy for the Tsar to experience that someone was still concerned about him in his misfortune, and that one could not be grateful enough to the

Kaiser for this show of goodwill. The Tsar had suffered all the misfortune with steadfastness and calmness, he was in good health and his nerves were in very good order. The old gentleman spoke with great contempt of those people around his monarch. 'You can imagine that it must be a real boon for the Tsar to find himself in the company of decent people. Just look at his environment, no intelligence, everything below the average, no heart and no feeling.' ... Among all the Russian gentlemen there was an unbelievable lack of enthusiasm with regard to the war ... The Tsar seems to be inclined to peace. May God grant it that it may come about soon and that we will come to live again in calmer times, so that the menacing fire torch of an all-out European murder war will disappear from the horizon. I can well imagine how the newspapers will distort this latest of the Kaiser's surprises beyond recognition. It will give them material for several months of extravagant conjecturing. The thought of purely human feeling, of wishing to offer compassion to a monarch who has been humiliated and crushed by misfortune, of giving him courage, of possibly even encouraging a peaceful resolution, of making clear to him how necessary it was for Russia to give her people peace and justice, would probably not occur to any of these newspaper writers and scribblers.

I will never forget this evening and the day that followed it. The whole thing was too strange, almost like a fairy-tale. The significant encounter, the changed mood of the Russians who formerly were so proud, the grey solitude, the far-off bay, a flickering of gratitude from the very sovereign who, exactly a year earlier, spoke these proud words: 'One does not attack Russia, it is not a state on whom one declares war, it is a Continent'—and who now with a groping hand reaches towards Germany's firm baton—all this left a deeply moving impression...

The *entrevue* is over and before us rises the question, as gigantic and dark as the sphinx: What will follow from these hours?

How different this journey is from those in the Norwegian fiords. This time we are not seeking the stillness of the world of glaciers and the light nights. We are travelling about, turning the rope of politics whose end is lost in the fixed constellation of the future and which will lead our Fatherland with its 60 million people towards the unknown.

May God grant that it will be for their good.

Danzig, 30 July 1905

The friction between Germany and England has unfortunately increased in a threatening way. The visit of its Channel Fleet to the Baltic announced by England can only be interpreted as a demonstration. I do not know how these affairs will turn out and be resolved. On the English side the most malicious things are being said, the most dreadful lies are being propagated, and Germany is being depicted as the most evil spirit on the face of the earth. The first shot fired between England and Germany will be the signal for a general European massacre involving atrocities one shudders to imagine, and yet there is absolutely no reason why this is so—there is no vital interest involved, neither country is threatened or injured by the other and should it come to fighting, no one will know why things came to that pass. The future ahead of us looks dark. May Germany have the strength to put up with difficult times as well.

Saßnitz, 3 August 1905

We certainly do live in a time of grave political crisis. There is no need at present to fear the worst but there is enough inflammable matter around, you are quite right about that. The worst part for us is England's jealousy about our expanding commerce and industrial development.[19] If one looks at the English newspapers one is shocked at the systematic and hateful propaganda against Germany that is to be found in the papers of all the parties. The press is really bloodthirsty and would like nothing better than to destroy us root and branch so as to be able to dominate and exploit the world without restriction. These newspaper writers and noisy trouble-makers do a great deal of damage and have no conscience about playing with fire. Should it come to fighting they certainly won't need to risk their own skins; they'll stay peacefully at home, dipping their pens in poison and gall, and letting others kill one another.

Berlin, 22 August 1905

The Japanese-Russian peace negotiations seem to have ground to a halt, and the slaughter in Manchuria will probably soon be resumed.

Nothing much has changed about the general political mood among us or around us. All the other nations are pretty unanimous with regard to complaining about Germany and spreading the filthiest lies about us in the world. I think that nothing could create such excitement in the whole world as the prospect of Germany getting thoroughly beaten up. Everyone is claiming that we are the trouble-makers and nobody understands that Germany wishes for nothing more than to be left in peace.

Sweden, Tulesbo, 28 September 1905

Yesterday the local pastor was here in order to visit M, a very pleasant man, decidedly liberal, intelligent and well-read. We had a long conversation abour religion by M.'s bedside, and I was pleased about the views he presented. In our country he would have been ordered before the cardinals' assembly a long time ago for such views. He takes the view that the human soul continues evolving after death, that there is an interim realm; he thought that by means of sympathy of minds the soul after death was drawn into circles in tune with it and that higher spirits look after the souls of the deceased to teach them and to raise them to ever higher spheres. What would pastor H. say about this fellow priest! He has read a lot, also the writings of the German theologians. He was familiar with all the Ancients, Origin, etc., the Buddhist teaching, he was extremely knowledgeable about all the different systems of religion and had an open mind towards all of them. I was most surprised to find such a man in the solitude of a small pastoral province.

Bergen, Norway, 7 July 1907

The Kaiser is very cheerful and very kind. The political outlook also seems to be better than the weather. The invitation from Uncle Eduard, which is couched in very friendly terms, signifies without doubt a shift in the English government's school of thought about us. It is not entirely clear to me what has brought about this change; I don't know whether it is the state of affairs in France, or those in India or resistance on the part of the government in London. There must be some important reason or other; in any case this invitation is a symptom. In consequence I believe that the next few weeks will pass peacefully.

Today is Sunday and we began the church service with the obligatory curse from the Old Testament and then as consolation listened to a sermon about faith based on the text 'Whoever has faith will be blessed, but whoever does not believe will be dammed'. The author of the sermon sought to prove that we cannot give ourselves faith—that is basically the doctrine of predestination—that in effect God gives faith and subsequent salvation only to certain human beings, while everybody else, no matter how much they may torment themselves, remains forlorn, one of the most barbaric and miserable teachings that exists. Once again I felt a real horror at this kind of religion and would just like to know what the poor sailors thought about this analysis, that is, if they thought anything at all!

I have got to feel my way gradually back into this life of which I had already pretty well lost the habit but it is actually quite good that I am taking part in the trip for several reasons; I don't consider it to be a pleasure trip, it is a duty like any other, but I believe that the Kaiser is pleased that I am of the party as he often expresses himself very openly to me—which is something that he needs to be able to do.

GHQ Berlin, 4 August 1907

Writing the date just now it ocurred to me that there is a certain similarity between today's 4 August 07 and the same day 37 years ago, 4 August 70, only the last two figures turned around. On 1 August 1870 I experienced my first battle, near Weißenburg. How long ago it was, and how clearly it stands before my eyes nevertheless.

The *entrevue* between the Kaiser and the Tsar seems to be going according to plan. Naturally the press is drawing the most ludicrous conclusions from it. In my opinion it is not of significant political importance. The interests of countries are not determined by encounters between monarchs, they follow their own course and lead consequently and inevitably to collision or to understanding. As far as I am able to judge the world situation is looking threatening at the moment. Our western neighbour is too busy in their own house for making aggressive politics and England appears to be becoming entangled itself in its far-reaching coalitions. As long as we remain calm and strong we have nothing to fear; however, both are necessary, especially the latter. A weak Germany would be the greatest danger to peace in Europe.

Norway, Bergen, 18 July 1908

If I am not going with you on all your paths, it is because I have a very real profession and need to have both feet firmly on this earth for as long as I want to do justice to it. You know this, after all, and understand it well.

Norway, Bergen, 14 July 1910

It is half-past-ten at night, I am sitting by the open window and I am writing without light. The sun is still gleaming on the highest mountain peaks, our ship is lying in the shade. Never in my life have I seen a more beautiful panorama than this evening; it simply is beyond description. The deep violet shadows of the mountains, the peaks illuminated in red, the rose-coloured snow fields—as Goethe says: 'Sets fire to all heights, calms every valley'. I had the impression as if these mountains, covered with light, glowing with love were shining towards their Creator and as if His Eye must be resting upon them in quiet delight. How magically beautiful is this Norway when it is bathed in the light of the sun and the love of God.

Molsheim, 19 June 1911

Moving around the country suits me very well. I feel completely fresh and well, have no trace of any kind of complaint, neither when riding or during long journeys in the car, nor when climbing the occasional slope. This morning I rode first of all to Oberehnheim.[20] The air was so clear that one could quite clearly see the heights of the Black Forest, while on our right the chain of the Vosges stretched out with its lovely wooded hilltops and numerous castle ruins. Then we drove to the monastery of Odilie's Mount[21] which is renowned far and wide and which, from its position on the mountain peak, offers a wonderful panorama of the Rhine plain and the Vosges foothills. It is a very ancient settlement which was mentioned in Karl the Great's time in 800AD. The mountain top is surrounded by a wide, 10 kilometre-long Cyclops-type wall, the so-called Heathen's Wall, dating from ancient Celtic times and consisting of gigantic piled-up square stone blocks. One can hardly grasp how human powers could have moved them; it is one of the most remarkable constructions of its kind both in its extent and massiveness. In places the wall is 10 metres thick and just as high. It is incomprehensible how people could have begun to raise the stones, some of which weigh many tons. A kind of summer vacation place with a *pension* has been set up in the monastery and receives a lot of custom. It is a monastery for lay-sisters who in their black habits and starched white bonnets serve the guests. In the afternoon we were on the Kaiser Wilhelm Fortress[22] where our lectures are held. Tomorrow we are going to Zabern,[23] the day after that to Dieuze and then to Metz. I think I shall hold the closing discussion on Monday, the 26th, travel to Cologne on Tuesday for a tour of inspection of the HQ of the Railway Command and return to Berlin on the 28th.

Baleholm, 16 July 1911

A few days ago I had a very interesting conversation with His Majesty about religious questions. He had no time for clergymen, condemning their narrow-mindedness and orthodoxy. In his opinion, death meant the start of a further development; he had thought a great deal about these things and is much more liberal in his views than one would have believed. He is searching for truth and all this business of empty formulas fills him with horror. He doesn't want religious development to stand still but wants it to move forward and feels the need for religion and science to be brought into accord. He described how he had told the clergy that when children see and hear about the development of the world in the *Urania* and then hear, in their religion lessons, that God created the world in six days, seeds of doubt must be sown in their minds. 'If you clergy do not move forward science will disregard you, and if you have nothing new to say the stones will cry out.'

Telegraph from Moltke to the Kaiser

Berlin, 23 May 1912

Please accept my deeply felt thanks, Your Majesty, for the most gracious gift of an inkwell for my birthday, and the benevolent words that accompanied it. The root of my strength[24] lies in the confidence which Your Majesty has so often shown me, and which was once more expressed today. All that I have been able to achieve is due to this. I pray God He may give me strength to continue to prove worthy of this highest honour.

Your Majesty's most faithful and obedient servant.

General von Moltke.

GHQ, Berlin, 18 August 1912

Even though the weather was not very promising we did actually go for the flight on the *Hansa*; unfortunately its distance had to be shortened from that originally planned. We drove out on Saturday morning to the hangar in which the enormous ship is kept. With a length of 110 metres it took up almost all the length of the hangar. The weather was dull and cloudy, the wind pretty fresh, but at least it wasn't raining. The ship's captain told me that test balloons had shown at a height of 800 metres a strong wind which was blowing with a speed of 15 to 16 metres per second and that he reckoned that towards midday strong gusts would appear. For this reason we would only make a trip lasting several hours and be back in the hangar by midday. At eight o'clock we went on board and the ship was dragged out of the hangar. It has a very roomy cabin in which 16 people could sit comfortably and we were only 8. One has a comfortable wicker chair in which one sits by the large open window and looks down on the world. There is no draught and absolutely no vibration. A steward is on board who has a small pantry with cold food and a small cool-box in which the wine rests on ice. There are small tables on which one can spread out maps or eat one's food. The saloon is very pretty in a clear light and high enough for me to stand comfortably.

The ascent was wonderful. After the ship had been turned nose-to-wind the order was given to the teams to let go of the mooring ropes, the propellers began to turn and the gigantic vehicle rose slowly into the air. One only realized this through seeing human beings, houses and trees, etc., becoming smaller and smaller and the overall view steadily widening. After a few minutes we had reached a height of 300 metres which we maintained throughout with only slight alterations. The journey took us straight over Hamburg which was shrouded in a dull haze of smoke and fog; the Alster river sparkled clearly through the smoky air. The wind was strong, about ten metres per second, but as the ship's own speed is 21 metres we nevertheless made good progress. The *Hansa* possesses four propellers in each of its two gondolas. Between the two gondolas is the cabin, connected via a narrow footwalk to the front and rear gondolas which, however, passengers are not allowed to use. One sits in the cabin just as one would in a Pullman carriage, the propeller noise does not disturb and one can carry on a conversation quite easily. Now we are over the harbour with its innumerable ships and small steamers shooting hither and thither and ceaselessly churning up the water. All the vessels greet the *Hansa* with their sirens, we wave our handkerchiefs out of the window and down below people stand with upturned faces and wave back. Then we move downstream over the Elbe. The view over the many slopes of Blankenese with its light-coloured shining villas and the ships moving through the water beneath us is delightful. Crowds of people gather to wave greetings up to us; from windows and roofs they wave with white cloths. At a single glance one can take in the many harbour inlets, the docks and the quays, all around are smoking chimneys and the screeching of the cranes reaches our ears. The noise of working activity is unceasing, industry and commerce weave and spin. Ships are unloaded and loaded, bundles of goods are transported, the railway tracks glitter and the trains creep along them like black caterpillars, gradually the city disappears behind us, we follow the course of the powerful stream, see both its banks, dredgers at work, the islands and navigation signs. On this great road carrying world trade the ships proceed, the fast steamer swooshes through the water making use of the ebb-tide, we overtake it with ease, the trains on shore cannot keep up with us. And so we continue downstream as far as Cuxhaven where the ocean, leaden-grey in colour, lies before us. We have covered 130 kilometres in two hours. But coming towards us over the sea there is a blue-black wall, clouds chase past us, often enveloping us and blocking our view, the wind grows stronger and we have to turn back if we are not to be caught up by the approaching gusts. Such a great pity but there's nothing for it because this is not a military operation but a pleasure trip and we must not endanger the airship. Now we are driving before the wind. The engines are at half-speed but still the countryside below passes by in an ever-changing panorama. We are travelling at 120 kilometres an hour. It is admirable how the ship responds to the rudder. We descend to a few metres above the surface of the water band then rise again into the heights. A wonderful feeling, thus to hover in the air like a bird, to go higher, to descend at will, and always in regular flight without any vibration. Now we are travelling overland in a north-easterly direction, leaving the river behind us. Now beneath us lie rectangular fields, houses and farms and grazing cattle. The effect of the airship on the animals is interesting. Horses grazing in the paddocks raise their heads and with streaming tails and manes tear away at a gallop, the cows and sheep too, everything rushes away as if all that mattered was to save their lives. The chickens in their runs behave as if they had gone mad. They flutter and fly against one another, press themselves flat on the ground and rush into their coops to hide. From above we look down into the woods, notice the stands like straight lines, here and there a few roe deer, which rush for cover in a thicket, a few storks which fly away frightened across the meadows. Everywhere fright and terror among the animals, only the people stand still and greet us and wave upwards. We fly over the coastal moorlands of Holstein, heath, fields, copses, hamlets and individual farms alternate with one another. Now we are over Elmshorn, then we head for Barmstedt whose low church tower I can recognize from far away. There in Vossloeh where as children we consumed mulled ale and bread and butter, and the beech wood in which we used to play around with a vague feeling that it was enormous! Now we take it in with a glance, a green island in the landscape. Now we see the winding Pinau and beyond it, Rantzau. There, on its little island, stands the old house of our happy childhood surrounded by green and water. I know every inch of it, every inch on which we played, the trees on which I carved my name. The windows behind which I lived and the bridges we used to cross. How unchanged it all is and how deeply buried in the memory. There is the garden where I spent many a winter night in the snow waiting to shoot the hare which came at night to the cabbages, the pond with lots of Crucian carp, the old pine trees at the top of which W and I used to hide when we were skipping the drawing lessons, the Bornholt mill, the court-house, the judge's house, everything is there. All visible from above, all arranged like a toy, and here, too, again children who interrupt their games and gaze upwards, and are probably very happy just as we were and who also think that this wonderful existence will never end—just as we did!

Hansa's propellers clatter over this old, cherished patch of earth and water, we turn round and ride again the whole length of this piece of the past. The propellers clatter and in their sound I hear again the children's joyful cries, the voices of my parents, the rustling of the leaves, the murmur of those past times. How distant, worlds distant, the time lies behind the man who now hovers in the air above and feels how the past, present and future all intermingle: If it didn't sound so banal I would like to say 'If anyone had told us that in those days!' And we must tear ourselves away for the weather is catching up with us on the wings of the storm. We turn around and in ten minutes we are over Altona, then Hamburg and now already over the hangar. On the ground in front of it there lies a white sheet with a red arrow indicating the wind direction, for we have to land against the wind in order to prevent it catching the gigantic hull sideways. The teams of men are standing ready to catch the descending bird. Now we turn into the wind. The nose of the airship descends lower and in an oblique, gliding flight we sink down, closing with the green grass below. The mooring ropes are thrown out and caught by the teams, the engines are silent. At a run the soldiers drag the airship towards the hangar, line it up and then the propellers turn once more and at a quick pace *Hansa* dives through the enormous hangar doors into the innards of the hall, stops and is secured. We climb out, all conscious that it has been a wonderful trip. Two minutes later the weather we have been fleeing so fast reaches us and the rain rattles on the hangar's corrugated iron roof. Safe and sound at exactly the right moment! Beautifully timed.

Karlsbad, 21 July 1914

I am pleased that you have seen Dr Steiner and spoken with him. You always find it so inwardly strengthening and refreshing to speak with him. I would also be pleased to see him in August if he should come to Berlin.

Now the decision is to be made on Thursday! I am slowly becoming quite sceptical about all this!

GHQ, Berlin, 27 July 1914

This morning I spent a long time with Bethmann. I have just come back from there, and in an hour I have to be at the Neue Palais which is where the Kaiser will be at three o'clock. The situation is still very unclear.[25] It won't get any clearer for some time, and it may be up to a fortnight before we will know, or be able to say anything definite. Do spend the rest of this time in Bayreuth. You need have no concerns on my account.[26] I got through yesterday excellently, which was admittedly very different from the day spent at the Karlsbad Spa, and I feel fit and well.

2. Helmuth von Moltke's Appraisal of the Political Situation Three Days before the Outbreak of War

Berlin, 28 July 1914

There is no doubt that no European state would show anything other than human interest in the conflicts between Austria and Serbia, if it were not for the danger latent in it of a general political debacle that today already threatens to unleash a world war. For five years already Serbia has been the cause of tension in Europe, which by now is exerting pressure on the political and economic life of the nations concerned that is becoming intolerable. Austria has until now endured, with a forbearance bordering on weakness, the constant provocations and agitation directed at the undermining of its statehood by a people who have gone from regicide[27] in their own country to the murder of an Archduke in a neighbouring country.[28] It was only after the latest horrific crime that extreme measures were taken to cauterize, with red hot iron, the abcess that was threatening to poison the body of Europe. One would think that Europe would feel obliged to show gratitude for this. The whole of Europe would have breathed a sigh of relief if its mischief-maker had been appropriately chastised, and peace and order had been re-established in the Balkans. But Russia took sides with the offending country. It was this that turned the Austro-Serbian issue into a thundercloud that threatens any moment to burst over Europe.

Austria has made it clear to the European cabinets that it has no territorial ambitions in Serbia, nor the intention of seizing any of its assets. It merely wished to force its unruly neighbour to accept the conditions necessary for peaceful co-existence and which Serbia, as experience shows, would not keep to, despite all its solemn promises, unless forced to do so.

The Austro-Serbian issue is a purely private conflict which, as has been stated above, would be of no serious interest to anybody in Europe, and would in no wise threaten peace in Europe, but would, on the contrary, consolidate it, were it not for the fact that Russia has got involved. It is this which makes the position threatening. Austria has only mobilized part of its forces (the Eighth Army Corps) against Serbia. Just sufficient to carry out its punitive expedition. In response to this, Russia is making preparations to mobilize, in the shortest possible time, the army corps of the Kiev, Odessa and Moscow military districts, a total of twelve army corps,[29] and is taking comparable preparatory measures in the North as well, on the borders of Germany and the Baltic. Russia has declared its intention of mobilizing, if Austria invades Serbia, since it could not tolerate the crushing of Serbia, even though Austria has declared that it has no intention of doing so.

What will inevitably be the consequences?

If Austria moves into Serbia it will confront not only the Serbian army, but also a greatly superior Russian force, thus it will be unable to pursue the war against Serbia without taking measures to secure itself against Russian intervention. That is to say, it will be obliged to mobilize the other half of its army, for it could not possibly submit unconditionally to a Russia that is prepared for war. However, the moment Austria mobilizes its entire army, a conflict with Russia will be inevitable. That in turn will put Germany under an obligation, as an ally, to join the fray. If Germany wishes to keep its word, and to protect its ally from annihilation from superior Russian forces, then it too will have to mobilize. This will lead to the mobilization of the remaining Russian districts. Then Russia will be able to say, 'I am being attacked by Germany', and thus secure the support of France, which is bound by treaty to join the war if its Russian ally is attacked. The much-vaunted Franco/Russian Defence Treaty, which theoretically only exists to forestall any German aggression, is thus brought into effect, and the civilized states of Europe will begin to tear each other apart.

It cannot be denied that there has been skilful manipulation on the part of the Russians. With constant assurances that they are not yet 'mobilizing forces', but only making preparations 'just in case', that 'so far' no reserves have been called up, they are actually preparing for war so well that if they do officially mobilize, they can be ready to march in a few days. This places Austria in a desperate situation, while leaving it to bear the responsibility if it takes measures to protect itself from a Russian surprise attack. Russia will say, 'You, Austria, are mobilizing against us, so you clearly wish to make war on us'.

Russia assures us that it has no intention of harming Germany, while knowing full well that Germany cannot stand by idly in a conflict between its ally and Russia. Thus Germany too will be forced to mobilize, and Russia will again be in a position to say to the world, 'I did not wish to go to war, but Germany forced it on me'. This is how events will inevitably unfold unless what one might call a miracle occurs to prevent, at the eleventh hour, a war which will annihilate the culture of almost all of Europe for decades to come.

Germany does not wish to unleash this dreadful war. The German government knows, however, that the deeply rooted feelings of allegiance, which represent one of the finest characteristics of the German disposition, would be fatally injured, and that it would stand in contradiction to all the sensitivities of its people if it did not come to the aid of its allies at a moment when their very existence is in question.

According to reports received, France has begun to make preparations for a possible mobilization later on. It is quite apparent that Russia and France are working in tandem. Thus if conflict between Austria and Russia is inevitable, Germany will mobilize, and be prepared to fight a war on two fronts. It is of prime importance for the military measures we have planned, if this should be the case, to obtain clarification as soon as possible as to whether Russia and France are willing to let it come to a war with Germany. The longer our neighbours continue with their preparations, the quicker they will be able to complete their mobilization. Thus the military situation is becoming more unfavourable for us daily, and if our opponents are allowed to continue their preparations undisturbed, this could have dire consequences for us.

3. Letters from Helmuth von Moltke to Eliza von Moltke after the Outbreak of War

Extract of letter written in Luxembourg, 29 August 1914

... I am happy to be alone and not at the Court. It makes me quite ill to hear how people are talking there. It is heartbreaking how unaware the great man is of the seriousness of the situation. There is already a kind of 'gung ho' attitude which I despise. Well, I shall calmly continue to work on with my good people. We have only the serious business of our duty to do, and no one is in any doubt how much there is and how hard it will be to do.

Luxembourg, 7 September 1914

A great decision will be taken today. Our entire army, from Paris to the Upper Alsace, has been engaged with the enemy since yesterday. If I had to give my life today for the sake of victory, I would do so with joy a thousandfold as thousands of our brothers will do today, and as thousands have already done. What rivers of blood have already flowed. What nameless misery must come to countless innocent people, whose houses and property have been burned and laid waste. I am often overcome with horror when I think about it, and I feel as if I should answer for this appalling situation, yet I could have done no other than I have.

Luxembourg, 8 September 1914

I can hardly express how extremely heavily the burden of responsibility has weighed on me in the last few days, and still does. For the great struggle along the whole front of our army has still not reached a decisive conclusion. It is a question of maintaining or losing what has been gained with indescribable sacrifices, and it would be terrible if all this blood should have been shed without a significant gain. The dreadful tension of these days, the absence of news from the far-distant armies, the consciousness of what is at stake, all this is almost beyond human endurance. The terrible difficulty of our situation often seems to me like a black, impenetrable wall. This evening, some more favourable news came from the front. May God grant that we once more achieve success with our reduced numbers.

The guards have once more been involved in heavy fighting, and have apparently been reduced to half their number. These are dark times, and this war has already claimed nameless sacrifices, and will continue to do so. The whole world has conspired against us. It looks as if it were the task of all the other nations to destroy Germany once and for all. The few neutral states are not well disposed towards us. Germany has no friend in the world. It stands quite alone, relying on its own resources.

The outcome of today's battle will decide whether we remain here. Not for long in any case. The Kaiser must move into France, closer to the army—he must be in enemy territory, like his troops.

Luxembourg, 9 September 1914

It is looking bad. The fighting East of Paris will end unfavourably for our side. One of our armies has to retreat, the others will have to follow suit. The hopeful prospects at the beginning of the war will turn into their opposite. I have to bear what is happening and will stand or fall by my country. We are bound to suffocate in this battle against East and West. How different it was when we gloriously opened the campaign a few weeks ago—to be followed now by bitter disappointment. And how we will have to pay for everything that is destroyed ... You know better than anyone else how hard all this is for me to bear—you who altogether live in my soul.

4. Helmuth von Moltke on the Retreat from the Marne

Berlin, summer 1915

I have never been under any illusion over how difficult the battle would be that Germany would have to fight through once a conflagration in Europe broke out. This is set out in detail in my annual memorandum to the Chancellor on the military and political situation, not least in the one in which, three years ago, I requested the last reinforcement of the army, which regrettably was not carried out to the extent I wished.

The most momentous decision that I faced as Chief of the General Staff was as to whether Germany should fight the anticipated war on two fronts, defensively, or at least on one front, offensively. After detailed investigation and studies, I decided in favour of the latter course, and drew up the armies so that the offensive in the West could be carried out with the strongest possible forces, and a simultaneous defensive war in the East could be fought with the mimimum number of troops. There was some hope that a decisive action could be fought quickly in the West. This, indeed, was necessary to secure freedom of action in the further course of the war, but it could only be expected if the French army could be fought in open combat. An attack on the fortified eastern border of France would in all probability lead to a long-drawn-out set-piece war, and delay any decision. This view was borne out by what happened to the sixth and seventh armies during the war. This made it necessary to circumvent the French fortified lines which, given the numbers of men to be moved and the space available, could only be done by passing through Belgian territory.

Thus far, my assessment coincides with that of Count Schlieffen. My view of how to execute this plan was significantly different. My predecessor had drawn up his troops in such a way that the right flank of the German army was to pass through Roermond, i.e., would cross not only Belgian, but also Dutch territory. Count Schlieffen took the view that Holland would confine itself to a protest, and would otherwise allow a violation of its territory to proceed unhindered. I had the gravest misgivings about this view, and did not believe that Holland would take such a violation lying down. Furthermore, I could see that a hostile Holland would so weaken the German flank, that it would forfeit the necessary striking power against the West. In my opinion, the advance through Belgium could only be carried out if Holland remained strictly neutral.

Although I did not know what position England would take in a war that pitted Germany against Russia and France, I considered it more than likely that this state would take sides with our opponents the moment we infringed Belgian neutrality, all the more so since England had already declared, in 1870, that this would lead it to declare war. It was clear to me that this alone made it absolutely essential to maintain Dutch neutrality, and I took on board all the difficulties that must result for our deployment and advance if we were not to cross Dutch territory. Immediately our mobilization was declared, I gave the Dutch Ambassador in Berlin a solemn guarantee that Germany would strictly observe Dutch neutrality. I believe that events proved me right. One need only imagine how things would have turned out if we had had to deal with a hostile Holland, whose coastline was open to the English, and what would have happened in our action against Antwerp if Schelde had not remained neutral, and how many troops would have been needed to cover our advance into the West? I was convinced then, and remain so today, that the campaign in the West was sure to fail if we had not left Holland out of it. Moreover, it was clear to me that whatever happened we would have to keep this country as a kind of airpipe for our economy. Thus if we kept Holland neutral, then England, having declared war on us, ostensibly to protect a small, neutral country, would itself scarcely be in a position to violate Dutch neutrality.

It has to be admitted, however, that the planned advance through Belgium was made much more complicated by the decision to avoid Holland: the layout of the railway lines made it necessary to extend the deployment of our troops with the right wing up as far as the Krefeld area. It became necessary to move the strong 1st Army which was later to carry out the outflanking movement southwards past Aachen. There was only one crossing between Lüttich and the Dutch border at Vise, which lay out of range of enemy fire. In order to overcome the enormous technical difficulties resulting from this procedure, I had theoretical studies done over a period of years on the logistics of advancing with our army corps along only one road, and I believe that, in this respect, the trips that I arranged for the General Staff have paid off. The taking of Lüttich early on was of the greatest importance for the execution of the planned operation. The fortress had to be in our hands if the advance of the 1st Army were to be at all possible. This consideration led me to the decision to take Lüttich by surprise. All the previous drafts of the operation featured a more systematic besieging of Lüttich: first, the drawing up of troops as planned, then the advance along the whole line followed by the encirclement of Lüttich and an artillery bombardment. But these plans also provided for the advance of the right wing of the army through Holland. The siege of Lüttich would undoubtedly have cost a great deal of time and troops. The Belgian army would, in the meantime, have been able to mobilize and draw up their troops, and we should have had to deal with a Lüttich that was prepared for war. Furthermore, one would then have had to reckon with the destruction of the Verviers-Lüttich railway line, whose preservation was of prime importance for our advance through Belgium. With the surprise attack which I had planned, everything depended on the swiftness of the attack. I had reconnoitred the area around Lüttich, and had established all the roads along which columns could advance against the town within, without crossing the field of vision of the outer fortress. There were five such roads: officers had been trained to lead the columns in on local patrols, also by night, and were constantly kept up to date. Despite the prevailing prejudice against conducting operations with troops that had not yet been mobilized, I had singled out five brigades from the Territorial Army for this operation. The important thing was to carry out this attack before the interlinking elements of the line of fortification could be built up.

It was quite clear to me, that if the operation should fail, I would stand accused by the whole military world of having sought to accomplish something impossible, and in venturing an infantry attack on a modern fortress, have demonstrated my complete incompetence. Yet it was precisely the fact that Lüttich was a modern fortress, i.e., one that did not include an inner circumvallation, that led me to conceive the plan of penetrating into the inner part of the fortress through the gaps in the outer fortification.

I was indeed staking all on one venture with this operation, and thanks to the bravery of our troops, I won. They will not build fortresses like that again in the future.

It was only once Lüttich had fallen that the railway became free for the advance of the 1st Army, and furthermore, the Belgians had had no time to destroy the Maas railway line. This represented an enormous gain, as the course of events was to show later, when the railway line via Lüttich was the only line available for our troop movements.

The underlying idea for the operations that followed was to push the Belgian army, if at all possible, southwards and away from Antwerp, and likewise, the French army, which I expected to find between the Maas and Sambre south-east and away from Paris, by surrounding its left wing. While the first five armies were to wheel towards the South from Metz/Diedenhofen, the 6th and 7th Armies were to cross the Maas between Nancy and Epinal in order to join up with the 5th Army again to the south of Verdun.

We knew nothing of French intentions before the outbreak of war, and likewise had no firm information on their plans for deployment. We had not failed to notice the strong emphasis on the offensive approach which was apparent in French military writing of recent years. We had no indications that this idea would be realized by attempting a strong thrust on either side of Metz. It was only when large numbers of French troops advanced between Metz and the Vosges after the French had completed drawing up their troops, that this became clear.

I had directed the 6th Army, with the 7th under its command, to retreat initially in the face of the French advance. I was concerned to allow the enemy to advance as far as possible South of Metz, in order then to attack both its wings from the North and South with a much greater prospect of achieving a decisive victory.

It was the declaration by the commander of the 6th Army that he could not allow his troops to retreat any further without undermining their morale, that he simply had to attack, which prevented this intention from being carried out.

The battle in Lothringia was fought before the 7th Army, and the reinforcements for the 6th Army, had fully arrived. It resulted in a complete tactical victory, but the pursuit of the enemy came to a complete stop at the Maas, when the planned breakthrough between Nancy and Epinal did not take place. It was here that it became clear for the first time how strong prepared defensive positions with full field equipment could be, a phenomenon which made its mark on the whole course of the war after the Battle of the Marne. It soon became clear that the defensive line set up by the French between Nancy and Epinal could only be broken through by advancing the 5th Army.

While the first five armies were making victorious progress across the Maas and Sambre, the situation in the East made it necessary to send reinforcements, for the Russians had been able to invade East Prussia quicker than expected, and before we had been able to achieve a decisive victory against the Anglo-French armies. My intention was to draw these reinforcements from the 7th Army, which, like the 6th Army, and despite a long and heavy struggle, had been unable to make any progress at the Maas. It was the unequivocal dispatches from both armies that they were constantly outnumbered by the enemy, and that their own losses were so great, that any other deployment would only be possible once their own numbers had been restored, which caused me to take two corps from the German right wing after the fall of Maubeuge, and to send them East. I recognize that this was a mistake, and one that we would pay for at the Marne.

The messages we got about the deployment of the French armed forces during the advance through northern France all suggested that Paris was being virtually emptied of troops. The reports from the armies had all referred to 'retreating in disarray', and 'signs of the opposition disbanding', and the General Staff had repeatedly emphasized that 'ruthless pursuit' would result in the complete annihilation of the enemy.

It was only in the last days of August that we received reports of the transport of French troops from the east of Paris, having apparently been withdrawn from the front with the 6th and 7th Armies. The 7th Army was then redeployed to St Quentin with the intention of engaging them on the army's right wing. It now looked probable that the French would advance from Paris against the right wing of the 1st Army. Reports of this were passed on to the armies on the right wing, and they were directed, either on the 28th or the 29th August—I don't have the records with me—to draw up their positions as follows: the 1st Army between Oise and Marne, the 2nd Army between Marne and Seine. At the same time the 1st Army was instructed not to advance any further towards Paris than was compatible with its freedom of movement. When this instruction reached the 1st Army they had already crossed the Marne with some of their forces. They asked for permission to continue their pursuit for one more day in order to consolidate their gains. But it was at the same time re-emphasized that it would be necessary to regroup in echelons and secure themselves against attack from Paris.

There followed the French counter-attack against the right wing of the 1st Army and the front of the 2nd, 4th and 5th Armies. To counter the threat on its right wing, the 1st Army drew two corps from the left wing behind the front line towards the right wing. This left a 25-kilometre gap between the 1st and the 2nd Army into which three English divisions penetrated, whereupon the 2nd Army withdrew its right wing.

On 7 September we received reports from which it was clear that the 1st Army was in a very difficult position. It seemed necessary to give instructions for the eventuality that it might be overrun. I therefore sent Lt.-Col. Hentsch[30] to the 2nd and 1st Armies. He was supposed to assess the situation, but was not given the task of issuing orders for the 1st Army to retreat. He was, on the contrary, to give them instructions if they proved unable to keep their present position to withdraw to the line Soissons/Fismes, from there to re-establish access to the right wing of the 2nd Army—and thus to close the gap which had been created. My radio message of 10 September at 10 p.m. to the General Staff of the 1st and 2nd Armies: '1st Army to stand by as rear echelon. Encirclement of the right wing of the 2nd Army is to be prevented by means of attack', shows how far it was from my mind to give Lt.-Col. Hentsch the order to let the 1st Army simply withdraw behind the Aisne. The 1st Army maintains that Lt.-Col. Hentsch conveyed the order to them to retreat, but this is contested by Lt.-Col. Hentsch, who told me on his return that, on his arrival, the directions for the army's retreat had already been prepared. It is clear from the fact that the 1st Army was unable to re-establish contact with the 2nd Army at Fismes that the 1st Army was no longer a free agent. It was obliged to retreat with its left wing towards Soissons instead of its right, so that the gap between it and the 2nd Army could not be closed. This had to be done later by the 7th Army which had, in the meantime, arrived.

I drove to the General Staff on 11 September. I had given orders that the 3rd, 4th and 5th Armies should stay where they were. I believe that this order, which I dictated at the 4th Army General Staff, may be found in the 4th Army's records. I did not pass it on from there for the following reasons: when I came to the General Staff of the 3rd Army, the Commander-in-Chief reported that his Army was no longer capable of holding the territory between the 2nd and 4th Armies if the French should attack him. The Army had suffered such severe losses that he was sure the French would already be attacking it on 13 September.

I thus had to decide to give the 3rd Army a shorter line, which in my opinion they would be certain to hold. This would only be possible if we withdrew the army. This meant that the 4th and 5th Armies also had to withdraw. The regrouping of the 3rd, 4th and 5th Armies on the Reims/Verdun line meant that the front line would be considerably shorter, and should make it possible once the line had been reached to withdraw troops from the front to reinforce the right wing. Since it was necessary to act quickly, I gave the order at four o'clock in the afternoon on 11 September for the armies to withdraw to the following lines: 3rd Army to the line Thuizy (exclusive)—Suippes (exclusive), 4th Army to the line Suippes (inclusive)—St Menehould (exclusive) and the 5th Army the line St Menehould (exclusive) and eastwards. Once these lines were reached they should consolidate and hold their positions. This resulted in a front line of only 20 km. for the weakened 3rd Army, and a total front for the armies 1 to 5 of about 150 km. Since the recent French attacks on the left wing of the army had been repelled, it was to be expected that the five armies would be able to reach their allocated positions without difficulty. Unfortunately, the 1st Army was unable, as reported above, to link up with the right wing of the 2nd. Likewise, the 5th Army reported it would be unable to hold the line at St Menehould, and would have to withdraw to the forest of Argon. (See the 5th Army's documents of 11 September.)

Thus the regrouping of the army on the line I had intended did not come about.

On 13 September, I ordered the withdrawal of one corps each from the 3rd, 4th and 5th Armies to provide reinforcements for the right wing of the army in the west, and in order to close the gap between the 1st and 2nd Armies. This became necessary because the 7th Army had only just begun to reach St Quentin.

On 14 September operational command was transferred to General von Falkenhayn, and at the same time my quartermaster-in-chief, General von Stein, was named General in Command of the XIV Reserve Corps.

Thus ended my military activity.[31]

5. A Document that could have Changed World History

(i) Rudolf Steiner's Prefatory Remarks to the Pamphlet The Question of War-'Guilt' [32]

The German people must confront the truth about the outbreak of the war. This truth can be the source of the strength it will need to take the action which is now necessary. The seriousness of the present situation requires that we set aside all concern that may be expressed by one or other party about revealing the events that took place in Germany before the outbreak of the war.

This publication is intended as a contribution toward the presentation of the truth of these events. It derives from the man who was right at the centre of what took place in Berlin between the end of July and the beginning of August 1914, the Chief of the General Staff, Colonel-General Helmuth von Moltke. From this contribution it will be clear just how far it may be said of this man that he stood at the centre of these events.

Herr von Moltke's widow, Frau Eliza von Moltke, is fulfilling an historical duty by not withholding these documents from the public. Anyone who reads them may come to the conclusion that they constitute the most important document to be found in Germany on the beginnings of the war.

They characterize the mood which made it seem in military circles that the war was inevitable. They set out the military reasoning behind its development in the early stages in a way that brought upon the German people the condemnation of the whole world.

The world expects an honest confession of the truth from the German people. Here it has one, written down by a man whose every word bears the stamp of honesty and who—as will be seen from the documents—was quite incapable of wishing for anything but the purest subjective truth to flow from his pen at the moment of writing.

And *this* truth, if read aright, amounts to a complete con-demnation of German politics. A condemnation which could not be more scathing. A condemnation which points to quite other things than those that are taken for granted by friend and foe alike.

It is not the actual causes of war that one will find set out in these documents. These may be sought in events which naturally go back a long way. But what happened in July 1914 sheds a true light on these events. This light reveals the collapse of the house of cards that was German politics. One sees people that were involved in these politics of whom it may be said that any proof that they wished to avoid the war was superfluous. One can certainly believe that they wished to avoid the war. It could, however, only have been avoided, if *they* had never got into their positions in politics. It was not what they did that led to disaster, but rather the whole nature of their personalities.

It is shattering to read in these documents how, at the decisive moment, German military judgement is met by German political judgement. The political judgement is quite incapable of assessing the situation, having reached its own nadir, and the consequence is a situation, about which the Chief of the General Staff writes: 'The mood became more and more excitable, and *I stood there quite alone*'.

One need only stop to consider what follows in these documents from that sentence to the next: *'Now you may do as you wish'* ...

Yes, indeed, that is how it was: The Chief of the General Staff stood there quite alone. Since German politics had reached their nadir, the fate of Europe on 31 July and 1 August 1914 lay in the hands of a man who was *obliged to do his military duty*. And who did so with a bleeding heart.

Whoever wishes to judge what really happened must factually, and without prejudice, confront the question: How did it come about that there was no other power in Germany towards the end of July 1914 that could decide the fate of the German people than the military alone? If indeed it was so, then it was necessary for Ger-many and for Europe as a whole to go to war. The Chief of the General Staff, who 'stood alone', could not have avoided it.

The calamitous invasion of Belgium, which was a 'military necessity' and a political impossibility, shows the extent to which everything had been allowed to sway in the balance of military judgement during these times that preceded the outbreak of war.

The present writer put the following question to Helmuth von Moltke, with whom he had been friendly for many years: 'What did the Kaiser think about this invasion?' The reply was: 'Until a few days before war broke out, he knew nothing about it: for being the type of man he was, it was to be feared he would blurt it out to the whole world. This could not be allowed to happen, for the invasion could only be successful if the enemy were completely unprepared.' 'And did the Chancellor know?' 'Yes, he knew about it.'

These things *must* not be concealed by those who know them, however reluctant one may be to disclose them. I need hardly add that from the whole tone of my conversations with Herr von Moltke, I am under no obligation at all to keep these things confidential, and that I know that I am acting as he would have wished in disclosing them. They show how German politics were drifting to their absolute nadir.

One is *obliged* to point to these things when discussing to what extent 'guilt' attaches to the German people. This 'guilt' has its own peculiar quality. It is the guilt that attaches to a people whose thoughts were not of politics at all, and the intentions of whose 'superiors' were kept obscured from them by impenetrable veils. A people, moreover, whose apolitical disposition was such that it could not guess that the pursuit of its policies must lead to war.

It must also seem incomprehensible that even some time before the war words were spoken in an official capacity from which one could only conclude that Germany did *not* have the intention of ever violating Belgian neutrality, whereas Herr von Moltke also told me, in November 1914, that the person concerned must have known of the intention to march through Belgium. *That* question as to whether the German people could have taken steps to prevent the outbreak of war in the year 1914: that question is completely answered by these documents. Things would have had to be set in motion a long time before if the events of this year were to have found Germany in a different state to the one in which it was. Given the condition in which it found itself, nothing else could have happened than what did. This is how the German people must see its destiny today, and the power that flows from this insight must guide it on its further path. The events which took place *during* the terrible catastrophe of the war demonstrate this no less that those which are recorded in the documents in this pamphlet. Yet it is not my task to speak of *that* here, since it is my duty only to provide an introduction to these documents.

It is clear from them that the deciding factor was not the assumption that France or England would violate Belgian neutrality if Germany didn't, but rather the assumption that France would fight a defensive war behind its eastern front, a war which had to be avoided. This standpoint had characterized the whole of German planning for the contingency of war for several years, and this standpoint must, of necessity, leave the decision in the balance of military judgement unless political work had been carried out over the same period enabling quite different forces to be brought towards such a decision. This did not happen. Instead the country was allowed to drift towards a situation that made it necessary at the decisive moment for any form of political judgement to give way before the military. The key issue lies behind what the documents highlight on this point: the appeal 'to the German people and the civilized world' drew attention to it. The German Reich was 'placed in the context of world events without a substantial mission that justified its existence'. This mission should not have been such that only military power could carry it. Indeed, it could not at all have been based on the *exercise of power* in the outer sense of the word. It could only have been directed towards the *inner* development of its culture. Having such a mission, Germany need never have built itself up on things that placed it in competition, and then in direct conflict, with other empires, empires to which it must, of necessity, succumb in the exercise of power in the outer sense. A German Reich should have developed policies that disregarded the outer exercise of power. It should have developed the politics of true culture. There should never have arisen in Germany, of all places, the thought that whoever considered such politics of culture to be the only viable ones would be an 'unpractical idealist'. For the world situation in general is such that any form of power politics must inevitably turn to purely military power, and the fate of the German people should never have been left in the hands of the latter alone.

In these documents a leading personality gives a simple account of what he experienced and the actions he took at the end of July and the beginning of August 1914: and this account sheds a clear light on the tragic destiny of the German people. It shows 'how German politics at the time were like an empty shell, and how having reached their nadir, the politicians were *obliged* to allow any decision on *if* and *how* the war was to be started to lie in the hands of the military administration. Anyone in a position of authority in the military of that time could not, from a military point of view, *have acted in any other way* than they actually did, because from *this* point of view the situation could only be assessed in the way it was. For in all areas apart from the military, Germany had manoeuvred itself into a position where it was incapable of action.'[33]

The conclusive proof of this may be found within the documents of Helmuth von Moltke. They contain the words of a man who saw the 'forthcoming war' as the greatest misfortune to befall the German and, indeed, the European peoples: a man who had contemplated this disaster for years, and who, at the critical moment, found himself in a position where he would be in breach of his duty as a soldier if he delayed the outbreak of war, even by hours. Over a period of years before the war I was able to observe how this man devoted himself to the highest spiritual ideas with ardent yearning, how his disposition was such that he was touched by the least suffering in any other being: I have heard him speak about many things, but hardly ever about anything of military significance. In a remark such as the following one from his records it is indeed not *he* who is speaking, but rather the military way of thinking *through* him: 'In my opinion, the highest art of diplomacy consists not in maintaining peace at all costs, but rather in constantly shaping the affairs of the state in such a way that it is in an advantageous position to embark on a war.' In much the same way, the explanations that Helmuth von Moltke himself gives as he writes down these notes about the development of humanity and of Europe are overshadowed by military thinking. Against this background, it will be understood how he could write in his notes: 'Germany did not initiate the war, it did not embark on the war out of a desire for conquest nor out of any hostile intentions towards its neighbours. The war was forced upon us, and we are fighting for our national existence, for the survival of our people, and our national heritage.'[34] I could never believe other of this man than that if he had been obliged to say anything different from the words above about the 'coming' and, in his opinion, inevitable war, he would have left office long before the war. As things were, military thinking in Germany could arrive at no other conclusion. And this conclusion *condemned* Germany to be in conflict with the whole of the rest of the world. The German people will have to learn from this disaster that *its* way of thinking must be a different one in the future. From a military point of view the war could only appear necessary. Politically, it was unjustifiable, indefensible and futile.

How tragic it is indeed that a man is *obliged* to turn his hand to a deed, the responsibility for which makes his heart bleed, and yet which he takes to be his highest duty: a deed which outside Germany *had to be* considered as morally reprehensible, as a deliberate starting of the war. Thus world events collide in a sphere of life in which the idea of 'guilt' should be seen in a very different light from the one in which it is commonly seen by everyone today.

There was talk of German 'warmongers'. Rightly so, they were present. People also say that Germany never wanted the war. Rightly so. For the German people did not want it. But the 'warmongers' would never have been able to precipitate the war in the last few days before it broke out, their efforts would have got them nowhere, if it had not been for military planners seeing no alternative. After all, these documents contain the sentence: 'I am convinced that the Kaiser would not have signed the order for mobilization if the despatch from Prince Lichnowsky had arrived half an hour earlier'. The political mood was *against* war. But the political mood had become powerless, *vis-à-vis* military considerations. And it had even become powerless in the face of the question of *how* to deal with the East or the West. This did not depend in any way on the political situation at the time in question, but rather on the extent of military preparations. There is a widespread myth about a privy council or some such which is said to have been held in Potsdam on 5 July and in which the war is supposed to have been planned out. Now von Moltke, to whose military judgement the decision was entrusted at the end of July, had gone to take a cure at Karlsbad in June and only returned from this at the end of July. Until the end of his life he knew absolutely *nothing* about any such privy council. He took the decision out of purely military considerations. There is no doubt that what came to expression in the situation in Europe in July 1914, and which eventually gave rise to military considerations turning out the way they did, can be traced back to events that took place over the course of years. There are many individuals in Germany who must carry the blame for these events, but they brought these events about because they saw the being of Germany expressed in the outer exercise of power and glory, not because they wanted to stir up a war. And those people who did wish to incite a war would have been checked by the prevailing inclination towards peace in political circles during those fateful days of July: their efforts would have come to nothing if those things had not come about during the days after 26 July which had, from the outset, forged the chain of events in Germany which led directly to war. The decision lay with Herr von Moltke, and—as is clear from these documents—he had nothing to do with any warmongers. Often enough I heard him speak after his dismissal in such a way that it was clear that one would never have paid any attention to warmongers from whatever quarter. When asked about Bernhardi[35] he delivered a rebuff which stated quite plainly: he could have written all the books he wanted—no one who mattered in our circles would have paid any attention to that sort of thing. I would never record such a remark here if it were not fully supported in these documents; moreover it is fully supported by numerous conversations I had with Herr von Moltke during the war. Previously, as stated above, he had hardly ever referred to military matters in conversation with me. I am very well aware of how attitudes such as those of Bernhardi can influence those who are in positions of authority in an indirect way, and how influential people can be who are not in positions of authority. But von Moltke was in a position of authority, and what he did he did out of his own conviction. One can disregard all suggestions that he was influenced by warmongering, though it was undoubtedly going on. The *immediate* chain of events which led to Germany's declaration of war began with the assessment of the situation in Europe from a purely military point of view, which Herr von Moltke came to on his return to Berlin. All other factors which people regard as immediate causes of war were ineffectual, and could not in themselves have led to what happened.

Thus these documents may be seen as conclusive evidence that it was *not* military judgement as such, *neither* was it the completely inadequate political judgement on the German side in 1914, that led to the war, but rather the fact that there was no political activity which could prevent exclusively military considerations prevailing. Only if there had been such in the year 1914 could there have been any other outcome. Thus these documents are a terrible indictment of German politics. This perception must not remain hidden.

It may be that the publication of these documents will be

objected to on the grounds that they conclude with the words: 'they are only intended for my wife, and should never be published'. Helmuth von Moltke wrote these words in November 1914 in Homburg where he wrote his account of events. There is nothing in what is published here which I did not know in November, and which I had not heard after November from von Moltke himself. By the same token, I was never sworn to silence on any issue raised here. On the contrary, I would be in breach of my duty to publish what may not be withheld if I remained silent about what I know. I would *have* to pass on the information in these documents even if they did not exist, and I would be *able* to do so because I was aware of *all* of it before I read the documents. In agreeing to their publication, Frau von Moltke shows her understanding of an historical duty; and from the period of extreme mental anguish that began for her husband after his dismissal, she knows that she is acting for and not against his intentions.[36] This man went through unspeakable suffering. He accompanied in his soul every fluctuation in the fortunes of his people at war until his death. Thus his words that the documents were 'only for my wife' may be seen as a proof of the absolute honesty and integrity of what was written. At the moment of writing this man believed he was writing only for his wife: how could even the least prevarication flow into his words! I can say this in public only because I knew the man, a man whose lips never uttered a subjective untruth.

Why were these documents not published earlier? This question might be asked. Well, time enough was spent vainly trying to gain a hearing for them among those who needed to hear them in order to direct their actions. They did not *wish* to hear this. And they were not interested. It was not their 'business'. *Now* it is for the public to know.

Written in Stuttgart, May 1919
Rudolf Steiner

(ii) Helmuth von Moltke—'Reflections and Memories'

Homburg, November 1914

The European war of the year 1914 did not come unexpectedly to anyone who looked out into the world without the prejudice of diplomacy. For years it had been on the political horizon, like a storm cloud; the tense European situation was bound to discharge, and there could be no doubt that the conflict between two major European states would unleash the war in which nearly all of Europe became involved. It was a necessary consequence of the treaties and agreements made between the members of the two power blocks which provided for ties between all the states in the event of war. It was certain that Germany would actively participate in any war that seriously threatened the existence of the Austro-Hungarian monarchy and it was equally certain that France would stand by Russia's side. For years the Entente had been hostile towards the Triple Alliance. However, it was not to be expected that the latter would fail when put to the test, and that Italy would not meet its alliance commitments. As late as one year before the war the already existing agreements between Italy and France had been revised and renewed, and in spring 1914 these agreements were ratified. Italy had agreed to provide Germany with two cavalry divisions and three army corps in the event of a war between Germany and France; General Zuccari, who had been put in charge of these supply forces, had paid me a visit in Berlin and the Austrian General Staff was to be involved in transporting these forces. Everything had been agreed in detail. In addition, a marine pact between Germany, Italy and Austria had been ratified according to which there was to be a joint operation of the Austrian and Italian navies, to be joined by the German ships present in the Mediterranean at the outbreak of war. All these agreements had been formulated so clearly and unambiguously that Italy's commitment to the alliance could hardly be doubted. The official documents pertaining to these, the declarations made in the name of the Italian government which had received the King's consent, are filed in our archives. Nevertheless, Italy broke its word. It declared its neutrality and casually set aside its obligations. A more ignominious break of a promise can probably not be found in history. Germany and Austria stood alone when the war broke out.

British diplomacy had managed to steer clear of any binding treaties and to safeguard its policy of a free hand. Although there had been agreements made between England, France and Belgium for the possible event of a co-operation, England could rightly maintain that it had not entered into any binding state treaties. So while there was no certainty over England's position in the event of a war breaking out, it was nevertheless very likely that it would be found on the side of Germany's enemies in the event of a war between Germany and France. The chance of getting rid of an uncomfortable competitor in the world market, of stepping in where there was a prospect of squashing Germany together with Russia and France by superior power; the long-term policy of insidious agitation to encircle Germany initiated by King Edward VII,[37] the hope of destroying the feared German fleet and thereby achieving sole rulership over the world oceans, of attaining world rule—all of this made it likely from the start that England would range herself among our enemies.

The hopes of our diplomacy of establishing good relations with England, which for many years had been the compass needle determining our policies, were bound to prove misguided as soon as the brutal English interests found a way of pushing through. England had always found ways to hide its self-seeking actions under a cloak of morality.[38] Thus in this case, too, the violation of Belgian neutrality by Germany had to serve as a pretext for declaring war on the latter.[39] While it may be doubtful whether England would have immediately joined actively in the war against us if this violation of Belgian neutrality had not taken place, it is certain that it would have intervened as soon as there was a risk of France being overpowered by us. None of the Continental powers, least of all Germany, would have been allowed by the traditional practice of English politics to become so strong that a risk of hegemony might arise. Maybe it would have been more convenient for England to delay its intervention until the Continental states had exhausted themselves in war, maybe this is what the state leadership envisaged initially. However, the fact that England would have in any case—sooner or later—acted against Germany had to be reckoned with under all circumstances by any objective observer. All the courtship efforts of our diplomacy *vis-à-vis* a state which, like England, pursued exclusively its own interests, were doomed from the outset. It would not have been so difficult to recognize this even before the outbreak of war. I think that it would have been easier to reach an agreement with France or some settlement with Russia than obtain a certain promise of neutrality from England. But our gaze was focused on England, as if hypnotized, and when it declared itself against us right at the beginning of the war, we were faced with the superior power of our enemies, together with Austria, and no other allies whatsoever and without any preparation that might have enabled us to win such a war.

The outbreak of the European war had been delayed over years because of human fear. It was that which caused all the governments to avow repeatedly that all efforts were directed at maintaining peace.

It would have been better for us to courageously face the events to come, the war that was unmistakably upon us, and to prepare for it diplomatically. In my opinion, the highest art of diplomacy consists not in maintaining peace at all costs, but rather in constantly shaping the affairs of the state in such a way that it is in an advantageous position to embark on a war.

This was the immortal achievement of Bismarck before the wars of 1866 and 1871. He was for ever concerned about the possibility of a coalition between France and Russia which has now come about and is forcing us into a war on two fronts. That the German nation had a clear sense of the hard times facing the Fatherland is borne out by the approval of the armaments proposal requested by the General Staff and the Ministry of War in 1912.

The General Staff had been reckoning on a war on two fronts for years. That it would become necessary at the moment when the rivalries between Russia and Austria in the Balkans would develop into open conflict was obvious enough. We all knew that France would necessarily take part in it alongside the Tsar's Empire, to whom it had provided billions to assist its preparation for the war. The question might be asked whether Germany would not have done better to leave Austria to its destiny instead of taking upon itself the tremendous gravity of the expected war in loyalty to its alliance. It has been stated repeatedly that the break-up of the Austro-Hungarian monarchy could, after all, not be prevented, and that Germany had actually no grounds to plunge into the adventure of a war that, as everyone knew, was going to be severe, for the sake of Austria. It has to be admitted that Germany, had it abandoned the allied monarchy, might have initially been spared from the war. Yet apart from the fact that the German people would not have stood for such felony, I hold that abandoning Austria would have also been a political mistake that would have revenged itself upon us in a very short time. The Anglo-French policy of isolation was primarily directed at Germany. It would have continued if Germany had split from Austria and in a few years we would have been at war with the same coalition which is attacking us now, but then without, or possibly even with, a hostile Austria. Then we would have stood completely alone. This war which we are engaged in now was a necessity which has its foundations in the world's evolution. Nations as well as individual people are subject to its law. If this world evolution, which is commonly referred to as world history, did not exist, if it was not guided by the plan of world evolution according to higher laws, then the evolutionary theory which is generally recognized with regard to that which lives on the earth, would not be applicable to the highest living being—the human being—as part of a people. If that was so the whole of world history would be nothing but the confused result of all sorts of coincidences, and any idea of a plan in its evolution would have to be refuted. In my view history shows that there is such a plan. History shows how the various cultural epochs give way to one another, how every people has a certain task to fulfil in the world's evolution and how this evolution follows a progressive course.

Thus Germany, too, has its cultural task that it needs to fulfil. However, the fulfilling of such tasks does not come to pass without friction as there are always resistances to overcome; these can only come to expression through war. If it were to be assumed that Germany would be destroyed in this war the whole of German cultural life, which is necessary for the further spiritual development of humanity, and German civilization, would be obliterated; humanity would be thrown back in its overall development in the most ominous way.

The Latin peoples have already passed the zenith of their development; they cannot carry any new fertilizing elements into the evolution of the whole. The Slav people, primarily Russia, are still too far back in their culture to take the leading role in humanity. Under the rule of tyranny, Europe would be reduced to the state of spiritual barbarism. England pursues only material aims.[40]

A spiritual progression of humanity is only possible through Germany.[41] That is why Germany will not succumb in this war. It is the only people that can lead humanity towards higher aims at this time.

These are momentous times in which we live. This war will bring forth a new departure in history, and its outcome will prescribe the path which the whole world will have to follow in coming centuries.

Germany has not brought about this war, and it has not entered into it out of a lust for conquest or with aggressive intentions against its neighbours.

The war was forced upon it by its opponents, and we are fighting for our national existence, for the continued existence of our people, our national life.[42] In that we are fighting for true ideals while our opponents are openly expressing that it is their aim to destroy Germany.

Never before has a more righteous war been waged by any state and never has it affected a people more strongly moved by ideal aspirations. As if by one stroke all dissent, all party differences, all material interests subsided with this people, the people stood together solidly, and everyone was willing to sacrifice his worldly goods and his blood for the Fatherland. The high idealism of the German people which even the materialistic current of many years of affluence could not destroy, victoriously blazed the trail. The people realized that there are higher and more precious aims than material affluence and it turned to these with the whole ardour of the Germanic nature. Such a people is invincible.

The outer cause of the war was the murder of the successor to the throne of the Archduke. As soon as it turned out that Austria made far-reaching compensation claims to Serbia, Russia joined up with the murderers. It feared that it would lose its reputation in the Balkans and its position as protector of the Slavs if it delivered Serbia to Austria without support. Therefore Russia was decided on war right from the start and soon began its preparations for the mobilization which were at first kept very secret. In my view Russia only wanted to gain time when it declared shortly afterwards that the meanwhile publicly ordered mobilization in the southern military districts was only directed against Austria, and that there was to be no mobilization against Germany. While the mobilization efforts were in full flow the Minister of War[43] assured the German Military Attaché[44] on his honour that there was no mobilization. It is known that subsequently, while our Kaiser attempted to mediate in an honest manner between Russia and Austria, Russia was also ordering the northern military districts to mobilize. It is true that the Tsar declared that this mobilization was not directed against Germany, that Russia did not want the war against Germany, but in doing that it expected us to expose ourselves to the arbitrary will of a fully-armed Russia without having made our own preparations for war.

That, of course, was impossible for Germany. As soon as Russia started to mobilize its entire army we were also forced to mobilize. Had we not done it, Russia would have been able at any time to invade our unprotected country and make it impossible for us to mobilize at a later time.

There can be no doubt to anyone unprejudiced that it is Russia who let this war flare up. It knew exactly that Germany would not allow its ally Austria to be destroyed, but had gained time through its treacherous actions and had already progressed very far with its mobilization when Germany started its own.

As I have already stated the General Staff had studied for years a simultaneous campaign against two fronts. The plan to advance through Belgium was worked out by my predecessor, Count Schlieffen.

This measure was justified on the grounds that it seemed practically impossible to force the French army to accept a decisive battle in the open field without violating Belgium's neutrality. All our information pointed to a scenario where the French would fight a defensive war behind their strong eastern front, and that we would have to prepare for a series of protracted sieges if we were to make a frontal attack against that very strongly fortified position. Count Schlieffen even proposed to swing the right wing of the German army through Southern Holland.[45] I changed this plan in order not to force the Netherlands, too, on the side of our enemies, preferring to face the difficult technical problems of forcing our army's right wing through the narrow space between Aachen and the southern border of the province of Limburg. In order to accomplish this move we had to take possession of Lüttich as fast as possible. That is the reason for our plan to take this fortress by storm.

The General Staff also repeatedly debated whether it might not be better to wage a defensive war. It was always rejected as it precluded the possibility of speedily engaging the enemy in his own territories. It was taken into account that Belgium would protest against our crossing but would not mount an armed resistance. That explains the form of the ultimatum I drafted to the Belgian government which guaranteed the King the integrity of the monarchy. The passage in this which granted Belgium the prospect of territorial enlargement in the event that we were amicably received was deleted by the Foreign Office when the ultimatum was delivered.

Certainly many objections can be raised against marching through Belgium, but the course of events in the first few weeks of the war showed that this forced the French, as we had intended, to meet us in the open field, where they could be defeated. Our failure to overwhelm France with the first attack was due to England's fast intervention.

The assault on Lüttich was a bold undertaking. If it failed the moral setback would be severe. I ordered it mostly in the hope that we would gain posession of the railway between Aachen and Lüttich before it was destroyed. In this we succeeded, and the fact that we later secured in addition the line to Brussels and St Quentin proved invaluable.

On the day before our mobilization we had received a telegram from London stating that England had formally promised to France to secure the protection of the French northern coast against German attacks from the sea. The Kaiser asked for my view and I declared that we could well afford to promise not to attack France's northern coast if England would guarantee to remain neutral. I held that the war with France would be decided on land and that a naval attack would not be necessary if England assured us neutrality in return. This telegram was probably England's first attempt to dupe us, or at least to delay our mobilization.

In response to the news on 28 July or 29 (?)[46] that a general mobilization had been ordered in Russia the Kaiser issued a proclamation of 'danger of war'. At 5 p.m. on 1 August His Majesty orderered a general mobilization throughout Germany. August 2 was the first day of mobilization.

I was on my way back from the palace to the General Staff when I received the order to return to the palace at once as important news had arrived. I immediately turned back. At the palace I found, apart from His Majesty, the Imperial Chancellor, the Minister of War[47] and some other gentlemen.

The Imperial Chancellor, who, as already indicated, considered it the most important aim of his policy to create good relations with England, and who, remarkably enough, had still believed up to that day that the general war, or at least England's participation in it, could be prevented, was evidently greatly excited by the content of a telegram just received from the German ambassador in London, Prince Lichnowsky.[48] His Majesty, the Kaiser, shared his delight. The telegram stated that Lord Grey, the head of the British Foreign Office,[49] had told the ambassador that England would pledge herself to prevent France from joining a war against us if Germany in turn were to pledge herself not to commit any hostile action against France. I must mention here that France had ordered a general mobilization on the same day we did and that this was known to us. As I said, the mood was joyous.

'Now we only needed to fight against Russia!' The Kaiser said to me: 'Now we simply post our entire army to the East!' I replied to His Majesty that this would be impossible. The deployment of an army of one million men could not be improvised but was the outcome of a whole year's arduous preparation and could not be altered once it was all laid down. If His Majesty insisted upon marching the entire army eastwards it would not be an army ready for battle but a chaotic mob of confused armed people without supplies. The Kaiser insisted upon his request and became very irritated; he said to me among other things: 'Your uncle would have given me a different answer', which hurt me greatly. I never claimed to be equal to the Field Marshal. No one, but no one, seemed to entertain the notion that it was bound to lead us into a catastrophe if we were to march our entire army into Russia, with a mobilized France in our rear. How on earth could England, even if it was willing to do so, ever have been capable of preventing France from attacking us from behind! My objection that France was already in the process of mobilization and that it was impossible for a mobilized Germany and a mobilized France to amicably agree not to harm one another, made no difference, either. The mood became more and more excitable, and I stood there quite alone.

Finally, I succeeded in convincing His Majesty that our plan of deployment, with strong forces against France and weaker defensive forces against Russia, must be carried out if we were to avoid disastrous confusion. I told the Kaiser that once our deployment was complete any number of strong reinforcements could be transferred to the East, but that the deployment plan itself was not to be altered, as otherwise I could not take responsibility for the operations.

Hence a reply despatch to London was drafted which said that Germany was very pleased to accept England's offer but that the original deployment plan, also on the French border, would initially have to be carried out for technical reasons. However, we would not harm France provided that she remained quiet under England's control. I could not get any more than that. The nonsensical nature of England's proposal had been clear to me from the start. Already in earlier years it had been brought to my attention by the Foreign Office that France might possibly remain neutral in the event of a war of Germany against Russia. I had so little faith in this possibility that even then I stated that, if Russia declared war on us, and France's position was in the slightest doubtful, we would have to declare war upon her immediately. Now I demanded, as a guarantee of France's willingness not to strike against us, temporary possession of the fortresses of Verdun and Toul. This suggestion was rejected as a vote of no-confidence against England.

In the course of this conversation I had reached a state of near despair. I saw that these diplomatic measures which threatened to impede the progress of our mobilization would lead us to disaster in the impending war. I have to add here that our mobilization plan had provided for the occupation of Luxembourg by the 16th division on the very first day of mobilization. It was imperative for us to secure Luxembourg's railways against a French attack as we needed them for our deployment. I was all the more shattered when the Imperial Chancellor now declared that the occupation of Luxembourg must not take place under any circumstances as it would constitute a direct threat to France and would make the guarantee offered by England illusory. While I was standing there, the Kaiser, without asking me, turned to his aide-de-camp and ordered him to send a telegram to the 16th division in Trier at once, ordering it not to march into Luxembourg. I felt as if my heart would break. Once again there was a risk of our deployment being plunged into disorder. What that meant can probably only be fully appreciated by one familiar with the complicated and minutely detailed efforts involved in drawing up a deployment plan. In a situation where every single train is planned to the minute any alteration was bound to have disastrous consequences. I tried in vain to convince His Majesty that we needed the Luxembourg railways and would have to secure them. I was dismissed with the remark that I would have to use other railways instead. The order was upheld.

So I was dismissed. It is impossible for me to describe the mood in which I arrived home. I was as if broken apart and shed tears of despair.[50] When the despatch to the 16th division confirming the order issued by telephone was submitted to me, I threw my pen down on the desk and declared that I was not going to sign it. I cannot put my signature, my first after the mobilization order, under an order refuting something that was prepared in accordance with a well-thought-out plan, and would immediately be received by our troops as a sign of uncertainty. 'Do what you like with the despatch,' I said to Lieutenant-Colonel Tappen.[51] 'I am not signing it.' Thus I remained sitting in my room, in sombre mood, until I was ordered back to His Majesty's palace at eleven o'clock at night. The Kaiser received me in his bedroom. He had already been in bed, but had risen again and slipped on a coat. He handed me a despatch from the King of England in which the latter declared that he knew nothing of a guarantee on the side of England to prevent France from joining the war. Prince Lichnowsky's telegram must have been based on error or he must have misunderstood something. The Kaiser was most upset and told me: 'Now you may do as you wish.' I went home at once and telegraphed to the 16th division that the advance into Luxembourg was to be carried out. In order to show at least some motivation for renewing this command I added: 'because news has just been received that France has ordered general mobilization'.

This was my first experience in this war. I am convinced that the Kaiser would not have signed the order for mobilization if the despatch from Prince Lichnowsky had arrived half an hour earlier. I have never been able to get over the impression of this experience. Something within me was destroyed that could never be restored. My confidence and trust were shattered.

The surprise coup against Lüttich was scheduled for 5 August. On the evening of that day a message came in from there which suggested that the operation had failed. At any rate our troops had not got through to the town.

I had to inform the Kaiser of this. He said to me: 'I knew that would happen. This advance against Belgium has lumbered me with England against us in war.' When news came through on the day after that we had taken the town, I was kissed all over.

After the initial fast and successful advance of our armies through Belgium towards France we suffered a set-back as a result of attacks from vigorous French and English forces from Paris against our right wing. The 2nd Army had to call back its right wing and the 1st had to be called back altogether. The situation was critical. I had gone out to the army supreme commands. While I was with army supreme command 4 a radio message from the 2nd Army arrived, informing us that strong French forces deflecting eastwards were attacking the 3rd Army. I wanted to leave the 3rd Army in its position, likewise the 4th and 5th. When I came to army supreme command 3, General v. Hausen[52] explained to me that he could not hold the line allocated to him as his troops were no longer operative. Therefore I was forced to give the 3rd Army a shorter line further back while at the same time taking the 4th and 5th Armies further back in order to restore a closed army front. I had to issue a command to that effect there and then, at my own responsibility. It was a hard decision which I had to take without seeking His Majesty's permission beforehand—the hardest decision of my life which cost me my lifeblood. But I envisaged a catastrophe, had I not taken the army back.

I arrived back at headquarters at three o'clock at night in Luxembourg. On 13 September I informed the Kaiser of what I had ordered, stating the reasons. The Kaiser did not take it with bad grace, but I had the impression that he was not completely convinced of the necessity of the retreat. I must admit that my nerves had been badly shaken by everything I had experienced and that I probably gave the impression of a sick man.

On 14 September in the afternoon General von Lyncker[53] appeared at my office and told me that the Kaiser wished to inform me of his impression that I was too ill to carry on leading operations. His Majesty had ordered that I should request sick leave and return to Berlin. General v. Falkenhayn was to take charge of operations.

At the same time General von Stein, who had up to that time been my head quartermaster, had been dismissed and put in charge of a reserve army corps. All this came over me without any preparation.

I immediately went to General Falkenhayn and informed him of His Majesty's orders. He was completely surprised. Together we went to the Kaiser who told me that he was under the impression that my two sojourns at Karlsbad spa had weakened me and that I needed to recover. I said to the Kaiser that I believed that it would not make a good impression on the army or abroad if I was sent away immediately after the retreat of the army.

General von Falkenhayn concurred with this view. In response to this the Kaiser suggested that Falkenhayn should act as supreme quartermaster and that I should stay on pro forma. Falkenhayn stated that he could only take charge of the operations if he had a completely free hand. I could not but agree with this. Hence I stayed on at headquarters while everything was taken out of my hands and I was left like a bystander without any influence whatsoever. I took this martyrdom upon myself and covered all further operations with my name, for the sake of the country and to spare the Kaiser from any speculation that he had sent away his Chief of the General Staff at the very first setback. I was aware of the disastrous consequences this would have.

Later I asked His Majesty to send me to Brussels to assist with the occupation of Antwerp. I could bear it no longer to be present at headquarters completely inactive and pushed to one side. The Kaiser approved my request and I travelled to Brussels and from there to the headquarters of General von Beseler. I was there three times, and back several times in the main headquarters whence my unrest about the further operations drove me again and again. I was able to procure some supplies, bridge trains as well as a territorial army brigade for General von Beseler. I was in Fildonk at the time of Antwerp's capitulation. The Kaiser had authorized me to finalize the capitulation in the event it happened, and I had conferred that authority on Beseler to whom alone it was due. After the capitulation I returned to headquarters. I had nothing left to do now, was finished and in near despair over my bogus position. I went to the Kaiser and told him that I could no longer suffer this state of affairs. He was surprised when I explained to him that I was totally excluded and said that he still considered me the actual leader of operations. After I had explained the facts to him he said that this was not his intention and that he would take steps to remedy the situation; he would think things over and make amends. On the next day I succumbed to an inflammation of the gallbladder and liver and was forced to retire to bed. The soul commotions of recent weeks, my desparate mood and situation had rendered my physical organism disposed to illness. When I had been laid-up for eight days the Kaiser came to visit me and sat by my bedside for an hour. He was very kind and gracious but did not refer again to my offical concerns. Two days later I received a second visit. He offered me the use of his apartments in Schloß Homburg, advising me to spend some time there in order to recover. He also exhorted my second aide, Colonel Köhler, to look after me well and was very gracious again. I departed for Hamburg one or two days later, on 1 November.

On 3 November the order appointing General v. Falkenhayn my successor was signed. I hung in the air without any official function whatsoever.

I have written all this down quickly, without recourse to any notes or other materials. There may be errors with regard to dates, etc., as a result. In addition I was still sick when I wrote these things down. They are intended for my wife only and must never be made known to the public.[54] The martyrdom I have suffered was great. I believed that I owed it to the Kaiser and to the country. May God forgive me if I have acted wrongly. I am completely convinced that the Kaiser never became aware of what he had done to me. Even after my dismissal his disposition towards me was gracious and kind.

(iii) Entries from the Diary of Wilhelm von Dommes*
Between 28 May and 9 June 1919[55]

28. V.

Around midday received order through GHQ [General Head-quarters] North (Fritsch) from SC [Supreme Command] to go to Berlin and attend meeting with General von Winterfeldt about publication of Moltke's notes by Dr Steiner.

29. V.

Ascension. Telephone conversation with Winterfeldt who thinks it necessary I go there quickly. Accordingly I set off early (5.30 a.m.).

30. V.

Arrived Bln. [Berlin] 9.00—meeting with Winterfeldt. Then to Frau von M. [Moltke]—latter touchingly pleased I had come. Very depressed by pangs of conscience over publication. St[einer] put it to her that her husband *wished* for the publication (spiritual worlds—letter from there!)[56] Fr. v. M. read all this out to me. Book is already printed, and partly distributed due to indiscretion. Very bad things in it. From there to Winterfeldt. Read book through with him once more, and decided to go to Steiner in Stuttgart. 7.00 at the [...] with Dr Naumann, who also knew about it, and with Hans Adolf Moltke (*chargé d'affaires*, Stuttgart).[57] In touch about withdrawal—8.00—back with Fr. v. M. both daughters there.[58] Fr. v. M. very depressed. Completely in agreement with my proposal to go to Stuttgart, indeed pleased about it. Telegram ... to Steiner, and made appointment for Sunday midday.

---

*Wilhelm von Dommes (1867–1959) held a post in the General Staff's political division around the time of the outbreak of War, and his relationship to Helmuth as well as Eliza von Moltke was one of mutual trust. It was v. Dommes' intervention with Rudolf Steiner in Stuttgart on 1 June 1919 which caused the latter to withdraw the Moltke pamphlet. See Rudolf Steiner's letter to Helmuth v. Moltke's widow of 6 August 1919 (page 252).

31. V.

Rather awkward connections by rail since no ticket to be had at first (. . .) 5.20 departure for Stuttgart.

1. VI.

8.30 Stuttgart. Hotel Marquardt. 10.00 meeting with *chargé d'affaires* counsellor von Moltke. He had succeeded in holding back publication. He got Dr Steiner to agree since his father's vote as head of the family and the Foreign Office will be withheld [?], never to release it.

2.15–3.15 and 4.30–8.30 with Dr Steiner (Landhausstr. 70). I brought him letter from Frau von Moltke.[59] I put it to him that there were three factual errors in M's notes. 1. violation of Belgian neutrality; 2. assumed French tactics (not defensive, but offensive) and 3. the idea of marching through the Dutch province of Limburg. Read him a memorandum on this subject. Explained how M's notes are in two parts; 1. Political part, good; 2. Part written when tired and ill. Notes partly inaccurate (. . .) partly merely personal (31 VII–1 VIII and 14 IX ff.) Publication can achieve nothing significant at present, merely a small sensation. Can only demonstrate the astonishing incompetence of the men in charge. In Bethmann's case this is correct,[60] not in the case HM or Moltke—one would be doing them a deliberate injustice. Can this be the intention? Can it serve any good purpose that M[oltke], a true friend and servant of HM, and a man who honestly loved his country, betrays his king and master and harms his country by the publication of extracts from his memoirs casually quoted out of context.[61] He himself would come across in the most unfavourable light possible as a small-minded egocentric individual whose own petty suffering makes him completely forget his country. He was the opposite of this.

Both the documents and the foreword give a completely false picture of the genuine and unblemished character of HM—the family [Moltke] are appalled by the publication. Highly undesirable political consequences may result. Frau von Moltke is suffering pangs of conscience because husband's 'soul' is supposed to have requested publication.[62]

Steiner replied: In the light of my remarks there was no longer any reason to publish. He had wanted to impress our enemies by publishing truths that were uncomfortable for us. Then they would have had to say: If these things are freely admitted, then the other point, namely that Germany was not pressing for war, must also be true. He had wanted to show: This is just how bad the German leadership was 31 VII–1 VIII. But he had not considered that this would include an incorrect picture of HM and M himself. These points were less important to him. The notes and their foreword are no longer relevant from his point of view, if I could assure him that they are incorrect on these three points of fact. I gave him that assurance. On Frau von Moltke's behalf I then mentioned the request of the 'soul'. Reply: Souls only possess a subjective feeling consciousness (or some such). The soul therefore fully believed in the subjective truth of what was written.[63] If this condition was no longer valid the same would hold good for the request.[64] Finally I said to St. that the family would deal with the financial implications of the withdrawal of the book from circulation. I would convey this to Hans Adolf Moltke. St. agreed.

I formed the impression that St. is a completely straight and decent man who is loyal and wishes to do good. Conversation was interrupted from 3.15 to 4.30 since Steiner had business to attend to. He then spoke very interestingly about the threefold social order, which he explained was a specifically German social form. He spoke of his own non-party political development, about the Moltke family and so on. What was remarkable, was the unfavourable opinion that he had formed of HM. I demonstrated the inaccuracy of such an opinion, and showed him where he could find material with which to revise it. We spoke in full confidence and parted on a friendly basis.

There remains to clarify the question of the copies which have already disappeared owing to an indiscretion. There are supposed to be a maximum of 20 of these, of which twelve are in the hands of members of the Federal Committee.[65] St. promised to do everything to retrieve the copies, and to exclude the possibility of further indiscretions.

Evening with H. A. Moltke. Notes on the conversation with Steiner in the notebook with my files.[66]

2. VI.

I intended to take the morning train listed in my timetable. It didn't run. Letter to minister Moltke. Breakfast with H. A. Moltke in Stuttgart pub. 6.15 eve[ning] back to Bln.

3. VI.

Arrived in Berlin around 10.00. 11.30 reported on results to General Winterfeldt. 12.30 Frau von Moltke. She was once again touching and suffered terrible pangs of conscience and was *very* nervous. Very happy about the result. Unfortunately her family and others (Minister Naumann) are being very reproachful towards her personally. This is very understandable if one is not aware of all that preceded publication.

4. VI.

9.00 with Minister Naumann in the FO. He agreed to my solution of the financial question (purchase by H. A. Moltke) (...) 4.45 Frau von Moltke.

9. VI.

[Whit Monday] Beautiful Whitsun weather on both days. Contrast with world situation.

(iv) Unsustainability of General von Dommes' Objections[67]
by Jürgen von Grone

Rudolf Steiner made his views known to Frau von Moltke (...) on the three points which von Dommes raised against the publication shortly afterwards. Initially he did so in a letter to her dated 6 August 1919.[68]

It there states: 'It was very sad that the publication of the notes was made impossible in this way. I need not tell you in detail what Counsellor von Moltke brought about with the Foreign Office, since that in itself would not have led me to acquiesce.

'The decisive factor was von Dommes' intervention. He came and explained to me that he could *prove* that three points in the notes did not correspond to the facts. He spoke in considerable detail about these three points. This put me in an extremely difficult position. I asked von Dommes if he would be willing to swear on oath to the inaccuracy of the three points. He assented without hesitation. (...) There is nevertheless no doubt that [von Moltke's] soul still believes in the accuracy of the notes.'

In a later letter written by Rudolf Steiner to Frau von Moltke on 19 June 1920 the following words may be found: 'With regard to the publication which was so insidiously forestalled at that time, the thoughts coming from that side cannot be any different yet from what I said earlier in Berlin. This would only become possible if there were an opportunity to publish. But there are people like Tomes [Dommes] still lurking in every corner. What a lot of ugliness he came up with at that time!'

As is well known, these notes were then published at the end of the year (1922) in the second chapter of the Moltke book under the title 'Reflections and Memories'. At that time Rudolf Steiner dictated to me the last paragraphs for Eliza von Moltke's foreword on the arrangement of the contents of the 'Memories, Letters, Documents' in the most telling words.

There one can read: 'First come the documents [Chapter 2 and Chapter 5, (i) of the present edition] which can present a factual and true picture to present-day readers of the events which took place at the end of July and the beginning of August of 1914 in Berlin. At the centre of this first part stands Moltke's own record of his recollections of the decisive events and of their political and military significance. One may be sure that these recollections will give a picture of the outbreak of war which, despite its brevity, will be more revealing and significant than anything which has been written on the subject so far. The picture presented in future historical writings will, I am sure, be much closer to this portrayal than to the others. Then follow the documents which graphically illustrate Moltke's development [Chapters 1 and 3 of the present edition] up to the point in his life where he had to take a decision which was harder than any that had confronted anyone he knew, either present or past.'[69]

It is quite clear from these paragraphs that Rudolf Steiner considered the objections raised by General von Dommes—who, incidentally, was serving in the Operations Division of Supreme Command in 1914—to the publication of these notes as a complete distortion of historical events.

To these three points one may make the following brief remarks: the Schlieffen Plan had always provided for a comprehensive defeat of the opposition in France in open combat by means of an outflanking movement in the event of a war on two fronts.

This *inevitably* required—i.e., even if the enemy did not itself advance through Belgium—that the Germans marched through Belgium, thus tacitly accepting a violation of Belgian neutrality. On this point I would refer to the basic work on the subject, written by the Freiburg historian Gerhard Ritter who died two years ago, *Staatskunst und Kriegshandwerk* (Statesmanship and the Craft of War), and in particular to his book *Der Schlieffen Plan* in which he critically examines the origins and further development of the plan. In both these he refers to the critical attitude of the younger Moltke to this plan.

General von Stein, who was Moltke's closest associate as Quartermaster General in the Supreme Command, bears witness to the fact that Moltke renounced the option of violating Dutch neutrality. In his letter of condolences to von Moltke's widow after his death, von Stein refers to a 'great deed' of Moltke's. At the time, he could not say more about this deed, but there is no doubt he meant Moltke's restraint on the question of marching through Holland.

There were two important motives for General von Dommes'
intervention:

1. The obvious inclination to avoid admitting what was originally
intended in the Schlieffen Plan, i.e., the violation of Holland's
neutrality. This was a taboo subject for years as the historian Ritter
also points out.
2. The 'preface' to the 'Reflections and Memories' of Moltke. In
these remarks Rudolf Steiner had highlighted the complete failure
of the politicians in the German Reich, and this was unacceptable to
influential circles.

Rudolf Steiner summarizes his criticism of German politics in the
following words: 'Thus these documents may be seen as conclusive
evidence that it was *not* military judgement as such, *neither* was it
the completely inadequate political judgement on the German side
in 1914, that led to the war, but rather the fact that there was no
political activity which could prevent exclusively military considerations prevailing. Only if there had been such in the year 1914
could there have been any other outcome. Thus these documents
are a terrible indictment of German politics. This perception must
not remain hidden.'

The three objections which von Dommes raised thus only served,
for the reasons given above, to make the timely publication of this
pamphlet before Versailles impossible.

(v) The Sauerwein Interview with Rudolf Steiner for Le Matin *about the Events that led to the First World War, October 1921* [70]

'You know that if one were to believe your opponents, the Chief of the General Staff first lost his head and after that the Battle of the Marne through your involvement.'

This is the question I asked the famous spiritual researcher and sociologist Rudolf Steiner, German-Austrian by birth. I have sincerely admired this man for over 15 years now and my feelings towards him are those of a friend. It was a matter of great satisfaction to me at the time to translate several of his theosophical works into French. Whenever my travel arrangements permit I take the opportunity, when passing through Basel, of paying a short visit to Dr Steiner in Dornach.

On this occasion, too, I had met him in the impressive and tremendous building which has been called 'Goetheanum' by his pupils, in acknowledgement of Goethe as the precursor of spiritual science. I have already written in *Le Matin* about the man as well as the building and its wonderful position on the last foothills of the Jura mountains, crowned by the ruins of ancient fortresses.

Rudolf Steiner had just returned from Germany where he had given lectures about his teachings to enthusiastic audiences of several thousand people in Stuttgart and Berlin. On the same day in Dornach he received a group of 120 theologians with whom he had begun discussions on questions of theology and religion. Most of these theologians intend to embark upon creating new forms of religious life on the basis of Dr Steiner's teachings.

Dr Steiner was at that time working on the mighty wooden sculpture representing Christ and the succumbing forces of seduction, Lucifer and Ahriman. This is one of the most impressive creations I have ever seen; it forms the central conclusion to the smaller domed rooms in the Goetheanum. While I was watching the people who were coming up the hill in small groups as dusk was falling in order to listen to the lecture, Dr Steiner told me about the attacks of his opponents. Clergy people, nationalist Germans and fanatical followers of various religions fought against him with every conceivable weapon at every opportunity.

The fear of the truth

When I asked him directly about General von Moltke he directed his intense gaze at me, his face lined with the traits of forty years of the most arduous spiritual striving.

'What you are saying to me does not surprise me. There are people who are doing their utmost to drive me out of Germany or possibly even out of Switzerland. There are many different reasons for these attacks. But insofar as they are aimed at my relationship with Moltke, they have a very definite purpose. They are directed at preventing the publication of some notes Moltke wrote down before his death for his family and whose publication in book form I intended to arrange in agreement with Frau von Moltke.

'These memoirs were due to be published in 1919. Immediately before their publication I was visited by a personality[71] who was in charge of the diplomatic representation of Prussia in Stuttgart; he came to tell me that this publication was impossible and that it would not be wanted in Berlin. Later a general[72] came to see me who had occupied various posts near General von Moltke and Kaiser Wilhelm II and now presented the same arguments to me. I protested against this and wanted to ignore them. I thought that I might turn to Count Brockdorff-Rantzau who was present in Versailles at that time; but nothing could be done. My efforts remained unsuccessful for the further reason that at the same time Frau von Moltke was presented with arguments she was not able to ignore.

'Why those fears? These memoirs are definitely not an accusation of the Kaiser's government. But it can be understood from them, which is possibly worse, that the government of the Reich was in a state of total confusion and that its leadership was incomprehensibly frivolous and ignorant. Those responsible are adequately described by a sentence I have written in my preface: "It was not what they did that led to disaster, but rather the whole nature of their personalities".

'I may add that this was occasioned by the peculiar circumstances which brought it about that in the end the total responsibility for crucial decisions came to lie on one man, the Chief of the General Staff, who felt compelled as a result to fulfil his military duty, because politics had reached a nadir. I never discussed military or political issues with Moltke before his resignation. It was only later, when he was seriously ill, that he naturally spoke candidly about all these matters to me, and, as this will interest you, I will tell you what he himself told me and what can also be read in his unpublished memoirs.

'At the end of June 1914, Moltke, who had been Chief of the General Staff since 1905 [1 January 1906], went to Karlsbad for his health. Up to the time of his death he knew nothing about a Potsdam Council meeting on 5 or 6 July. He did not get back to Berlin, with his health restored, until after the ultimatum to Serbia. After his return, he said, he was firmly convinced that Russia would attack. He clearly anticipated the tragic development which matters were going to assume; that is to say he believed that France and England were going to take part in the world conflict. He wrote a memorandum for the Kaiser[73] in which he outlined the necessity for certain measures to be taken. The plan of the German General Staff in its main lines had been laid down a long time previously. It had been devised by von Schlieffen, Moltke's predecessor. You know its principal features: the launching of great masses of troops against France, in order to secure a quick result in the West at any cost; and the dispatch of a weak defensive army against Russia, which was to be replenished after operations on the western front had been completed.

Beguiled people

'However, von Moltke had altered his predecessor's plan in one important respect. Whereas Schlieffen had mapped out a simultaneous march through Belgium and Holland, Moltke had given up the idea of going through Holland in order to give Germany a chance to breathe in case of a blockade.

'When Moltke arrived at the palace on 31 July he found himself in the midst of utterly confused people. He had the impression, he said, that he had to make a decision all on his own. The Kaiser did not sign the mobilization order on that day, an order which, in Germany, is tantamount to a declaration of war, for as soon as such an order is given, everything, including the first military operation, takes place at fixed hours, automatically and inexorably. William II contented himself for the day with declaring a "state of danger of war". The next day, Saturday, 1 August, at 4 p.m. he had Moltke summoned again, and during the next six hours the following drama unfolded.

'Moltke finds the Kaiser in company with Bethmann-Hollweg, whose knees were literally shaking, the Minister of War von Falkenhayn, General von Plessen, Lyncker and some others. The Kaiser expresses himself vigorously against the Chief of the General Staff's plan. He has, he declares, received very good news from England. England would not only remain neutral—it was King George who had informed him—but she would even restrain France from taking part in the war. Under these conditions it was logical to hurl the whole army against Russia. No, Moltke replied, the plan must be executed in East and West just as it was conceived if we were not to cause a horrendous disaster.

The technical reasons

'Moltke is not moved by the objections raised, he refuses to change anything. He maintains that immediate action must be taken in the terms of the mobilization order. He does not believe in the English despatches, and holding in his hand the mobilization order which has just been signed, he is dismissed, leaving behind the others in a state of total confusion. Thus it came about that the decision about the outbreak of war had to be taken for purely military considerations. On the way from the palace to the General Headquarters his motor car is overtaken by another from the palace. Moltke is summoned back to the Kaiser. The Kaiser is more dismayed than ever. He shows his Chief of the General Staff a despatch from England. He sees in the despatch positive assurances that the conflict will be limited to the East and that England and France will be neutral. "The army must immediately be given orders not to proceed in the West", he concludes. Moltke replies that one must not subject an army to a series of orders and counterorders. Then the Kaiser, with Moltke standing by, turns to the aide-de-camp[74] and gives him orders to immediately convey to the command of the 16th Division in Trier the order not to invade Luxembourg. Moltke goes home. Deeply shaken, for he envisages that the greatest catastrophe will ensue from such measures, he sits down at his table. He declares that he cannot make the countermanding order needed to carry out the Kaiser's telephone order.

This order is submitted to him for his signature by an aide-de-camp. He refuses to sign it and pushes the document away. Until eleven o'clock at night he remains sitting there in a state of dazed exhaustion in spite of having returned in good health from Karlsbad. At eleven o'clock there is a knock on his door. The Kaiser wants him back at the palace. He goes there at once. Wilhelm II, who had already started going to bed, puts on a dressing-gown and says: 'Everything has changed. A disaster is pending. The King of England has just stated in a new despatch that he had been misunderstood, and that he could not enter, either in his name or in France's, into any commitment whatsoever.' The Kaiser ends by saying to Moltke: 'Now you may do as you wish.' Now the war begins.

Ominous signs

'During the month of August I saw General von Moltke only once, on 27 August in Koblenz.[75] Our conversation was about purely human concerns. The German army was still advancing victoriously. There was no reason either to speak about what had not yet come to pass. The battle of the Marne took place later. I had not seen Moltke again up to that time. It took place under conditions which were bound to deeply shake Moltke's expectations. In manoeuvres he had several times carried out a cautious advance on the right wing which might be used for an advance against Paris. Three times Kluck,[76] who had the supreme command over the right wing, advanced too fast. Every time Moltke said to him: "If in real operations you advance as fast as this we shall lose the war." When Kluck's army was about to be surrounded Moltke was struck with a terrifying premonition: Germany might have lost the war. This to me appears to be an important part of the "Psychology" of the war's progress. When von Moltke returned to headquarters on 13 September he gave the impression of a deeply shaken man. The people around the Kaiser considered him sick. From that time, it was in reality Falkenhayn who commanded the army without having the official title. Later, when Moltke was confined to his bed, Wilhelm II came to pay him a visit. "Is it still I," he asked the Kaiser, "who am conducting operations?" "I believe indeed that it is you," Wilhelm II replied. So for weeks the Kaiser did not even know who was the true commander of his troops.

'Here is another illustration of the opinion that was entertained of Wilhelm II by his own entourage. One day, when von Moltke was describing to me the feelings of deep suffering he experienced in going back through Belgium after the fall of Antwerp, I spoke to him for the first time of the plan of attack by way of Belgium. "How did it happen," I asked him, "that a Minister of War could bring himself to say at the Reichstag that there had never been a plan for invading Belgium?" "This Minister," Moltke replied, "did not know my plan, but the Chancellor was familiar with it." "And the Kaiser?" "Never on my life," said von Moltke. "He is too much given to talking and too indiscreet. He would have told the whole world about it!"'

(vi) *The Core of the Problem in Seven Points*
An undated memorandum from the literary estate of Jürgen von Grone

1. On the day of mobilization on 1 August 1914 the relationship of trust that existed between the Kaiser as Commander-in-Chief and the younger Moltke as his Chief of Staff was broken. The Kaiser interfered in the process of drawing up the troops on the basis of a misleading telegram from London. When he took up his position as Chief of Staff, Moltke got the Kaiser to promise that he would not interfere unnecessarily in military matters. This promise was broken. 'Trust and confidence were shattered', as Moltke himself wrote. This remained so when, on the evening of the same day, the Kaiser said to his General: 'Now you may do as you wish', once the King of England had declared his country's alleged guarantee of French neutrality as erroneous.

2. The Chief of Staff's intention to bring the campaign to a victorious conclusion in the battles on the border with France failed because his clear orders and instructions were not followed by the Commanders in Lothringia, and the General Headquarters of the 1st Army on the right wing.

3. The fundamental order of the Supreme Command on 27 August was repeatedly ignored by the General Staff of the 1st Army, Colonel-General von Kluck. In particular his army did not take part in the battle of St Quentin as, indeed, it had not previously done so in the battles at the juncture of the Sambre and the Maas. On two occasions the attacking French army was able to evade crushing defeat. In the beginning of September the same General Staff took the decision to avoid Paris towards the south and south-east. Its task of protecting the right wing of the army as instructed by the Supreme Command was disregarded. The Commanding Officer in Paris, General Gallieni, at once recognized his big opportunity to attack the flank and the rear of the German Army, and Generalissimo Joffre began a general offensive on 6 September. 'Négliger Paris' as Gallieni put it, was to prove a costly error. The Battle of the Marne developed under the most unfavourable operational

conditions for the German Army. The retreat of the 1st Army into the area directed by Supreme Command on 4 September left a gap of 25 km. between the two armies on the right wing at the Marne, east of Paris.

4. Colonel-General von Moltke had for some time seen the need to establish an operational control unit close to the right wing of the army (Rethel). This did not take place because, after the crisis of confidence between the Kaiser and his Chief of Staff, it was not considered desirable to separate them. On the other hand there were considerable technical difficulties (telecommunications) involved in moving the whole headquarters. This critical factor is well documented.

5. Only thus did it come about that Lt.-Col. Hentsch was despatched to the front, and, without specific orders from von Moltke to order the retreat of the two armies, brought it about on arrival at the two army headquarters that both armies on the right wing of the army began a retreat in the hours when the battle was to be decided. At the headquarters of the 2nd Army, Hentsch had maintained that the 1st Army was about to be surrounded at any moment without himself having checked the true state of affairs there. The decisive factor was that on 9 September Hentsch emphatically declared, in the headquarters of the 1st Army, that the neighbouring army was 'reduced to dregs' although he had to know that it was, in fact, completely intact, and even engaged in an attack on its left wing! This is what brought it about that this 1st Army, which was already in the process of attacking the enemy on its flank, left the battlefield undefeated.

6. 'Two hours longer and the victory would have been ours. The French had prepared the order to retreat for despatch!' These were the words of the younger Moltke in reaction to a situation that was unparalleled in the history of war.

7. The perfectly understandable theory that there was a complete failure of both political and military leadership in Germany [put forward by Walter Görlitz] thus requires a corollary. It is historically true that once the relationship of confidence that existed between the Commander-in-Chief and his Supreme Commander at the outbreak of war was broken, the younger Moltke was subsequently prevented from dealing quickly with high-handed behaviour on the part of his army Commanders. The Supreme Commander was simply no longer free to decide even the exact

location from which to carry out the conduct of operations that was his task.

Addendum to Part One:
The Image of Helmuth von Moltke in Twentieth Century Historical Writing
by Jens Heisterkamp

The first publication of Helmuth von Moltke's 'Reflections and Memories' which are reprinted in this edition (page 101), came at a time when the undigested military defeat and the harsh terms of the subsequent peace had created a climate in Germany of the most violent agitation and nationalist excitement. One particularly noxious element was the myth of the 'stab in the back', the alleged betrayal of the German army which in reality had been undefeated, and was let down by the politicians. In the search for someone to blame for the defeat, attention was drawn among other things to von Moltke and his conduct at the Battle of the Marne. Soon after the end of the First World War, there was a plethora of writings[77] which analysed the loss of this fateful battle, and not infrequently came to the conclusion that Moltke was personally responsible. In the spring of 1921, a hostile publication by General von Gleich, *Rudolf Steiner als Prophet* ('Rudolf Steiner as a Prophet'), made disparaging remarks about the relationship between the spiritual scientist and Helmuth von Moltke. At the time, these calumnies were vigorously rebutted by Jürgen von Grone and even by Gleich's own son, the anthroposophical researcher of cultural history, Sigismund von Gleich. When von Moltke's widow published his *Erinnerungen, Briefe und Dokumente* ('Memories, Letters and Documents'), it was an attempt in the context of these events to give the public a clear basis on which to come to a judgement about the former Chief of Staff.

Some time later Ludendorff, who had aquired the status of a folk hero during the First World War, and whose career had been furthered by von Moltke, defamed his former Chief of Staff in a particularly impudent manner. Already during the war Ludendorff had become an increasingly schismatic character, who pointlessly delayed the end of the war, and ruled dictatorially in Germany. He worked as an influence hostile to Middle Europe by his contribution to the enthronement of Lenin in Russia, and by his purely tactical order for a ceasefire facilitated by the American President, Woodrow Wilson.

In Ludendorff's review of the First World War in the year 1922,[78] there was, as yet, no criticism of Moltke, but it was already strikingly anti-semitical, and inclined towards crude Teutonic ideology and the glorification of the struggle for survival. It was only under the influence of his later wife, Mathilde von Kemnitz, who was remarkable for her racist and explicitly anti-christian writings, that Ludendorff developed the delusion of Moltke's 'occult guidance' by Rudolf Steiner, which was supposed to have taken place in the context of a large scale 'Masonic plot' against Germany.

In 1934 Ludendorff published his book, *Das Marne Drama, Der Fall Moltke-Hentsch* ('The Marne Drama, The Case of Moltke and Hentsch')[79] on this delusion.

Altogether, National Socialist activity in Germany after 1933 acted like a beacon for the increasing resurgence of attacks on Moltke, the most radical of which again disparaged the relationship between Moltke and Rudolf Steiner. In January 1933 a particularly vicious and libellous article appeared in the *Leipziger Neuesten Nachrichten*[80] which was rebutted by Marie Steiner in the weekly periodical *Das Goetheanum* as well as the political drama *Die Marneschlacht* by von Cremers, which had its first preformance at this time.[81] In 1934 a certain H. Graf von Moltke made disparaging remarks in *Die Deutsche Tragödie an der Marne*.[82]

It is a credit to Jürgen von Grone that he quickly countered these calumnies and in particular that he set the record straight on the role played by Moltke in the Battle of the Marne. In a series of articles in *Stuttgarter Neues Tagblatt* in 1933 he reconstructed the sequence of events in the battle and concluded with a complete rehabilitation of Moltke.[83] As one of the earliest anthroposophists (who met Rudolf Steiner in 1906), and as an active officer in airborne reconnaissance, who had received the rare distinction 'Pour le Merite', von Grone was as if predestined to champion the cause of von Moltke's individuality. Thus after the death of Moltke's eldest daughter, Astrid von Bethusy, in the year 1961, it was he who was entrusted with von Moltke's literary remains.

Already towards the end of the 1920s Albert Steffen had attempted to protect Moltke's individuality and to include him within the spiritual ambit of the anthroposophical movement, although in a very different manner from von Grone's studies of military history. In his drama *Der Chef des Generalstabs*, Steffen raised an artistic monument to Moltke. In it he also sensitively portrayed the motifs of that 'unwritten mystery drama' (Johannes Tautz)[84] which unfolded in the relationship between the Chief of Staff and Rudolf Steiner during Moltke's earthly life.

Despite various efforts to correct them, the widespread untruths about Moltke have stubbornly kept their place in historical writings. A crass example is to be found in the historical standard work entitled *Biographisches Wörterbuch zur Deutschen Geschichte* (Biographical Dictionary of German History) under the title 'Helmuth von Moltke':

> In failing health, inclining towards anthroposophical thought, without a firm belief in victory, he was unable, after the beginning of the First World War in the Battle of the Marne, to maintain the unity of his command structure, and broke off the battle before it was decided. Thereafter, on 14 September 1914, control of operations was handed over to the Minister of War von Falkenhayn...[85]

Apart from the untruth about Moltke's state of health before the Battle of the Marne, it is remarkable that even this respected scientific work does not hesitate to establish a suggestive link between Moltke's relationship with Anthroposophy and the loss of the Battle of the Marne.

It is quite clear that the personal rivalries from Moltke's time in the General Staff are working on in German military history today. In addition to von Kuhl,[86] this applies particularly to Wilhelm Groener, who was in charge of troop deployment under von Moltke. In his book *Der Feldherr wider Willen* (The Reluctant General) which appeared in 1930, he already attributed the loss of the Battle of the Marne to Moltke's apparently labile personality. Walter Görlitz adopts a similar approach in his standard work on the German General Staff.[87] In the chapter dedicated to Moltke, his attitude is already apparent in the title, 'The War without a General'.[88] This is followed by the usual characterization of Moltke as an allegedly sceptical, brooding and brittle personality.

This image is also perpetuated in the various publications of the Fischer School, which, in their attributions of war guilt, tend to depict Moltke as a warmonger.[89]

While it is true that Moltke is presented more objectively in other standard works on the First World War,[90] it is primarily thanks to the Israeli historian Yehudah L. Wallach that these allegations are refuted in accordance with all the rules of military history and replaced by an objective appraisal of Moltke's personality. It is indeed remarkable that it should be an Israeli historian who should write one of the most well informed and thoughtful books on military thinking in Germany.[91] In particular, Wallach refutes, with admirable attention to detail, the oft-repeated allegation by Moltke's enemies that he 'diluted' the Schlieffen Plan by making changes to it. On the contrary Wallach arrives at the very interesting conclusion 'as if the already deceased Schlieffen bore a much greater responsibility for the failure than the Moltke who was still alive'. Wallach is also able to demonstrate plausibly that Moltke's chief accusers, von Kuhl and Groener, each have strong personal motives for deflecting attention from their own inadequacies by their allegations against Moltke.[92]

One of the most objective portrayals of Moltke in recent German historiography may be found in Sebastian Haffner's book *Das Wunder an der Marne*[93] (The Miracle on the Marne). It is striking that this portrayal chooses to set out the crucial events both of the outbreak of war and of the Battle of the Marne in the form of dramatic reconstructions—rather like Steffen's approach. Substantial passages in this feature Moltke's own words culled from his *Erinnerungen, Briefe und Dokumente* (1922).

While Haffner breaks with the traditional picture of the General as a 'nervous wreck', it is unfortunately restored in another recent dramatic reconstruction of events. Rolf Hochhuth's *Sommer 1914*,[94] which appeared in 1989, features Moltke alongside many other key figures, and also makes use of parts of Moltke's own notes, but having a blanket prejudice against all the military, does not allow a differentiated image of Moltke to emerge.

Against the background of this brief outline of the history of portrayals of Moltke, his life may appear like an open secret, which wishes to be revealed from under its web of prejudice. Moltke's tragic role in one of the most fateful battles of European history, and his personality, which was so different from the cliché figure of a German general, both give his critics ample opportunity for attack. His yearning for deeper knowledge in particular, and his personal relationship with Rudolf Steiner, led many narrow-minded 'experts' to make judgements typical of those which are common as soon as one moves beyond the realm of the commonplace. It is not only conventional German historians whose powers of comprehension are tested by the fact that a German general should have a close relationship with the spiritual scientist, Rudolf Steiner. Clearly there are a number of anthroposophists who can find no other explanation for the apparent high esteem in which Steiner held Moltke, than that this represented an all-too-human 'weakness' on the part of the initiate.

For German historians, and for the anthroposophical movement, the substance of the destiny of Helmuth von Moltke still remains to be discovered.

PART TWO

And those souls who are here and are able to understand me at this moment will never ever forget what I have tried to express: how significant it is that this soul is now taking up into the spiritual world what has flown through our spiritual science for years now, in order that it may become strong and effective there.

Rudolf Steiner on 20 June 1916

Editorial Comments

In 1957 Emil Bock produced a first typed copy of the following documents which hitherto only existed in handwritten form. Before going to print these were checked against the originals by Rudolf Steiner and Helene Röchling, respectively. In several instances minor inaccuracies of Bock's versions needed correcting. In the case of letters and messages 30, 53, 54, 58 and 59, written down by Helene Röchling, it was not possible to check against the original. The corresponding originals by Rudolf Steiner are filed in the archives of the Rudolf Steiner Nachlassverwaltung in Dornach. Message 61 is only available in typescript (by Emil Bock); it was produced on the basis of an original also filed in Dornach. In view of Helene Röchling's as well as Emil Bock's conscientiousness it can be assumed that deviations from the original documents, if any, are minor; hence their inclusion in this volume seemed justified.

For additional editorial commentary and notes, see notes section to Part Two on p. 302. *The note numbers do not appear in the text. They refer to the letter numbers.*

[r] = date on which Eliza von Moltke *received* a letter or document

Listing of Letters, Verses and Documents

L = Letter from Rudolf Steiner
A = Answer to a Question (to R.S.)
V = Verse or Meditation by Rudolf Steiner
M = After-death message written down by Rudolf Steiner
LR = Letter from Helene Röchling
LMR = Letter from Helene Röchling with an after-death message
MR = After-death message written down by Helene Röchling
N = Note by Rudolf Steiner
NB = Note by Emil Bock

1. To Eliza von Moltke (L/12 August 1904)
2. For Eliza von Moltke (A/14 August 1904)

3. For Eliza von Moltke (A/1909)
4. For Helmuth von Moltke (V/1914)
5. To Eliza von Moltke (L/20 December 1914)
6. To Helmuth von Moltke (L/20 December 1914)
7. To Eliza von Moltke (L/31 December 1914)
8. To Eliza von Moltke (L/26 January 1915)
9. To Helmuth von Moltke (L/9 February 1915)
10. To Helmuth von Moltke (L/30 March 1915)
11. To Eliza von Moltke (L/March or April 1915)
12. For Helmuth von Moltke (N/26 May 1915)
13. For Eliza and Helmuth von Moltke (N/3 August 1915)
14. To Eliza von Moltke (L/18 August 1915)
15. To Eliza von Moltke (L/1 September 1915)
16. For Helmuth von Moltke (N/1 September 1915)
17. To Eliza von Moltke (L/23 September 1915)
18. For Helmuth von Moltke (N/23 September 1915)
19. To Helmuth von Moltke (L/23 November 1915)
20. For Helmuth von Moltke (V/11 December 1915)
21a. Verses spoken by the Bier (19 June 1916)
21b. Metamorphosed Verses Spoken by the Bier (20 June 1916)
21c. Memorial Address by Rudolf Steiner (20 June 1916)
22. For Eliza von Moltke (V/20 June 1916)
23. To Eliza von Moltke (L/24 July 1916)
24. To Eliza von Moltke (LMR/9 August 1916)
25. To Eliza von Moltke (LMR/12 August 1916)
26. To Eliza von Moltke (LMR/6 September 1916)
27. To Eliza von Moltke (LMR/13 September 1916)
28. To Eliza von Moltke (LMR/26 September 1916)
29. For Eliza von Moltke (MR/19 October 1916)
30. To Eliza von Moltke (LMR/2 December 1916)
31. To Eliza von Moltke (LMR/16 December 1916)
32. To Eliza von Moltke (LMR/8 January 1917)
33. To Eliza von Moltke (LMR/18 January 1917)
34. To Eliza von Moltke (LMR/29 January 1917)
35. For Eliza von Moltke (NB/1917)
36. For Eliza von Moltke (N/31 August 1917)
37. For Eliza von Moltke (M/January 1918)
38. For Eliza von Moltke (M/29 January 1918)
39. For Eliza von Moltke (M/8 February 1918)
40. For Eliza von Moltke (M/1 March 1918)
41. For Eliza von Moltke (M/23 March 1918)
42. For Eliza von Moltke (M/22 April 1918)
43. For Eliza von Moltke (M/14 May 1918)

44. For Eliza von Moltke (M/24 May 1918)
45. For Eliza von Moltke (M/22 June 1918)
46. For Eliza von Moltke (M/7 July 1918)
47. For Eliza von Moltke (M/15 July 1918)
48. For Eliza von Moltke (M/28 July 1918)
49. For Eliza von Moltke (M/2 August 1918)
50. For Eliza von Moltke (M/8 August 1918)
51. For Eliza von Moltke (N/8 August 1918)
52. To Eliza von Moltke (L/12 August 1918)
53. For Eliza von Moltke (MR/30 August 1918)
54. For Eliza von Moltke (MR/11 October 1918)
55. For Eliza von Moltke (MR/11 October 1918)
56. For Eliza von Moltke (MR/14 December 1918)
57. For Eliza von Moltke (MR/27 January 1919)
58. For Eliza von Moltke (MR/27 January 1919)
59. For Eliza von Moltke (MR/28 January 1919)
60. For Eliza von Moltke (MR/27 March 1919)
61. For Eliza von Moltke (on or around 1 May 1919)
62. For Eliza von Moltke (L/3 May 1919)
63. For Eliza von Moltke (M/3 May 1919)
64. To Eliza von Moltke (LR/10 May 1919)
65. Appeal by R. Steiner (May 1919)
66. To Eliza von Moltke (L/28 May 1919)
67. To Eliza von Moltke (L/6 August 1919)
68. For Eliza von Moltke (M/20 September 1919)
69. To Eliza von Moltke (L/before 19 June 1920)
70. For Eliza von Moltke (M/26 October 1920)
71. For Eliza von Moltke (M/29 October 1920)
72. For Eliza von Moltke (M/16 February 1921)
73. For Eliza von Moltke (M/May 1921)
74. For Eliza von Moltke (M/June 1921)
75. For Eliza von Moltke (M/around June 1921)
76. For Eliza von Moltke (M/December 1921)
77. For Eliza von Moltke (M/2 February 1922)
78. For Eliza von Moltke (M/9 August 1922)
79. For Eliza von Moltke (M/8 December 1922)
80. For Eliza von Moltke (M/beginning 1923)
81. For Eliza von Moltke (M/12 March 1923)
82. For Eliza von Moltke (M/28 July 1923)
83. For Eliza von Moltke (M/13 January 1924)
84. For Eliza von Moltke (M/17 June 1924)

1. Letters and Verses from Rudolf Steiner to Eliza von Moltke and Helmuth von Moltke 1904–15

1. Rudolf Steiner to Eliza von Moltke

12 August 1904

Dear Madam!

Please do not think that I intend to keep up my habit of writing as few letters as possible in relation to *you*. Some time I'll tell you in person why this first one is arriving so late. In future I will write to you very regularly.

Please treat the enclosed document as absolutely confidential. In matters like this I am merely an instrument of Higher Beings whom I revere in complete *humility*. Nothing is my merit, nothing is dependent on me. The only thing I can claim for myself is the strict training I have undergone which protects me from any fantasy or illusion. This has been my first rule. What I experience spiritually is therefore free from any imagination, any deception, any super-stition. But even of *that* I do not speak to many. People may con-sider me an illusionist; yet I can differentiate perfectly between truth and deception. And I know that I need to follow the path I am following.

When you make the exercises your own that are outlined in the enclosed document, dear Madam, do not start before 19 August or after 3 September. Thus is how it is written in the 'Signs of the Heavens', as the occultist refers to them. In case you should not be able to begin between 19 August and 3 September—and any day during this period would be possible—it would be necessary for you to contact me again for a later period.

I often recall the delightful hours I was able to spend at your home. I have come to feel great affection for your husband and have great hopes for his spiritual future. Sometimes people walk along special paths; but many different paths lead to knowledge.

I hope you will have an agreeable time in Silesia and enjoy the inner peace you need.
With my very best wishes
Dr Rudolf Steiner
Berlin W Motzstrasse 17

2. Answer to Question for Eliza von Moltke

Berlin, 14 August 1904

In comparison with much else that is offered this report is really excellent in all its descriptions of outer circumstances. However, it needs to be noted that *dalai* refers to the as yet undifferentiated *spiritual* substance from which the physical substance has evolved. In contrast to the differentiated physical substance the spiritual must be imagined as undifferentiated, fluid, as an all-penetrating sea. The term *Dalai Lama* is derived from the idea that the soul of this being is not in the physical but in the spiritual, and that the physical body of the Lama is *only* a *picture* of the soul.

This soul itself, however, is deemed to be the Buddha, who has spiritualized himself in this way after his death. Such a spiritualized human being is called Bodhisattva; and the Bodhisattva of the Buddha Avalokitischvara (abbreviated Avalokita). Dalai Lama therefore really means the 'supersensible Lama'. What the author says about the the 'Third Eye' can be considered quite correct. Originally the 'Third Eye' meant the 'Eye of the Spirit'. However, very often superstitious people relate it to an external thing, like the monocle in this case, instead of the truly spiritual. And it is quite possible that people around the Dalai Lama interpret an old teaching, which is no longer understood, in the manner described.

3. Answer to Question for Eliza von Moltke from the year 1909

Berlin, 11 December 1909 [r]

During sleep we are unable to see on the astral plane because in this state the astral body and the 'I' do indeed leave the physical and the etheric bodies but nevertheless remain connected with the latter by a connecting thread. During sleep certain forces fluctuate to and fro within this connection. During ordinary sleep these forces paralyse the astral senses, which *each human being* possesses. The aim of development is to learn to make the astral senses *independent* of the physical and the etheric bodies. One does not actually create them through initiation, but, to put it precisely, one learns how to use them.

After death the paralysis caused by the physical and etheric bodies ceases and consciousness in the astral world begins to awaken. This is indeed like a slow awakening in the spiritual world. One feels free of the physical body and the 'I' begins to perceive. This applies to *everyone*. With respect to *this* there is no difference at all between the initiate and the uninitiated after death. The only difference between the two is that the initiate has better orientation as well as a deeper understanding of what is happening in the spiritual world. But this is already true to a very high degree when a person has absorbed knowledge of the spiritual world during his physical life merely in the form of logical (as opposed to actually perceived) truths. One discovers this in the case of all individuals who die with such knowledge but never actually attain initiation during their earthly life.

What I have said here about consciousness after death is a fact. The clairvoyant encounters the dead in the spiritual world and he finds them really awake and fully conscious of their environment. They also become aware of what is happening on the earth (in the physical world) insofar as this is imbued with soul and spirit. However, for the perception of purely physical processes in the physical world they avail themselves of the sense organs of incarnated individuals; this is always possible. However, even that is not an absolute necessity, because every physical process has a spiritual counter-image (like a kind of negative exposure) and this is *always perceptible to the dead without any mediation whatsoever.*

4. Three Meditation Verses for Helmuth von Moltke from the Year 1914

Siegen wird die Kraft,
die vom Zeit-Geschick
vorbestimmt dem Volk,
das in Geistes-Hut
zu der Menschheit Heil
in Europas Herz
Licht dem Kampf entringt.

Glauben will ich,
Wissen darf ich
Dich in des Geistes Schutz,
der brütet über Europas Mitte
dem Volke seines Geistes Ziel.
Es lenk'zu Dir meinen Glauben
Jahve
Es schenkt Dir liebend meine Wissenskraft
Christus.

Was habt ihr Truggedanken, Blendgesichter,
zu tun mit Hohem, was ich *soll*;
Die Geister wollen's doch von mir.
So schaff ich der eig'nen Seele Feindschaft,
Mich zwingend zu kräft'gem Denken,
mir aus dem zagenden Herzen,
das stark mir dient, *will* ich es nur.

*Victorious will be the power
Which by the fate of the times
Is predestined for that people
Who, protected by the spirit,
Will, for mankind's salvation,
In Europe's heart
Wrest light from the battle.

I will believe,
I am permitted to know
You to be under that spirit's protection
Who broods above Europe's centre
Giving that people its spirit aim.

---

* Translation by J. Collis

May Yahveh
Guide my faith to you.
Christ
Lovingly gives you my power of knowledge.

You deceptive thoughts, you false apparitions:
What have you to do with that great thing that I *must* do.
It is the spirits who want it of me.
So, in forcing myself to be strong in thinking,
I make an enemy of my own soul
Through my timid heart,
That serves me strongly if I but *will* that it shall.

5. Rudolf Steiner to Eliza von Moltke

Dornach, 20 December 1914

Dear Madam!
While sending the enclosed to your husband I would like to express
to you, too, that I am often with you in my thoughts. Standing firmly
in our certainty of the spirit will give you the strength you are so in
need of now. Your soul strength will pour out over your physical
existence, which is marred by fatigue and its consequences, for
reasons we well understand.

In my letter to your husband I have expressed the thoughts I wish
to convey to you at this moment. As far as actual events are concerned, as well as our legitimate hopes, I cannot say anything different today than what I have expressed in recent times.

I will be very happy to be able to see you again in January. I will
probably not be able to hold the lecture before 14 January. However, I think that I might be in Berlin a few days before that date. I
will certainly visit you on the day before the lecture if you wish. I
will let you know my arrival date in Berlin.

Please give my warmest regards to Countess Bethusy and her
children.
With best wishes
R. Steiner
The enclosed letter to His Excellency is really not just intended to
be a consolation but rather is a reflection of things that have come

before my soul, in spite of the fact that many a thing has happened since mid-November that presently has the effect of causing *later events* and can therefore *not* be perceived outwardly. But it is here as *cause*—quite as expected.

6. Rudolf Steiner to Helmuth von Moltke

Dornach, 20 December 1914

Excellency may be assured once more by these lines that my thoughts are often with you. Such serious events as those of our time, when looked at from the outside, could easily give rise to the impression that the spiritual impulses, of which one can speak out of spiritual knowledge, might prove to be erroneous ones. And yet this is not the case. It remains an irrefutable fact before this spiritual vision that the Genius of the German people stands with his torch held high, hopeful and confident, and that the forces coming from this side are together with your thoughts about the course of events. Your thoughts, Excellency, have been the instrument needed by this side of the spiritual world for many years now. Even if the physical course of events now appears to contradict this it is not the case *in reality*. In the spiritual realm it is still the thread of your thoughts, Excellency, which shapes the course of events. I am certainly not saying this to just express some words of consolation. That I would consider utterly contemptible. I say it because it stands before my soul like this. And although you are not actively involved with events in the physical world it is nonetheless true that whatever will turn out to be *beneficial* for the further development of things is connected with your work; moreover, your thoughts live right into it.

Excellency, you have suffered greatly. But in truth suffering is also the ground from which the powers of the spirit must weave the salvation of the earth. Through your suffering you are serving the great cause which the German people must serve now. One day, when what is the present now will be the past, those who want to understand will know for certain: that your thoughts and intentions as well as your suffering were part of the necessary seed from which the future mission of the German people will flower. The task which lies ahead of this people is so significant that it may only be accomplished through destiny's solemn working.

In the knowledge that even now your personal destiny is intimately connected with the destiny of the German people I may stand by every word I have ever spoken in this context. When one beholds the necessary future of the German people with spiritual vision, momentary failures—even the severe ones—cannot shake one's conviction, and neither can temporary successes. Calm is maintained in the face of adversity and likewise jubilation does not break out as soon as this or that goes well. Individual people can *appear* to have been removed from a particular incarnation before they have achieved what was predestined; this is because they come back in future incarnations; a people however does not lose the conditions of its mission before this mission is fulfilled. Your strengths, Excellency, are strengths in the organism of the German people. The calmness of soul you are able to cultivate now will sustain your strength and heighten it; and if you succeed in maintaining this calm, you, too, will become conscious of the certainty of spirit which is so deeply inscribed in the grounds of your soul.

Spiritual certainty must be awaited in calmness of soul. It is bestowed from light divine heights; our calmness of soul makes it possible for the spirit to work in us. My thoughts will endeavour to humbly ask from the spiritual world that many a doubt you have voiced in recent times may be taken from you as soon as the time is right. Indeed the spiritual powers are working in you, Excellency, through important impulses; hence they will also disperse your doubts if you await their grace and blessing in calmness of soul; all certainty depends on this. With these words I have tried to express what stands before my soul when I think of you in faithful devotion. May you always be assured of this.

Yours, R. St.

7. Rudolf Steiner to Eliza von Moltke

Dornach, 31 December 1914

Dear Madam!

You will have received my answer to your question with the telegram sent by Frau Röchling. When I say that there must not be any interference in the workings of the spiritual impulses this should always be understood to mean that nothing should be undertaken on the part of His Excellency that could *remove* him from what is predestined to him spiritually. However, uncovering the truth *vis-à-vis* the authorities named by you would not cause anything to happen that could be at odds with the right approach I have outlined. The more clearly the authorities concerned understand the true picture the better it will be. Whatever effect the revelation of the truth may have initially, it will be beneficial in the end. It makes no difference that the matter is to be handled by someone close to you: it is the cause itself which counts; whoever can serve it should do so, no matter how he is related to the people connected with it.

Please also convey to His Excellency that I am often with him in my thoughts and that I would only repeat to him today what I conveyed to him in my last letter. The time of waiting seems long; but the course of outer events is the absolute counter-picture of this need to wait, the fullest confirmation possible, is it not?

The events themselves are *waiting* until something happens which can bring about a favourable turn, so that the actual course of events may be directed in the sense of the spiritual impulses working through His Excellency once again. After all, these impulses have worked *beneficially* into the mission of the German people and will continue to do so. And whatever is *not* connected with these impulses will not take a beneficial course. However, this will only be understood *later*. I have to say it again and again: What I have told His Excellency and you, dear Madam, in this respect continues to stand vividly before my soul. Hence I must consider it right for His Excellency to summon his forces in calmness of soul, the forces which connect him so strongly with the spiritual world, that world which in the present cycle of time conferred upon the German people a mission that cannot be taken from it by any foe. The better His Excellency manages to attain *this* calmness of soul for the summoning of his forces, the less he bars his access to the spiritual word by brooding, the more beneficial it will be for that which must come to pass.

I am very happy to hear from you, dear Madam, that your husband has responded well to the words of my last letter. As I said already, I could not but affirm them today. I hope to be able to come to Berlin a few days before the dates set for my lectures and to see you and your husband on that occasion. In the meantime please

convey my heartfelt greetings to him and be assured that my
thoughts are often with you both, the thoughts of
Yours, truly
R.St.
In the morning of 31 December 1914.

8. Rudolf Steiner to Eliza von Moltke for Helmuth von Moltke

Berlin, 26 January 1915 [r]

The Genius of the German people shows himself with his torch
raised to him who directs his thoughts to him with the feelings
which spring from the love for this people. This gesture of the
Genius is the way in which he wishes to reveal himself. This gesture
is, as it were, the word—the silent word—through which this Genius
wishes to give expression to the destiny of the people and the good
grounds for confidence. He will be able to come near to us, he will
pour light and warmth into our soul and strength into our heart, and
spread calm over our being, when we imagine him with this gesture,
for this is the gesture with which he shows himself to him who
approaches him to ask him about the destiny of the people, even if
the one approaching him does not imagine him with this gesture. In
other words, one may approach him without this inner picture of
him, and he will show himself by virtue of who he is with this gesture
of hope; but for approaching him it is helpful to picture him to
oneself with this gesture. The gesture is something which he has in
relation to the one who approaches him, this gesture is like a word
of strength which he speaks again and again. This gesture which he
has in relation to us is not to say that he has it at all times, just as in
the physical world someone would not repeat the same word over
and over again, but will call it out again and again to him who needs
it for his working. When the Genius is pictured with this gesture, it
is akin to reminding oneself of a word of encouragement, and
through this memory one comes near to him.

Whatever peace and strength has flown into us through spiritual
forces in such manner that we experience it *consciously* will *remain*
within us even if we do not always succeed in becoming conscious of

this peace and strength. There are certain to be times when this consciousness exists. We should always be satisfied and grateful for what has flown towards us, even when failure occurs from time to time. Especially when we accept such failure with equanimity, success will be all the more certain. The strength which emanates from the spiritual powers, is emanating from them even when we are unable to be conscious of it, but this consciousness will arise so that we may gain in strength and certainty. What His Exc. experienced on Saturday is very important, and it is good to recall it from time to time; the experience will come back when the recalling of it paves the way for its renewal.

What comes before my soul again and again—to the present day—is an *affirmation* of what I have said; the Genius with the raised hand and torch will carry and lead his people; and this Genius is with you, Exc., and never will the plea addressed to him by another in your name be unheard by this Genius. So may this plea for ever be directed to him.

9. Rudolf Steiner to Helmuth von Moltke

Dornach, 9 February 1915 [r]

I would like to tell His Excellency in a few sentences what has been placed before my soul while thinking of you in spirit, from that side of the spiritual world known to you:

'Human beings work in the world through their outer deeds in the ordinary course of life; but when something spiritual is to be realized through physical happenings significant things may be achieved when a human being not only performs his deeds but connects *himself* with the course of events in such a way that he bears patiently what appeared to him hard to bear, and for which he needs to overcome himself. This is what you have rightly achieved. It is very positive that things have not reached a state of detachment where one's own will would have been in opposition to what was willed by the outer world; that in fact everything has been done not to drive this detachment beyond what was effected from the *other* side. Such deeds are deeds of the soul life, and in that they are *crucial* forces for helping to bring about a favourable outcome. It is *significant* that a man exists who is willing to bring personal sacrifices to the true love of the cause, who *knows* himself connected with the cause in such a way that he willingly bears personal suffering for *reasons of serving the spirit*. In such a mood of soul the forces of the spirit can work; and these *must* work for things to take a favourable turn. The guiding powers of the spirit are able to gather forces in this personality during the time of an apparent distance from the events, and these forces will be needed in the time before us.'

I have put these words in inverted commas for a good reason. There is nothing in these sentences which I have just thought up. These intuitions are rather an affirmation that I may speak to His Excellency as I have indeed done in these times which have afforded you such hard trials. My thoughts often go towards you and then to those sources of the spiritual life which shape the direction of earthly events, and then I may always bring back the satisfying vision of your connection with the spiritual world. May you feel with your whole being how what has been brought about through you is in unison with the spiritual world, and may you recognize in the consciousness of this unison the inner spiritual support which is infinitely more secure than any outer supports man might find for his existence. Knowing oneself to be at one with the willing of the spiritual world gives one's soul the power of certainty in the course of one's life, however disconcertingly the events of outer life may be raging around the vessel of one's life. I know for sure that you may experience this; may it spread throughout your soul and fill it with utter clarity. Such is the way in which I often think of you, Excellency, and I will continue to do so as your devoted
R. St.

10. Rudolf Steiner to Helmuth von Moltke

Dornach, 30 March 1915 [r]

The following thoughts emanated from the soul of the personality once so close to His Excellency whom we discussed repeatedly in recent times as being close to the Folk Spirit; I will write them down according to their meaning, not verbatim:

1. Helmuth von Moltke, around 1912

2. Helmuth von Moltke, 1891

3. Eliza von Moltke, 1897

4. Kaiser Wilhelm II with family, 1893

5. Tsar Nicholas II with family, around 1895

6. 'Peoples of Europe, guard all that you hold most holy' (von H. Knackfuß)

7. Helmuth von Moltke, around 1870

8. Wilhelm II, 1918

9. Helmuth von Moltke, around 1910

10. Wilhelm von Dommes, around 1910

11. Helmuth von Moltke, around 1910

12. Jürgen von Grone, around 1945

13. Helene Röchling, around 1915

14. Rudolf Steiner, 1915

15. *Astrid, Adam, Else and Wilhelm von Moltke*

16. Eliza von Moltke, around 1910

17. Helmuth von Moltke, July 1914

18. Eliza and Helmuth von Moltke, around 1914

19. *Helmuth von Moltke on his deathbed*

When I—the soul—look back at past events in which I was involved then I can see that in the past we were led by a more unconscious feeling power of soul which now needs to reign more consciously in the incarnated souls. I would say: I was guided by the belief that that which is rightly intended must prevail even if outer circumstances resist it. After all, I was always guided by the strength of thinking and not by what was expressed in outer circumstances. Even when it did not *appear* to be the case at times, this is how it was, even when it did not appear like that to my own self. Such a thought must now consciously enter the soul of the younger bearer of my name: for this I generate the forces with which I penetrate into his heart, bringing warmth to him on whom my spiritual gaze is resting. When he comes to recognize that which seems like heaviness in his heart as a sign that healing forces are wanting to come through, a veil before him will drop and much will be revealed that is presenting him with riddles now.

*

These words seem particularly valuable and important to me because I received them after having been inclined to the spiritual spheres in a certain mood of searching for several days, namely with the feelings that 23 March brought to me. Among other things this searching brought to me the above. My thoughts are directed towards you, Excellency, so that you may feel that the power of the spirit is together with you. I do not merely know this to be the case in a general sense, in relation to the power of the Folk Spirit, but it also appears to me in such special manner as described above. I wish to bring home to His Excellency again and again that the soul which waits in calmness and makes this waiting a positive inner mood will eventually feel the power of the spirit with which it is united. Over time such calmness will open the soul to the feeling power of cognition for that which exists objectively, which can be seen with spiritual eyes, and is not just desired or wished for you by another soul.

'Among other things' I wrote earlier. I am referring to the intuitions from another side and of a different kind. In the days just passed things have happened which conceal more important matters than would appear from the outside. Now the question has to be asked: In what way do these very recent events reveal the full truth of what had to be said over and over again from the viewpoint of the spirit? Because this is precisely what they do. These are events which are designed to strengthen man's faith in the supreme power of the spirit especially because they are so likely to shake what is merely a superficial kind of trust. In the being of the German Folk Spirit there is life, a life essence that shines out to the future, and this genuine true life will be the perishing of those who would destroy this life. What I have told you in connection with this thought and with you yourself, Excellency: it is confirmed, not because I might wish to maintain what was said once for outer intellectual reasons but rather because all *further* spiritual experience *too*, to the present day, points in the same direction. While one would not expect this to be any different, it may nevertheless be noted as a spiritual fact simply by virtue of such a fact being real.

I have summarized in these aphoristic sentences what has been clearly placed before my soul in these last few days in many guises. May His Exc. take these thoughts even in their abbreviated form as a sign of my faithful devotion,

Yours,

R. St.

11. Rudolf Steiner to Eliza von Moltke

Dornach, end of March/beginning of April 1915 [r]

Dear Madam,

When I directed my thoughts to His Excellency, your husband, in recent days, to beg for inner peace for him so that he may feel the blessing powers of which I have often spoken, above him, that which came before my soul then, again and again, was an *affirmation* of the spiritual perception about which I wrote in my last letter to him. This is not a new perception but rather a renewed beholding of what was beheld then; however, the fact that the same is revealed to repeated contemplation is proof that that which is offered for renewed contemplation may be taken as an objective solace as well as a command to *hold fast* to what has been held so far. One needs to remind oneself over and over again that it is the very feeling of suffering which is a sign for the proximity of those powers I have often characterized. They want to reveal themselves, and what is still needed is the *equanimity of soul* wrought out of suffering. For sure, times are difficult now; but this must not change our thoughts about the matter. All I can do is continue to be with His Excellency and yourself in my thoughts.

Regarding your son's injury, to which Frau R.[öchling] referred, I can only say from the distance that the ischia-type pains are a side-effect of the injuries suffered, and not something separate.

I hope to see you again during the week after next week, around 14 April. Until then please be assured of my most devoted thoughts, Yours, R.S.

12. Notes for Helmuth von Moltke

Dornach, 26 May 1915 [r]

Notwithstanding all that is happening outwardly, inwardly every-thing has remained as I have always described it to you. Keeping up one's courage, mastering the difficulties, this is what needs to be done without fail. With respect to this, new spiritual experiences confirm the earlier ones. And if the will is quietly strengthened and upheld it will be possible to achieve what has to be achieved. Our trust in the world's spiritual guidance will only grow strong enough if it is hardenend and steeled by experiences in the physical world which, if they were merely taken to be such physical experiences, might make us faint-hearted. After all, trust in what is spiritual demands that we nurture it whatever may be happening in the physical world. If I were to write down today what has been revealed to me spiritually in the time since we last met the description would not look very different from what has been given earlier. And actually it is this very fact which makes it so significant, so hopeful. There are certain details which are new but as far as the general thrust is concerned nothing has changed. Therefore it is necessary to hold fast to what has been understood to be the right course so far.

What is experienced in the *satisfaction* of the physical world as such has run its course, has fulfilled its task, what is *suffered* has an inherent causal power; it leads beyond itself. This is not altered by the fact that suffering, too, has its causes. It is, as it were, the seed of that *light* which wants to be borne out of darkness. And this *light* really does continue to appear in the way it did in all those difficult times of suffering in the past. And all the spiritual beings of which we have spoken keep on pointing to this light, signifying that in it solace and strength and peace are to be found.

The Spirit of the German people is with this light and whatever this Spirit places within the gleam of this light will eventually find the path. This spirit remains the Spirit with his torch raised, and those who were around him continue to be around him and whoever is protected by him is well protected. These are the spiritual facts of which we have often spoken; and what I have been allowed to know today serves to confirm my seeing of these facts.

13. Note for Eliza and Helmuth von Moltke

Dornach, 3 August 1915 [r]

Note:
The spiritual being of which I have often spoken provides the following, which I relate faithfully with regard to content and meaning, if not in the exact wording which is difficult to capture:

The more the soul, into which a year ago important and significant thoughts for mankind's evolution were implanted, succeeds in keeping up its deep conviction that the right path was chosen at that time, and the more it imbues all its feeling with this conviction, the more easily it will find the path where the power of the spirit that accompanies this soul can be felt. Doubts enter into human thinking. This is necessary since souls would not become strong without doubts. But this soul must concentrate all its powers so as not to think about its doubts during a short time of inner contemplation, when it rests within itself in quiet expectation. Such moments radiate their power to the whole of life and they make the soul ready to unite itself with the power of the spirit.

The reasons for the *apparent* contradiction between outer facts and that which in this case is both inner spiritual truth and reality will be revealed at a time to come which will actually prove that the apparently contradictory course of events had been necessary to do justice to what was willed by the spirit. Looking calmly at everything the soul in question had to experience in the course of the year just passed, looking contentedly at what happened *through* it so that it may find its way: that is what will ignite its spiritual light. Because from a higher spiritual point of view that which happened happened so that this soul might find the path allotted to *it*. This path is, after all, a very special one and it would not lead to its goal if it were not laced with the thorns of destiny. What happened in the past was right; and the future will prove this rightness.

The time which is occupied by meditation should be dominated by the feeling: these are the moments in which my soul surrenders itself by means of its own strong will to the working and weaving of the spirit; in *this* case the particular Spirit that has often been referred to will be with this soul; it is *also* with it *during times* when it is beset by a spirit of uncertainty and refuses to let shine into itself what really *is*. The Spirit's power of grace that is to flow into this soul will find its way into it when the soul, in moments of complete equanimity, is able to forget everything that comes towards it from outer life. Then it should be possible to think and feel in the following way, for however short a time: this or that happened; this or that affected me; I am letting it all rest for the time being; no matter how strongly I may be connected with it in outer life; for a while I am looking at it as if I was watching through a window street life of no concern to me. If one succeeds for a short time to look at what is one's concern as if it was of *no* concern, *equanimity*, inner calm, is attained. When *such* a mood really takes possession of the soul, then what is given for meditation may draw the soul up to that place of the spirit where one first feels, and then knows, that one is coming closer to the spirit. It is in accordance with a spiritual law that these words are directed anew at the soul in question after the first anniversary of the great events. This serves to confirm the fact that the Spirit's connection with this soul is the same today as has been made known many times already.

*

As for other matters it can only be stated today that the direction of things is still the same as has often been described. However, this very fact should strengthen one's confidence. There is good reason to stand confidently by what has been shown to be right so far.

14. Rudolf Steiner to Eliza von Moltke for Helmuth von Moltke

Dornach, 18 August 1915 [r]

Notes:
From out of the spirit that has often been referred to:

He who is predestined to go through his life with his soul not just following the protecting and guiding spirit unconsciously, but truly in the knowledge that: this spirit is here, he spreads his light over my soul, must get used to the idea that he has to overcome many a difficulty in life which is spared those whose karma does not lead them to encountering the spiritual world. The soul in question must find its life's path in just this way. That is why it has to experience how difficult it is to live on the threshold where the spirit meets with the human soul. This spirit is there, shining his protective light over the human soul. And this light is different from what people often imagine the light of the spirit to be. Therefore the experience of this light will often give rise to feelings which *appear* to reveal the opposite of what they really effect. In such cases the soul may feel as if it had been *abandoned*. Yet such feelings of abandonment and many related inner states bear within them the seed for the strength which leads to the spirit with even greater certainty. What is important is that such souls never lose sight in their spiritual eye of the fact that their karma has destined them to *search* under arduous conditions in order that, when they do *find*, they may be strong enough to really hold fast to what they have found and truly make it the light of their soul. After all, when the spirit leads a soul unto himself he has to lead it along a special path, a path quite different from the common road of ordinary human habit. When souls such as the one in question are through their karma connected with great historical events, it is essential that such souls accept with courageous inner calm every situation they are made to experience in relation to these events, so that the right spiritual relationship to these events may be attained. The protecting Genius is dealing with a soul who would not benefit at all from being led to overcome all hindrances in life with ease. It is the adversities which are to make it ready for living in nothing but Truth. The soul must pass through the arduous path of Truth so that it may rightly feel the power of the spirits of error. It is all too easy for the human soul to succumb to the temptations of the spirits of *deception* if it is not strengthened by suffering *disappointments* in calmness and equanimity. Therefore retain your strength and calm through the adversities of this path which is a spiritual path towards an aim which cannot but be the fruit of this strength and calm. A soul which is sought by the spirit on special paths must likewise find the spirit on special paths.

*

There would never have been *light* in the universe if the light had allowed itself to be deceived by the darkness out of which it had to be born; and the light of the human soul shares the destiny of the World Light. The light of the soul, too, must overcome the power of darkness.

As for other matters, the same applies as was discussed earlier. The duration of time changes nothing in the inner nature of what is happening. As to their inner nature, outer events are going in the same direction as before.

15. Rudolf Steiner to Eliza von Moltke

Dornach, 1 September 1915 [r]

Dear Madam,
May I send you the enclosed notes for your husband? They are records of what stands before my soul, not just once, but repeatedly. Whatever outer events may bring: the direction of what is spiritual proves that what has happened so far is right. It is really good that it was possible to hold out, and the patience needed for that will bear its fruit. I do feel for you when you say that 'perhaps a little less patience might be more helpful in this situation'; yet I know for certain that a way towards the light could be found even if things happened which rendered such patience impossible. There is good reason to trust in this light. Something could only be lost if setbacks were to lead to discouragement. It is not the setbacks which matter but only the consequent falling into despondency and doubt. *You*, dear Madam, will find the way.
Yours very truly
R.St.

16. Notes for Helmuth von Moltke

Dornach, 1 September 1915 [r]

Notes:

Just as before the anniversary, the Folk Spirit is lending support to his people in complete confidence; and this spirit's gaze also stayed directed at the soul on which it was focused at the time when the all-decisive first steps towards the great event had to be taken. Since then there have been times where one might have become despondent if one drew conclusions only from outer facts; but no matter whether outer facts appeared more or less favourable—one's questioning gaze was directed towards the Spirit of the people: he showed in the sign of his raised torch that there was good reason to *remain* confident. And similarly the Spirit's protecting gaze *remains* directed at the soul in question, as in earlier days. This Spirit's relationship to this soul in active life more than one year ago is unchanged today, when through periods of temporary renunciation this soul should be faithfully guided to an awareness that quiet persistence will lead it on to the path which will *eventually* be recognized as having been the right one. Right also in the sense that the soul will know: even that which *apparently* led me away from the predestined goal is *in reality* bringing me closer to it. However, it is necessary to follow the right direction on the way, in loyal endurance and out of the strength that can only grow from within one's own soul. The instrument for the right path is created by the *feeling* that will not allow its inner forces be blunted by outer obstacles. Certainly souls may also become strong when—for a while—their forces are strengthened by outer events; but there are also souls which can only gain their right strength by overcoming obstacles, because this strength has to be greater than that strength that arises through favourable outer events. When these souls are not defeated in the inner struggle *necessary for them*, when they see *straight* in the spirit whatever happens—seemingly unfavourable to them—to their left and right in the sense-perceptible world, then they will find *their* path. Then, too, the Spirit whose gaze is directed at them will find the path. From the point of view of the Spirit the same must be said today as was said more than a year ago. And when it is said today: await in calmness the Spirit's light and his guidance on to the right path, then this is in truth and reality the same as could be said in complete confidence more than one year ago in different outer circumstances. My thoughts will thus follow the direction that I have often indicated.

17. Rudolf Steiner to Eliza von Moltke

Dornach, 23 September 1915 [r]

Dearest Madam,
The enclosed briefly captures some of what has been placed before my soul in recent times. Perhaps you would pass it on to your husband. I will always be with you in my thoughts. And you will not lose the courage which supported you through such difficult times and will also give you strength for the future.
Yours always,
R.St.

18. Notes for Helmuth von Moltke

Dornach, 23 September 1915 [r]

Notes:
The enduring of karma is certain to be of the greatest benefit to the soul; bearing it in a way that the soul may understand: I must endure because the strength I need for my next life's task can only be gained by bearing adversity in equanimity. The soul in question must steer towards a point in life that could not be attained without the guiding power of the spiritual. The Genius who guides his people towards something very definite in the seemingly indefinite will not abandon this soul if it remains confident that the stars will shine again even if they are obscured by a storm which seems to persist. This soul has gained great strength from the fact that a whole year has passed in a mood of renunciation needing much patience.

In the physical world many a thing that appears now to be a gain is in fact a loss. And the true gain will be, *surely* be, somewhere different from where some now believe it to be. To make this gain a true gain this soul had to follow a path that was at times quite different from what seemed to be its *outwardly* predestined path. This soul had to be placed against events in a much more spiritual way. Even now the riddles which the Genius with the raised torch poses to his people cannot be solved by a view confined to *outer* events.

The soul in question has found a way of remaining faithful to the direction of the spirit through heavy trials and it has found this way before the year was up; this is of the greatest significance for the soul. Because it had been given the task of following the light even where the light wanted to hide behind the clouds.

The strength thus gained will find its time of application. Strength which has not been gained through favourable outer events but has acquired its direction through inner trial and trust in the spirit, is of immeasurable value at the present time. This was important a year ago; this is important at the present time. It is necessary for the soul in question to hold fast strongly to its direction, unswayed by the fortunes or misfortunes of the time, and to move towards the guidance of the Spirit whose torch is raised over the destiny of his people and similarly over the personal destiny of this soul.

At the beginning of August 1914 a mighty call resounded from this Spirit, one of the calls which cannot remain free of tragedy in the stream of eternal necessities; but time will show that, in relation to the course of events historically, what was done then, was of the utmost importance.

The soul which found the power to decide in favour of what was of the utmost importance has, in its inner being, never been separated from the course of events. This soul's connection with these events accords with a resolution of the Spirit, and just as, initially, the soul was destined to follow 'the Call of the Time' from the Spirit, it was further destined to stay connected with this Spirit, and provided it would find the strength to hold on to listen out for the 'Call of Eternity'. Continuing on this path will lead to the right goal.

19. Rudolf Steiner to Helmuth von Moltke

Stuttgart, 23 November 1915 [r]

Your Excellency spoke during my last visit at your house about the obstacles in the way of gaining inner certainty about the spiritual world. Allow me to put forward the following in this respect.

These obstacles have to be there. They are not the workings of hostile powers but a gift from powers that want to bestow on human beings the gracious gift of true insight. We need inner forces to attain certainty. These are strengthened by difficulties, especially, too, by doubts. Everything a human being encounters in the way of such difficulties is transformed into inner forces. The human being himself can do no more than this: to let come to him in inner calmness and humility what is brought across his path by the powers of destiny working through him. Knowledge and insight come to man from the realm of the spirit like a light that breaks through dark layers of fog to envelop him in brightness. It comes to him as a gift that he has to await. Yet such 'awaiting' does not mean that he has to wait until a certain point in time; and that he must live in uncertainty until this time comes. The time for inner certainty is always there. Man must only develop the right mood of awaiting. Then the portals of certainty will open.

Your Excellency is now living through the time where the paths of destiny are shaping into the riddle of life. The powers whose mission is the spirit guidance of man hold sway in the paths of destiny. Through your spiritual guidance the destiny of your own inner life has been interwoven with the guidance of the German people for this era. The destiny of the German people is connected with the deepest and loftiest aims of humanity's evolvement in the world. The threads of such a folk destiny, in particular, are not straightforward. They must often become entangled. The path of destiny leads through trials. Trials which lead to the brink of World Mysteries. To the abyss where the great question 'To be or not to be' comes before the soul. Where apparent darkness spreads before one's gaze. But at the abyss there stands the Genius of the German people and his torch is not lowered but raised up high. Whatever may come to pass, the way to the light will be found. And obstacles and difficulties will merely signify that the forces will grow, to find the path, to follow the Genius.

Anyone who is connected with this path of the people as you, Your Excellency, are connected with it, will find reflected in his own life path that of the people as a whole. You were destined by the spiritual guidance of humanity to lead the German people to a certain stage of its task. The fact that you have, at a specific point, come to an *apparent* halt, signifies only that new strengths have to be gathered. *In reality* you were always *ready* to devote your strength to the events of the time. After all, in reality things are very different from what they present to the outer senses. Outwardly you are not connected now with the scene of events; yet in the depths of your soul you are; and in these depths are gathered and strengthened the forces which you will need when the powers of destiny call you again. And destiny will need these very forces of yours and is preparing them within you so that they may be used at the right place. Your path is a path that must be followed by everyone who has a serious task to carry out. It can be summarized in these words: Await whatever comes with calm and be 'ready' when called.

I cannot but view favourably the way the great events of the time have developed so far. Even everything that has become difficult up to the present, that, too, is favourable. In the higher sense the most unfavourable outcome would probably have been for everything to come to pass without hindrance. There is many a dark cloud still on the horizon, many a thing that will seem surprising on the surface is yet to come. But the Genius holds his torch on high. And the *direction* of the whole is, after all, the one that has been imprinted in your soul for years now, Excellency. And this *direction's* source is the benign guidance of Central Europe. At this point a beholder of the spiritual can perceive your connectedness with the spirit. At this point destiny placed the gateway through which it guided the spiritual powers to your soul. Through your deeds you have affirmed your connectedness with the spiritual world.

It is, after all, the secret of the spiritual world that the most apparent things also prove to be the most hidden. The spiritual world is completely apparent in your soul; and the most important thing is: to see what is revealed in the right light. In reality man is *never* uncertain about the spiritual world. There are only two impediments which can make this spiritual world *appear* uncertain, just as *in daytime* there are only two impediments to man's seeing the sun. The first is when the sun is concealed by a layer of cloud. Similarly the light of the spirit can be concealed by the outer events of life. Yet this is only possible for a certain time. The sun will always break through the clouds again. The other impediment is when a person shuts himself off against the sun within the four walls of a house. So, too, the walls of doubt, of brooding, can enclose the human soul. But just as a layer of clouds or the walls of a house in the physical world cannot cause uncertainty about the existence of the sun, outer events and possible doubts should *not* deceive man about the existence of the spirit. A human being, even if he cannot see the sun because it is covered by clouds, will still see the plants which could not exist if they had never had light from the sun. Even if he cannot see the sun through his four walls, he will still see *himself* within these four walls; and he can *know* about himself that the sun has had an effect on him. Since he would simply not be there if the sun had never shone on him. Thus man can direct his gaze at his own soul in the midst of doubt and uncertainty; and even if, for a while, he cannot see the sun of the spirit: *this soul* could simply not be there if it were *not* there by the grace of the spirit's sun. The *power* of the sun *lives* and *works* in man even if for a while he cannot see the sun; the power of the spirit's sun shines in the human soul no matter what doubts and uncertainties this soul may surround itself with, and which, basically, the soul builds up for itself.

I am writing these lines to you, Excellency, on the morning of the 23 November between six and eight o'clock after my soul has dwelled with you a great deal. I have written them as I was compelled to write them from an inner urge.

Take them as a sign for my deepest devotion
Yours, R. St.

20. Verse for Helmuth von Moltke from 11 December 1915

Wenn Ruhe der Seele Wogen glättet
Und Geduld im Geiste sich breitet:
Zieht der Götter Wort
Durch des Menschen Innres
Und webt den Frieden
Der Ewigkeiten
In alles Leben
Des Zeitenlaufs

When quietness smooths the waves of soul
And patience expands in the spirit:
Then the word of the gods
Moves through the inner being of man
And weaves the peace
Of eternities
Into all the life
Of the course of time

2. Helmuth von Moltke's Death

21a. Verses Spoken by the Bier on 19 June 1916

I.

Was vielen Menschenseelen
In tiefen Geistesgründen nur
Ein unbewußt Erleben bleibt:
Daß sie des Weltgeschehens
Bewegungs-Macht in's Antlitz
Mit innerm Auge schau'n:
In dieser Seele ward es
Die furchtbar-ernste Willensfrage;
Als durch Europas Schicksalsmächte
Der Menschheit Prüfung kam,
Und Zukunft rang mit Gegenwart.

Der helle Stern der Hoffnung,
Gehalten von des Volkesgeistes Armen,
Er strahlte über diesem Haupt.

II.

Was vielen Menschenseelen
In tiefen Wesensgründen nur
Ein abgedämpft Erfühlen bleibt:
Daß sie des Menschenrätsels
Erschauernde Kraft im Herzen
Durch innern Kampf erleben:
In dieser Seele ward es
Das schwerste bittre Lebensringen;
Als fern vom großen Schicksalsfelde
Des Weltengeistes Mächte
Sie in sich selbst berufen mußten.

Der Sorgenstern des Glaubens
Erstrebt von Wissensgeistes Sehnen,
Er bebte da in dieser Brust.

III.
Was viele Menschenseelen
In tiefen Herzensgründen jetzt
In schicksalschwerer Stund' ersehnen:
Daß in der Zeiten Wirren
Aus Geistes-Sphären helfend wirke
Ein Geist von Volkesliebe übervoll:
Er Wird in dieser Seele
Aus lichten Weltenhöhen strahlen;
Erlösung andren jetzt zu senden,
Wird ihm Erlösung sein,
Da er durch Todespforten hingegangen.

Der Sonnenstern der Liebe,
Errungen schwer in Pflicht- und Leidesleben,
Er glänzt aus diesem Geist.

I.
What for many human souls
In deepest grounds of spirit
Remains an unconscious experience:
That they are looking into the countenance
Of the motive power of world events
With their inner eyes:
In this soul it became
The awful earnest question of the will
When destiny powers of Europe
Brought trials on humanity,
And the future wrestled with the present.

The bright star of hope,
Borne in the arms of this people's Spirit,
It shone above this head.

II.
What for many human souls
In deepest grounds of being
Remains a muffled feeling:
That in their heart they are experiencing
The awe-inspiring power of mankind's riddle
Through their inner battle:
In this soul it became
The hardest bitter wrestling of life
When far from the great field of destiny
World spirit's powers
Had to summon it into themselves.

The troubled star of faith,
Aspired to by spirit-knowledge-longing,
It trembled within this breast.

III.
What many human souls
In deepest depth of heart now long for
In this destiny-burdened hour:
That in the turmoil of this time
May work from spirit spheres with helping hand
A spirit overfull of love for his own people:
Within this soul he will shine down
From light-filled cosmic heights;
To send redemption now to others
Will be redemption now to him
Now that he has passed through the gates of death.

The sun-star of love,
Hard-won in a life of duty and suffering,
It shines forth from this spirit.

21b. Metamorphosed Verses Spoken by the Bier
20 June 1916

(The first verse remains the same.)

2. Strophe
Was vielen Menschenseelen
In tiefen Wesensgründen
Ein adgedämpft Erfühlen bleibt:
Daß sie des Menschenrätsels
Erschauernde Kraft im Herzen
Durch innern Kampf erleiden:
In meiner Seele ward es
Das gnadevolle Lebensleuchten,
Als fern vom großen Schicksalsfelde
Des Weltengeistes Mächte
Sie zu sich selber führen mußten.

3. Strophe
Was viele Menschenseelen
In tiefen Herzensgründen jetzt
In schicksalschwerer Stund' ersehnen:
Daß in der Zeiten Wirren
Aus Geistessphären schaffend lebe
Ein Geist, dem Volkesstreben zugewandt:
Er wird in meiner Seele
Hinab zum Erdenleide schauen,
Verständnis andren jetzt zu geben,
Wird ihm jetzt Leben sein,
Da er in Geistesweiten aufgenommen.

Second Verse:
What for many human souls
In deepest grounds of being
Remains a muffled feeling:
That in their heart they are *suffering*
The awe-inspiring power of mankind's riddle
Through their inner battle:

In my soul it became
The grace-filled shining of life
When far from the great field of destiny
World spirit's powers
Had to lead it unto themselves.

Third Verse:
What many human souls
In deepest depths of heart now long for
In this destiny-burdened hour:
That in the turmoil of this time
May *live creating* from spirit spheres
A spirit turned towards his people's striving:
Within my soul
He will look down to earthly suffering;
To bring to others understanding
Will now be life to him,
*For he has been received in spirit spaces.**

---

* Editor's highlighting denotes metamorphosed sections of the text

21c. Memorial Address by Rudolf Steiner of 20 June 1916

My dear friends!

Before coming to the subject of our deliberations today I feel impelled to speak about the great painful loss which we have suffered in these days on the physical plane. As you will know, the soul of Herr von Moltke passed through the portal of death the day before yesterday. It will be the task of others, of future history, to give full appreciation to what this man was to his people, the supreme part he played in the great destiny-laden events of our time, and the important and deep impulses of human evolution which inspired his deeds, his work in the world. After all it is impossible these days to present a fully exhaustive picture of anything, especially where it relates to the time in which we live. But as I have said already I shall not speak today about what others and history itself will have to say, although it is my innermost conviction that in future history will have a great deal, indeed, to say about this man in particular. But some of what is before my soul at this moment can and should be said here, even if it is necessary for me to express this or that in an allegorical rather than actual sense; the latter will only be understood gradually. This man, and this man's soul, stand before my soul like a symbol of our present and immediate future, born out of the development of our time, truly a symbol for that which should happen and must happen in a very real, very true sense of the word.

We emphasize again and again that it is truly not an arbitrary desire by certain people to incorporate what we call spiritual science into the culture of our present and immediate future; this spiritual science is a necessity of our time, and that there will be no future unless the substance of this spiritual science flows into man's evolution. And here, my dear friends, you have the great and significant phenomenon we need to look at now as we remember the soul of Herr von Moltke. In him we had a man, a personality, among us who stood in the life of the present in a most real and active sense, this life which has evolved out of the past and has now reached one of the greatest crises humanity has ever faced in the course of its conscious history, a man who led armies, who stood in the centre of the events which formed the starting-point of our destiny-laden present and future. And at the same time we have in him a soul, a man, a personality who was all of that and sat in our midst, seeking knowledge, seeking truth with the most holy and fervent thirst for knowledge imaginable in any soul of our times.

This is what should now come before our souls. Because this makes the soul of the personality who has just passed through the portal of death an outstanding historical symbol, in addition to all that it represents historically. The fact that he was a leader in external life, that he served this external life and yet found the bridge to the life of the spirit which is sought by this spiritual science, that is a deeply significant historical symbol; that is what may implant a wish into our souls, not a personal wish, but a wish born out of the necessity of our time: may many many more in his situation do as he did! This is what is so significant and exemplary, and I want you to feel it, to experience it. However little one may speak of this fact in the outer world is of no importance at all, in fact it is best not spoken of at all; but it is a reality, and what matters are its effects and not what is said about it. This fact is a spiritual reality and makes us understand: this soul had within it a feeling for rightly interpreting the signs of the times. May many of those who are perhaps still far distant in one or another sense from what we call spiritual science follow this soul.

For this reason it is true: that which flows and pulsates through this spiritual-scientific movement of ours has received from this soul as much as we were able to give it. We should keep this well in mind, because I have often spoken about it here. It means that right now souls are passing into the spiritual world who bear within them what they have absorbed here from spiritual science. When a soul who occupied such an eminent position in active life passes through the portal of death and now dwells up there in the world of light which we are meant to learn about through our knowledge, when we know it to be up there, in other words, when that which we are seeking is carried by such a soul through the portal of death, then it becomes, through the association it has formed with such a soul in particular, a deeply significant and effective power in the spiritual world. And those souls who are here and are able to understand me at this moment will never ever forget what I have just tried to express: how significant it is that this soul is now taking up into the spiritual world what has flown through our spiritual science for years now, in order that it may become strong and effective there.

All this can certainly not lessen in a trite way the grief we suffer over such a loss on the physical plane. Suffering and grief are called for in this case. But suffering and grief will only become great and significant, will only become effective forces in themselves, when what underlies them is properly understood. And so what I have said should be taken as an expression of grief at the loss on the physical plane which the German people and mankind have suffered.

22. Pontifex Meditation for Eliza von Moltke on 20 June 1916

Eine starke Stütze-Kraft
In Erdelebens schweren Tagen
Das Erbe vergangner Erdeleben
Die wir nicht einmal nur gegangen
Die wir in Zukunfttagen
Wieder wandeln werden
Du gabst mir—was ich—
Was wir *in künft'gen Tagen*
Getreulich Menschheitdiensten
Wenden wollen.

(Gelassenheitsfrucht in Seelenstille)

A strong support and strength
In burdened days of earth experience
Heritage of former earthly lives
Through which we passed not only once
Which we in future days
Will pass through yet again
You gave to me what I—
What *we*—in future days
Will to transform
Faithfully in service of mankind.

(Fruit of composure in stillness of soul)

23. Rudolf Steiner to Eliza von Moltke

Berlin, 24 July 1916

My dear Frau v. Moltke!

Before my departure I would like to write this to you. As a whole everything at present is a continuation of the effective harmonious state I was able to describe to you as having resulted from the struggles which were hard but have essentially been won for now. Especially clear is the decisive will to consciously feel from time to time the connectedness—especially with you—brought about by the mediation of the spiritual in recent years. 'This should continue; what there is now should be the continuation of it': this is how I sense his very thoughts. I myself always find a complete connection with him now through the 'fruit of composure' verse I have given to you. His working along the lines I described to you is growing together more and more with his being and is becoming more effective. Everything emanating from the precious soul now is harmonizing, since one can sense that he attained it in his soul. I also believe that I have clearly perceived this thought: 'I hope that she'—and here you are meant—'can feel my being around her'.

So let us continue our work in the direction indicated.

With all this I hope that you will recover and that the present calmness will lend you new strength. My thoughts are with you.
Sincerely,
R. St.
My best wishes to the countess and her sons.

3. After-death Messages from Helmuth von Moltke, and Relevant Documents

24. Helene Röchling to Eliza von Moltke

Mannheim, 9 August 1916

My very dear Frau von Moltke,

I hope you are well when you receive this letter. I was asked to tell you today that the dear soul is enjoying the bliss of attaining greater knowledge, emphasizing again and again that everything is to continue as before. The need to be together with the family is great, more intense than it used to be. The soul lives partly in the circle known to you, and partly flees from that in order to dwell with his family. Continue creating that kind of togetherness on Saturdays that has always been achieved in recent times.

What is being done from a particular quarter is felt to be extremely helpful. Everything that has been said should be continued. The soul can always be found by using the words of the meditation given to you; they get through to the soul.

There is strong involvement with the Isidoric Documents (Decrees). In addition the struggle with the power known to you, which started being active two years ago, is still going on. Apart from that there is no struggle, rather a working in the sense of spiritualizing what is happening in material life and of influencing matters peacefully in that way.

The connection with you, dear Frau von Moltke, is very strong indeed and it may be possible for you to feel and sense this. It is a strong and rich life filled with work, without struggle, because the bliss of knowledge has now become the most important and significant of all experiences.

(...)

Your faithful Kundry—the Great!!!*

---

* See Foreword, p. x.

25. Helene Röchling to Eliza von Moltke

Mannheim, 12 August 1916

My dear, dear Frau von Moltke!
I have just arrived back and my very first task is to convey greetings
to you: Intense spiritual work that is to serve the age is difficult for
the dear soul but *not* painful, great efforts are needed because
human beings do not wish to receive the thoughts. In order to give
direction to this there is intensive work going on with regard to the
earlier incarnation. For present circumstances this is a continuation
of our (i.e., all of you together on Saturday night) earlier work (on
the physical plane). You should not worry because this work, which
was initiated in this context, belongs to what is dear to him. In
general there is no cause to worry because this way of being together and working under present circumstances is preferable to him
to what it was in the earlier conditions here (phys. plane).

(All this taken down as dictation. Now the following two notes
are added.)

[Notes in Rudolf Steiner's handwriting.]

Being with the family: he has a *need* always to determine himself
when to devote himself wholly to the family circle.

These worries achieve nothing, besides stopping him sometimes
from choosing the time because he is pressurized. But he does not
view circumstances (the matter of your son [H.v.R.]) with concern
now, but with the intention of helping her (you are meant by that
[H.v.R]) and through this the cause itself.

*

In explanation of the above I would like to say to you that he knows
about your worries but that they are hindering his work. For
example, your worries are drawing him away from his work, he
rushes to you and therefore cannot keep to the times he arranged
for working with a particular personality. It creates a certain
amount of unsteadiness. From where he is he does not consider
your worries to be that important, they are earthly worries. He
needs to work in a greater context and therefore you are asked to
turn your thoughts to him as has been indicated. The fight with the
person alluded to earlier is still going on. However, he *wants* this

fight and carries it on with strict determination. It is important that you, dear Frau von Moltke, help him. It is possible that your forces were needed when you were feeling so weak. That is why you must try to drive away your worries. Being together with you strengthens him because it was through you that he was given knowledge, hence it helps him a lot when you work with him. That is what I wanted to say to you. I will probably go there again on 2 September and will be able to give you further messages then. In case of something urgent and important I could go for two days. I willingly make myself available. Otherwise just on 2 September. I hope that you will soon be quite well. My loving thoughts are always with your dear daughter and the dear departed soul.

Your faithful H.R.K. a. Gr.!!!

I am *very* sorry that I cannot come now!

26. Helene Röchling to Eliza von Moltke

Mannheim, 6 September 1916

My dearest Frau von Moltke!

Having just returned I hasten to tell you: Retrospective of previous incarnation pursued vigorously. In the course of that a glance at the Belgian-French-Russian corner, and this was linked up with the events of 14 August. In this context there was a rather remarkable, very difficult request for thoroughness from his side. He inquires about all possible relationships and experiences the conquest of spiritual cognition (that means he penetrates these relationships with spiritual cognition); in other words there has been another hard time but he fully recognizes that this is *necessary*. Intense participation in current affairs for which he is seeking the spiritual counter-image (i.e., seeking the reason for the present evil, the spiritual basis). It will probably become even worse.

Relationship to the Folk Spirit and his environment as before. Repeated requests for exact clarification of the facts which were often embellished here in order to save his feelings.

He is always attentive to your thoughts and follows them closely. (Hence the importance of your way of thinking.) He views the change that has taken place (Hindenburg) somewhat differently from how he did here as he recognizes the capacities for what they

are and no longer overestimates them. In 14 days there will be more news about what is probably already indicated today but is not yet certain enough: the karmic relationship with Lehmann.
Many affectionate greetings
(…)
Your faithful K. and G. esoterically
Helene Röchling exoterically

27. Helene Röchling to Eliza von Moltke

Mannheim 13 September 1916

Dearest Frau von Moltke!
Dr Steiner sends his very best wishes. There is nothing very different to report. Work is proceeding steadily: 'Worked steadily on previous incarnation. *On his side* forces which already affected events, which come from his work.' Relationship to Lehmann incarnation cannot be expressed yet, perhaps possible soon when I have been there again.

The soul is not asking any direct questions yet but this will come. He now recognizes that events can only serve human progress when they lead to the spirit. In other words, the exact opposite of the present situation. In the beginning it might have happened like that, before the counter-forces got to work.

Such influences (as referred to above) might already have worked in relation to the H. event. However, present events ought not to extend to war-like undertakings. Morality ought to be the decisive factor.

(…)

Goodbye now, dear Frau von Moltke. I will send you the name by telegram as soon as possible. I am not sure whether it will be possible as early as Saturday. I expect that there will have to be some research in the annals of the Akashic records.

My thoughts are with you both and the dear departed soul every day. My best wishes to all of you and the Countess.
Yours faithfully
K.a.G. es!
Helene Röchling (ex)!

28. Helene Röchling to Eliza von Moltke

Mannheim, 26 September 1916

My dear Frau von Moltke!
I enclose a note. The message is that his work is extremely taxing. Difficult and taxing from here, too, because the potential for error is great in these confused times. Very occupied with the last incarnation. There is already a certain influence on events, but in a completely spiritual way, different from how one imagines it here. The effect is to clarify and enlighten in order to work on the intentions. His lingering with the family always proceeds in the same manner; therefore please continue with everything as indicated.

Last time Lehmann was in Rome, too, with the soul in question. You were there, too. More about this next time. Also your last inc. You should rest a lot—and think of him in the way prescribed.

He is not spending a lot of time with Lehmann because L.[= Kaiser] is nothing (zero) over there!!! He is at the service of the old General Field Marshal.

(...)
My best wishes,
Your faithful Kundry

29. Rudolf Steiner to Eliza von Moltke

19 October 1916

It is the clearest mission of my 'I' to work on the European relationship between the Germans and the Slavs. For that it was necessary, during the Nicholas incarnation, to bring about a separation from Europe for the future eastern Slavs. The Greek-Catholic Church, as herald of what was to happen later for the eastern Slavs, was brought about through the Church politics of my 'I'. At that time my 'I' did not want the separation. But it was heavily influenced by a high-ranking church dignitary who wanted to get me out of the way and take my place. This relationship caused my position with regard to him in his present incarnation. In my present incarnation my 'I' was directed towards this 'I'. Now this relationship is completely transparent to me. I also know now what to make of the warning that came to me from the East on 14 August. It had to happen like that. When my 'I' in September 1914, after my journey, gave the command to pull back the troops to Hausen, all the old resentment affected my consciousness—which was used by Ahriman—which had built up against me in the previous incarnation, because many who held positions in the headquarters were in Capua in their previous incarnation—now the time was coming when my work on the physical plane was to come to an end. For it was my karma that my 'I' should not attain a clear understanding of my relationship to the people with whom I was connected in my earthly position.

Now my 'I' became the connecting medium for the forces assembled around the German Folk Spirit which had to bring the outer advances to a halt.

This apparent regression was in truth a victory over Ahriman. My physical departure from the earth was another such victory over Ahriman. To bring about ruin he let the thought arise to use me against the Romanians. But no soul that carries within it the spiritual impulse was to intervene in these matters. There will be an intervention from the spiritual world at the right time and my 'I' will be involved in it. But first that right time will have to be prepared from here. Hindenburg's appointment and everything connected with it is the work of Ahriman, and it was not *willed* to be otherwise here. Here one does what matches the intentions of the spiritual powers and not one's own wishes.

30. *Helene Röchling to Eliza von Moltke*

Mannheim, 2 December 1916

My very dear Frau von Moltke!
Having returned home last night I would like to report the following:

The growing light around me makes me realize that this last earthly life of mine was an intensive schooling for me. Through this earthly life I was meant to absorb something into myself that I was not allowed to understand fully *in* that life but only *now* where I may look at all the events from without through my soul's eye. What I caused to happen through my actions in the August and September days created in me a condition where the Guardian of the Threshold was right at my side. The seemingly fantastic visions I experienced in September were His approach. I had to stay on earth after this, because, if I had passed through the portal of death earlier, the light around me would have become so dazzling that I would have needed 34 years here before I could have intervened in earthly affairs. I will be able to become a helper through what I have suffered on earth, even now, but through more spiritual means than I would have believed possible on earth, since spiritual means are the only right ones for Central Europe. It will be seen how these will gradually come in special ways, and especially through outer misfortunes. But criticism is permissible.

What 'she' is to me now I can only describe like this: she is holding together that part of me which must still work in the earthly sphere, which hovered around me through 'her', with what I must experience here; without this holding-together I would experience much greater difficulty in relation to the light pressing towards me. That is why everything must continue as arranged after my departure from the earth. Because in this way many things which would otherwise affect me directly, and which would require a great deal more time to live through, come to me as if through filtered light. This relationship has been fixed and determined by the effects of the previous incarnation where 'she' developed the Nordic Germanic and I the Latin Roman element. Our life together *must* go on.

What I am permitted to do will break through at various points in earthly life and it will be experienced as thoughts in human beings which will bear fruit. However, a few people at least must first understand that criticism can mean a greater love than mere 'silence'—especially that silence in thinking which is to blame for so much of what is happening now.

This is what I had to convey to you. I was told in person that at the special request of the departed soul your incarnation should not be revealed yet.

All the new things which are now being arranged were naturally not approved of. I will go there again on Thursday; please let me know if there is any message.

The return will probably take place just before Christmas. There is still work to be done on the Group* so that the artists can carry on their work. You are asked to be patient and to understand that there is no other way.

I will telephone this evening. My very best wishes to you,
Yours, K.

31. Helene Röchling to Eliza von Moltke

Mannheim, 16 December 1916

My dearest Frau von Moltke!
This is the message:

What I called the German Folk Spirit on earth has now become the fullest spiritual reality for me. He is engaged in strenuous battle with a number of ahrimanic beings. Without this battle the full spiritual character of the German people could never play its part in human evolution.

I am gaining increasing insight into the nature of this spiritual character. I am totally reconciled now to my last earthly life. In the latter my consciousness was not sufficiently awake to understand that an apparent failure can in reality be a success. The strength you were to me (Frau v. Moltke) is now a solid ground beneath me. If you had not often needed to contradict me I would now only see dimly what is around me. Now I have to create thought centres so that insights arise in certain individuals on earth. Soon I will know *how* I can bring this about.

This is a verbatim account of what was given to me. The departed soul is helping the one whose departure has caused so much to happen.

The recently departed soul is still completely asleep.

(. . .)

Farewell, my dear Frau von Moltke.
Thinking of you always,
Yours, Kundry.

---

* Wooden sculpture of 'The Representative of Humanity' holding the balance between the adversary forces of Lucifer and Ahriman.

32. Helene Röchling to Eliza von Moltke

Hamburg, 8 January 1917

My dearest Frau von Moltke!
I would like to tell you the following:

'The passage through my last earthly life happened earlier than it should have done according to all the conditions of the preceding and significant Roman incarnation. But it resulted in the right relationship with Liza who, in turn, had to incarnate in this time. Our recent life together on earth is to be the starting-point of our working together for the spiritualized evolution of humanity. While on earth I lived and shared in various kinds of errors committed around me. (In his official position). The reliving of these errors continues to be relentlessy hard, indeed, for me, but it also brings me joy, because through it I gain strong forces which I am using some of the time now to create the centres for a spiritual under-standing of the world situation on earth. Acquiring these forces also gives me a strong feeling of power and is a favour for me.

There is nothing at all to be hoped for from what human beings on earth mostly strive to achieve. In 50-80 years nothing that is esteemed highly now will be so regarded then. I am happy to live in increasingly new understanding. What streams up to me through my participation in the anthroposophia is nourishment to my soul'.
My very best wishes, too
(...)
Yours faithfully,
K.H.R.

33. Helene Röchling to Eliza von Moltke

Mannheim, 18 January 1917

Dear well-beloved Frau v. Moltke!
What a surprise it was to meet your dear son here on my return!
That he of all people should come to Mannheim!
But first of all the most important:

There is now a great need to wholly absorb inwardly the anthroposophical development of the world. 'When these concepts are within me as a body of strength I can fulfil my task of creating centres in those human souls which are up to the tasks that the time demands.'

Complete truth no longer exists now anywhere on earth. It is untruthfulness which exists and shyly keeps away from scrutiny. Souls are full of deformed concepts. Were the spiritual world to intervene directly in the sense of a total change of course, a time of even greater materialism would follow. Lucifer, in particular, is working continuously to effect such a change of course in the wrong sense. He is stronger still than the German Folk Spirit. He will not always be. Once I am sufficiently imbued with the concepts of the world's evolution to impart them comprehensibly to those who have arrived here before me (this refers to the circle around the old General Field Marshal and Bismarck) my influence on earth will be perceived in various places. It will be possible soon.

Liza ought not to worry. What she herself means is indeed what I am saying now, even if here much has to be put differently from what earthly words would express. (He means the contradiction you often had to present to him in the context of his review.)

(...)

As far as you are concerned, he asks you to continue the 'I'-exercise and also to do it in reverse, in other words let the streaming light stream out again (let darkness enter). Persevere with *that* until the Dr comes. I will receive instructions by telegram on the 26th and will pass them on to you straight away. I will go there again, probably on the 29th, depending on the message. Have patience for a little while longer now, the time of waiting is nearly over. As to your son, we will do our best to make him comfortable. I will not talk to him about Dr Steiner's message. We are *very* pleased that he is with us. For me he represents a bit of jointly experienced Anthroposophy, even if nothing is said about it. It makes me feel so at home! To have the company of a soul in the house which knows these matters!

My best wishes to both of you, dearest twins*
Your faithful Kundry.

---

* Astrid and Else

34. Helene Röchling to Eliza von Moltke

Mannheim, 29 January 1917

My dear Frau von Moltke!

The following was added: Intense spiritual work still going on as described earlier; the soul is now engaged in living through the first period, about 10 years ago, of theosophical communications. There is now, however, full recognition of all the absorbed truths which were met with doubt and contradiction at that time.

He has now come to recognize his mission in its entirety.

(…)

I hope to come to Berlin myself in February. My best wishes to you! Now you will soon have our dear Dr Steiner there. Friday morning Dr Steiner's arrival in Berlin! Nevertheless I remain your faithful Kundry, even though the commissions will not go through me any more, unfortunately.

35. Notes by Emil Bock from Lost Notes of Eliza von Moltke from the year 1917

(Berlin) 7 May 1917

The Field Marshal (the 'old man') sends this message:

The Mysteries have moved into the ether. We were the last ones to conduct wars in the old spirit. Now Ahriman is fighting a desperate battle in the ether, and the battle on earth is only a shadow image of the ahrimanic battle. It can only come to an end when the Germans have found themselves. They will find the way up and the way down. They will have to discover a new Olympus and a new underworld. The Zeppelin is a mockery of Olympus,
The Submarine the fear of this underworld.

*

The 'old man': ancient Greek. Highly esteemed in the Nicholas era. Against the separation [of the Western and Eastern Church]. Intruction over there: like a solemn cultus.

Nicholas wanted spiritualization of the Church. Pseudo-isidoric decretals imposed on him.

*

Berlin, July 1917

The 'old man' helped carry spiritual culture from the East to the West. He was in Hibernia on an expedition in the second, third centuries after Chr.(?) And what the Field Marshal brought to Hibernia was received back by Nicholas in the form of visions. They spoke to him and guided him.

Oskar Hertwig's lecture to the Kaiser. The cutting up of animals. Helmuth beside himself. Hertwig a savage in earlier incarnation. Helmuth understands now that this lecture was arranged for his sake. At the papal court of Nicholas, O.W. was a negro who played a special role as servant in the Kaiser's half black-magic affairs [in his incarnation at that time].

Now Umi needs him for his purposes. (This happened during the lecture to the Kaiser.)

In the twelfth/thirteenth century BC we were incarnated together with Umi. Umi was a Black Fever healer then. This his last incarnation. Then, in 111 BC, Umi inspired the Field Marshal who was then an initiate in the Greek Mysteries. Then the Field Marshal worked into the Nicholas life, just as Umi worked supersensibly into 'her' in the Nicholas era.

Umi suggests to Novalis his over-appreciation of the Jesuits. The 'old man' translates what he has received into mathematical guidelines.

Laurentius—Field Marshal (in connection with the Uriel note)
Umi to Astrid: We are in the Light
Like Gold in the Earth

Beginning (?) August 1917 (Berlin)
Agrarianism: Luke
Industry and Urbanism: Matthew
Military: Mark
Priesthood: John

(Apparently Frau von Moltke asked a question following the lecture of 31 July 1917—*The Karma of Materialism*, Lecture 1, 'Forgotten Aspects of Cultural Spiritual Life'. Firstly about African Spir, a Russian who had settled in Central Europe. Then about agrarian society and industrial man. At the end tentative classification of the Luke Gospel with the agrarian ... and the Matthew Gospel with the industrial type. This question leads to further Gospel classifications as well as to the resumption of the after-death messages:)

Conversation Nicholas—Umi

Nicholas: Why did I not insist on it then?

36. Two Reports from Rudolf Steiner about St Odilie

Dornach, 31 August 1917

The Convent of St Odilie was originally a heathen Mystery Centre that was to be led to Christianity under Saint Odilie. 150 years before Nicholas I the Alemannic Duke Eutycho (Eticho I.) lived on Odilie's Mount; he had a daughter, Odilie, who was blind, and because of that her father wanted to kill her—she was blind in order to be illumined during her baptism. She was miraculously saved on *several* occasions; once she fled from her father's persecution, protected by her later born brother, to the hill which lies opposite our Dornach building. On her return she was once again miraculously saved, and after that the transformation of the old Mystery Centre to a Christian convent took place. Here started that ecclesiastical stream which Pope Nicholas in particular had striven to propagate; this stream was to be totally opposite to the Byzantian stream; later on there was a continuous correspondence between Odilie's Mount and Pope Nicholas. The destruction of this stream was the aim of Duke Eticho; he was in the service of the Merovingians. From this convent the Christian essence spread over the entire Occident, hence Odilie's Mount in Alsace has been the centre of so much fighting.

From a letter of Eliza von Moltke to W.J. Stein:

Arlesheim, 27 December 1927

I am very pleased to be able to answer your question properly. You ask whether I know which hill Dr Steiner is referring to when he said on 31 August 1917: '... the hill opposite our Dornach building'. I am able to answer this question very precisely as Dr Steiner asked me during my first sojourn at Dornach in late autumn 1917 to accompany him on a walk to the *Eremitage* and then said to me at the very place from which one can see the Dornach building from the window 'This hill is the place to which Odilie fled'.

37. Message of January 1918

Dornach, January 1918

Having my letters from the century's beginning read out to me released a special power in my soul. My 'I' was not very well prepared for entering into this incarnation, this earthly life. In its subconscious there were most oppressive spiritual notions. The impulses of centuries of European evolution played an unconscious part in my 'I'. My soul knew much. The physical abilities covered over all these inward impulses. My 'I' was meant to be totally transformed as a result of bringing to this incarnation completely different world impulses from those of my previous incarnation. This caused a situation where my feelings which unconsciously carried the effects of earlier impulses in many cases did not register pleasure in the face of what my 'I' had to think.

When my soul now experiences my earlier feelings with greater perception, it knows that it would not be able to grasp these at all if 'she' had not brought me the spiritual thoughts whose repercussions can now unite with these feelings. 'She' was connected with me in an earlier incarnation through karma. But this connection was mainly attributable to karma. Only in this incarnation was it brought to perfection through our connection in thinking. That is why I can dwell so easily in 'her' thoughts now. What 'she' now thinks strengthens my soul; I experience it as encouragement which mildly flows into the experiences that must be undergone to build the foundations for the future out of what has passed.

Let 'her' know that the pains I must suffer now have a completely different meaning than they do in physical life. One suffers, but one understands the need for it. 'She' should remember that, and during difficult times, entertain the thought that all is 'good' for the right aim. My 'I' now also beholds the 'aberrations' and 'confusions' of my last earthly life. In the physical world these drove many a wedge between 'her' and my soul. But all this served to tie 'her' soul more closely to mine.

The personality that brought confusion was obsessed by a spirit which guided his instincts. Such spirits are allowed by the leading spirits of the world in order that human souls may become stronger through overcoming obstacles. The best parts of my looking back over my life relate to what 'she' has done for me by helping me out of my confusion. Now I look back over these events as on something which has taught me a lot. They were not part of what connects 'her' to my soul; but I may learn a lot from it for the very reason that it more or less passed me by without my soul participating strongly. In that way I experienced something on earth in which my soul hardly participated. In the spiritual world such events are like something from which one learns, yet with no further involvement.

'Her' thoughts will now always be able to live in mine because 'she' brought me spiritual interests in this last incarnation. I am able to live in all the forms when 'she' thinks them. And this living in the 'forms' will contribute to my soul's and other souls' coming back at the time needed for our future work in the world. 'She' has acquainted me with the thoughts about the demise of the age of materialism in the course of the nineteenth and the beginning of the twentieth century. Here the spiritual impulses for a new era on earth are already waiting. The repercussions of the old era will still have to run their course on earth. The souls who have achieved great deeds on earth such as that of the 'old uncle' [the older Helmuth v. Moltke] are now among the new impulses waiting.

Now I understand how the 'Folk Spirit' meant really well for me. But in my last years on earth I could not yet understand his good influence. He drew me towards my tasks; yet he also drew me towards difficult experiences on earth which were necessary.

'She' often witnessed the struggles of my subconscious. It was a wrestling with spiritual impulses. They entered my head, and my head was not sufficiently prepared for understanding what was already prepared in my heart for such understanding. In my heart I bore an understanding for the spiritual world but I did not know it and I kept saying to myself: If only I could 'understand'. I believed that I needed to scream for 'certainty' and did not know that this 'certainty' was already in my heart and that it was only my head that did not want to let it enter into my ideas. My task now is to reverse all this. Now I am working on understanding what I believed then and I can now see the 'certainty' of what I resisted believing then.

A lot needs to be done to penetrate these matters. Through my karma I was also connected with people in my earthly life who could not muster understanding for the new era on earth in their bodies. I could not develop the right ideas about this either with my head. Now I am freeing myself of the concepts which have given me fruitless feelings about my connection with such people. I now look at the illusions of many people with whom I was connected and recognize them as illusions, whereas during my earthly life I still believed that something favourable could be gained from illusion. I expected the Folk Spirit to be not only with my task, which he was, but with the illusions, too. After all there are many illusions still living on earth. And because they are alive they have real power.

People on earth are finding it so difficult now to read the signs sent them by the spiritual world in the shape of particular earthly happenings.

'She' should know that 'she' and my soul will work together, whatever happens. Some of it will be unexpected, and of this I have only an inkling now, because whenever I want to dwell on particular aspects, the great world impulses to which my soul will be devoted come rushing in. I also see all the details of the Nearer [sic]; yet a powerful light reveals them all to me in a great context. A lot of the details continue to be beyond my understanding. That has to be; for what is understood prematurely paralyses the soul.

The spiritual thoughts in which 'she' lives are like the moon, lending a soft glow to the light around my soul; I need that. The thoughts of loved ones still living on earth are to the one living in the spiritual world—if he can perceive them—in an outer world which he may illuminate. This creates a mildness in his environment which does not blind him, whereas many a thing in the spiritual world blinds him when he cannot gaze at such thoughts. The spiritual thoughts which have come towards me during my last decade on earth also contribute to this mildness around my soul. If I had not received those I would nevertheless have to receive all of it now. For I was destined to absorb all that. But I would have to absorb it without the mildness, and then it would be a singeing fire. It is also a great help to me that I can understand how such things are connected.

After all, certain thoughts can only originate on earth, but those living in the spirit do need these thoughts. What is experienced in certain regions of the spiritual world is still awaiting the future. The soul does not bring it down when it takes hold of itself anew. Being in the spirit is of a twofold nature: mere being and conscious, active being. The conscious, active being must often wait until it can perceive the mere being. Many of those living in the spirit are unable to understand this. I can only understand it through the way I now live with earthly happenings. It is true, one gains strength out of waiting for certain things until mere being has been transformed into conscious being.

'She' now perceives much in a way that enables me to see forms with 'her' as well. Thus the soul living in the spirit is afforded a 'freedom' it would not otherwise have *at this point.*

In recent times many of the impulses I received some time ago as individual experiences have condensed into one single experience that lends great inner strength to my soul.

On earth people frequently believe that they can judge things which can only be decided upon when normal judgement is suspended and it is possible to weigh, as if with a set of scales, which reasons weigh heavier. It is not only a matter of having the right reasons for something but of actually recognizing the ones of heavier weight. What is decisive in the world is not just what is right but what is of heavier weight. (Note: The latter flashed through the soul like a thought that came to be understood.)

[On the back of the last page in R. Steiner's handwriting:]
'Cyrillius and Methodius'.

38. Message of 29 January 1918

Berlin, 29 January 1918 [r]

When my 'I' looks back over the last few weeks it is filled with a powerful impression. Through 'her' it has experienced many a thing that happened on the physical earth but is related to the spiritual life and spiritual forces on this earth. My 'I' lives in 'her' thoughts and, through experiencing 'her' thoughts, it also acutely experiences what these thoughts themselves experience in physical earth existence. This is very important for my 'I' now, for my 'I' still needs such a connection with the earthly existence. It is precisely things like these which this 'I' must bear up into the spiritual world from the earth existence. There are many souls here for whom my 'I' has to act as messenger. I have to understand certain things in the world and certain things within myself if I am to enter into my own task in the right way now. I have been able to penetrate to the last 15–16 years of my last earth life with relative ease, by means of the contemplative understanding needed here. However, 16–18 years ago a great change took place in my soul. I experienced it in the depths of my soul then, but only fragments of it entered my consciousness, and even those fragments bore little resemblance to what was happening within my soul. A lot remained completely unconscious. Only the thoughts planted in me through 'her' give me the strength to understand matters in my retrospective view in the way I must understand them to fulfil my task. These thoughts produce new forces within me and through these forces I understand. And I must find my own self through learning to understand my earthly life's experiences, those which remained unconscious then. In my last years on earth these experiences were stored up within me; they did not rise up to my conscious understanding. Now that the earthly sheath has dropped away I may gradually build up a consciousness capable of understanding. Thus the pains I suffered in my last years on earth are now becoming the source of my growth, of my increasing strength. However, it is important to me that 'she' *knows* that; for if she knows it 'she' thinks it and when 'she' thinks it I feel ever strengthened by this thinking for finding my present direction. In addition I gain more and more views of earlier incarnations. And I need such views. For the present and the future must be found with the help of the past. What 'she' experienced in recent times in 'her' thoughts has been nourishment for my soul. The soul needs such nourishment to rightly find 'itself'.

It is, after all, my destiny to view the various circumstances of life which relate to personal matters in context with greater world impulses. I beg 'her' not to be offended if I have to consider many a thing that is so close to 'her' heart now in that manner, too... Much of what is said now would not have been told me if I had had to experience it in the physical way. There is something demonic in the personal context in which we stand. A lot is connected with that. Only 'she' is up to these demonic forces. But may 'she' keep her eyes open to it all. For a lot is yet to happen. One can and should not imagine anything definite in this direction; but it is necessary to be awake to many an inner connection revealed by outer events.

My own soul only came 16–18 years ago into the karmic stream in which I belong together with 'her', to the extent where the soul was able to take hold of it. And what then was taken hold of by my soul is presently taken hold of by my consciousness. In human life the soul can take hold of something long before consciousness takes hold of it. The bodily organisation is often an obstacle to understanding consciously what the soul has taken hold of already. For consciousness requires for its instrument a certain organization, be it a physical one between birth and death or a spiritual one between death and a new birth. The soul alone may well experience something but not be able to understand it consciously. However, man can only comprehend the experiences of his soul through his physical body if this physical body can be imbued with the fully developed spirit-organism. Yet it is often the physical body itself which presents an obstacle to that. It is bliss to realize in retrospect that the suffering one has endured originated there.

The suffering one has endured presents a very different picture when one looks back on it at a later time. 'She' has had to share very intensely in a lot of suffering. May 'she' now regard this relationship to the suffering I endured in the same way in which my soul must now regard it. That will establish the right karmic relationship between us both. My soul is finding the way to 'her' even though she has much to bear now. I want to bear it with her; it is possible. Thus many a judgement will be rightly directed.

Wakefulness is necessary, in the narrow as well as in the wider contexts. There is a lot of chaos on earth. The spiritual, however, is as if blunted. Human beings will first have to prepare their souls by developing a feeling for the spiritual world. Then the spiritual world—waiting to be understood—will be there to help.

The birthday greetings written in May 1901 are newly enlivened. They were written from out of the depths of the soul. They become ever more true the more one lives into them. They reflect karmic connections. They are written to express what souls may say to one another again and again. During my life my feeling often turned towards James 1, 17: 'Every gift which is truly good and every perfect present descends to us out of the higher world from the Father of lights in whom there is no alternation and no phases of light and darkness.' and James 2, 14–26: 'What use is it, dear brothers, if someone says he has faith and does not act in accordance with the faith? Can faith by itself help him?' and so on, and especially: 'So it is with the faith: if it is not proved by works, by itself it is dead.' In 1901 my soul did not yet understand these words; yet they were experienced in the depths of the soul; then the soul sought for deeper understanding; but the physical body was an obstacle to such understanding; the urge to understand was there but the ability to understand was not. That is what had to be suffered. The body is no obstacle any more. Gradually the pain of suffering is fading just as the seed of a plant fades when it must bring forth the new plant. And already the new plant is growing.

39. Message of 8 February 1918

Berlin, 8 February 1918 [r]

The 'I' looks at its tasks. 'She' looks below in the stream of world events; with 'her' thoughts, my 'I' follows the stream; the fact that it is 'her' thoughts that work upon my 'I' enables me to follow this stream in powers of soul that can unite with mine. Even if my soul can perceive more than is accessible to 'her' below, the things which 'she' is familiar with support other perceptions in me which are unfamiliar to 'her'.

There are also other earthly thoughts which come through to me; with these, however, there is always something I have to overcome before I can unite them with my being. These do not have such a powerful way with mine as do 'her' thoughts. I find it good now that 'she' knows of the necessity of a reincarnation before the end of the century. My gaze and my efforts must now be directed towards this.

In the East there is now chaos. The previous incarnation in the ninth century cut me off from the East. But I do, nevertheless, have a task to fulfil there. 'She' must help me. I was obliged in 1914 to go not to the East, but to the West. That was a repetition in another form of what happened in the ninth century. At that time I contributed to cutting off the East from Europe. Now I had to go to the

West in order to build up a relationship with the separated West. In the East my task can only be a spiritual one. In the context of the present spiritual constellation it seems good to me now that I was scarcely drawn into an active role in the battles in the East. This enables me to make spiritual connections with many eastern souls. The chaos there will only gradually take on the forms that it must eventually come to. My view of the tasks that come to me from the East is unobstructed to the extent that I have worked directly in the West and only indirectly in the East. Thus what was puzzling down there is now clear. The East is awaiting a task for which I must prepare myself by the next century. Earthly institutions must then be founded which will be an image of spiritual ones. 'She' and others who are linked with us are to work together on this.

A spiritual wilderness is now spreading over the earth. The 'old man' can see this now, too. How he will stand in relation to the task that lies before us is not yet clear. In the twentieth century there will be a great deal of materialism which will be even more powerful in the twenty-first century. But everywhere there will be centres of spiritual will and deed. That is where the task will lie. In the 'forms' of Dornach which I can now feel, I can see lines which are preparing something which in future will enable one soul to understand another more inwardly.

'She' now also has a great many difficulties to face. Wakefulness is needed. I cannot see everything very clearly in this area. But I can see a crisis. In essence there is much that has built up over many years which is now moving towards a crisis. While I was alive I faced this with some anxiety. This anxiety now has a baleful effect when I look at the critical situation. 'El' must be supported. I am able to do so because I had a great deal of love for her in life. This love is now a bond which links me to her. Nevertheless, it is essential to be wakeful on earth.

It has a warming effect on me that 'she' now has 'it' with her again. Now is the time for something spiritual between them to join on to what was there before, which is important for the future and for the task. There is more at work in 'it', than 'it' itself knows. This has to do with the fact that 'it' was also an intermediary to the spiritual world for my soul. We had to go through spiritual experiences in which there was much that was unconscious. 'It' has to remember many things from those days. By this means, 'it' will be able to help a great deal in the present and in the future. 'She' will need much wakefulness now. In the company of 'it' this wakefulness will gain in strength. When the two are together there lives a force in my soul which serves to make me strong for the 'task'. The company of these two also enables me to get more intimately in touch with things of a family nature. The events of our family life have to do with the fact that we are brought together by many a painful experience, for many blood relations of ours are to be held together. My soul has had to relearn a number of things during its earthly life, just in this respect. And it is so that wherever the soul looks back at a place where, during earthly life, a new lesson had to be learned or had to accept a disappointment, it is as if a window is opened to it, which without this lesson or this disappointment would have had to remain closed. With 'El' ...

In the time to come, I will be able to join 'her' in the spirit particularly well when she reads to me from the letters to 'her' the passages with which my soul was most strongly united. Then I will be able to be active in 'her' thoughts, in order to support 'her' wakefulness. Whatever happens, 'she' should follow the dictates of 'her' understanding; if one does not always *appear* to come to the right thing, it is only *apparently* so and later, subsequent events will show what was right.

'Her' concerns are also felt in my soul; but this should not disturb her, for my soul is willing to share this; and 'she' should know this. It was already so easy for me to come to 'her' in the days when 'it' was expected, and it is so now too. May they remain together as long as possible, though without wishing to force anything. The lecture on Tuesday came to me almost in its entirety, but it did so as if through a blue mist. Nevertheless, I could already read the contents of the lecture beforehand, as if they had been written in the Akashic Record by an old Rosicrucian.

The greatest misfortune is the harbinger of the greatest redemption: many who are on earth will learn of this, but will only gradually come to experience it. Spirits who now strive to work in souls on earth freeze in spiritual coldness that works like fire, and consumes the effect. The lecture cycle on the 'Folk Souls' should become known outside the Society, too, but in its present form it can only be understood by very few.

40. Message of 1 March 1918

[Berlin] 1 March 1918 [r]

My soul lives in 'her' thoughts. The world truths that she has so far grasped and the world secrets that she has beheld have now become part of 'her', and form part of her being, enabling 'her' to become ever more conscious in the world of the spirit. Through this consciousness, the thoughts which she devotes to my soul stand before me like configurations of light. Thus there is always a way to 'her'. Let 'her' know that we live together, let 'her' see in this the impulse that is developing for our working together later. Something will develop out of this which has its origins in our family karma. What now fills 'her' with concern is a power here which is working together with the great experience that has recently passed through my soul. Umi once appeared in the spiritual atmosphere which unfolded around us at the turn of the last century. He is a spirit who has been connected with us for thousands of years. In the 'revelations' which come [sic] to us at the turn of the last century he came to the point where, by means of the working of our own destinies, he should reach his position clearly in the spiritual world. At that time, he penetrated into the physical world by means of revelations in order to prepare my soul for consciousness of the spiritual world. I had to consciously find the thread which lay woven through our karma for so long. I was not to continue on my way through life in dull unconsciousness of the spiritual world. All this is, however, also connected with many other things. It is now possible for me to view objectively what is going on in the small details and in the major events of life on earth. Early sufferings are often the starting points for processes of spiritual development. Let 'her' be aware that I am with 'her', let 'her' see what is happening now as necessity. 'She' must not let her heart be troubled by events, but must connect her thoughts with the fact that by means of these events, things of the future are coming to pass, which must come to pass. The spirit must destroy many things in order to build anew. On earth one sees the destruction, yet in the destruction is contained already the seed of renewal.

We often see pass away
What on earth has been built

Yet what is truly coming to pass
Seen rightly in the spirit
Reveals in earthly night
To the seeking light of the soul
The developing might of spirit
And sufferings are not
What on earth they seem
They are in full truth
What they spiritually mean
In the kingdom of soul clarity

'El's' individuality was connected with us differently to that of 'it'. 'El' must first bring into consciousness how she belongs to us. She must find the strength to be conscious out of suffering. She is now holding back an old power in order to gain a new one. My soul must be with her so that 'she' may find the right way. Events can be confusing. Wakefulness will lead to what is right at the right moment. No good is done by saying at the outset: 'This and this should happen', one must wait and see what circumstances require.

Looking back at the moment of my 'rebirth', at the beginning of this century, is the lifeblood of my soul; looking back at the time of suffering before my present entry into the spiritual world gives me the spiritual air I breathe. Thinking through with 'her' what karma has woven through us over the centuries gives light of day to my soul. Let 'her' see the manner in which I live with her in this way. I must hold fast to these great connections in my soul, so that I can live with those things which move her in the realm of time. For the being who is no longer embodied, those temporal things which come up to him from those who are close to him on earth, enabling him to share in their lives, are like the objects in a room for one who is living. The latter cannot see these objects, however close they may be, unless the light of the sun shines into the room. In the spiritual world, this sunlight is provided by insight into the great spiritual connections. In earthly life one might have the perspective even as an older person of a few decades. Out of the body, one must direct the gaze of the soul across centuries. And this gaze across the centuries must be illuminated by the understanding which one has been able to acquire through contemplating ideas of how things relate to one another in the greater dimension of the spirit. I must constantly bring to life such thoughts in my soul. In the physical body, the memory enables one to reach a thought that one has once had. In the life of the spirit, one has constantly to re-enliven the thought with one's own life of soul, just as, in life on earth, the physical body must constantly breathe in fresh air. Thus it is also good when tried and tested thoughts keep coming up from those who are still living in the body.

41. Message of 23 March 1918

[Berlin] 23 March 1918 [r]

It was from the East, then, too, that the storm came, when a Christian impulse had to be pushed back, which was not yet to begin to work in Europe. The human souls in the East were quite different from those in the rest of Europe. Ninth century. 'She' said: 'The Easterners will mature later. They may not yet cause a disturbance in our circles.' 'She' stood at my side in those days and believed that the development of Christianity had to go through several phases in the course of time. We acted accordingly. The thought was alive in my soul: 'Through "*her*" you must yourself awaken'. When I *now* breathe in 'her' thoughts, *this* thought always returns to my soul. Thus the old bonds are renewed, which were so firmly tied then at the time when Europe's destiny was foreordained.

In 1914 we confronted the effects in the East of what had been done in the ninth century. 'She' stood beside me in July when my soul was in turmoil with the things that came from the East. Ever since the Romans, we have been in this turmoil. The bora, which came from the mountains of Montenegro, and took hold of the ship, is an image of that turmoil. I wrote to 'her' at the time: 'The ship is keeling over'. The whirlwind came in 1914 also—I was surrounded by people who stood in the whirlwind. The years that followed enabled me to reach the understanding which 'she' had prepared for me and which I was only unable to see through because of the obstruction of the earthly body. 'She' supported my thoughts that renewed our karmic bond. Now 'she' is my guardian on the physical plane, that takes its toll on 'her' health. But that is because 'she' must help to bear a part of my destiny.

'She' is concerned about 'El'. She does well if she asks herself how can 'El' be helped out of difficulty. 'El's' spiritual nature was surrounded by all that had to come from family karma because this family karma was so closely bound up with world karma. Thus 'El' had much that was unconsciously at work in her soul which would not permit her to come to full self-consciousness. She felt herself *at the same time* both inside and outside the family. Through all this, 'El' will find 'her'. Since the beginning of the twentieth century there was so much that had to be readjusted in the way that we stood within the common destiny. 'El's' character, too, had to undergo a metamorphosis. She had to be tested. 'She' needs only to think that much will only come to fruition in the course of time. If one strives to do what is right, then in this doing what is right one should have a feeling of sureness, for it is often only very much later that it becomes apparent that one has acted rightly, when things have matured in the course of time. Let 'her' feel in her present physical weakness how strong 'she' actually is. My soul can sense this. The physical weakness comes from the resistance to the demands of the spirit.

> Out of obstruction the spirit seeks
> For strong supports, which may bear it
> As in the dawning, the light reveals itself
> As the bearer of the forces of destiny.
> With spiritual bonds, both here and there
> We shall strive together
> To seek both now and ever more
> The meaning in true life.

There is much on earth today which is going into the twilight. Human beings will not desire the light until they recognize that it is the dawning which surrounds them. The storms are still coming from the East, which came in 1914. I now recognize what was meant then with the reference to the 'Folk Spirit'. It was to be found in the storm. And the storm was blowing through my soul. That is how 'she' saw me in the difficult days when decisions had to be made. She never failed then in the days of disappointment to keep alive in me a consciousness of the 'Folk Spirit'. My bodily nature put obstacles in my path. My conceptual understanding could not grasp what was going on in my soul. 'She' 'kept watch' over me then. In those days she truly learned to 'keep watch'. If 'she' can remain wakeful, then the good will come about in many areas. The 'good' is not always what seems to be so from close to. Let her in no circumstances be anxious whether this or that is done rightly or not: wait and see how circumstances turn out; they will reveal what one should do under given circumstances.

Now the matter of L. is coming up. That is something that has to do with many things at the present time which indicate the prevailing twilight. It is no individual case. Those who think like this benighted soul are obsessed with what is destined for ruin. Everything must be done to prevent others being confused by them. When the crisis broke, many things came about because of the baleful influence these people had on others. We were karmically linked with many such people, and some of the things that we have now had to deal with were there to enable us to loosen our karmic ties to them. We must become free of them until, in the next incarnation, we are in a position to enable others also to come to a right judgement of them. Such people are 'blind in soul' for the new things that are to come. What dulls their spiritual sight is the fact that their bodily nature bears within it the very spirit which must now be left behind. They bear the stamp of the spirit which should only have held sway until the seventeenth century. The facts need to be made clear about the being of such people. This will prove to be a difficult earthly task. It is from the spiritual world that the battle is to be waged against *this* spirit. Only when this spirit is vanquished will it become clear how it releases its hold on those people over whom it had gained power through their vanity and ambition. The consequences will be different to what many people imagine. Circumstances will be such that many people will be unable to feel vain and conceited about what they would like to. Their pride will then be transformed into another quality. They will be neurasthenics of a particular type. They will be unable to deal with either themselves or the world. They will become a nuisance in the sense that many will consider them very 'talented' on account of their other qualities. But in reality they will be 'imbeciles'. They will be 'imbeciles' in the same sense as we used it in our earthly conversations about a person who was considered by many to be 'very talented'. It is, in fact, just this kind of imbecility which makes it possible to be possessed by another spirit.

Spiritual people often have difficulty forming a conscious judgement about what lies in their soul. This is something my soul can vouch for, since I suffered in the later years from being unable to judge what was going on inside me. It wanted to come to the surface, and could not. But among those who came to false conclusions about me were those who could easily form a judgement because spirituality was remote from their thoughts, and they succumbed to the belief that judgements that had their origin elsewhere were in fact *their own*. Yet I was often obliged by karma to come together with just such people. For their way of thinking is a continuation of what began to develop in the ninth century. Such people are not familiar with Europe because they have been unable to penetrate through from the superficial layer of circumstances which has developed since the ninth century to the layer beneath which had, at that time, to be placed in a state of dormancy, but which must *now* bring its powers to the surface.

The Christ impulse must now take into itself those qualities which it then had to lay aside for about a millennium owing to the circumstances prevailing in Europe. The 'old man' says: Of all the things that filled my soul in my last earthly life, the most important to me now is the sense of certainty which enabled me to feel sure of myself in certain matters. For everything else on earth is taking on new forms now, and one can only carry on into the next life what is founded on this sense of certainty in the individual personality. Speaking in this way, the 'old man' is listening to what I bring to his soul out of spiritual science. And because he is a 'strong force', it is important that [this] can be brought to him. From previous incarnations he still bears within him something of a Christianity which is not so remote from the multiplicity of spiritual beings as the Christianity which had to be brought to the West in the ninth century, and which even led to the belief in the multiplicity of spiritual beings being condemned as heresy. In the future, however, a human being was no longer to wish to establish an immediate relationship with the 'highest Godhead'; he was to learn that there are many spirits in hierarchical order, for if he did not do so this very 'God consciousness' would make him proud. In centuries gone by there was no alternative but for human beings to imbue themselves with this 'one God consciousness'; they would otherwise not have been able to develop sufficient strength of ego. This may, however, no longer continue without itself becoming a source of pride. Human beings do not know what makes them proud. But this is how it happens.

We may not approach the East with purely economic thinking;

we have to think in such a way that the East can reach a spiritual understanding of the Middle European. Otherwise 'the Beast' will be unable to spiritualize itself. The brutality which is now emerging in the East is only the fearsome shadow cast by a light which would work its way through the darkness. We need to bear the thought within us: in the East many people are 'waiting' who must be 'found', for they would be able to 'understand' if one spoke to them in the right way. Any attempt to reach an understanding with those 'people of the East' who have become 'western' is futile. The 'West' corrupts these people, since they eradicate their own being when they take into themselves the 'West'.

42. Message of 22 April 1918

[Berlin] 22 April 1918 [r]

'El' has developed the right mood in herself. When she strives to be inwardly calm and allows what is happening to pass by her like the events of the outer world, she will find a way through the difficulties that lie before her. She is helping to bear the family karma—it all belongs together—and Uomi, who once approached us, has now attuned himself again. He will be relieved by much of what now must be borne. We must become free of our connections with certain souls with whom we were only to go a portion of the way. By means of his peculiar destiny U. has connected us with them. But he is becoming free. His task was merely to build a bridge to the others. He will find his redemption in our sphere. It now seems that I will shortly be able to see the whole of this in context with the eye of my soul.

It is always a great help to me when 'she' and 'it' can send their thoughts together as well as they do now. These thoughts are borne to me by a deep understanding, and they have the necessary warmth.

The general situation on earth must develop in such a way that people can see: things cannot go on like this; we have simply not seen what is most necessary.

One thing stands now before the eye of my soul. After Nicholas the process of development began which had its spiritual origin at that time, and which is now coming to its conclusion with material confusion. Nicholas had to be born again at the end of the epoch, which only began *after* his death. After this death humanity in Europe was so imbued with the seeds of materialism that one was obliged to give it what it unconsciously wished for: the soul without the spirit. Nicholas would not have permitted this. Look at my karma. Nicholas died and was born again in an age that was not connected with his innermost being. He was thrown together with people who were not with him before 867, who indeed fought against him at that time. Now here they were again. He was among them, but he was as isolated as he was on the ships in 1896. But he knew only of the external world that was not his inner world; he had his inner being, but he knew it not. He could feel it in the natural beauty of the North, in the pictures of Sicily. What my soul at that time could not see I can now see in retrospect. For after that 'she' did those things which proved to be my resurrection, and whose fruits I now have, I have them for the new time which is to come. For the 'spirit' must once more be recognized by humanity, but suffering is still to come on the earth: much suffering. For people must recognize that they have come to an impasse. My soul had to feel that impasse. In those days there stood before my soul: the Beast; the Beast. Now I can see: the spirit was lost. What is alive in the purely material development is: the Beast, the Beast. 'She' must think all this through. For my soul must think this with 'her'.

Already in 865 'she' was the element around me which represented the 'spirit'. She made me prick up my 'spiritual ear' at the time to the fact that it did not wish to hear 'quite rightly' that 'spirit' was evil and made one proud. What later caused me so much suffering was that in me which at the time was full of the opinion: 'the spirit makes one evil'. Then came Nicholas's soul development after death. This soul walked with 'her' in the spirit. But the ordinary karma had not been fulfilled. Uomi had to keep the connection alive on this side. He kept the balance on both sides, but then he was able to come through. He penetrated into my consciousness. And after the resurrection, he gave me a 'push towards the spirit'.

In doing so, he will ripen towards his own redemption. Thus only was it possible to bring our personal karma into harmony with the karma that we have by virtue of being placed in the world. It was as if the family was on an island; surrounded by the surging waves of the world. 'She' was already more inclined towards the 'island', while I was still being swirled about by the waves.

The image of the coast of Dalmatia, where the ship is being tossed about between East and West, stands before my soul.

'El' was drawn into the observation of all this while young, and having a sound understanding. She must work through to *herself* in all this: in doing so she can become very capable. To be wakeful is worth a great deal. My soul is now so close to them all.

My soul could not put into words what it felt in 1914; it could not even put it into words before my death on earth. What later happened already then cast its mirror image in my soul. The confusion which now reigns on the earth was present then in my soul as a reflection. But no more could be said to me than: 'there will be setbacks'. I could not have endured any more without the will-power in my physical body at that time being completely paralysed. Look at Austria now; read what it says in my letters. The written text says something quite different. But this came as a reflection of what later was to come about. It is all now much clearer to the eye of my soul. If I had had this vision then, what would have happened to my will power? I could not have endured *being obliged* to *act* in the face of what was to come. I would have frozen, and what *had to be done* was, after all, a *necessity*. Down below, it is quite rightly being said to people: history is being dreamt, indeed, to some extent, even being slept through. My soul had to dream along with this dream until its earthly end. But this dream must not go on being dreamt on the earth. And I was also not permitted to go on dreaming it. So I had to pass quickly through my death on earth, which had, after all, long been in preparation. And yet: everything that has been prepared for me here would not have been possible without my swift death.

'It' was instrumental in many things. All this will bear fruit. But we must find the strength to be able to consider those things which have no future as just that. Be awake to what in the present bears the future within it.

43. Message of 14 May 1918

[Berlin] 14 May 1918 [r]

It is often granted to me now to be around 'her'—when 'her' thoughts go to me; recently I have also been able to weave around

'El' a good deal—one can do so from here when thoughts encounter each other; there is then a kind of intertwining of the thoughts from here and from there. Unfortunately, 'El' has thoughts which are not sufficiently calm; often questioning thoughts. Then it is more difficult to be with her. I can now see the karmic connection with 'El' more clearly, although there is still much in it which is obscure to me. Two incarnations ago, she was connected with us. But at that time she saw a great deal of the world which is now creating turbulence within her. She got to know many people then who were demonic. That made it so difficult for her now to establish straightforward relationships with the people who crossed her path. The people whom she encountered unconsciously always remind her of spiritually opaque situations. It will be possible that I can remain close enough to her thoughts to lead her to clarity. In such special tasks, we can also strengthen our forces for the greater tasks. But there are so many people now incarnated, and some already excarnated, who are will-o'-the-wisps. People who unconsciously and obscurely remind each other of demonic workings. And these memories clothe themselves among those who are alive on earth in materialistic ideas; among those who have died, they appear as shadow images. Both these work together to lead humanity now into an impasse. I can experience things very clearly when I can unite myself with 'her' thoughts. For they are straight, definite, energetic thoughts. One can hold on to them as if they were rods. I can feel how much is being said about me in many circles. People are indulging in thoughts which are supposed to clear the others of blame. When that happens, then I seek for 'her' rods to hold on to. Let people say that I was hasty in July and August of 1914—without this hastiness, there would have been general confusion. However much I was personally affected—the haste came not from me but from the confusion, in which the thoughts of the others worked.

I can see this clearly now. One could have delayed the march of events, but not prevented it. In my situation, however, I was not permitted to delay events. A world historical karma has been at work since September 1914 that could not come to play without what I had done preceding it. Now people should be in a position to see that the forces of the spirit must be taken up by souls on earth. But they will not see this for a long time yet. They will have to learn from the sad course of events.

I am only present at the anthroposophical lectures when 'she' is, I cannot do so otherwise—but the content streams up to me all the same. Knowing the content and being present are two different things. I can be there when I can take hold of these rods. Then I have not only the content, but also the strengthening of soul. 'She' simply belongs to me—that has been decided since the ninth century. Rasputin has become apparent to me. His is one of the most complicated souls. Scarcely a human soul at all. Always with Ahriman. But never dependent on him, rather exploiting his forces. The forces he bears within him are almost exclusively forces which belong in earlier centuries of earth development. He has a terrible desire in him for reincarnation. One cannot understand him at all when one has the powers of memory in the spirit land that I have. One can only behold him. What clings to him spiritually is great. It sometimes appears as if he is split into many beings who all strive greedily for incarnation. He is very different in his spiritual form from other excarnated beings.

It is granted to me to spend a good deal of time with the 'old man'. He is interested in what I can tell him of spiritual science. He transforms this into mathematical guidelines. Some things become clearer also to me in this way.

Let 'her' sometimes become quite still inside, as if she would free herself from her present thoughts—and listen inwardly—I will then try to be in 'her' thoughts. Many things will have to be decided in this way.

The conversation on what had to do with me came through to me. I was there. It is good that such things are attended to consciously. Even though it is not yet time to act, the thoughts that one now has will be useful in the future.

Heavy clouds are gathering in the South. The East remains obscure for earthly vision. To spiritual sight it is clear. For me in particular. For what is now happening is a direct consequence of what began in the ninth century. The people of the East are conserving their forces for the future. Such forces, which are being conserved for the future, work in the present as a very spiritual element. But this spirituality reveals itself as if through a mask. It appears chaotic; but in the chaos there are life forces which are very effective even now. In this East there will be people one day who will speak a very particular language. People will believe they are speaking of earthly matters; but in reality, they will be speaking of spiritual matters. And one ought to be able to understand them in the rest of Europe. But this will require goodwill. One will have no longer to be bound by words. One will have to learn no longer to listen to what people are saying, but rather to be attentive to what people are. The time is coming in which one will have to learn to distinguish whether it is someone from the East or someone from the West who says something. Though they may be saying the same thing, it will, in fact, be quite different. One will have to learn to understand not the words, but the people. I must live in such thoughts now; for the next earthly life will give me the task of saying to people: look at what you are, do not merely listen to what you are saying. 'She' has gone through a great deal in her life in order to be able to stand by me in such a task. Spiritual science is now being heard by many an ear which cannot rightly hear; but there are souls among these who 'experience' what they do not 'hear' due to the background noise of daily life.

Nevertheless, much will be audible within this background noise for those who are nearby, which requires wakefulness. 'El's' illness has also given me the opportunity of weaving in her thoughts.

44. Message of 24 May 1918

[Berlin] 24 May 1918 [r]

The power of the words which 'she' allows me to experience with 'her' enables me to find my way to the others who belong to us: their hearts are beset by deep anxiety. But I must be with them in this, for their hearts must find the strength to live with the circumstances on earth in such a way that they see them with earthly eyes; what this seeing can bring about in their hearts will create the foundation for our working together in the task we have before us. One must learn from one's suffering. You permit me by means of these letters to look back on the earthly life gone by. In doing so thoughts arise in my soul that our karma has made it possible for us to live in close communion of soul. We are very close. Thoughts which are now becoming feelings in 'El': these are thoughts that my own 'I' had several years ago. In the depths of her soul, 'El' is now thinking much that I also thought years ago. At that time, she did not think as I did. Behind the karma which she is now living through lies a much deeper one. This says: she must find her way to my soul so that she can join those who will be working with me later. Time lay between me and her. However, the separation brought about by this time will be overcome. There are thoughts in the spiritual world order which have to find their way through to us.

But we must also work our way towards these thoughts. There is always something like a veil between the human being and the truth: many an apparently insignificant outer event in life is symbolic of this. I stood before the Tsar. Before the representative of the power which after the ninth century had to be confined to the East. I was placed there in the physical body with the painting that has me speak words to do with the opposition of West and East. Words whose origin in thought went back hundreds of years before my birth this time; I spoke. The words which I spoke were a veil. For there was a feud between me and the Tsar. I had to throw down 'the gauntlet'.

The soul can learn so much when it can see the truth through the veils. I have a great deal still to do in order to place the truth of Europe before my soul. And yet it must be so. Let 'her' read aloud a good deal from the cycle on the Folk Souls. Where Russia is mentioned. These thoughts help to crystallize what has come before my soul from the depths of the riddle of the being of the world.

'It' should frequently read lectures about death and rebirth. Thus complementing each other we can all work together. I can then also bring many thoughts to the 'old man' who transforms them into mathematics. He is now coming to a karmic connection with 'El'. But this does not yet stand clearly before our souls. It goes back to an incarnation before the last one.

Now there are thoughts coming which are flowing randomly. One cannot gain control of them so that they can be united with one's soul. I am now more often able to be with us all. When I call to life the memory of an object which is in one of 'her' rooms, it is quite easy now. The hand of the 'old man' is now such an object. And a couple of times I was able to be there because during the reading aloud of the passage with the picture before the Tsar my memory led me to the picture in 'her' room.

It is as if many a suffering we have been through now wishes to give form intensively to the thoughts we think together. People on earth must learn from events, that thoughts are facts. Very subtly I am becoming aware of something now—though it is still unclear—which requires 'wakefulness'.

During my journeys on earth, I came across many images of the world. Those which I am able to re-enliven in my memory provide a background for what must now become thoughts in my soul. I looked into nature. Nature gave me access in my soul to much that I was unable to reach with my understanding. My soul had to understand a great deal without the use of my powers of reason; for it had to lead me to take action. What I had to do in 1914 could not merely be thought out in the way one is led to think by earthly conditions. My letters of the end of August and the beginning of September stand before my soul. They direct the gaze of my soul in that time to my unconscious. It was looking for the right way. Something is expressed in earthly terms in these letters which is quite different from this perspective. Not on my account, but to avoid people on earth getting the wrong idea about important things, let them be destroyed. Also what I wrote to 'El'. Let 'her' decide what should be destroyed.

In *this matter* let 'her' think only the cause. Then other influences will not disturb the thoughts which I 'share with "her"'. In *this matter* they should not be present, however well intentioned. A picture of what happened in 1914 will be needed by humanity when the time comes. People will say incorrect things about this time as never before. The truth will also be very difficult to understand. Much had to be done then about which, even though it was quite right in the context of human development, many people said quite wrong things at the time, and about which they are even now not only saying but also thinking wrong things, since they know no better.

Rasputin with demons around him. He is filled with desire for a swift reincarnation. He wishes at first to appear somewhere in the West, in order to drive out demonic powers with demonic powers. There are so many supra-animal elements to this human being. People on earth ought to strive to decipher the riddles of such elemental forces, rather than merely passing judgement on them out of 'old concepts'. Soon other demons will appear as 'incarnated human beings' in the company of this peculiar being. While he was still on earth, he said to many people: I let the god in me speak. He uttered quite rightly what he felt, but he did not recognize that what spoke in him was sometimes an eastern spirit of progress, and sometimes a terribly ahrimanic being. There are many in his retinue who, since 1879 have had to oppose the forces of Michael. He is a spirit of denial, but also a spirit out of whose denials will come affirmations for humanity.

In Central Europe questionable spirits are weaving evil threads. These threads will become entangled. Care must be taken that at least a few heads remain clear. They must preserve their clarity for later times.

45. Message of 22 June 1918

[Berlin] 22 June 1918 [r]

My thoughts are seeking yours: 'hers', 'his', and 'El's'. Trouble lies ahead which would be a burden to my soul if I were not able to see it in the light of spiritual science, and to see in everything a higher purpose. While I was on earth, it was difficult for me to go along with all that had been determined for 'El'; had I not met with spiritual science, I could now still only feel that I had been right then, and that all this should not have come about. Knowledge of the spiritual world has enabled me to see that these karmically determined personal experiences are connected with the way in which we are placed within the context of the unfolding of world history. At the turn of the century Uomi announced himself. This being was to be the mediator between us and the other individualities from whom we were to become free in this incarnation. In this manner U. will also attain his freedom. He is also familiar with the demonic world which played into the sphere of our life through 'El's' experiences. What 'El' did then kept demonic beings at bay. For I was to remain on course. I was not to be drawn away too early from the ahrimanic powers to which I was connected by my karma. I was to liberate myself after death. Had it been so that I was to become free while still 'in the body', then this could only have happened unconsciously. And then the full extent of the freedom would not have been there for the task that is to come to blossom in the next life. But the fact that everything came about as it did unites me in thought with you. And so I can see that the events are 'right' even though much will follow that will cause anxiety and disquiet. Let 'her' know that I am with 'her' in what she does, and that *now* she cannot do otherwise. I shall send strength into 'El's' thoughts, so that their restricted point of view can be broadened. 'El' indulges in the world of feelings; she thinks too little, and yet believes that she is thinking a great deal because she takes her dark feelings for thoughts. 'El' must go through severe trials. But as a soul she will gain much from this. Her soul life has plunged deeply into the world of mere feelings. And she must become free from this. She should learn to cultivate interests other than personal ones. She shows so little interest in things which are not connected with her personal interests. Perhaps this is not quite right from the perspective of the physical world but from the perspective of the spiritual world, it is right. But, in overcoming her life of feeling, 'El' will completely unite her karma with ours, for she belongs to the task we have in the next life.

Demonic beings are now also very active in world karma. Rasputin is seeking for a new manifestation on earth. He will appear in many forms, and ahrimanic powers are closely connected with his desire for earthly existence. Keep alert for many things that wish to take a hand in world events from this side, too. They will appear in great events; but they will also be apparent in some things which do not seem significant, but are nevertheless symptoms. The events of the ninth century are now passing in their own peculiar way into the sphere of existence in which they express their effects on the earth as if in reverse. In the ninth century we pushed back to the East what was of no use for the West and Central Europe. But it continued to live in the East. Since then, it has lived in the souls of the people of the East, but now it is disengaging from the people, and is becoming like an auric cloud rolling from East to West. What is thus rolling like an auric cloud across Europe from the East during the course of the twentieth century will take shape at the end of the century in such a way that it will be our task to take hold of it. Humanity is being prepared more and more for the realization that one cannot be happy with what is to be found solely on the physical plane, though everyone is seeking for it there. People will have to cease looking for this happiness and will have to realize that what comes from the spiritual world must flow into everything that the human being experiences on the earth. It is only the combination of earthly and spiritual experience which will produce what is desirable for humanity. But this cannot be made clear to the human being of today. And our task will be concerned with acquiring the forces by means of which the interrelationship of spirit and body can be made clear in social and political life as well. It will be the opposite task from the one we had in the ninth century.

It is possible for me to be with 'her' a good deal now. When 'she' copies out my letters. And also when she is reading aloud.

Things will soon improve for 'it'. Over the years, 'it' has had experiences in the depths of 'it's' soul which will find expression in this way. 'It' has dealt with these experiences subconsciously. From there they are penetrating into consciousness, and are having their effect on the organism. 'It' needs only to keep really calm and to think frequently: things are moving in the calmness of my soul which will one day permit me to be of service in the task.

'El' strives impetuously towards everything which she wishes for, but finds she is nevertheless too weak. She must constantly strive to find herself. But it is hard to find oneself if one is too often preoccupied only with oneself. Nevertheless, much has flooded into her soul that has been a school for her, and which will raise her up beyond purely personal experience to experiences which are generally human. She has connected herself with a life situation which she cannot yet penetrate with her consciousness. She has been in it with a dulled consciousness. But she will still have to understand what she has been through.

She will have to learn from everything how powers can be released which will enable her to take her place within the task. Her soul is presently experiencing much that her 'I' will gradually have to take hold of. The human being has experiences which can only be understood when one is in a position to see them as a revelation of the forces of destiny working in the spirit. Such experiences are often the most painful, and yet also the most necessary. Such truths are as if written in letters of brass in the spiritual tablets which are gradually revealing themselves to me as fruits of my own sufferings which were imposed on me in the physical body. My power of thinking is gaining strength now in the memories which my soul reveals to me of everything which 'she' brought to me and experienced with me. What comes to mind now of my travels, my soul had already described then while I was in the physical body, but in such a way that it was not quite rightly united with my consciousness. Only now does my consciousness correctly embrace what my soul described at that time. My soul beheld the spiritual auras of the landscapes infused with their elemental beings; this soul described them, and when these descriptions reach me now, I can experience consciously what then presented itself unconsciously to my soul. Through these unconscious experiences Uomi made his way to us. 'She' sensed that something spiritual wanted to come into our sphere of life, and 'she' prepared a path for this spirit into conciousness. That was my spiritual rebirth. 'She' had understood my soul; 'I' was unable to understand my own soul because my 'I' was obliged by the karma of Europe to attend to so many things from which my soul would gradually have to liberate itself. In this incarnation which has just gone by, my soul had to take a different path from my 'I'. When the human being is in the physical body the 'I' is much closer to the physical world than to the soul. And so it is also with 'El'. Her soul can scarcely reach her 'I' at all. This 'I' reflects a life to her of which the soul can only retain the fruits for the spiritual world. According to a necessary, but painful, law, many things are experienced as pain in the physical body which can later work as a guiding light in the life outside the body. 'El' is now making her way to 'her'; I also went on this way. Only 'it' had trod this path before this last incarnation. 'She' is our gatherer.

My 'I' now yearns to follow the further course of earthly events through 'her' wakeful thoughts.

46. Message of 7 July 1918

[Berlin] 7 July 1918 [r]

These 'dark shadows' which affect 'her' mood of soul: they now speak to my soul of the consequences of days long gone by. They have to do with karmic relationships. It is not yet clear where the causes of these shadows have their origin in days long gone by. Much can be explained when one can see through to the origin of these causes. But these 'shadows' are also extending their influence in another way. There is a certain something in 'her' soul. At that time 'she' unconsciously 'gazed' deep into my soul, and what came to me through 'her' was, seen externally, rather like anxiety. In reality, seen from the point of view of the spirit, it was something different. It was a resolve which 'she' had to come to for karmic reasons. She had to come to my aid so that my soul could find 'the path of the spirit' in our later time together. 'The spirit wishes to return to him.' These were the words of 'her' soul in the unconscious. And 'she' sensed this call, but at that time through the soul mood of the 'dark shadows', she could only experience it as if through a veil. I was in danger. There would have been terrible consequences for my latest time on earth if 'she' had not cleared the path to the spirit for me. Moreover, together with 'her' I had to remain on the path to the spirit.

All this she then sensed unconsciously without thinking it consciously. In her subconscious, 'she' could feel the approach of a catastrophe for me. 'She' had the unconscious desire to turn this aside. My own soul could also unconsciously experience something of all this; it was reflected into my consciousness in the feeling: I can only be happy with 'her'. This meant at the same time that I had to avert a catastrophe through 'her'. Thus we came through a difficult moment in the course of our lives at that time. Let 'her' think with me now that we were both called upon at that time to plant important seeds for the future. 'She' was of course only later able to carry out what, at that time, gathered like a nightmare over 'her' soul; but 'she' did carry it out. A karma which would otherwise have taken a very different course was thus transformed in a very positive way.

But such a transformation always results in shocks. 'El' was affected by these shocks. Affected, however, only because it lay in her karma to be so. But my soul will find strengthening thoughts for 'El's' soul in the very fact that I am now able to see such connections. It is 'good in the right sense of the word' that 'she' thinks about such things on earth, and my soul does so in the spirit. In 'her' wakefulness, 'she' will find what is right. We still have many a knot to unravel.

From a field of spirit which was hitherto unknown to me, the old question appears before my soul in a new light. The question: how am I situated in the course of world events. Now the name and the words of the 'old man' have been uttered to the German people. His soul willed it so. These things are all connected. How they are connected I will not see until later. A chaos is brewing up, but behind the chaos there is spiritual light. Yet human beings are weak in their will. Ahriman is strongly active.

His power can now only be weakened by the knowledge: the physical misery that is spreading must help us become aware of our spiritual lack. Physical distress must be seen as the lesser of two evils: the consequential evil which is to take away the evil that caused it.

47. Message of 15 July 1918

[Berlin] 15 July 1918 [r]

In the ninth century 'she' is by my side. She had a picture of what was to come. It was incumbent upon my soul to push the knowledge of the spirit to the East and to detach the impulse of faith from the impulse of knowledge of Christianity for Europe. At that time the people of Europe had not yet matured to spirit cognition. Yet at the same time they were not suited to the instinctive life of faith of the people of the East. Over the heads of the latter there was preserved a gnosis in the form of rigid dogmas and Mystery rites which they did not understand. It was the orthodox teaching of the East. Some of the ancient knowledge of humanity was preserved in it. But this knowledge was not intended to penetrate to the people themselves in the East. It was intended to float above them like a cloud. Their childlike imagining was to develop further under this cloud. This was their preparation for the future. In Europe, however, from the ninth to the twentieth century knowledge of the material laws of the world was to spread. It was a mighty ahrimanic wave that was to wash over Europe in that way. So it was necessary to strongly anchor human hearts in the mere power of faith in order that the connection with the spiritual would not be lost altogether. But up to the nineteenth century the wave of materialism increasingly grew in force. 'Believing' in the spiritual was condemned to untruthfulness. We were placed into this current in the nineteenth century. 'She' carried in her heart the unconscious conviction which had remained with 'her' from her life in the ninth century. 'She' had something in 'her' innermost being which said to 'her': things cannot go on like this if earthly civilization is not to lose all connection with the spiritual. We had found each other again in this nineteenth century. The forces of life from the ninth century had led us to each other. But our mutual understanding had to be striven for. The 'old man' was at a high level spiritually. However, in his earthly life he was not able to free himself of the ahrimanic influences. My soul was placed by his side on account of being connected with him a long way back.

But this soul of mine did not find through him the spiritual in the realm of earth. This it was to find through 'her'. 'She' always felt this unconsciously. 'She' felt that something had to be brought to me without which I could not live. But 'she' became anxious about me because she saw me totally enmeshed in ahrimanic entanglements. Had I remained in there without connection to the spiritual a catastrophe would needs have befallen me. My physical body could not have resisted it. Because it had concealed within it the spiritual impulses of the earlier earthly life. They bore the desire to find the spirit again. But in all that surrounded me there was nothing that could let me find the spirit. Hence 'she' had to become anxious about me. That marked our life in many ways. 'Her' seeking for my way to the spirit; my difficulties in understanding what I actually wanted. My soul remained unsatisfied in the outer earthly life. At times I considered myself condemned to inactivity. Yet I would not have fared any differently under different outer conditions of life. Any situation would have left me unsatisfied; for I could only have been satisfied through the spirit coming closer. 'She' knew all that.

Where the unconscious holds sway to such an extent, demonic forces find easy access. That's how it came about that 'El' grew up in a spiritual sphere which introduced many a demonic element into her life. All this will be karmically compensated by future efforts. But we need to look at everything in utter wakefulness. There will be many a knot of destiny still to emerge. Due to the fact that Uomi's destiny has been tied up with ours for many ages we have to resolve many a matter by spiritual means. It is good that 'it' is so untouched by all that is ahrimanic in earthly existence. That's why the good spiritual powers are keeping close to 'it' and find in her a place of rest.

However, earthly destinies will continue to work confusion into my current thought streams for a long time yet. For I was solidly placed into these. 'She' will have to continue to mediate there. The earthly people of Europe have a lot to learn still from events. The people of the East have to learn from themselves.

The nature of events in Europe is such that people are placed in their midst without their inner soul destinies being connected with these events. The painful outer life runs its course as something that becomes more and more alien to the souls. But people will have to understand that this is the situation. People will have to find *themselves* through these events. They will have to learn to measure everything differently. They will also have to learn not to let things grow over their heads. At present events are taking their course, guided by the ahrimanic powers, and people do not understand this course, but allow themselves to be carried along. They do not wish to hear although they could only hear from the spirit now what it is that could guide them. They believe that it should be possible to solve the questions of the future in earthly institutions alone. However, now is the time when a wave of the spiritual will have to be incorporated into human affairs. The Anglo-American nature will misapprehend this spirit and fight against it. It will be given materialistic forms. That will be the part of the world which will become more and more soulless. Marcher's soul is coming increasingly close to me. It is also gaining ever greater clarity about what needs to happen. Many thoughts about future tasks are exchanged between my soul and the 'old man'.

48. Message of 26 July 1918

[Berlin] 28 July 1918 [r]

Two events are forcing themselves before the gaze of my soul. Between the two is my search for 'her' soul in this past earthly life. In the ninth century 'she' stood by my side, as a man, with the map of Europe in her mind. 'She' acted as counsellor. It was my task then to conceive of ways to separate the East from the West. Many people were involved in this separation. 'She' formed a view of all of these in 'her' mind. But in those days there was still a closeness to the spiritual world. One was aware of the comings and goings of spiritual beings. Yet the inhabitants of Central and Western Europe were striving away from the spiritual beings. Already at that time they needed to prepare for materialism. But for us in the ninth century there was a lot of directly perceptible spiritual influence. The 'counsellor' would often say then: 'The spirits will withdraw from Europe; but later on the Europeans will long for them. Without the spirits the Europeans will make their machines and their institutions. They will excel at that. But in doing so they will breed in their midst the western people who will drive ahrimanic culture to its highest peak and take their place.'

There was among those beings who communicated with us like human beings, but who did not incarnate as human beings, Uomi. The 'counsellor' said: 'He must not leave the Europeans' side, he will suffer greatly from the Europeans' contempt for the spirit. We must redeem him.' Then the centuries in which materialism spread more and more came over Europe. The spiritual essence of Odilie's stream survived only in a few individuals then. By then 'she' was in the spiritual world together with my soul. In my soul the bond was growing with a Europe that was becoming more and more ahrimanic. The 'counsellor' became 'guardian'. The 'guardian' knew my soul in his unconscious spiritual depths. The 'guardian' was put by my side in my new earthly life. Now the 'guardian' searched everwhere for ways of restoring my soul to the realm of the spirit. In my earthly life my gaze was at first directed to the physical world. Yet I strove towards the spirit in my innermost soul. Hence the world could give me nowhere what my soul longed for. I became involved in situations in the world into which I did not fit. My 'guardian's' inner gaze was directed at my soul, for ever feeling: What is all this to us? What are we doing among those people and in those situations, with everyone wearing masks. My soul consciously wanted to find its way into these circumstances; but my 'guardian' sensed something foreign in all the involvement with these affairs. Yet the purpose of it all was that we should find ourselves through that which was foreign to us.

Then, in 1914, 'her' guardianship had become significant. That is when everything happened which deeply affected European affairs. Then European karma, to which we had been so deeply connected since the ninth century, came to fulfilment. Then 'she' as 'guardian' became wholly filled with the thought that had unconsciously been forming within 'her' over decades. Then my soul became so deeply connected with events in Europe and at the same time so totally cut off from the people who were outwardly connected with those events. Then all her 'guardianship's power' came to my side. It was all so very intense since the future task was forcing its way into that life, the task which was being prepared by the momentous events of the present. The bond between 'her' soul and mine was already prepared at that time for the future, through the very way in which destiny had placed us into the present. All that had been forming in my life over many decades through 'her' was concentrated in this moment when 'she' stood face to face with this great turn in my destiny. Outer circumstances placed me into outer life events; but the 'inner man' was formed in my evolving relationship to 'her'.

Now the thoughts of my letters are coming before my spiritual gaze as true soul light. Nearly every sentence is now turning into something different from what it was when I wrote it down. The soul wrote words which consciousness understood in a far more external sense than the impulses emanating from the soul. The soul wanted to express in words a relationship of one thousand years; the consciousness of this earthly life could not yet understand what the soul sought to express in words. The consciousness was to learn from its own soul. 'Will this consciousness be able to learn from this soul?' is what my 'guardian' was unconsciously thinking anxiously. There was always this thought in the depths of my 'guardian's' soul: 'Will this consciousness be able to find this soul?' My soul was always a question to my 'guardian'. And the 'guardian' wondered: 'What do I love in this soul? There must emerge in this soul what I love in it.' This is what was speaking in my 'guardian's' depth of soul. Then my 'guardian' brought close to me that which taught my consciousness 'to find my soul'. Also the last years' great sufferings were only stages on the path of finding my soul through my consciousness.

The 'dream in Ragaz', 15 August 1884: my consciousness wrote it down so naïvely at that time. However, as early as three decades before the catastrophic events loosened my soul, in the eighth month of 1914, this soul already wanted to say to me: 'Look, I am forming pictures out of the most insignificant events from without your body'. My soul always followed its own paths beside my consciousness. But this soul let me write to my 'guardian'. He understood in our concealed love that he had to foresee that 'soul' which was bound to find the spirit. We were both as if homeless. Both in environments with which we could not quite cope. We had to search for our own selves within worlds that were so strange to us. And the dream itself was, despite its pictorial nature, a fundamental symbol for all the momentous events with which my soul was connected. At that time I jumped 'into the abyss' in my 'dream'; three decades later I did it in reality. Such connections exist; but human beings are not allowed to just simply understand them. The fact that they later experience in the tough school of life what has long taken place in the soul in pictures—prophetically—and cannot be understood: that is what the evolvement of the physical life is based on. In truth this physical life is dreamt; behind the scenery of one's life spiritual beings are bringing it forward in the manner destined for this life. Uomi ocaasionally allowed us some insight into these things; we were only allowed to understand him half-way.

49. Message from 2 August 1918

[Berlin] 2 August 1918 [r]

Retrospectives of this life which teach my soul how outer events demanded the inner spiritual light. The conditions of previous lives—they paved the way for everything. When the Michaelic times of the earth began my soul needed the 'guardian' who had acted as such for a long time. What does Michaelic times mean? It means: the spiritual light is shining over the earth, but in such a way that souls may only find it in freedom. If they themselves do not plant the longing for the spiritual into the physical forces of the body, the spiritual in them will turn into cleverness in the material sense, it refines the material forces of the body, and this then appears as intellect; it refines the forces of instincts and drives, and it will not become morality; it becomes calculated egotism instead of morality. When the spirit is striven for consciously the power of Michael will come to man in all the materialistic striving of the age. My 'guardian' unconsciously felt the power of Michael. This 'guardian' was led to me—destined by virtue of an ancient con-nectedness—in the years of Michael's descent. Our life together, our struggles, all our striving became a picture of Michael's Age. I was compelled to see a lot of things which the reason bestowed upon me by the earth could not comprehend; 'she' had to uncon-sciously always direct her 'guardian's' soul towards the radiance of Michael in order that we could become human beings who were seeking. For in this age of time nothing is bestowed upon man unless he is seeking. Michael is a comrade-in-arms who can accomplish a lot but who is not to make it easy for his gifts to reach mankind.

50. Message of 8 August 1918

Berlin, 8 August 1918 [r]

Soon after we found each other again she called up in my soul the thought structure of the world's spiritual evolution. I had to write down like a thought sketch what was, after all, connected with the innermost core of my soul. Then, some time later, 'her' efforts provided for me in concrete form what 'she' had previously called forth in the very depths of my soul as thought sketch and which had remained unconscious. Thus 'she' placed herself at my side with the spirit knowledge 'she' had brought forth from earlier earthly lives.

In the ninth century her role was more that of 'guardian' than that of 'counsellor'. In those times it was the need to establish the occidental Catholicism which compelled me to cast an ancient doctrine of the spirit into a form appropriate to the occident. However, 'she' kept watch so that I could find in a new form in the twentieth century what had been lost in the ninth century. From very far-off times we carried this knowledge through the ages. We had gained it from different methods of initiation. But we had allowed it to flow together in times long past. This thought sketch stands before me like the 'light of my soul'. It really was my 'I' which shone towards the meaning of this thought. Without my knowing it my soul was seeking the direction of this light with burning intensity.

Now it is comprehensible, 'her' question to me whether people's superficiality was not deeply unsatisfying. But I had to live in this superficiality. I had to pretend to myself that the superficial was not superficial. 'She' was frightened by the fact that I was living in an environment that was foreign to me and that there was something in me which secretly strove away from it but which I could not understand. It would have led to catastrophe if 'she' had not brought the knowledge of the spirit to me. But it was also necessary for me to be placed into the world where superficiality reigned. For I was connected with this world through the world karma of the ninth century. What I had to do in this world was a historical necessity. The germ of the spirit will have to be laid into this world in the future, too, until it can be found by those people who are willing to take it up.

A lot will have to be said still about everything that happened in

1914. How often I dwelled with those who have plunged from their height in Russia due do the events of that year. How little did my brain-bound intellect foresee what was in store for those with whom I spent time in earthly splendour. My soul is looking into the web of ahrimanic illusion I took for the truth in those days. Yet I did not even understand my own self at that time with my brain-bound intellect. Now my soul recognizes in all the words of the early letters unconscious inklings of understanding that 'she' was to be my 'guardian', that 'she' was to cause my soul to find itself. All I had to bear in the end in earthly pains, earthly disappointments and earthly fears: all that had to be confronted by the soul that had re-united with the spirit. The message from the spirit came to me. Already several decades ago the thought *sketch* rose up before me from the innermost depths of my soul. After all, all of this was within me. And yet my own earthly intellect which did not measure up to me caused me to say again and again in the last few months of my life: if only I could experience it, if only I had a little experience of the spirit. What there was within me, what out of my love for her I naïvely stammered in words, taking it to be my own thinking, the core of my soul: I wanted to have it from outside; yet I carried it within me with such certainty without ever knowing of it.

But let her know now that 'her' life work was built upon her knowledge of my soul which she had preserved from previous earthly lives; my soul which had been driven back to her in this life. And now, where my gaze reaches further back, beyond the first exchange of letters, I can see how I had been searching for 'her' even before meeting her in the physical body in this earthly life. The words 'now I surely have firm ground under my feet' and 'what results from losing one's inner hold and succumbing to self-doubt': now, from the perspective of the great connections of life, light is shed on to these words I wrote down from out of my brain-bound intellect without knowing that the substance of my soul's deeper forces was flowing through them. It was 'she' who caused them to emerge, dimly, in her role as my 'guardian' and who suffered much in life and wrestled to raise them into my soul's consciousness.

'It' was then bestowed upon us because 'it' was disposed to always retain a connection with the spiritual world and was there-fore able to transmit Uomi's messages to us. Uomi will now soon have found the redemption he is seeking.

Let all those who belong to me often send their thoughts to me as they are able to; then their thoughts are here and I am with them. We can best serve the world by seeking what is destined to us in our spirit-island-existence. For the world our task will be a new one. Thoughts will have to unite for this task. But what is also needed is that we do not allow ourselves to be confused by the stormy chaos of the world.

'El' will always be well advised to consult with me with regard to important feelings.

51. Note of Rudolf Steiner about the Message of 8 August 1918

All the details are of significance
1 November 1877: Germ of anthroposophical thinking.
10 August 1877: Announcement

52. Rudolf Steiner to Eliza von Moltke

Berlin, 12 August 1918

Dear Frau von Moltke!
Concerning Countess Bethusy's sickness I would like to confirm that this is connected with the events of 1914 as you suspected. I think that she will soon be completely recovered. It is probably not necessary to carry on endlessly with supplementary feeding, although the measures taken so far were excellent. In view of what one was able to observe during the countess's presence here, the course of events you described is not surprising. As a whole I would not be too worried about this patient in particular because her beautiful inner soul constitution makes her capable of overcoming many a thing that others would not overcome so easily.

I am glad that your other daughter [Else] is also better now. In the meantime her father's soul has affirmed quite strongly what I had already told you in relation to Frau Else. The soul is with you and it pleases him to dwell in the harmony of thinking between the three of you. 'It will give me especial pleasure to think in harmony with "her" in the near future; the time in which I once searched for "her" is now before me in perspective; dwelling in "her" thoughts I will gaze at this perspective.' That is now a *consistent* mood, with no details working into that mood yet. I hope that it will be possible for me in the near future to get through to you with what there is to be communicated. I am glad that the cycle of time devoted to reading the letters could be drawn to a close and hope it will be followed by a momentous development.

I will always be with you in my thoughts; you may be certain of that, and Frau Röchling will surely also hear from you.
With my best wishes,
Yours, Rudolf Steiner

53. Message for Eliza von Moltke

30 August 1918 [r]

How magnificently the painting of my soul life emerges as a whole as my soul is contemplating those last, deeply sorrowful years on earth, back to the time when it found the 'guardian' and 'counsellor' from the ninth century! In those last years 'she' stood by my soul, strengthening all that which had to be strengthened for this soul but could not be raised into thought by the physical body. Through 'her' my 'I' could retain what my own body could not take hold of. Thus it could turn into strength when the physical body was discarded, and enable my soul now to understand some of the 'why' of my last earthly life. That is when my 'I' had to be placed in the midst of the world-historical connections of Europe. It had to be related to people who had no real wish to know about these connections; these people were destined to detach themselves from my 'I' which was connected with them from earlier earthly lives. Then 'she' turned from 'counsellor' to 'guardian'. It is the light of knowledge, of sound self-knowledge, which now illumines my soul when I recognize from the letters how she placed herself in the midst of this mass of people as 'guardian'. It is the light of true self-knowledge which now illumines my soul when 'her' words from the early days resound so powerfully: 'What does that life of yours mean among those people?' There were many instances where I forced myself into non-comprehension, but this non-comprehension was only superficial. In the depths of my unconscious these words of warning fell on fertile ground. And the forces from earlier lives that enabled me to find 'her' also made it possible for the deeper layers of my soul to absorb the effects of her working by my side in this life. The outer course of my life was determined by the circumstances and the people around me. However, in looking back my soul now recognizes in the light of true self-knowledge how little was the strength that those circumstances and those people could afford me in order to really pursue the course of that life. That it could be pursued at all was made possible by 'her', through her soul's eye seeking to introduce into the outer life certain elements of that world which to the earth is supersensible. Without those elements my physical body would have been broken before it was allowed to break.

It is my task now—the task of my true self-knowledge—to search for the light and strength which comes from perceiving 'her' office of counsellor and guardian. In the same way in which one needs to nourish and clothe oneself on earth, so one needs to form one's soul body in this world here out of what flows from such true self-knowledge. And when I receive again and again the intuition of such self-knowledge, the strength to dwell with 'her' and 'it' and 'El' issues forth from my soul.

At present I am not to share in other endeavours of spiritual science on earth but solely in what 'she' is involved in. For spirit cognition is the binder, the spiritual bond between my soul and the 'guardian's', and that is why my soul should be attuned a lot in dwelling with her and with her efforts for spirit cognition. This is what holds our karma together. And that needs to be held together because it is the preparation for the future time on earth. However, 'she' should not neglect to direct her thinking to what is now hap-pening on earth. For it reaches my soul more easily when it has been transformed into 'her' thoughts. And in the near future there will be forces sent from here into earthly events as has already been begun. It will be difficult because even when 'the divine thoughts are sent to their earthly provenance', the 'earth does not want to accept these thoughts'. Hence these thoughts and influences will make many detours and meanderings; and much of this kind will look very different from what is imagined. This and that will happen and it will not appear as if it had been influenced by the soul world, and yet it will be so, for what has to happen will in many cases happen by way of detours.

I notice in 'El's' thoughts that she now comes close to me in soul. She is now able to think of me in a way that enables my soul to dwell in her thoughts enduringly. Thus I will be able to help 'El's' soul to find her way through the confusion which is still ahead of her. 'El' is karmically connected with me in such a way that her thinking of me will provide a lot of help for her at this time.

The possibility of looking into past times is the result of the letter retrospective. 'El' can be seen there in a certain context with Uomi. It was through her sister rather than through her that this connection was able to enter into our sphere.

Frequently searching in loneliness—an obscuring power—striving in the opposite direction. It makes many things invisible.

54. Message for Eliza von Moltke

11 October 1918 [r]

That my soul may bring the future before its gaze: that is my striving. For the task is there awaiting me; it must be understood. When 'she' unites herself with me in her thoughts my soul gains a lot of strength for directing itself at this very task for she is growing towards this task through our karma together. However, for that it is always necessary to look into the past, with clarity and without reservation. Through the circumstances of our lives in the ninth century the two of us, 'she' and 'my soul', were connected with Central Europe. However, 'my soul' not only had to connect itself with that which was passing in European history but also with all that which was emerging for the future. In the human environment in which my karma placed me through my profession and physical descent all thinking was focused on what was passing away. Then, towards the end of the seventies, there arose from the depths of the spiritual life, quite unconsciously, the impulse to 'search' for the being which spiritually belonged to me through karma: it was 'she'. It truly was an unconscious 'searching'.

My soul beholds this in utter clarity now. And this soul is looking back over all those years in which 'she' and 'I' were searching for that living connection in the spirit that had arisen between us through earlier struggles and manifold circumstances of life but had been obscured by the facts of the sense world.

This 'searching' was not yet completed when the great moment of suffering came to pass and 'she' was with me when Europe's destiny was placed upon my soul in the context of making a rapid decision. *That* created a strong connection between her soul and mine.

Then there arose the other time of suffering when I was removed from the context into which I had been placed through this incarnation just passed. However, it was *that* which guided my soul to the spirit and bonded it tightly to 'her' soul which was placed beside mine in the spirit. My body had to suffer because it still had to be part of the world from which the spirit wanted to remove me.

'It' grasped the supersensible connection in this incarnation; in that 'it' was helped by the U. individuality who is striving to fulfil its own life path of redemption by doing so. A certain amount of darkness through error is necessary at this time. But there is always some light in such darkness. The German people can only fulfil its mission through the spirit. Through the events of the ninth century and their repercussions during my last incarnation 'my soul' was bound up by deepest forces with the destiny of the German people. But this people was not on its own path. It was on a path imposed upon it. And because of all that it evolved on this imposed path there was only one route to salvation: 'military willing'. A soul as deeply connected with the German people as mine could not but turn to 'military willing'. For as a result of the imposed path this 'military willing' was the only thing suited to lead to the 'right' in the world context. However, now this 'military willing' was faced with an utterly obscured political willing.

My willing and that willing: it resulted in the tragedy to which my soul was bound to succumb. When the obscured willing removed me from these circumstances, the real outer decision was made. What happened subsequently and is happening now was preparing to happen since that point in time, and not before. When I was still living in my physical body I did not see the need for being thus removed; it made me suffer. Now I can see that it was necessary. In the light of everything I had come to believe through my previous and this last incarnation I felt my removal as devastating. But at the same time the spirit opened the door for me through which I could not enter fully until my physical sheath was no longer around me. But at the time when I collapsed in pain and suffering the spirit spoke in the hidden depths to the German people: *you* must not abandon me; but those who deem themselves its leaders know nothing of the thoughts I wish to bring to this people in the world context.

And while my soul was suffering from all that was happening in the physical world it decided for the spirit. However, those whose gaze was directed at the physical affairs did not want to be with me any longer. From that day onwards the path to the spirit was paved through 'my soul's' deep suffering. It is on this path that the task lies towards which all future thinking must be directed.

55. Two Further Messages for Eliza von Moltke

11 October 1918 [r]

My thoughts also strive towards 'El' in this way; to tell her—'El'— about how she has begun to work together for the future task by entrusting herself to a destiny which has brought her suffering.

Let her consider that in the experiencing of earthly destiny a connection to the spiritual can be made. Then the strength to bear it is given. Then one knows that the connection to the spirit is pre-pared through conscious bearing of pain. 'El' is destined to help us in our tasks. The path of suffering has led her back to us. Let her find strength in these thoughts. For that I often send my thoughts to her. And let 'her' be watchful. What was resolved in this regard still applies unchanged today. It must always be remembered that the spirit must always strive to reach human beings, even at this time, but that human beings are shutting themselves off from it. That is why the messages coming to earth from the spiritual realm espe-cially now are interpreted wrongly. What would be needed now is a *total* change of direction, a declaration of belief in the will of the spirit before the whole world would be needed, and all people are thinking about is how things might be achieved without turning to the spirit. A new order without the spirit can no longer be fruitful. It can only bring illusion and people should not seek illusion any longer.

Mankind is predestined to turn to the spirit now; it will work when humanity turns its consciousness towards it; humanity will fall into ever greater confusion if it denies the spirit. The spirit always works in the unseen; whoever is with the spirit knows this. It will be revealed when human beings seek Him [sic] in the unseen.

*

A strong impulse for knowledge has arisen for my soul from the return of thoughts I had addressed to 'her' in letters. It is, after all, the contemplation of self which is needed above all for spiritual progress. In the subconscious of my soul I was seeking for 'her' with all my powers of soul because I had tied the course of my life strongly to 'her' in earlier lives. It has been and continues to be the greatest help to my soul to have placed before my souls's eye that which was obscure in my soul in earthly life—struggling for words to express the deeper life connection—and is now illumined in the light of the spirit and irradiated by the thoughts which are coming from 'her'. From that will rise the strength I need for the future task. Already in the near future my soul will be involved from the realms of the spirit with many a thing that happens in the European context. If the influence of the spiritual on earth appears to be felt so little at this time it is because the spirit often has to work in ways which cannot be grasped in the physical world.

The present working of the spirit in Europe's destiny—its seeming ineffectiveness—is a consequence of the fact that many a thing is being prepared right now. The great calamity is still to yield its gift of blessing. I only grasped this necessity through my suffering, when the spirit had left my physical body. 'She' is my soul's 'guardian'. It was for 'her' that I needed to search in the seventies in order that my soul could find in the chaos of tense world affairs that position in the spiritual world which leads to the right task. Preparation for many a thing which is now coming to pass...

56. Message for Eliza von Moltke

14 December 1918 [r]

The transformation in the world of the senses is great; and my gaze is directed at 'her' and 'it' and 'El'—hard times may come over the sense world. But we should trust in the strength of the thoughts that connected us together and that were imbued with the essence of spirit understanding. Through this essence they will carry us over abysses and heights of destiny. It has often been placed before my soul since it left its body that the world I had to serve as a result of karma in my last incarnation was bound to run into confusion so that the fruitful new could emerge to take the place of the unfruitful old.

'She' clearly recognized the brittle nature of that which was old in so many places. My 'I' had to serve the old in my last incarnation. That was 'our' destiny. At a decisive time in world history my soul was standing between the representatives of what was old and decaying. The storm of the immediate future cast its shadow into this soul. My subconscious went on a very different path from the one my ordinary consciousness was allowed to follow due to the way I was placed into these events.

Spiritual science could not be heard when the 'dice were cast' but only when the 'dice had been cast'. Could things have taken a different turn ... that is what my 'I' sometimes wondered in earlier times; now it is long past asking such questions. It was my destiny to find spiritual science *wholly* only later. What lay before was the preparation. Only the suffering connected me so strongly to her soul that she became one with my soul. First in the subconscious, which was in truth with the German Folk Spirit, and then, when the physical sheath had dropped away, in the half-conscious. This consciousness was, after all, tied to a decaying outer world through karma. 'She' placed herself into this outer world with an impartial gaze. In doing so 'she' paved the way to the spirit for my subconscious. Uomi acted as mediator because he needed to strive for his own redemption. He is still having to find his way through the confusion that is taking the place of the old order and will create for the gullible and the illusionists new illusions to replace the old ones which were part of my outer world. For it is not a matter of replacing the old order with something different, and it is not a matter of different people occupying the positions of their predecessors, but a matter of finding the impulses for decisions in different recesses of the soul, from different sources of the spirit.

Human thinking has become like the working of a machine. Thus the impulse of destruction is carried into the world out of human heads. When my conscious 'I' had to put this machine in motion, an apparatus of destruction was put in operation. In this respect everything is different in its inner nature and essence from what it would appear to be from outside. However, even in the world of the sense-perceptible, the consciousness of what things are inwardly and in their essence should never be lost completely.

The 'truth' ought to be revealed to the world as soon as it is possible to do so. A lot of good fortune could arise from that. The effect will be that some people will have to understand in the end that they will have to *hear* differently. For in their souls people are now hearing everything as if through the clatter of the machines of this age. Ahriman-America should not have the only voice; Lucifer-Bolshevism should not be allowed to do the only deed. However, as no one knows any different from what the stupefying and spirit-alienating institutions of 'modern science' have been teaching people, a real 'enlightenment service' is needed above all else. A lot would be gained if a number of people were to admit to themselves that they cannot but commit wrong actions in the world if they apply what they owe to 'modern thinking' and were to realize that a new way of thinking had to be adopted. In the next few years only wrong can arise because people's heads are full of wrong. To adopt such thinking would be the right thinking and would be healing to the world to the degree in which there can be healing in the man-ifest outer world.

57. Message for Eliza von Moltke

[Dornach] before 27 January 1919 [r]

The soul sickness brought to me by my physical sheath before it was taken from me, was fear, fear of what the German people are witnessing now. It was a sickness of soul, as my mouth often expressed when others referred to my physical ailments. My unconscious was raging against my consciousness, demanding a solution to the riddle: why was I placed into the gruesome necessity of this age? How many people are saying now: Germany is to blame for this world war. To spiritual vision, which I am only able to apply now after the physical sheath has dropped away, the question is a very different one: could this catastrophe have been averted in the position into which my physical person had been placed by karma? My soul, unconsciously acting through the forces of the ninth cen-tury, was surrounded by personalities that understood nothing of what was happening around them. These personalities forced me to think many a thing consciously that my soul negated unconsciously. And 'she' nurtured the strength of the unconscious within me. After all, my soul was imbued with the impulses of the ninth century to the extent that it could perceive how what was good in these impulses were denied by a Europe that had turned materialistic. What is good cannot be developed by materialistic force and thinking but by the new spirit knowledge. My physical environment had no connection with this new spirit knowledge. It was only 'she' in my environment who stood for this over decades.

What clarity I have gained indeed through the retrospective afforded me my means of the letters through which 'she' continued her work on me. What these war events signify in relation to the necessities of historical evolution will only be be comprehended by a major part of humanity when it will be apparent what Europe is becoming under the influence of the West. Does not the outcome of the war show up the necessity of its outbreak? Austria, without which Germany, as it should be, is unthinkable, is now showing that the forces that ought to be holding it together are non-existent. These forces had been non-existent for a long time. Austria continued to exist, nonwithstanding the fact that it could not exist by its inner structure. Just as a dying man has to try and save himself by a last medicine, Austria tried to do so by the Serbian ultimatum. Was this good or bad? This question was often raised and continues to be asked. However, it was a question of necessity for Austria. And the way in which Austria fell shows that it was a necessity; it may be regretted that it was a necessity. It may equally be regretted that it [the ultimatum] had been sent off; but it cannot be denied that it was a matter of necessity. It may also be regretted that Germany did not protest more strongly against this ultimatum; but such protest would have been tantamount to a death sentence over Austria. That could have been executed by world history, but it could not be executed by a physical person who had been put in my position through destiny. Likewise, this person was not allowed to decide not to lead the war for Germany. Had it not been waged, Germany would have become by virtue of its impossible politics what it has become now by virtue of the unfortunate outcome of this war. Germany, as it was at the beginning of 1914 as a result of materialism, was an impossible construct. And because it was an impossible construct it brought forth the whole of the impossible politics of the Kaiser and others with whom I became involved on the physical plane through destiny. And thus this destiny brought it about that I actually had to wage war against German politics.

Rising up from my subconcious I felt: in actual fact my enemy in this hour of war is the Kaiser together with those who had been misguiding him for so long in his unfortunate political endeavour. German politics, which brought forth nothing to give Germany a content worthy of its people, produced a situation in which it was impermissible not to engage in war. For Germany had become similar to Austria. It had not built up the inner strength necessary for maintaining the structure of the empire. In both of these structures the spirit was urging towards form; but the leading circles wished to know nothing of the spirit. It ought to be considered what would have happened if in July/August 1914 the general mobilization of Russia had not been met by a declaration of war. Suppose we had remained passive: what has become of Germany now in the course of four years would have happened all the same, albeit in a different way. Whoever is able to see that materialism has ruined noble forces in the inner nature of Germany will also see that all that happened was bound to happen. Central Europe has betrayed the spirit; the spirit will rise from the chaos. Western Europe and America will experience through its victories what Central Europe is experiencing through its defeats, and what Russia, too, is experiencing through its defeat. These things are manifesting everywhere in a different form. But they do manifest in *their* particular form. Now it is worded like this: German militarism has been destroyed. However, this is wrongly put. German militarism had to become an empty vessel, without spiritual content. And as such it could not but destroy itself because it had not been called up to defend something of value which it cannot give itself but which it ought to serve. German militarism wanted to fight for Germany; but what was Germany fighting for in the shape of the people who led its politics? No word of significance was ever heard from any quarters that should have acted in the place of the military. German militarism fought for Germany; but Germany, as it was, fought for—nothing. That's why the spirit of Bismarck and the older Moltke stood apart through those years.

This catastrophe could not be averted. Whoever believes that it could have been averted judges the situation by its illusory outer appearance in which I, too, was caught up. Only 'she' saved my inner being from this illusion by spiritual means. For this was and is our shared karma. In July 1914—enveloped in the illusion in which the leading politicians were living—I was not allowed to justify the war in the way I should have done. Suppose the Kaiser had said: We do not want this war—and in his utter indecisiveness he would not really have dared to say so—I should have said: If you do not want this war you are bound to not want yourself. In that way the situation would have come to a head. In the face of such necessity action had to be taken. It is easy and has always been easy to maintain that the *Entente* did not want this war. It did not need to want it for it came about through it without being wanted by it. We *had to* wage it even though we did not *want* it, for it would indeed not have come about without us, but we were not allowed to bring about by our own will that which would have happened even without the war and has now happened through the war. The statesmen of the *Entente* could do this and that to avert the war. It could not be stopped by such action. Germany was able to avert it but was not allowed to because in that it would have committed suicide. It was Germany's destiny not to murder itself but to be murdered. The *Entente's* resentment will be great for in actual fact it is angered that it was forced to become the executive power of world history and that Germany and Austria did not murder themselves.

My soul is concerned but not saddened about the destiny of my loved ones. 'She' will be guardian and my soul will live in 'her' thoughts. In recent times she brought about a positive turn with regard to these things. Many a hardship must be suffered. But the right and the good will arise from such hardship. 'It' is also standing firm in the storm—in equanimity of soul. And my thoughts are reaching easily to those 'it' is thinking. 'El' is labouring, but she will find herself. My soul should be with her soul. The other children will find their way through 'understanding'. My thoughts on that are not yet fully formed. There is something uncertain there. But let the strength be alive in 'her': 'she' was strong in so many respects; let 'her' continue to be 'strong' and watchful.

I, too, will be included in the ranks of the accused and that is when the defence will have to be made, when the time is right; in view of the confusion reigning now this could only be after a challenge, otherwise—wait. Whatever is done in that direction must be effective and must not just fall flat. However, for it to be effective people will first have to see many a thing they are not seeing now and do not wish to see either.

*

Also preparing what is happening on earth. I was given the task by my karma and as a result of world evolution to be involved in the hour of decision. In the retrospective view all this involvement is now connected to my entire life and it brought me light, a lot of light, so that I was able to view the two great moments of my last earthly existence together: the time when 'she' stood by my side when the world historical decision was placed upon my soul and the time when this soul was preparing to seek for 'her' who was destined for me from a previous life on earth. No great fuss and pretence and no amount of elevating of certain personalities can ever substitute for the necessary inclination to the spirit.

58. Message for Eliza von Moltke

Dornach, 27 January 1919

The world has sunk away for which my soul thought it must fight; The world for which one really had to fight—it cannot sink away: it is the world of the spirit. Human beings only need to let it come near them. The old Germany to which our humanness was attached in an outer sense: it exists no longer and what appears to have survived of it will also disappear. Those of short sight who only apply their earthbound intellect are saying now: we are *guilty* of this terrible catastrophe. Those of even shorter sight are silent on this interpretation. My soul was freed from the physical sheath at the right time by the grace of destiny. For my soul could indeed not have suffered the present state of the community that formerly was Germany. It would have been unable to summon the only thought appropriate at the present time: this catastrophe of humanity was a necessity, it had to come to pass. We have not caused the war; but it was our task by destiny to be the first to perish in this catastrophe together with our old unsustainable state existence, and to see that the new has to be built from out of the spiritual. Beyond all the hardship we experienced we have to *find one another*, we who were brought together by destiny during a certain period as a result of our karmic connection. We are connected through ancient karmic ties. The hard times we experienced are bound to strengthen these ties.

'She' was placed by my side through ties of karma. Unlike me, 'she' was not tied to the time in which we live by external factors. 'She' truly guided my higher being out of what I had to leave behind. 'She' guided it to the spirit. 'It' never belonged to this age. Her calm nature stood above the age. 'El' revolted against everything to do with this age like an inwardly revolutionary being. The sons carry enough substance within to find themselves in the thought that the old order must be abandoned. All of this will strengthen the ties which connect us. Into the conciousness of my loved ones I direct my sense-free thinking. Do not worry; trust in the spirit of the inner power of all that is truly human. Now you are witnessing that which is human falling to pieces. But there is nothing in these pieces that the human spirit should have built upon; it has to build upon itself. I can speak like this to you from here; I could not have done it while in my body. Trust in the spirit that works within you. The German Folk Spirit has not failed; it would have also led to an external victory if in the last four years there had been enough people willing to learn from the events, willing to change. So now they will change through the hard necessities of misery. The *Entente* victory is a Pyrrhic victory, that means a victory where the victor loses more in the end than the vanquished. It appears different right now.

The 'old man' is not saying now: my work of 70/71 has been destroyed; he says: at the time we did what necessity dictated; nevertheless we paved the way for the spirit. The sadness that all (or all that was old) is gone is the sadness of one who elects to feel sadness over doing what leads him to an experience: an experience of having his eyes opened even though it is painful. Therefore, my beloved ones who are connected with me by karma, trust in the human spirit that dwells within you. Then the spirit whose blessing is upon me now will also find his way to you. I want to be more to you now than I could be in my earthly life. Just observe how human beings condemn what was done by our side in 1914; the Spirit of the German people does not condemn it because he did it himself; yet there have been many in Germany since 1914 who turned away from the German Folk Spirit. It is they who removed me or allowed it to happen. That was the beginning of the collapse. In those horrendous days around the end of July/beginning of August my soul alone had to bear the weight of all decisions; all the other parties responsible failed—and when they then acted against their destinies and did not allow to continue what had been placed upon my soul through their guilt, they paved the way for the collapse. Destiny as karma is a necessity, but its individual paths can be subject to change. Great earthly suffering would have been imposed on me had I not been removed. Yet even then I would have been freed of my earthly body in time by the grace of destiny. Even then I could not have been 'victorious' in an outer sense. That this should have been possible was my *necessary* illusion. There will be 'set-backs': these words made me shudder inwardly at the time. But they would have come. And if I had still been involved with these set-backs: the war would have ended earlier and for a short time immeasurable resources would have been available for a recon-struction, resources which are now lost. A 'terrible' peace would have come, but a far less terrible one than the present peace is in truth—a peace over which my body would have collapsed already at that time. However, my destiny, so I have been told, is the symbol of the German people. It is granted to me now to take this view because in those free of the body the personal can be detached even if the view concerns something personal.

With kind regards,
Your faithful messenger, H.R.

59. Message for Eliza von Moltke

[Dornach] 28 January 1919

My beloved ones, observe carefully the thoughts which arise very quietly within you; my soul wishes to dwell in these thoughts. This is because I can translate into eternal thoughts what oppresses and tortures mankind today in the passage of time, eternal thoughts which will contain the soul when it believes that all support will be lost in the turmoil of events and the turmoil of human willing in these times.

My soul, too, was placed into turmoil, and what was wavering then is now broken. However, what is placed in Time breaks but human souls live in that which is breaking. They preserve what is experienced in the breaking and transform it into eternal values which they then preserve in order to transform these into the work of later times in human evolution. Destiny will bring us together again at an important time; to perform in unison of body and spirit the work which mankind will be in need of. There will be repercussions of the turmoil in which human beings find themselves now, in deepest suffering. We will be able to transform into deeds what our souls have absorbed from the spirit, what out of their bitter experience they were able to craft into impulses, for deeds that will be performed when they will be surrounded again by new bodies for new times and will dwell again among people who feel within themselves the repercussions of our present-day turmoil.

Recognize that what came to pass as a result of my decision in July/August 1914 was historically necessary for human evolution. What earthly people are searching for in concepts of 'guilt' was necessity, iron necessity. Here, in the place of eternity, spiritual beings speak differently from human beings down below, who only see the things through veils and thought corpses. Here the beings speak of necessities which the earthly people will only fully understand in half a century's time. Then that which is now before my soul's eye as a picture of the future, will be living substance, that to which my gaze is directed, the source of the thoughts which I am sending into you [sic] in order that you may listen to them when you are calm within and listen in that inner peace for what my soul may speak to you in the spirit. For that 'she' was the bridge, and for that 'she' is still the bridge now. During my sojourn on earth I was able to trust in 'her' in my innermost heart; and I may trust in 'her' even more now. My soul feels strength when 'she' thinks of me. Let 'her' feel in wakefulness that my soul is speaking in 'her' thoughts.

60. Message to Eliza von Moltke

[Dornach] 27 March 1919 [r]

'She' will understand what it was that tormented my soul when it was still feeling through the physical sheath. Already then it was tormented by what is now sweeping over the earth and which my 'I' could not have lived through in the physical world. 'She' will understand that my soul had to depart. Now 'she' has brought it about that the life reflected in my letters has come before my spiritual eye. For the soul that signified finding itself, strengthening itself. If only 'she' could feel completely how warmly the soul's grateful thoughts are streaming towards her. Much of the future lives in these thoughts—a future which joins my soul and 'her' soul for work together. It stands now before my spiritual eye as if at some distance. And when the spiritual eye looks away from this future picture and the soul feels itself to be in the present, then it seeks also to direct the spiritual gaze of those connected with me, those close to me, to the picture of the future. My loved ones suffer in these times which have come to pass. But let them regard the many people of the present day who remain deaf and blind in spite of the current hardship. People do not receive the rays of the spirit. Thus those who do wish to receive them must also suffer. This suffering is of deep significance. The sufferings of the dullards are not as great as they would be if everyone were dull.

My soul is especially close to the 'old man' now. He witnessed the decay of what he built up. He had understood long before that this would happen. He knew early on that illusion instead of truth had reigned in this building. That, too, was a historical necessity. We who had to wield the sword were working on a vessel without contents. But in this life we were entrusted with safeguarding the good that had survived from previous centuries. Now something new must come. Something new on the rubble of the old.

'El' is suffering. If only 'El' could feel how my soul is seeking her's. I am often with her. She is progressing inwardly; but she is finding it hard to follow the ways of her soul consciously. For her, too, the time will come. I call into her [sic] again and again: 'Wait patiently; look for the meaning of suffering and you will be looking for what makes your soul greater.'

1914 stands before me. There are two points of view from which my soul beholds 1914. One is that everything had to happen the way it did because there was no one in Germany able to think politically—thus the ruin was born out of 1914. So Ahriman achieved for once what he was after. Now there will be no salvation until it is realized spiritually that Ahriman was involved. Already in the ninth century he instigated what he subsequently achieved in the twentieth. He was often spoken of in the context of my demotion in 1914—that was well spoken. His aims were characterized very well by these words. Because if my body had not received its leak [sic] through the Commander-in-Chief at the end of July, the days of September would have taken a different course. Everything else followed from the former event.

The other viewpoint is the impulse for the future concealed in the events. There was something morbid in all European institutions. The élite lived in what happened on the surface; but below there was a worm eating away. And that is how people fell deeper and deeper into untruth. No one wished to see the worm. At a time when party-political passions were flaring up terribly beneath the surface it was stated that no parties were 'known'. That was the calamity indeed that they were not *known* while they existed to a greater extent than ever before.

Through 'her' my soul turned to the interests of the spiritual life. There one lived in reality. There the great viewpoints of human evolution were given. There one could see the purpose of continuing with what had begun for Europe in the ninth century. This will be carried forward over the ruins. People will have to believe that at present the Christ is speaking new words from the invisible realms of the earth. But people will first have to prepare their hearts for hearing Him. Under His invisible guidance the New will arise, when people will no longer say that the sun is a fireball. Speaking like this is akin to saying that man's earthly face is made of wax. And yet, people believe that the sun is a fireball. They do not see the spirit which speaks to their hearts in the sun's rays: you deny yourselves if you deem yourselves to be merely earthly. But as long as people do not recognize themselves to be children of the spirit they will act misguidedly on earth and Ahriman will live in their instincts. He sees progress in destruction.

'It' contributed greatly to 'her' finding the way to my soul with the message of the spirit. 'It' remained distant from outer events in her soul. Today man remains just as distant from these outer events of which he feels that they are drifting towards their own destruction in order that the New may arise when they are destroyed.

No one who wanted to accomplish things in Germany in 1914 could have avoided the enormous genocide. Anyone who could have mitigated it did not want to accomplish anything serious, but wanted the illusion. And this illusion led to the present situation. 'Her' eyes are still looking at this destruction; my soul is with 'her' heart and that is where we are working for the future. There we already are beyond the 'shining appearance of the sun' which for earthly life needs to take place in etheric imagination. For the earth the Christ will appear when almost everyone has deserted Him, when they know little more about Him than His name. Then a New

Rome will arise in the hearts of human beings which will, however, be one with the New Jerusalem.

We have shown that we, as Germans, could no longer understand each other by bringing things to the point where we had to reach an understanding with the Turks. It is not the understanding which is at issue here; they are human beings, too. But we did not see that this understanding could only be a chimera. The greatest misfortune had to come, it is unfolding right now, so that the bridge to connect both worlds could be built. People who want to accomplish things on earth have to become builders of bridges (Pontifices).

61. *Message for Eliza von Moltke*

[Stuttgart] around or before 1 May 1919

It is necessary to make the facts clear. The situation is different from what my earthly 'I' wrote. At that time not the faintest thought of what was about to happen entered my soul. My soul thought about defeat and loss of territory but not about the collapse of the monarchy. Now everything is different. The facts need to be made clear. 'She' will find the best way of doing this in the physical world. It has to be said that someone had to act in 1914 but that none of the political advisers knew how to act. For years no political plan whatsoever had existed. What had been German political life all collapsed. Reliance could be placed only on military power and military decisiveness.

My soul was surrounded by people about whom I only gained a clear picture when the utter nullity of this company was revealed in July-August 1914. The Kaiser stood before me with the forces he had developed through black magic in Rome. These forces flared up again. My soul was particularly strongly exposed to the power of the magic flames on 1 August. Yet it could only experience this power unconsciously, hence the paralysis of consciousness. Falkenhayn was the tempter of the Kaiser as early as 856. Lyncker had knowledge of magical practices then. There are documents from that time in the Vatican today. 'She' took a defensive stance then. Her mood had been one of 'unconscious knowing' about these things for a long time. Many of the people in society are just reincarnations of people from the ninth century.

K. has half of his etheric body detached. This has to do with the effects of karma from the Roman period. It means that the temptations emanating from K. cannot be resisted when the souls of the people around him become weak.

My soul was often completely enslaved by the temptation from these quarters. When I walked away from K. my soul was full of thoughts of temptation. These thoughts would only be dispersed when 'she' spoke in a straightforward manner about these matters in 'her' own way. Without 'her' my soul could not have gone through this incarnation without being *obliterated* by these circumstances. 'She' came to my side. If 'she' had not come my soul would have been completely absorbed in the life of those around me. My 'I' would have had to wait until the next incarnation to know what it needed to know in order to go forward.

Now that 'she' had come to my side, things took a different turn altogether. In my environment I experienced the decadence of what was old and had turned into materialism, that from which there could be no salvation. It was that which enmeshed my soul. But 'she' guided my 'I' to the spiritual. Hence, though my 'I' was enmeshed in the decline, this did not result in having to wait until the next incarnation. The relationship to the spiritual lifted my soul's better forces from those of the decaying society and therefore saved my soul. My external person suffered a lot on earth after the Battle of the Marne. My 'I' was not able then to raise itself above the sufferings of the external person. But my life now is such that the sufferings of that person are not continued into the present. If I had not absorbed any thoughts about the spiritual before my death my earlier suffering would still exercise some power over me now. But it has lost its power even though my 'I' can see it clearly as an object.

That is why the instruction 'for my wife only' which was given by the external person is no longer binding, because it is necessary to clarify the facts. The German nation can only survive if *truth* is bestowed on it. But the others are also speaking untruthfully about my role in July-August-September 1914. They are not telling the truth about my earlier position in these events nor about my position in 1914. They say what they *want* to see; they have no organ to see the facts.

Schlieffen was a great strategist. However, not a military but a political strategist. He did not reckon at all with the inevitable consequences of his battle plan which gave the enemy the opportunity of viewing the German people in a totally wrong light. Schlieffen's soul cannot look at his own battle plan now without searing pain. Nor the 'old man' either. In the time following Schlieffen's departure my changes to this unfortunate plan could not be made effective. Only the dreadful idea with regard to Holland could be changed. The changes could not be far-reaching because all the generals believed in Schlieffen's plan. *This* plan is the cause of all the external collapse. But what was there to put against it, with the K. enveloped in the fog of his own former magic powers?

Everything that my soul had to do in connection with the mission regarding the painting was an after-effect of these magic powers: Peoples of Europe, guard what you hold most holy. The whole affair was ahrimanically inspired because Ahriman gained access through the powers of magic. The scales fell from my soul's eye and my 'I' was restored to health to see things in their true light by 'her' action in enabling my 'I' to read the letters, causing the picture of the entire Russian ceremonial feast to stand before my gaze.

An external victory would have meant the total downfall of the German people. Such a victory would have been followed by an epoch of Mammon, of terrible money-making and 'recovery' and all the nations would have combined forces to exterminate the German people. The 1914 war was the instrument for teaching the German people about deprivation and suffering, and therefore it will be possible to maintain the people's strength from out of deprivation and suffering.

When the truth about the outbreak of war becomes known the thoughtful Germans will start thinking about the ineptitude of their former 'leaders'. They *must* think in this way, because in times like the present wrong thoughts are the actual forces of destruction. Now I understand why in August 1914, when the defeat on the Marne was already signed and sealed, I was merely told: 'There will also be setbacks'. If I had been told more it would have paralysed my brain. 'She' saw more but could not dwell in her thoughts on what more she saw for she had to stand at my side, bringing strength. And anyway, what would have been the good of having the defeat at the Marne clearly in our vision in thought. One would have been at a total loss about what to do. No sensible action could have been taken in the clouded atmosphere around the Kaiser.

Now the spiritual eye of my 'I' is able to see what would have been the right thing to do in September 1914. Close-up formation of the army in the West to present an impenetrable defence; no regiment to be surrendered to the eastern front; conclusion of an immediate peace in the West with all the disadvantages this would bring; drawing attention to the Russian invasion to curb Austrian ambitions in Serbia. But we would have been 'ostracized' for such proposals at that time; they would not have been understood. What was most sensible would have been considered the most senseless.

It is only recently that my 'I' has been able to endure such thoughts. This endurance provides strength for the next incarnation at the end of the century. 'She' should live intensely with the thoughts that I can thus share with 'her'. 'She' should talk about these things with 'it'. The more intensely other members of our family absorb such thoughts without prejudice the better it will be. Then, after a while, they will find strength coming to them from within; and this strength will be the result of thoughts such as the ones referred to and which are before my soul now.

The German nation lives in 'untruth'. Many books are telling it 'untruth'. It does not matter that Bethmann, Jagow, Pourtalès *believe* that they are telling the truth from which they are so far removed. What does matter is that their wholly untruthful thoughts are destructive forces in the real world. If the untruthful beliefs were now replaced by a true one a purification of the German people would become possible. Those who presently speak so untruthfully before the German people ought not to be accused morally since 'they truly do not know what they do' and they never did know it; but they ought to be exposed in such a way that their inadequacies, their lack of goodwill to achieve insight, become known in the widest circles. That would help the people and it would help those who 'do not know what they do'. Because if they pass through the portal of death in this befogged state, no spiritual power whatever can save them from losing all their incarnations until the world's end. Through their untruthful thoughts they cut themselves off earthly events unto the end of the earth. However, if they could be made to understand their own inability now, if the mirror could be held up to them, a helping power could come to them after they die. This would be possible even for the most severely deluded person in the Supreme Command in the second half of the war.

In the second half of the war: what would my situation have been if I had experienced it on earth? Everywhere my 'I', the 'I' limited by the external person, would have had before its eyes the true face of those human abilities I had deemed great even though they were only small. My outer person could have never ever borne that. The second part of the war would have crushed my outer person. Spiritually my departure from the earth was a deliverance. It was important and significant how 'she' established the connection with the earthly. 'She' must keep her thinking along the lines predestined through these messages *and the earlier ones*. We are in the middle of a tragic time in life and will only find the right way in these tragic circumstances when we look at everything with the utmost clarity, waiting for the right moment to clarify the facts. The incompetent people who govern the German people now, devoid of any thoughts, cannot and must not stay. They have no inkling of the spirit. They do not even know that there is a spirit. But the German people can be put on the right path only through the spirit.

62. *Rudolf Steiner to Eliza von Moltke*

Stuttgart, 3 May 1919

My very dear Frau von Moltke!
Frau Röchling will come and see you in Berlin to ask you on my behalf for a copy of the notes of the dear, precious soul; I was very pleased to receive your telegraphic agreement to their publication. Believe me, I did not come to the decision to ask for your agreement *now* without truly considering everything within my reach. And we may be certain of the dear soul's agreement. *You will understand me* as far as that is concerned.

Frau Röchling will tell you what is happening here and *how* one has to work. *This* is the place we had to decide upon for getting our work going. There are thousands of people here already who have declared their support for the [gap in the text here: ideas outlined?] in the appeal and in my book *Die Kernpunkte der sozialen Frage* and called for their realization in the shape of my being called by the government. Well, this is of only ideal value initially because, firstly, no such thing will happen with *this* government and secondly, nothing could be achieved with this government anyway. But as long as this government does not disturb my associates and the people in my committees one can at least be certain that the new starting point in Stuttgart will be saved from the horrors of Munich and that fruitful seeds for the future can be planted in *complete level-headedness*, even in connection with the most radical workers' groupings. But, importantly: last Wednesday I said to the Minister of Labour here: 'Give me four weeks' time and don't work against me and you will see how it is possible to negotiate sensibly with the workers who will by then have understood how one needs to work towards the future in a *sound* way.' He replied: 'You are barking up the wrong tree; these people are hopeless. They pick out of your lectures *those* plums which are of use to them and fail to hear what doesn't suit them.' I replied: 'Well, these people pick their plums out of my proposals. But aren't there any plums in these lectures for you and your supporters? But you and your supporters are taking *nothing* from these plums. You see, that's how it is.'

However, we must be straightforward and direct in our work. And this entails above all publishing the notes of our dear soul. *You* will not consider it an exaggeration if I tell you that to the outside as well as the inside it is the only way for a healthy beginning towards a possible peace making. The present preliminary peace in Versailles is, of course, whichever way things may turn out, an utter impossibility. And without a possible peace Germany cannot revive socially but is doomed to disintegrate further even with the best possible institutions. German assets have shrunk to a mere percentage of what they were, and a very small one at that; there are certain to be further losses if social threefolding does not get established. However, in order to establish this absolutely essential social threefolding we need above all the *moral* credit of the non-German world. And no one in Germany has any inkling of *the degree* to which this has been lost. No one has any inkling what has happened in Germany and outside to contribute to this loss ever since those days when you, my dear Frau von Moltke, wanted to authorize H. to confer something to me which was to counteract those losses: in Germany no one is aware of any of it. This should have been prevented at the time by what H. was willing to do but then did not materialize 'because German resources would have to have been given preference *over* the Austrians'.

Herr v. Moltke, your nephew—the son of Julie v. Moltke—

attended a whole series of my lectures together with Minister Lindemann's wife; he also visited our branch here once.

I have just given you an outline of the situation. A letter from our dear precious soul is enclosed. It is a summary of many things; but it states literally what is told me in the same way *often* now.

I will have to continue working here for a while; then I will probably be able to come to Berlin if the thread of opportunities for travel doesn't snap earlier. Or something else happens.

The notes are to be printed here. I will write an accompanying essay. Would you, my very dear Frau v. Moltke, please convey your wishes with respect to this to Frau Röchling or write to me via her. The best thing would be if we had everything ready for the publication of the notes by the end of next week. I believe that the events to come make all this necessary and that these necessities can be met only *here*.

With my most heartfelt greetings,

Yours always,

Rudolf Steiner

Stuttgart, Landhausstrasse 70
(bei Kinkel)

63. Message for Eliza von Moltke

[Stuttgart] 3 May 1919

A Summary

My 'I' is contemplating the crucial events in the sphere of earth; and my soul is not only contemplating them—it is immersed within them. 'She' has made this possible for me through the life review my letters have afforded me. Through this I have found the right connection with the decades of my last incarnation during which my will was driven by the consequences of Europe's ninth century while my head knowledge could not keep pace.

'She' was destined to stand by my side then. My soul is indebted to 'her' for its eventual inclination to the spirit world. The time when I found 'her', found her again through the karmic connection in the last earth life: it was also the time when Europe had to find the connection to the ninth century. This connection, however, has nothing to do with the perniciously materialistic intellectual life into which all spheres of life were drawn in the second half of the nineteenth century. This wave of materialism carried the seed of self-destruction within itself.

In the ninth century Christianity was still connected for the people of Europe with a consciousness of the spiritual hierarchies and the spiritualization of the cosmos. From the tenth, eleventh centuries onwards man's view of life and the universe became increasingly bereft of the spiritual. The relationship to the soul became an outer one for the people of Europe, as exemplified by the relationship to the souls which incarnated in Herder or Goethe. What these souls willed in a spiritual sense did not become state culture anywhere. As far as public life in the states was concerned, Europe was wholly materialistic at the end of the nineteenth and the beginning of the twentieth century. We stood in the midst of all this.

'She' stood by my side. And 'she' was always aware that this European materialistic life had to be overcome. That was good. Now the wave of materialism is on the point of breaking. This breaking process will continue. The convulsions of materialism must reach their full term. In my last physical body my soul was not able to experience what only this discarnate soul can now experience in clarity, with the strength 'she' has given to my 'I', with my soul steeled through the suffering before my physical death.

You ask me: whether it is in accordance with or against my will that my writings penetrate to the public. My will must profess to truth since truth alone can have the right effect now. If my soul said 'no', an important truth would be withheld from the world. This must not be. The world must be newly developed from seeds which the world has not wanted to see up to now, from spirit seeds. It will as yet be necessary to give these spirit seeds to the world in a way that it may absorb them in its consciousness which has been utterly seduced by materialism.

What wanted to rule when my soul was dwelling in the physical body was bad, was given up to materialism. What has taken its place now is equally bad. It is equally far removed from the spirit and its reality. It will also break. But in chaos the spirit reigns. It is necessary now for the spirit to raise its voice. In misfortune it will be heard. No thinking being can believe today that anything new can spring from the old materialistic thinking. My soul wishes to be in your willing if you do now what must be done in accordance with the spirit.

In my physical existence I was confined to seeing my karma interwoven with the breakdown of materialism. Now my willing connects me to the resurgent weavings of the spirit. Seeds must be sown in the ruins. The lie of the age has led to ruin. Truth must lead to the building of the new. The spirit can only work in truth. At the end of July and the beginning of August I stood alone with my decision, abandoned by all politicians who were totally helpless at that time. What happened had to happen and it had been prepared for a long time. Truth must hold sway. Otherwise not only German culture will perish; the entire European world would perish, too, and Eastern Europe would have to be rebuilt from Asia. That must not happen. Europe must come to its senses and find its way to the spirit.

You, my closest family: my soul's will is striving to you. Bear with inner strength of soul the outer difficulties that come your way. Bear them, because this is the bridge between the realm of the past and the realm of the future. Stand upright in wakefulness of soul.

My soul is looking towards the future. Fruit will ripen before the end of the century but the seeds must be found now by people of goodwill. Europe's materialistic era will be like an interlude when the new Spirit Sun begins to shine for humanity.

64. Helene Röchling to Eliza von Moltke

Stuttgart, 10 May 1919

My dear, dear Frau von Moltke!
In the enclosed the Dr sends you the second appeal which is due to come out soon now. He sends his regards as well as the following answers to your questions:

1. What the soul said with regard to Harden's article of 5 May: that the soul suffered from untruths therein does not relate to the Marne Battle but to the assertion that the soul when down here was in favour of the war for a long time, had wished for it for a long time.
2. As to the motive for relating this matter now: as long as there was war no communication could be given; it was necessary to wait and see what the others would be doing and now the time is right;

because, now this matter is introduced between the preliminary peace and the final peace, the threefolding impulse must come in at this point in time in order to become effective.

3. Regarding the exoneration of Lehman [= Kaiser]: he is exonerated morally but accused intellectually; he shows himself as he was; and by virtue of *how* he *was* he is part of the causes of the war.

In faithful union with you, the soul, Dr Steiner and our cause for truth I am sending you my sincerest greetings.
Your messenger, H.R.

65. Appeal 'To The German People and the German Government', May 1919, by Rudolf Steiner

The German people can only create the basis for a healthy reconstruction of the social order by means of relentless exposure of the truth in regard to the facts connected with the outbreak of war in so far as they can be determined, and about the activity of the powers that set the tone in Germany during the war. It matters not what the rest of the world does; let the German people do its duty at last; let it now tell the full truth which has not yet been revealed. It owes it to itself and to its integrity to be ruthlessly honest before all.

The undersigned committee of the Bund für Dreigliederung des sozialen Organismus (association for the threefolding of the social organism), which, following Rudolf Steiner's 'Appeal to the German people and to the Civilized World', aims to liberate the forces which can lead to a reconstruction of the body social, and in order to make room for these forces, declares:

1. We demand a truthful representation of the events which led to the war, in particular of all that took place in the last few days before the outbreak of war in Berlin, regardless of whether this is acceptable from a crudely utilitarian point of view or indeed of whether as a result leading personalities are compromised. Officials or private persons who can contribute to the overcoming of the obfuscation of the causes of the war which was carried out by the leadership during the war and was not dealt with after the capitulation are called upon to make public what they know. Should

anyone require support in exposing the truth we are prepared to help.

2. So far as we ourselves are able we shall help the truth come out. We shall make it our own business to publish shortly the notes taken by Colonel-General Helmuth von Moltke on the events immediately before the outbreak of war that took place in Berlin, which Dr Rudolf Steiner will make available with the agreement of the widow of the deceased Colonel-General.

3. We challenge the relevant Government department to make it possible for the facts revealed in these notes to form the basis of a public inquiry to be conducted in all openness and covering all the relevant facts.

66. Rudolf Steiner to Eliza von Moltke

Stuttgart, 28 May 1919

Dear Frau v. Moltke!

The brochure containing the 'Reflections and Memories' is due to be published in the next few days. I am sending you the first copies I have received. I am enclosing two with this letter and will send the others at the same time by book-post. It will be of great significance that the material be published right now. This is truly what had to be done. May I ask you to regard what I have written as utter *necessity*. I checked every sentence with the utmost conscientiousness before committing it to paper. I also found it necessary not to go any further in my characterization of the departed one in order not to arouse too much opposition.

The soul says: 'Now it is important to stand firm whatever may come to pass. "She" will stand firm. Many questions will be asked. Those asking the questions must be answered like this: Why have you not asked these questions before? Then the answer might have been different. My soul lives in "her" soul. My soul seeks the thoughts of "her" soul. It will come to pass that people will seek their own inner counsel when they have tasted from the cup of bitterness and have come to understand *how* the war had become a necessity because the seeds were planted by human beings who must learn now to create everything anew. How good it was of her to give me access to my memoirs before the great catastrophe happened. It was wise providence.'

Dear Frau v. Moltke: I will send you more from this source soon. I must not hold up this parcel now; you should be the first to see the copies; just as I got hold of the first copies myself I learnt to my utmost horror that 'anthroposophists' had already picked up some of them yesterday. It is really terrible that no such thing as order can be established among the 'anthroposophists'. Please forgive me if you should already have come across the brochure from another source as a result of this misdemeanour, for which I have severely reprimanded the Managing Director of the *Bund für Dreigliederung*.

I am in the midst of a veritable crossfire here. The more that transpires of what I must do the more vicious the attacks become. Every evening a lecture or an assembly. The worst is yet to happen, and people just carry on with their souls asleep. This sleepiness of soul prevails everywhere in bourgeois circles and the Social Democrat leaders are part of these bourgeois circles. When one really looks through these things one is bound to conclude: for a new cause new people have to come into being. But this is *very, very* difficult. Nevertheless it *must* be done. It looks as if we may have made a good step forward last night, albeit with people totally unknown to us until then.

I was in Ulm the day before yesterday. In other words, once again on completely unprepared ground. On occasions like that one sees quite clearly: every day new abysses open up, new variations of hostility are encountered; all this must be met by the 'threefolding impulse' to create a new order. The explosive stuff that emerges at such assemblies: it is appalling! Mistrust everywhere; no one believes that anyone else could possibly have good intentions. Out of this most 'unsocial' of all states 'socialization' is to be effected! At the same time *this total* absence of any capacity of understanding the merest thing among people. *They simply do not hear* the essential message I want to put across. It seems that they are only capable of understanding things to which they have been accustomed for 30 years—right down to the word order of the sentences. Sclerotic brains, paralysed etheric bodies, empty astral bodies, totally dulled egos. This is the hallmark of the people of our time. Assuring you of my sincere and enduring friendship

Yours, Dr Rudolf Steiner

Stuttgart, Landhausstr.70 (bei Kinkel)

67. Rudolf Steiner to Eliza von Moltke

Stuttgart, 6 August 1919

My dear Frau v. Moltke,

Although I will return here quite soon I nevertheless want to write to you about certain things before my departure for Switzerland. For certain reasons I will not be able to send you communications from the soul before my return here. But this will be very soon. For this time it will just be what I can enclose in this letter.

It was very sad that the publication of the notes was made impossible in this way. I do not need to tell you in detail what Counsellor v. Moltke brought about with the Foreign Office, since that in itself would not have led me to acquiesce.

The decisive factor was Herr von Dommes' intervention. He came along and explained to me that he could *prove* that three points in the notes did not correspond to the facts. He spoke in considerable detail about these three points. This put me in an extremely difficult position. I asked v. Dommes if he would be willing to swear on oath to the inaccuracy of the three points. He assented without hesitation. This made for a very difficult situation in relation to the soul. The soul was *not* aware of the errors and was therefore in complete agreement with the intended publication. It only became anxious when the reflection of v. Dommes' views, which are the opposite of its own, came through to it. That could not be allowed to happen, this conflict of an individual here with the soul there. So what happened was not that the soul shrank away from the idea of publication but rather that everything had to be done to prevent a difficult situation from arising, where the dissemination of v. Dommes' views would cause people in the physical world to form a very different picture from that of the soul. There is nevertheless no doubt that the soul still believes in the accuracy of the notes. I am unable to gain access if I put a direct question about the issue of correctness. My dear Frau v. Moltke, when I have sent you the communications of the soul you will see that the situation is just as I have summarized it here. But let me emphasize this: there is no indication as yet that the soul does not wish for the publication to go ahead. However, there has been no inquiry either as to why the publication has not taken place.

For the sake of the soul's peace the publication had to be suppressed after Dommes' intervention. I lived through difficult hours with this man who thinks exclusively in military terms. He had no inkling of what I went through while he spoke: every word a prejudice; but full of rigid and inflexible judgements, just as if the world catastrophe had not happened.

My dear Frau v. Moltke: I feel for you, and everything you have suffered and are still suffering as a result of this event. Now I am longing to present this matter to the world in some way when I have talked to you. However, nothing must happen that does not accord with the interests of the soul. I certainly hope that the soul will express its wishes in this direction soon. The last messages focus strongly on Germany's arduous destiny. Typical comments: 'Everything was necessary after all; the suffering will be followed by an ascent. Slowly. We will be called on to do at the end of the century what we were not allowed to do now.' I asked whether the soul might have possibly erred in relation to Hindenburg and Ludendorff. But no answer was forthcoming. Relating Ludendorff's words from his pamphlet, which are obviously quite untrue, had a somewhat disturbing effect. But there was no specific answer in this context either. But often: 'Through *her* I learn much about the earthly; in *her* thoughts my "I" connects itself with the earth; my soul needs this.'

When I was in Mannheim recently Frau Röchling received a message from you that the Foreign Office had the brochure in their possession. Of course, this is totally untrue. The people concerned have declared *on oath* that the entire print run had been pulped. Do you see, even in these matters nothing but untruths issue from the Foreign Office.

In view of everything I had received spiritually before publication I could not but advise that the notes should be published, and it is an absolute fact that *no other reason* but the one stated by Dommes could have affected my decision in the end.

We will have to wait now until destiny brings us together again so that we can discuss what is to be done next. You can see, my dear Frau v. Moltke, that the soul has so far not suffered any disturbance through this thwarted intention to publish the notes. This is the positive side of the matter.

I would ask you to keep this in mind to try and fight your own disquiet, understandable though it is. It must be possible to find light in this darkness. Our time brings so much suffering. And what you had to experience in connection with these notes is part of this suffering, too.

In the hope of seeing you again soon.

Yours faithfully,

Rudolf Steiner

68. *Message for Eliza von Moltke*

[Dresden] 20 September 1919 [r]

Summary of many points

'She' should not believe that my soul is not inclined towards [sic] family. My thoughts are seeking my family's thoughts. My soul comes alive in their thinking whenever their thoughts reach me. But 'she' should try and make everyone understand how different everything looks from here. My thoughts are with all my loved ones and these thoughts will help them. However, the help provided from here must often be of a kind not immediately comprehensible to those on earth. Help must be provided in a way quite different from what people on earth frequently imagine. 'She' will find the right way as long as 'she' continues her efforts along the straight line which 'she' started when she brought the spiritual to me. When things happen in life which lead to concern among family members 'she' must entertain the thought that they had to happen as a result of our joint karma.

Our individual karma is determined by our participation in the karma of humanity. We found each other in this incarnation because we were now predestined to serve the karma of humanity through our being together in earlier incarnations. My soul was placed in the midst of this karma of humanity. And I could never have come to be who I became until my death this time without all the influences connected with my family's destiny.

My family was one of the elements that shaped my life. The other was the public sphere into which it had been placed. Now I must break the ties with the people with whom I was brought together by this public element. I remained connected with them from previous incarnations. But in the future their paths cannot be mine. The spiritual life that entered my existence will bring about this breaking of the ties. It will not be possible to help these people in the near future since they are chained with leaden weights to the consequences of their previous incarnations.

In my life before death I was still subject to many errors with regard to these people. But now I am able to see them in the light which my contact with the spiritual world afforded me before my death.

I entered into the war because it was a necessity. Had I not entered into it events would have taken their course as they did, albeit in a different manner. The revolution would have happened in Russia; the throne would have been toppled there in any case, but then the revolution would have spread to Germany and Austria. The war did not strengthen the power of the revolution, it weakened it. However, it also weakened the total strength of human beings. In the year 1914 the ahrimanic forces were very strong. Now they are more obvious; they destroy; but they are waging a desperate battle. A battle, indeed, which may be fought for a long time to come, but cannot end in their victory.

When the world comes to comprehend all of this it will also understand the need for this war. If only the world would not believe that the spiritual world can give help without human beings having to do something towards it. If you *believe* in the spirit you cannot despair of the spirit and if you act in the spirit you cannot despair in the long run.

Those who accuse me now want to cover up with their speeches the carelessness they succumbed to in 1914. What is necessary, however, is the uncovering of the truth. Such uncovering will reveal how the catastrophe of the war has arisen from the contempt for the spiritual, and what happened externally will be recognized as the consequence of this contempt for the spirit.

A great deal of what happened in the lives of those connected with me through family is the fulfilment of old karma which is redeemed therewith. Koennecke was connected with us in an earlier incarnation. We had to treat him badly then or else his existence would have been damaging. 'El' redeemed this karma. And that which in her own inner being assumed a form which enabled her to redeem it represents her arduous inner destiny. My thoughts are seeking her. She mirrors something in her own destiny which is related to my destiny from one side. Many a thing would turn out well for her, too, if she could seriously resolve to take the spiritual powers into her soul. She would have to work her way up from the struggles in which she masters her own being.

*

'It' should think intensely about the far-distant future which has been announced to me in the spirit after my death. Through the inner peace which she connects with her thinking she will gain a spiritual strength which will be very valuable to us when we need to act in accordance with what is predestined for us. There will be a lot of resistance; but the difficulties will be removed by 'it's' future ability to work out of the spirit. When 'it' and 'she' work together something is prepared from which strength for the future will develop. When they are united my soul's spiritual power is strengthened.

When my soul now beholds the consequences of the war on earth it wishes for human beings to become strong enough to recognize the truth. There are many dead here who were killed in action. They are asking: Why did everything happen in this way? What did we die for? From these doubts they will have to gain the strength to see things clearly themselves. Then they will be able to help people on earth. At present the discarnate beings understand better what comes from the spirit than the people on earth. But the discarnate beings have taken so little of earthly spiritual knowledge through the portal of death. And many a thing one has not absorbed there cannot be aquired after death. Even if one has little faith or understanding for the spiritual before one's death; as long as one just takes it into oneself: then it will be raised to understanding after death. Such are the experiences of my soul. Before death the body provided it with many a difficulty to consciously take the spiritual into itself [sic]; but it was within the soul when the body had dropped away. Then 'she' came with the letter retrospective, and this proved greatly helpful for sharpening the eye of the soul out of the strength afforded by *re-living* what had been lived through on earth. This letter retrospective brought to life what had been lived through together with 'her'; in that way I have now fully absorbed what 'she' experienced when my soul was still caught up in what came towards me in the outer world.

69. *Rudolf Steiner to Eliza von Moltke*

[Stuttgart] before 19 June 1920

Dearest Frau v. Moltke!

The *only* way of sending you a message is to send it with young Herr Bartsch. Unless something altogether unexpected happens, I shall be in Berlin for two days, on Sunday 20 June. In addition, either Saturday 19 or Monday 21 June. I am not sure whether you are aware of the circumstances to the extent that you know that I can only travel to Berlin if no one speaks of this journey.

You can well imagine that I would have liked to speak or write to you about our dear soul much earlier. However, there is simply no way of communicating now. Any indirect way could bring misfortune.

On the whole, the path to the soul had to continue to be sought as I described to you in Berlin last year. After all, things happen more slowly there than here. 'Why could not things also have happened differently?' This is often asked. But then the benefit of the letter retrospective comes into effect, and this, in context with the thoughts from spiritual science, results in a deep understanding that everything that came to pass was and is a spiritual necessity. 'One only needs to see what is *now* to recognize why it had to happen the way it did then.' 'Something completely new must arise from the grave of the old. Therefore the steps towards the grave of the old had to be taken.' 'The thoughts of my soul are thinking with "her"; thus they follow what is happening and only in this way can we work for the more distant future.' From these few words out of many more you may see that essentially nothing much has changed on that side.

With regard to the publication which was so insidiously forestalled at that time, the thoughts coming from that side cannot be any different yet from what I said earlier in Berlin. This would only become possible if there were an opportunity to publish. But there are people such as Tomes [Dommes] still lurking in every corner. What a lot of ugliness he came up with at that time!

I do not wish to urge you to journey to Berlin now. Because I would not go there myself if our apartment had not been confiscated. Hence I will have to do it after all. Up till now work is still proceeding here and therefore it is my duty to do it here. You will probably hear from Herr Bartsch how things are going.

Best wishes to your family. It is sad to have to be so far away now.

70. Message for Eliza von Moltke

Dornach, 26 October 1920 [r]

There is increasing clarity and truth around my 'I'. No more surrounding darkness keeps away what must come into my 'I' for enriched understanding. The relationship of my 'I' to the spiritual world and its search for knowledge is tied up with 'her', but this is good. Whatever 'she' thinks and feels in connection with the spiritual also lives in my soul. Thus it has been prepared through our earth existence. And in this way my soul will gradually receive everything it needs for the end of the century.

There is, however, the 'spiritual movement' down there. It has to be there. But where will the souls come from at the present time who will carry it further? The people who live on the earth now wish to receive the spiritual without effort—but they do not understand the practical at all, they consider themselves practical people and have no sense for it. That is why all the threads we have been wanting to connect together since the beginning of the twentieth century just break. The immediate destiny of the 'spiritual movement' will be that it will stand there like a plucked chicken. It will have all its feathers torn out.

My soul looks down at what it called the 'German Fatherland' during my earthly life. But there is no hope. The people are worn out. The 'spiritual movement' is spiritual substance without any reflection in human heads.

'It' helps me a great deal. She connects me time and again to the spiritual spheres out of which life conflicts arise, since in the entire series of my incarnations the being 'Umi' is active which had to remain 'spirit' for a certain period of time and yet had to work on earth. Now it comes about that the next incarnation at the century's end stands before my soul when 'it' concentrates strongly in meditation—and then this redeemed 'Umi' will again participate as a human being. But it will be necessary for all of spiritual science to flow into my soul so that my I may fully understand what is at stake here.

Often I think entirely in thought forms as Nicholas I. Oh! how well I see the deep truth of all this as well as the deeper connections.

My soul is permeated with everything that has come to me out of the spiritual movement. My 'I' is now living in this as in 'its world'. That is weaving together with everything I had to do and think in my last earthly life. My 'I' can no longer hold on to the details of the war. They have no important meaning anyway. The most important event was the great decision that had to be taken in 1914. It was a necessity. Because much of what had come into being by 1914 must now die away. The downfall is necessary. We were not allowed to attain victory. By such victory we would have devastated the world. So we had to leave this to the 'victors'.

This stands before my 'I' when it is totally objective. But then pains again come into view [sic], pains which passed through my soul in 1915 and after that. Then 'she' is always by my side. But 'my own' stand in the midst of the chaos. My soul makes tremendous efforts to bring consoling thoughts into what my I can experience through 'my own'. Then my soul suffers everything that comes from the 'enemies'. However, my 'I' needs that for its own purification.

'She' is thinking about what the spiritual movement represents. Then 'it' thinks in my soul, too. And my 'I' looks at this thinking. But these thoughts often remain too vague for the specific demands made by this world here. All this is bound up with the chaos reigning everywhere on earth.

'My notes'—they must be known—but it cannot be ordered from here, because not everything that has to be considered on earth works its way up here. If the world is to discover what happened in 1914 they must become known. The world is not yet inclined to understand that.

The notes ... where ... who is opposed to it ... perhaps ... (note: there is a gap here which cannot yet be bridged).

1914 is before me again. My fight with the dreadful powers of Ahriman. These really played an important part in everything that happened. At that time Ahriman was the strongest power around me. He could not have harmed me personally; but at the very moment I was 'dispensed with' Ahriman came to the surface everywhere.

What was done later was all brought about by ahrimanic

inspiration. Many of the individuals who were then in power were not human beings in the true sense.

This is clearly inscribed in my soul. And my 'I' can perceive it. This perception is particularly clear when 'she' unites her thoughts with mine.

What was said in spiritual science in 1914, before the war, should come to me through 'her'. When 'she' thinks it, it will be in my soul, too. And then it becomes an impulse for the future. What happened afterwards will then appear like a dark intermission. But this intermission will last for a long, long time. Only the end of the century will bring the solution to many a riddle. Until then, work must be done on earth, however much of the 'spiritual' should fall on infertile ground. The Evil is great and powerful on earth. The Evil will attain many apparent victories. The Good will often be presented as the Evil. That must be borne. Help and support can come from here but only to the extent that spiritual consciousness is created on earth through spiritual knowledge.

71. Continuation of Last Message

29 October 1920 [r]

'She' has mediated to my soul the course of my life; this is an important achievement. The 'I' gains strength and power by living in these events and looking at them. It becomes like a sheath for the soul, a sheath of transparent strength.

The soul is able to answer many questions through this life review which would otherwise have taken many years of soul work. And a lot must be accomplished speedily for the 'I' to be imbued with the aims and intentions of its future work at the end of the century.

The centuries which have passed since the last incarnation but one are passing before the soul. They are the school from which my 'I' needs to learn. The civilization of Europe spread from Odilie's Mount. This is also what carried my 'I' towards the South. The good spirit of my soul that became 'she' stood supportively by my 'I'. The two 'I's weaved together the Nordic and the European of that age. Both 'I's participated as spirit beings in the great time when so many Europeans moved to the Orient. It was then that the spirit whose seeds had been planted at the time of Nicholas became fulfilled.

After that things changed in Europe. The time of preparation for this last incarnation began. The time came when the outer intellect carried off all the victories. But this outer intellect on earth was merely the revelation of false magic. This false magic from Rome worked in the one who stood next to my soul in 1914 and threw all into confusion. He did not know the 'truth'. In his 'lower' soul forces he had a secret love for ahrimanic powers.

The thoughts of my loved ones often penetrate through to my sphere. The thoughts of my soul stream together with their thoughts. My strength wants to help them. 'El's' reincarnation history is manifold. She will have to do a lot of inner work to understand all the effects of previous earth lives in her soul. My soul will be able to help her. It is hard, however, to tune my thoughts into hers. 'El' loved me in life; but behind this love there was also a strangeness which made it impossible to become really close.

'She' and 'it' were objectively close to me. That is why my thoughts can now behold their thoughts in the spirit light. My 'I' does not always grasp these thoughts fully; often they are merely flames but one can feel what they are. They are tangible to the soul warmth in which the 'I' dwells here.

The 'old man' is spreading the threads of supersensible reckoning over the events of the centuries. Many souls who are connected with my life are here. The threads of reckoning act as 'initiation'. The 'old man' says: what was created in 1870/71 has been destroyed in the physical world. What we brought about then is dying away. But the Spirit of the Future must be born from earthly graveyards. The 'old man' perceives a spiritual awakening. But the whole extent of this is to be revealed to my soul in the future only. He says: now ahrimanic powers are counting on earth; but the *final* accounts will be made by other spirits in the far distant future. Prepare for the end of the century. In Odilie's stream, too, there was a lot of darkness. This is yet to be illumined fully by the light.

The 'old man' is able to absorb spiritual science from my soul. It works on him as light he longs to receive. He says: when my 'I' was on earth all this was in me as a vague feeling; now a veil has dropped from my soul, and the spirit can be perceived with clarity.

In beautiful moments 'she' absorbs very well what she has to conciously experience through my thoughts. 'Being wakeful', this is 'her' office. She should not feel aggrieved when this proves difficult. Even here, there are many things which are, as yet, difficult to make sense of. That is why it is not possible to make sense of everything on earth, either.

Through 'her' thoughts I dwell in the spirit and science that wants to work on earth. Through 'her' my soul seeks this connection. Wherever 'she' is my soul can be, too. 'My own' have worries. But enshrouded in 'worries' must be the seed of the future.

A scene in the General Staff Building stands before my soul. The false magician celebrated with the one who took my place. I was shaken in my physical being. At the time my elder son had the right thoughts about everything that was decayed. In the future he will understand these thoughts well. Many things were concealed from me when I was still enveloped in the earthly body. My earthly body withdrew at the right time. Darkness would have spread over my soul if it had been forced to experience in the life of the senses what it could only bear supersensibly.

Before taking any decisions 'she' should give herself over to the thoughts she can feel when 'she' can feel my thoughts, too. In this way her work of 'wakeful guardian' will be best accomplished. At the century's end all has to come together after all. 'Uomi' will then be human again. And he will be freed from the sphere where there is a love of false magic.

People on earth say: Moltke was not the right man in the position he held. This would have caused me pain if I had heard it while on earth. But now my soul sees differently. At the time my 'I' *had to be* in these [sic] positions. And the centuries have decreed it so. However, there was the insurmountable difficulty with the false magician. But this, too, was necessary for the sake of evolution. After all, Germany also hatched up a false socialism. But those of us existing in the atmosphere of the magician did not see the wrong where it really was but through many distortions. Hence Bismarck's soul had no interest whatsoever in the war. This is still the case. He does not understand much, either, of the 'old man's' calculations. It is not yet possible to see whether he will have a task at the end of the century. My soul is not perceiving the guidance of his life now.

Many thoughts from the earthly realm come to me through 'her'. From out the spirit science [sic]. The Dornach building bears a lot. The thoughts are good. But where are the people who absorb them on earth? All around desert, growing desert. My soul gains much from these thoughts. It grows with them. But the people on earth will carry on wishing for different things for a long time to come. The spirit is closed off to them. They denied the spirit in 869. The appreciation of the spirit which was to be inaugurated from Rome in 865 was of no avail. Besides the perception of the spiritual, something of the spirit of the Princes of Andlau is alive in Dornach.

72. Message for Eliza von Moltke

Stuttgart, 16 February 1921

My 'I' is quickened in its being when 'her' thoughts rise up from the realm of earth to the realm of spirit—again and again our last life together that 'she' has given to me in the series of letters rises up before my soul. That constituted finding. That is what strengthens my beholding of the distant past. 'She' was in Dornach. There 'she' had thoughts in which my soul was well able to dwell. There my spiritual thoughts connected with old soul being. Middle Ages. Odilie's Mount. The hill opposite the place of Goethe. It attracts my soul. Then the spiritual bridge to the existence in Rome is built. Europe's thoughts are seeking these places. 'She' was my soul's companion. What is seen of the earth today with all its spiritual ruins can only be understood by looking back to these times. In 1914 my soul became an instrument. But everything happened of necessity. The review proves it. The 'old man' had already brought the ancient wisdom of light to Rome. We shone it all over Europe. From the depths of this Europe a different spirit rose up. Indeed my soul longed for this spirit—but it only came to me in quiet seclusion—Brückenallee, then in the General Staff building—I stepped into the world—there was the ancient light but it had already turned to darkness. Ahriman was ruling everything there. One went along with it. My soul finally did what was necessary. But what was necessary was done in darkness. We did not actually want the war then. But we did not have the strength to see through these things. Now those who have survived from that time are not seeing through things either. Europe is craving for the spirit and yet it drives away the spirit. There is fear of the spirit.

12 September 1914. The hours of decision are before my 'I'. This

'I' only did what was necessary. Europe had to cast off its old garments. Now it will wander naked through human evolution for a while. What happened there: it was the result of the Nicholas deeds. From there my soul goes forward towards future times. End of the century. 'She' accompanies my soul. 'She' has embarked on the common path.

We need to move towards the new light. Yet that must first be understood. In the realms of the spirit it is shining towards me. On earth my soul was always enveloped by darkness when I stepped out of my secluded chamber into the world where Ahriman ruled forcefully.

In the ninth century there were many dark, shadowy figures. We hauled them along with us through the ages. They caused confusion everywhere. 'It' kept shadow figures away from us again and again. 'It' was not touched by the shadow figures. Uomi is fighting the shadow figures. He warned in many different ways. But Ahriman's powers were too great then.

*

I often dwell on my loved ones. They have been drawn into many a turbulence. But this is all destiny. It has to be suffered. Because we will all find each other in the end. The trials of our suffering will prepare us for the tasks predestined for us. End of the century. In earthly terms it is far away. But viewed from the spirit realm it is only a short span of time. Then my 'I' will be freed of the circle where it was confused. That is what Uomi, the one of the warning voice, wanted too—but it was too early for the last life on earth.

*

Are there questions to my 'I' about earthly being? The soul's eye is not very clear with respect to this. Many shadow beings appear. Incarnated souls can never be completely deciphered from here. What confuses you now: therein lives a being which comes from the darkest depths of the earth. The doctor wanted to carry it to Düsseldorf in 1908. But it attached itself too strongly to Cahnheim. So the doctor only carried the empty stones there. Ever since that time the spirit situated in Cahnheim wanted revenge. But his consciousness knew nothing of all that. It acted under compulsion.

But this spirit has remained on earth. It is related to the earth.

*

A being that wreaks confusion holds sway there. Liberation is needed.

73. Message of May 1921

[Stuttgart?] May 1921

'Uomi' was always keen to work into the earthly sphere; however, he could not fully penetrate into it since destiny willed it otherwise. There are dark beings from earlier incarnations. They wished for the confusion. In particular they wanted to bring about doubts in my 'I' in this incarnation on earth. Doubts of this nature affected the activity of my heart through my breathing. My heart, having been exposed to these influences for such a long time, then started beating irregularly. This, in turn, affected my judgement. My 'I' can now see my entire blood circulation like a great ocean of processes in the cosmos. From the planet Mercury vapours rise into this ocean; these are the forces of Digitalis. However, it is only the manifestations of karma that are contained in these material processes as well as in the actual substances. The circulation reflects the effect of my life in my last incarnation on all the doubts which still remained in me from my previous lives on earth. Yet these doubts had not only emanated from my 'I'; they are connected with all the events in Europe into which my 'I' had been placed over the centuries. These events put an end to the whole of European civilization.

There will be chaos—'she' had already seen it coming in her previous life and from this had grown her rejection of the completely ahrimanic conditions into which we had been drawn in the nineteenth and twentieth centuries. My 'I', because it carried all the heaviness of the past within itself, was full of passive doubts. Yet that was good. My 'I' is now able to throw off everything it was intertwined with in an outer sense—the 'old man' is wishing for this, too—in order to work with renewed forces towards the new life which is to emerge from Europe's chaos. It was not possible to succeed in September 1914. In Central Europe no forces of sufficient spiritual strength existed which could use such a victory in the cause of progress.

And it is *Digitalis* which—already annihilating the present—is already pointing into the future. It opened the doors to the spiritual world for me. It rapidly cut off the earthly thread of life. I had been suffiently shaken by doubts. My worst day was 16 May 1916; but the most important events took place in the subconscious; my 'I' knew little of that.

Question: How are things with 'El'?

It is difficult to understand the souls that are still in their earthly bodies—my thoughts strive towards theirs; but she has little strength to catch them; this comes to my knowledge here. In any case she must examine herself. Her doubts remain completely in the subconscious; in this regard especially she has inherited a lot from me. She must find her way out of the muddle by her own strength. However, I will continue to seek her thoughts in order to strengthen her soul disposition.

Now the hour of decision approaches for Central Europe. But there are no real men around at all. None of them is able to find the new note which now has to be struck. It is as if everybody were totally cut off from the spiritual world. 'It' is sending forth thoughts in which one feels comfortable to live. 'She' is brave. But there is nobody who understands. There is no need to be sad about it; but one must be awake and do what one can.

There are people sitting in Berlin who are cutting themselves off from the course of events in Europe. No one considers that an appeal ought to be made to the whole world. It is not possible to rebuild on how things were in the old days. The Germans keep on saying things which nobody else in the world understands. Now the Americans are appealed to; yet the Americans do not know what is wanted of them. In Germany no thought is ever completed. All thinking is done by halves. Bethmann's soul is almost completely extinguished. Like a paralysed soul whose spiritual eyes see nothing here. The last thoughts he entertained on earth are like a blindfold over his soul's eye. The same applies to many others who have entered this realm in recent times. I only gained the power of sight as a consequence of spiritual cognition coupled with the letter retrospective. With that 'she' gave my soul a great treasure. Everything contained in the 'Thoughts' I wrote for 'her' is true; however, the people with whom I worked are possessed by the ahrimanic power and do not want to see. Much happened in July 1914 of which I knew nothing at all. There were always people sitting in the General Staff who said: he does not need to know all that; we will handle that—let him stick to his affairs. I never became aware of all that intriguing against me. But now I have done. After all, the Kaiser had them all in his pocket; only a few there were who had him in their pockets. He really is a man of the deepest guilt; there was so little in him that was spiritual.

74. Message of June 1921

[Stuttgart?] June 1921

The earthly world is accessible to my 'I' through the thoughts sent to me from there, yet these thoughts contain more than those who entertain them as earthly people would know. In 'her' thoughts I see a lot of the present and also a lot of the future. 'She' is now thinking about many things that worry 'her'. 'She' ought to find solace and hope in the great thoughts of spiritual science. They will endure when everything that many human beings now attach themselves to will have passed away completely. People on earth know one another so little. My soul only really knew a very small proportion of the people that were around it on earth. It lived with a view to the spirit, it is true. But the earthly body did not follow suit. It believed too strongly in the temporal. At the moment of dying the earthly world sank as if into a deep abyss and the spiritual world became my soul's environment. I see worries in 'her'. These must be the shadows of thoughts about the future. But the thoughts of the future are light. Only their shadows thrown into the present are dark.

Light should be shone into the earth's darkness. The truth is being sought there. The time will come when it will need to be proclaimed. The people who know the truth and are still alive fear the truth. In Central Europe many people are afraid of the truth because they have lived a lie for so long; in the West people fear the truth because they would have to change their whole life if they admitted to the truth.

Only a humanity that understands what it is to live in the spirit will be able to bear the truth.

'She' ought to face the events to come with complete equanimity.

Things will happen which will change the direction of everything. My soul had turned against the old Latin heritage because it was too deeply enmeshed in it in its previous life. Counter-Latinism, that is what lived in me. In 1914 that worked as a positive force into what was predominantly ahrimanic. And now Latinism holds sway in Berlin. Goethe is far from Berlin. Already in ninth century Rome 'she' disliked that Latinism.

*

My loved ones are thinking of me. That is good, because it enables me to live in their thoughts a great deal. Thoughts are what one may retain here from the earthly element.

'El' is here strongly, but this is only coming to expression in her flickering element now. 'El' is suffering from the spirit creating unrest within her.

I am connected with 'it'. Just as I am with 'her'. All my loved ones have a lot to endure from the last earthly life. After all we lived as if on a spiritual island. How the others on the earth talk about that which was brought about by me. They talk as if it was something in which they had had no involvement. They really were in different worlds from that of my soul. That is why they seem to have forgotten everything, or else pour scorn over it.

That which was around me in 1914 was like a frightened creature that could not recover its senses. Those who were among the better people were frightened, and those less good full of fear. Such was the environment in which decisions had to be taken.

The shadow of fear which is so closely related to untruth is cast over everything today. Light should issue from what is German; but instead it is covered over by a black cloud of darkness. The bad is called good and the good is called bad. Many human beings are like automatons. Fear alone obstructs the progress of truth.

75. Message Without Exact Date
(following on from 21 June)

A somewhat older message:
Physical events are always images of the way things are connected spiritually. Digitalis: it was my deliverance. Without it my body would have had to suffer for longer. However, Digitalis is an

ahrimanic counter-force. It was in my karma that my soul should dwell extensively in ahrimanic human intentions during my life. Digitalis acted from the body to the soul to render powerless the ahrimanic forces. Through that I was greatly relieved. These matters look very different from the spiritual world from what they look on earth. My soul is constantly striving to enter into the thoughts of my loved ones. We need to unite together for the century's end. We will have joint tasks to fulfil then.

'El' will struggle hard. Her physical health is entirely connected with this. She does not express much of what causes her suffering. Maybe she does not even express it to herself. But nevertheless her suffering is entirely related to her soul. Hence cures aimed at the body will bring only temporary relief. Unfortunately I cannot reach the thoughts of the 'other'; would not be allowed either to effect anything via that route. He would have to be capable of taking decisions. One cannot will things for others. Bill could do with more backbone. For a man he is too dependent. He ought to pull himself together. Since my death my love for him has grown much stronger. He is close to me: that could help him. He has strong faith. May he uphold it. It is good. But he ought to become self-reliant.

In these times of confusion it is difficult for me to stay on my path and conduct my affair. What do the others know after all about the beginning of the war. When all the burden was upon me I had to take the decision while others carried out their stupid ahrimanically inspired acts. Their actions put everything in a wrong light. On my return home from Karlsbad I was told too little of what had happened. But if the nonsensical chatter continues as it does now, things will be very bad for Germany.

Everything appears in its grand context to me now. After the events of the ninth century my soul had to experience everything in the way it has done. 1914 is the fulfilment of 860—and everything that lies in-between. The whole period from the ninth to the twentieth century was a darkening of Christianity.

Ahrimanic powers intruded into what was originally Christian. They found easy access to the powers which the Kaiser wished to surround himself with. Anyone who knows about his time in Rome will understand this. He wanted the Spirit of Untruth around him. This spirit was everywhere. And it has stayed on now. Everyone wants to speak untruthfully because they consider the truth damaging to themselves. And they believe themselves to be representing Germany. What I have written down for 'her' was well inspired. My soul can stand by it all. There is nothing in there which could be impugned.

But the others cannot understand this because they isolated my soul so much. Many thought that they could serve their own aims when I was in Karlsbad. Most of them had lost all trace of a conscience in Rome. Now they talk of the 'Fatherland'. But such talk serves to anaesthetize their consciences which they lost in Rome. They have spent the time between the ninth and the twentieth centuries serving Ahriman in their souls. My soul had grown away from Rome. Was connected with Antlau [Andlau] at the Mount of Odilie and everything that belongs to that. Through this my soul became ripe for spiritual science. During my life other powers kept me away from it, that is all. But now everything is bearing fruit.

76. Message of December 1921

Stuttgart, December 1921

The vistas appearing before my soul are becoming more and more clear. But there are worries which play into this clarity—worries about the people of Central Europe. They are firmly in the grip of ahrimanic powers. Entire decades of my previous life are before me now. 'She' has helped me to experience this by means of the letters; through that action their contents, and also what they indicate about the whole character of my last incarnation, come up before my soul. It was a time devoid of spirit.

From Rome there had remained in my soul a longing for true spiritual cognition. In Rome one aimed at spiritual power. This is how it had to be in those days, because then we still had the great spiritual conceptions of ancient times. We had knowledge of the great sages of ancient times who were sent to humanity by the gods. From all of this a great longing remained in my soul. But there were people there, demon-like people. I met many of them around me in my last life on earth. That created a great deal of division in my soul. Finally, the prospect of the spirit! But it became so difficult to really grasp it. If there had been a stronger orientation to faith. But it wanted to be more than faith. It was a messenger of the true spirit— this is what comes before my soul now.

'It' had attained a completely different expression of strength from it. 'It' was filled with it. For this soul the spirit is self-evident. My soul often seeks 'its' thoughts now. There is a relationship with the earthly life. But there is such a relationship through 'her', too. This is necessary. However, the confusion one sees in earthly life is becoming greater and greater.

The truth about my position needs to be revealed. There should be no reservations. Times have changed. My soul needs to judge differently now.

My younger son's thoughts are brilliant. He knows what matters now.

Showing consideration for others now is not justified, because the people who were around me on earth consider themselves only.

What I did in 1914 I had to do. The world must know that. Germany was defeated; but the German spirit has not been defeated. However, the German spirit is asleep now. Simons has made awful mistakes. He is completely in the hands of those who do not actually want to see the truth.

The events on the Marne! Everything would have turned out differently if I had not been accompanied by the mistrust of those around me. I travelled to the front in a cloud of mistrust. There was a man who played a very evil part, who had wanted to introduce a heresy in Rome, and had to be punished very severely at that time. Now he acted out of revenge against my soul. He spread false news in [at] the front. But at that time everything was believed. It was I alone who was mistrusted by many.

And so I had to work in a cloud of distrust right from the beginning of the campaign.

The Kaiser was actually quite weak due to the forces working in him from his previous life.

The 'old man' speaks as if his earthly life, which brought him so much outer fame, means very little to him now. But his words carry weight. Sometimes he gets right through to the people on earth.

My soul often goes out to my children's thoughts. I feel concerned with their destiny. My elder son ought to remember me more often. If he recalled some of the things I told him in life he would be more aware of me and gain strength.

I can give him this strength because his thoughts are moving in a positive direction.

'Her' thoughts always lead me to the earthly world. I unite myself with the thoughts 'she' directs to me.

It gives me pleasure to look back into the time of my previous life. It was a time of great world thoughts. What those times left in me was what put me in that crucial position in my last earthly life. I bore great responsibility then. The time will come when the people who were around me then will disown me. 'She' must have no fear; battles will have to be fought. The people on the German side who wrenched the direction of the war away from me did not recognize the great questions of world-historical importance; they are still not able to do so now. That is why they distort the decisive responsibility that lay on my soul.

It is good that my soul was able to leave the earth before my earthly eyes would have had to see what burdens the German people had to bear. Through the final suffering my 'I' learned a lot, because from those pains it carried strong forces through the portal of death. They lend clarity to my soul now.

'El's' special destiny has made her particularly sensitive to the counter-forces connected with my and my loved ones' karma. All that is necessary is that these counter-forces be properly understood. They drive evolution forward through their activity. In the end these things make one stronger, even though one finds much to be bitter about because one cannot understand it properly at first.

When 'she' was in the regions where she saw a lot of that through which 'she' has helped me, I was particularly well connected with past times through 'her' thoughts. From vistas such as those the view into the future arises; the future in which we need to do our work so that the forces which will then be necessary for the earth's evolution may be gathered together at the end of the century.

'She' must not give way to fear when the times demand that much has to happen for the sake of the truth. Truth alone must prevail before the gaze struggling for clarity in the realm of the spiritual. In the context of the world as a whole only truth can bring strength.

*

Rome. Ninth century. European humanity wrestled in its soul with the thoughts of Asia. The Asian way of thinking was close to the spirit. But the Europeans had to do the earthly work. Then it happened, once when 'she' was with me, urging greater energy, that the Spirit of Peter appeared to me and demanded that I free the

European world from Asian thinking. It was the great hour of decision. But the other one, who brought me such suffering in my last earthly life, was there, too. He united himself with the powers of darkness because he did not want to understand the idea of the Christ. He said: O what should we care about the remote destiny of Europe.

I said: What concerns the world is a matter for human beings when the moments of decision arrive.
He: Peter is a person with whom I want nothing to do; he pushes me out of my path.
I: He went from Asia to Europe, from the spirit to the European cultivation of the spirit. We must follow him.

Then he went away and Peter's spirit was there again.

In my last life on earth the forces which were planted in my soul in Roman times emerged again. However, in the meantime Europe had forgotten the spirit. It has sunk into materialism.

In 1914 my thoughts could not but take the direction they did. If I had not pressed people 'forward' an even greater trial would have come upon my people. However hard these times are now they could have become harder still.

'She' must be strong. In 'her' strength there is a power of light which my soul needs. One needs to stick to the straightforward thoughts which guide us. Others want to distort these thoughts. But in the end this would only lead to disaster.

Let us seek the source of strength for the future by steadily developing what we have experienced. There is a lot of suffering in her; my soul shares it.

But even now there is a luminous glow when my soul is with 'her' thoughts.

77. Message of 2 February 1922

Breslau, 2 February 1922

The 'Spirit of Peter' was often before my 'I' in the ninth century. At that time it was he whom one had to follow in the course of Europe's cultural evolution. If the Asian way of thinking had been victorious then, a great spiritual darkness would have descended on

Europe; the greater part of humanity would have remained utterly impoverished in the spirit and only a few enlightened ones would have dwelt in separate spiritual colonies. He who gave me so much cause for worry in my last life on earth would have been happier in the ninth century for such a state of affairs to have come about. But the task was to devote oneself to bringing about the other state of affairs, and at that time 'she' stood at my side and understood that European thought had to be strengthened *vis-à-vis* Asian thought. All this resulted in the build-up of forces with which we still had to grapple in our last earthly lives. Those people who were around me then succumbed to the powers of Ahriman because they had no real interest in a European spirit. In their souls the thought lives that they would have fared better in the small spiritual colonies. So there were many souls around me in the nineteenth and twentieth centuries who were on spiritual paths very different from those my soul had to pursue. That is why spiritual science became a necessity for my soul; but then the ahrimanic people, with their intense hatred for everything truly spiritual, were again around me; they dragged my soul further and further away from it.

When the Battle of the Marne came nearer, the ahrimanic counter-pole grew especially strong. The ahrimanic people did not want any spiritual influence to come about in Europe. My soul was greatly burdened then. The outer calamity came nearer and nearer. Thanks to 'her' help my soul was able to escape through the narrow portal of life. The revelation of the realm of the spirit had come through 'it' many years earlier. That was the first prelude. To this was added spiritual science through 'her' efforts. And thus the connection with the spiritual world could be preserved in spite of the outer misfortune. Nevertheless, Europe's catastrophe was a necessity. My soul could not take any other decision in 1914. The truth about this may be obscured for a certain time but in the end it will have to prevail.

'She' is suffering from the present opposition from the ahrimanic people. All possible consideration should be shown to 'her' suffering in this way. A little 'waiting' will not make much difference. My soul lives in 'her' thoughts.

The times are serious for Central Europe. Hours of decision are at hand.

The Spirit of Europe has now to battle with much that is antichristian. But the ahrimanic people are calling what is antichristian,

Christian. What is antichristian is still strong because the true idea of the spirit and its world has yet to pass the test in Central Europe. There is still too little faith in the true spirit. And Central Europe cannot progress through unspirituality but only by the power of the spirit.

They were able to liquidate my body in 1914; but they will not be able to extinguish what my soul wanted to do. She, too, should stand firm on this firm point.

Many adversities are yet to come and pass by. But the light at the end of the twentieth century shines brightly before my soul.

The man who brought me so much anguish will find it hard to brighten up his soul. But my soul will suffer no more confusion through his. From now on my soul will be free from his interference. Christ, as the 'Son' of God's power, has, after all, never been able to recognize this soul of his.

Already in ninth century Rome the crucial question was whether Christ as the 'Son' should really pass into European consciousness. But even today there is far too little understanding of this in Central Europe. Therefore Central Europe can only slowly turn into the teacher of Eastern Europe. And this is what will have to happen if there is to be light. In Central Europe science, too, will have to become spiritual. Central Europe has yet to pass this test.

'She' should not worry about what cannot at present be because the time is not ripe for it. After all, many things can be disparaged but the truth cannot be done away with.

My 'I' is not affected when people say of me now: 'he was not good enough'. Those who say it have no idea what was at stake at the time. It was necessary to act and it was not possible to act in any other way. The great necessities in human evolution need to be understood, and great turning-points in evolution must not be judged out of sympathy or antipathy.

The unconscious fear of the truth which besets so many people today in calamitous fashion will lead to terrible disillusionment for many people who now live by spiritual anaesthetics alone. And especially 'she' has much to suffer from such people who wish to live by such spiritually anaesthetizing sleeping draughts.

78. *Message for Eliza von Moltke of 9 August 1922*

Dornach, 9 August 1922 [r]

'She' is giving me many thoughts from the world my 'I' has left. But 'she' is full of worry. These worries are understandable. In the spiritual world, however, they are experienced differently. There the greater interrelationships are seen. However, these are not yet in full clarity before my soul. That will come. The end of the century will demand that clarity from me and my loved ones.

The ninth century, too, breaks in more and more. And then the Middle Ages which my soul lived through in the spirit. The causes from my previous life placed my last life next to other people who outwardly dimmed my eyes for what was, and still is, ahrimanic in their nature. What happened in 1914 could not have happened in any other way. Very few people were in control of the world's destinies; I had to take the helm. My nine years in the General Staff were such in my earthly life that my soul may now dwell in beneficent solitude.

No one could have really prevented war in 1914. Rathenau's soul is tightly wrapped up, it cannot see yet.

Everything that was written [in] Homburg in 1914 is the complete truth.

But others are not writing the complete truth in this matter.

'She' will find the way which 'she' has to follow. Because our thoughts are finding each other.

The peoples of Central Europe are going through hard times now. They have lost their direction. This direction was prepared in the ninth century. 'She', too, was in Rome then. Was at my side. But the one who worked with magic means at that time became completely dark and lost his relationship to Christianity.

When 'she' listens to lectures in the wooden building I can hear, I can be present through 'her' thoughts.

Much was given to my soul through such hearing with 'her' thoughts.

If the German army had moved East rather than West in 1914, England would have found it easier to achieve her aims. Yet in the end everything would have happened as it did.

'It' helps me a lot when 'it' directs her thoughts to me. But this is also good for the future for which we all need to prepare ourselves.

Detachment from all those with whom destiny connected my last life on earth is now coming about. This detachment is effected by the knowledge of the spirit which streamed into me.

Uomi was indeed human once. But he served us; he has been connected for a long time with the destinies of our families. He worked supersensibly into their lives.

Those who spread untruths about many things today are easily believed because many people's sense of truth is impaired.

Before my last life but one a spiritual wave went out from Odilien from West to East. In the ninth century the work to be effected also had to be in harmony with this wave. At that time there was still a kind of false Mystery Centre in Central Italy. However, we did not recognize that it was a false one at the time. There were then many individuals in Rome who had trained there. The magic of the one whom I had to serve in my last earth life also derives from there. The pure Christianity that was still spiritual was to be turned into lots of dogma there so that Europe would lose its connection with the spirit. And around me in my last earthly life there were souls who had gone through this school. 'She' perceived at that time (ninth century) what emanated from this school. Thus 'she' was able to sense in the nineteenth century what called itself Christian but was not.

In 1914 one would have only been able to advance westwards with good luck if one had been carrying a new spirit there. However, when we set off nothing spiritual lived among those setting off into battle. There was a good power above us; but we did not want to set off in its name. Therefore this good power will have to wait until Central Europe is purified so that it may thereafter serve this power.

Uomi knew already more than 20 years ago that we do not recognize the spirit who wishes to show us the way. This non-recognition has defeated us. Heresy produced confusion. In September 1914 there was a spiritual fog over those around me. And my soul was unable to penetrate this fog. The fog was a continuing of the false Mystery Centre which was opposed to our work in Rome and which already at that time prevented us from doing what we should have done on behalf of a true Christianity in the spirit.

The 'old man' also comprehends these things now. So there is much understanding between his soul and mine.

79. *Message of 8 December 1922*

Berlin, 8 December 1922

People on earth are destined to live through difficult times. There is no power in sight which could intervene to make things easier.

I am with 'her' in my thoughts and 'her' thoughts live in my spiritual arteries. 'She' needs strength. May she feel the strengthening power of my thoughts. 'She' is up against my old earthly adversaries. Right now many old enmities dating from the ninth century are flaring up. 'She' stood by my side as counsellor then—filled with great courage and enthusiasm; and so she must experience the enmities which karma now brings. Only in this necessary way can the interrelationships brought by destiny be laid to rest. For a long time we had to be connected with our adversaries on the way, but now our ways are parting. Towards the end of the century we will be freed of our adversaries. We will accomplish a task of great significance to the world.

My eldest son will also have a task to fulfil then, just as Adam and 'it' will, together with us. It is good that my eldest son has explored the mysteries of the earth. Anyone who has penetrated the mysteries of the earth's grounds will receive his task in a future incarnation from *that* etheric sphere which specifically strengthens man's will. Von der Goltz is here and so is the 'old man'. Both of them understand that everything that happened had to happen, as my 'I' does, too: the war as well as the defeat and Germany's terrible destiny. Nevertheless for the 'old man' it feels as if the loss of what he had achieved through conquest wiped out a part of his earthly existence, even in his memory.

For some time now we have been looking at the demons who worked on earth in 1914 and who made use of some influential people to wreak havoc through them by creeping into their souls.

I see this picture: the helpless Kaiser in the days when war broke out. Helpless in his vanity. This is how he stood before me in the ninth century, too, when he wanted to introduce severest church sanctions into Western Europe instead of the spiritual life envisaged by 'her' and 'myself'.

He has remarried. The princess *had* to come together with him again, because she was the cleric who was his bitterest opponent in the ninth century. He could not have fulfilled his karma with her in his capacity as Kaiser. This is how destiny is shaped in the course of the world.

What appears highly significant on earth is often insignificant in the supersensible world and that which is insignificant on earth is often very important here.

My memoirs will be published. In this matter the thought experiences of my soul are with 'her', too. She will encounter opposition as a result. Let 'her' be strong. We had to have enemies. This has to do with the streams of destiny.

'Else' follows a path of her own. It is full of complications. Sometimes she strays from what is predestined for us. However, she will find her way to us in the end.

'She' has lived in the review of all I have written to 'her' in the course of my life. That made it possible for my soul to live through it all anew with 'her'. This strengthens the forces of my spiritual members.

My soul takes part in what happens to 'her' and is transformed into thoughts by her; this enables my soul to experience it. The thoughts of human souls on earth to whom one belongs are seen by the soul here, because the sun carries them into the supersensible world every day.

My soul is now entering a time where the struggles connected with my acceptance of the post of Chief of the General Staff are interweaving with karmic impressions from the ninth century; such scenes stand before my inner eye now. It was of the deepest karmic significance that I of all people had to carry the painting of the 'Peoples of Europe . . .' to Russia. In the ninth century we *really* did just that from Rome. At that time the 'I' of the Kaiser was opposed to it. Now, in the twentieth century, it had become a mere *picture*. In this way many things which have come to expression in public life in the twentieth century are mere pictures, not reality. For this reason many of those who have died in the midst of such events walk through the spiritual world like shadows.

'She' brought to me during my earthly life the reality of the spiritual while I was forced to live, with many of my professional colleagues, in an earthly world of pictures. One believed that one was accomplishing practical things together with these colleagues. In truth, one merely gave expression to illusory ahrimanic thoughts. For 14 years until 1914 the world was dominated by ahrimanic illusion; this paved the way for the luciferic period which began in

1914 and in which the feelings of human beings became entangled. This entanglement persists to the present day. Only a higher degree of devotion to the spiritual world can save people from it. We had enormous illusions about the Turks, for example. This led to the disaster that we even formed an alliance with them. Now destiny is fulfilling itself. What is not yet totally confused in Europe is now confused by the Turks. The world needs the light which can spring from western civilization and Central European culture and spirituality. Confusion will persist as long as this spirituality is denied.

Nearly everything that happens today stems from this confusion. For 14 years people lived in a world of illusory ahrimanic pictures, and now they have been for over seven years in a luciferic fog. This brings even greater confusion into people's feelings on earth. But here the light of Michael is shining and it could be found spiritually by people on earth if they were willing to dispel the luciferic fog. The third decade of the twentieth century will bring hard times for Central Europe. There will be certain 'signs' in the earthly-visible world which human beings should 'see'. This will be a hard test for them.

80. Message from the Beginning of the Year 1923

Dornach, beginning of 1923

'Her' good intentions and the courage 'she' showed in connection with the publication of the book are meeting with little interest. My soul feels deeply linked with 'her' deed but the people on earth have become so dulled now. Hence the enlightenment which this book could have brought about is not happening, unfortunately. And the souls who are already here in the spiritual world and who lived through it all on earth know what it is all about. These souls look down on the poor people on earth who are so tossed about by the painful events.

My soul is deeply connected with 'her' soul and the thoughts 'she' has in her soul are like clouds in which I live, warming myself, while at the same time feeling 'her' great suffering with her. There is plenty of suffering. Yet there is one great consolation. We are together. And also deeply connected with 'it' who is helping so much with her quiet courage and her great patience with life.

My gaze often goes back to the ninth century and beholds how things appear in a clearer light from there. 'She' was by my side then. 'She' had many ideas which needed to be realized at that time.

People called 'her' my 'spiritual counsel' then. What was started up then quivered through Europe for centuries. We had been connected with people then from whom karma only separated us in the last earthly life in order that we might stride out freely towards the end of the twentieth century, towards our task.

Oh, I want to pour strength into 'her' thoughts. Because the impact of the non-comprehending world was great. 'She' had to and has to put up with so much. There is simply darkness on earth. With regard to 1914 people cannot feel the truth. That is why people wrap themselves up in illusions, thinking that the truth can be set aside if it is rejected. Yet at the end of the day it will stride through people with giant steps. Hence my soul is in agreement with 'her' in helping the truth on its way through the book. I often send strengthening thoughts to my children from the spirit realm. May they feel these strengthening thoughts and greetings. They now have to help carry out that for which destiny led us together in our last earthly life. They will have to feel and understand that this had to be so. It was prepared when we lived through a great deal together in Rome, in more peaceful, yet already complicated, circumstances. Many veils are falling for my 'I' with regard to this time. The view is expanding and soon the time will come when the pictures which darkly rise up from that time like silhouettes will be completely bright. Then I shall be able to see a lot. Will be able to see a lot out of the past and thereby come to understand the present clearly.

The bond with 'her' is the strongest of all my connections. When 'she' concentrates her thoughts 'she' will be able to feel how my soul is with 'her'. The great difficulties of life must be lived through. We want to be together even now with our souls dwelling in such different places of the world.

My soul bears her suffering with her. It has to be so because karma has welded us together. After all, it gives the bond that links us much strength as well as much suffering. The picture of the future task remains before the spirit, after all. And the book which is met now with such incomprehension by earthly souls will work on further by means of the thoughts it projects into the course of evolution. It will yet be found that this book contains something quite different from the many other writings about the sad era of the war. It will be found that this book contains the unadorned truth whereas the others conceal the truth behind illusions. But at present the fog of illusions is still very thick, therefore the simple truth is not yet recognized. Nevertheless it will find its way despite the many obstacles it will encounter.

81. Message of 12 March 1923

Dornach, 12 March 1923 [r]

It is a difficult time now for the earth's inhabitants; 'she', too, can feel the vibrations of this difficult time, because 'her' thoughts are before my 'I'. There I can behold these thoughts. Up here thoughts are before one's 'I' just as objects were before one's eyes on earth. But the complete stream of thoughts is maintained. The entire past stands before my 'I'. The present only fits with great difficulty into this picture. It is as if everything were crumbling at the present time.

Nevertheless the future is there, too. One beholds it in the distance. But only the end of the century will bring it to the earth. Then the connections with the Nicholas era will have to be made. What was really intended then was the spiritualization of Europe. But it would have taken place too early. It was first necessary to endure everything that brought many disappointments to the peoples of Europe, thereby robbing them of their illusions.

From the Crusades right up to the time of our World War, all European thinking was full of illusion. Unfortunately in 1914, what was necessary had to be done out of illusion.

The fact that the world now knows how my soul thought in my last earthly life, how it acted out of iron necessity, gives my 'I' a satisfying feeling of warmth. One day these things will be judged correctly. It is not yet possible now. People do not look at the things but only at their own feelings.

'She' has to endure many knocks from all sides. 'She' is conducting my cause. My soul is living with 'her'. My comforting thoughts wish to reach 'her'.

'She' was by my side in the ninth century. Today's hostile factions were already forming at that time. Already at that time the opponents were working out their ideology against 'us'. 'She' always felt this during my last earthly life. Now it will hardly be possible for any of the opponents to be converted because what has been formed in repeated earthly lives remains very rigid.

In September 1914 the karma of my soul was detached from much that had long been connected with my 'I'. That is why the pains and sufferings which came upon me were so great. These were the consequences of the karma becoming detached. But it is for this very reason that the future will be less encumbered.

'It' will help a great deal through her heartfelt connection with the spiritual world. 'It' has fashioned this connection in a special way. 'It' transforms with her will what is spiritual in her eyes and ears and what is not spoilt in her through undermining thoughts. Hence she will carry into the future a spiritualized will and with that 'it' will be able to do a great deal.

My soul, too, experiences what is experienced by those on earth who were connected with me by blood. But many a knot will still have to be unravelled in this realm and many a thing has yet to be penetrated with clarity. But all of us will stay connected and become helpers in the unravelling of 'our' great life knot.

When 'she' is listening to lectures now my soul can also be there. In earlier times it was as if everything had taken place in one large room; now it is as if in a large meadow. But this meadow lies in isolation.

What 'she' does to refute the opponents' thoughts is good. Wrong thoughts must be prevented from emerging. They ruin earthly existence. But in this regard a great great deal will have to be done. Because today the truth is covered over with a thick layer of untruth and illusion.

The picture of the Roman time is forming with ever greater clarity before my soul. At that time 'she' had a lot to do with fending off the evil forces of magic that surrounded us on all sides. And many of the bearers of these evil magic forces were incarnated again at the beginning of the nineteenth century and also at the critical time. What was in them in those earlier days had an effect in 1914, too. These things will become a lot clearer than they are now. Because much of what tries to come before my soul with regard to these matters is clouded over. 'She' is still involved in the arduous earthly task; nevertheless, what she is doing will bear ample fruit for the time in the future when we will again work together a great deal.

'She' may draw comfort from the certainty that 'her' work is good. Through this work my soul's thoughts are guided in a direction where they may receive much spiritual light. It has always been like this ever since 'she' has acted for me on earth. 'She' moves in my direction and accomplishes much that I could not have done if I were still living on earth. But 'she' can do it, and that is good.

82. Message of 28 July 1923

Dornach, 28 July 1923 [r]

Everything connected with the feelings of 1914 is disappearing in the awful chaos of thinking that is now holding sway in Germany. People are losing themselves altogether. When the soul looks down on earthly happenings now it beholds a foggy cloud of souls.

In this foggy cloud 'her' soul appears to mine like a bright flame. But this flame can only shine into confusion and darkness everywhere. Because confusion and darkness is now earthly destiny.

'She' suffers greatly, too. A pile of rubble has taken the place of the former order among the Germans. The stones roll about and heap up on human hearts.

My soul beholds the suffering in 'her' soul. But then I direct my gaze to later times around the end of the century when we will work together to give humanity what it needs.

We have suffered much in the present in order to be able to do this work.

A world age has now come to an end.

It began in the ninth century, in Rome. Already then the 'old man' brought with him the impulse of ancient times. We were involved in bringing about what Europe needed. But there were individualities among us then who have come back now. They were the weights around our necks. The people in my vicinity had brought over their frivolous view of life from ninth century Rome.

We, my soul and 'hers', together with the others who belong to us, will continue our work in the spiritual world for nearly a century, for the impulses which must be given at the end of the twentieth century.

In Rome we were entrusted with the care of the spiritual life in Europe. This spirituality has gradually become less than perfect. From the site where 'she' dwells now in the mountains of Alsace and Switzerland, a great impulse also came forth throughout the Middle Ages.

Odilie is the name of a light that shone in the darkness from the Vosges mountain towards the German East.

What we had to inaugurate in the ninth century in Rome penetrated to that place. In 1914 that came to an end. At that time all spiritual-cultural interests had turned into economic ones. Europe had lost its spirituality. Those who should have been at my side to safeguard the spiritual had become vain and ambitious.

The confusion will become greater still. In this age there are as yet no new thoughts.

Many of those who were involved in the events on earth in 1914 have already arrived here. They all feel that the end of an era on earth had come and that they will now have to start afresh here to prepare for the future.

The heads of earthly people are empty now, and in their hearts they are at a loss. This must be so now because the spiritual was treated with utter contempt throughout the whole of the nineteenth century.

Thus the spiritual has become foreign to earthly man.

'She' has faithfully watched over things. But keeping watch is difficult now because the houses to be watched have been destroyed. The treasures are lying in the streets and even when a watch is kept robbers come and seize them because they are lying in the streets. People will say much that is bad about what happened in 1914. But it cannot be any different now. There is no respect or appreciation anywhere; there is only hatred and illusion.

People on earth will have to get from the spiritual world the new impulses they must have for faith and love, for they will not find them on earth.

Whole cities will crumble away; in many regions only the farmers will be left. It will be crucial that certain individuals are there who will still have the courage to create monastic-type settlements where the spiritual life can be cultivated, as earlier in hermitages.

In the innermost part of human souls the world has been in ruins since 1900; 1914 went through the world like a punishing wind. We were subject to the necessity of the world's vengeance. It all had to happen as it did in 1914. With good intentions we were cast into Ahriman's machinations. Everything charged through the darkness.

My soul is gaining increasing knowledge of these things. Along with this knowledge comes insight into the necessity of all that happened then.

Many innocent people are now suffering. But they will find the balance through karma. Even so the ahrimanic spirit had to be wiped out with a lot of blood.

In the nineteenth century people lived as if in a dream because they could not have borne to be awake. 'She' is thinking about many things now. 'Her' thoughts are with me. I live with 'her'. 'It' is pondering in solitude. But their thoughts carry many forces through the world. And *these* forces will be important one day when we will work together for a new age.

83. Message of 13 January 1924

Dornach, 13 January 1924 [r]

There is chaos on earth. Everywhere is dark. It is like a flood of unspirituality and sin. People are blind and deluded. The delusions of those who were connected with me in my last life are working on in my soul. 'She' suffers in this darkness. But 'she' is connected with my 'I'. The Michael-Sun has brought 'her' to me. I was able to be with 'her' on many occasions when 'she' feels rightly connected with the Michael-Sun. The 'old man' is turning away from earthly happenings altogether. He is completely remote from them. He considers that there will only be light again when new impulses enter humanity.

'It' is sending good thoughts towards my soul. A lot will come to fruition in this soul.

It is difficult to intervene in the thoughts of human beings. They are so confused by all that has happened. There is a great difference indeed now between the thought-beings who are preparing the future here and the ahrimanic beings who are creating deception on the earth below.

My soul often dwells with my family. It lives in their destinies. I can be with them when their thoughts are directed towards me. Many of the impulses from the Nicholas era are now resurging in the world. At that time 'she' proved herself an excellent judge of people. 'Her' understanding of people drove us forward.

However, the 'Europe' initiated then has run its course. It must be understood that this is the past, not the present.

The year 1914 will be inscribed as a year of terrible crisis in the evolution of the earth. There is thick fog where the events of that year are to be found in the astral light. Human beings will never clear away this fog.

We must live towards the future at the end of the century. We will then incarnate as people who will find the strength in their physical lives to work together with the gods.

By working together in this way many a knot will be unravelled which could never be unravelled by human beings in their present state. In 1914 we were completely forsaken by the gods. We abandoned ourselves to the machinations of spirits who drove us this way and that. The whole of Europe was subjected to this.

It was as if the river Rhine was filled with a whole army of ahrimanic beings who all had conflicting interests. They were joined by others from the river Weichsel who had allied themselves with oriental demons. All of this worked into human souls. One was bound to act in the way one did. However, things would have been very different if we had been able to follow Michael's will in its full content.

'She' is at the Goetheanum. Frequently her thoughts are such that my soul can be there, too. Indeed: if only this was heard: 'Practise Spirit-Remembrance', 'Practise Spirit-Contemplation', 'Practise Spirit-Beholding'. But this will only be heard by people when Michael is able to find in the astral light the trail which leads to the spirit-altar on which burns the astral flame that Ahriman fears. This will certainly not happen before the end of the century. As yet here are no eyes which can perceive the Christ walking in the ether light. Eyes that can only see what divides humanity will not be able to attain to such perception. From the East a huge wave of black clouds is moving towards the West. Only earthly impulses live in this. The Michael spirit despises these. And so humanity will want to dispense with leadership.

Everybody wants to live on the wreckage of the nineteenth century. The twentieth century demands a quite different attitude, but people do not want to submit to such a requirement.

There are many individuals incarnated now who have no soul. They become bearers of demonic powers. *These* can only be recognized when people have knowledge of the spiritual. And they do not want such knowledge.

If spiritual knowledge does not spread a time will come when black ahrimanic birds, hovering over the heads of people, will form a barricade between human beings and the spiritual world. These black birds of ill omen want to cut off the Light of the Michael spirit from mankind.

Human beings find what rays out from these black birds of ill omen of great benefit, because they think that the earthly world can thereby be improved. What underlies the hopes generated in this way is demonic in nature and has much to do with the fact that the birds, which ought to live seven miles beneath the earth, are raised above the heads of human beings. The dangers are very great indeed. The black birds of ill omen intend to spin a web of materialism around all mankind; this is to be followed by the cosmic materialization of actual thoughts and feelings, with the object of binding human existence to this materialization. In this way the 'greatest illusion' ever would take on definite cosmic reality.

It is possible to see in the astral light here what *may* happen but could still be averted if the following came to pass. Today the genuine spiritual world is still hovering above people's heads. The black birds of ill omen have only arrived at the level of the human diaphragm. They need not advance any further if the longing for the purely material makes way for the other longing for the spiritual. This is how it appears before my soul which wants to send out thoughts to push the black birds of ill omen back into the earth. May those close to me unite with my soul in these thoughts—many things could then still turn out better.

84. Message of 17 June 1924

Breslau, 17 June 1924

Looking at earthly worlds one cannot see much light—dark clouds of error, of being willing to live in error, rise up from human souls—so my gaze is directed only at my loved ones, those who surrounded my earthly sheath with love [sic], with whom I shared my life on earth. They are seeking the spirit in this confused life of darkness; their seeking acts as light-bearing warmth in my 'I' which seeks their thoughts; their seeking works as strength-bearing love in my 'I', which wishes to strengthen their thoughts. There my 'I' always finds the heartfelt spirit which changes into the mild light needed for experiencing of spirit-soul in the spiritual realms of life. We are not separated. 'She' should always reassure all the others of that, and 'it' should affirm it with her gentleness of soul and her heart-filled art in spirit-language. When consciousness of such feeling together both here and there resounds in my 'I', I feel it as a comfort, as liberation.

It is exhilarating for the spirit-enveloped soul which carries my 'I' to wander back to the times of fruitful working in centuries past, where in Rome the iron-giving spirit gave Europe its direction of soul and separated off from the Orient because of its mystical covering of fog. It was there where my 'I', and the 'I' which gave me such faithful support in my last earthly life, spoke these words:

I [the Pope]: Must we lose what spirituality has brought us by the descent of heaven to earth in the tidings of the Crucified One?

'She', the cardinal: What is outmoded must fade; death is but renewed life. I see the life of Europe rising out of Asia's decline.

I: It will be a hard decision.

'She': Nevertheless, it is willed by higher powers so that Ahriman is given proper direction into the life of soul which shall shine forth from Franconia to the East. It was told me by the Northern Lights which also possess a soul, as I lay in my own country one bright summer evening and listened to the voice of Gabriel who wishes to bring a new Europe to birth.

I: Are you certain?

'She': There can only be certainty where higher powers are speaking and I am certain that their message is clear.

I: Maybe they do speak clearly enough, but I also know that the centuries to come will weigh heavily upon our souls.

Such togetherness in an incarnation long past wells up now in my soul when my 'I' lifts itself from the ever-recurring question: Where did we stand in the crucial hour in 1914? As yet there is not much light coming up to me, but a lot is *darkening* up. People will continue to talk about 'guilt' for a long time to come. But I cannot see the concept of 'guilt' any more; what I see is an iron necessity: we had to do what we did.

And yet there is Conrad; my soul thought highly of him. Now my 'I' is repelled when it approaches him. It is repelled in this way by many individuals.

People speak of 'guilt'. In the land of the spirit it is meaningless to speak of 'guilt'.

Nevertheless, the link with the Nicholas incarnation is very strong. 'She' achieved a lot then. That is where the stream originated which we had to bring to a close in 1914. It had come to life in the ninth century; it had to die in the twentieth. My 'I' gave the earth in Europe a spiritual Rome in the ninth century. This pressed on towards the events of 1914. My 'I' could not take any other decisions. My 'I' needs to gain clarity over much that still confuses it now. Conrad is living too long. If this were not so he would not perpetuate the deed through writing.

My 'I' wants to live in the thoughts of my loved ones so that it may help them through the darkness of the times. Here my 'I' has many powers; but it does not yet have the ultimate power to communicate its strength to those it loves.

'She' is my messenger from the earth. My 'I' perceives the earthly life through 'her'. 'It' stands beside them and illuminates the way with her mild light. Then is my 'I' transferred into the earthly sphere in the best sense. This must be so. My loved ones down on earth are not consciously with me; but my 'I' is consciously with them.

Notes

GA = Rudolf Steiner Gesamtausgabe, the collected works of Rudolf Steiner in the original German. All quotations from Rudolf Steiner's work have been translated from the original sources. For a list of published translations of the relevant works in book form, see page 330.

Introduction

1. Otto Friedrich, *Blood and Iron—From Bismark to Hitler—The von Moltke Family's Impact on German History*, New York 1995.
2. Barbara Tuchman, *The Guns of August*, New York 1962.
3. See the essay by Jens Heisterkamp on page 130ff. of this book.
4. Trevor Ravenscroft, *The Spear of Destiny The Occult Power Behind the Spear which Pierced the Side of Christ and how Hitler Inverted the Force in a Bid to Conquer the World*, York Beach, Maine, 1982. Ravenscroft was a pupil of W.J. Stein (1891–1957), who was a student of R. Steiner and friend of D.N. Dunlop.
5. For example, what he brings forth about the alleged meeting of Stein with Hitler must be regarded as pure fiction. Likewise eighty per cent of what he has to say about the 'Moltke Communications', quoted by Friedrich. See page xxix of the introduction.
6. Tuchman, op cit.
7. C.G. Harrison, *The Transcendental Universe. Six Lectures on Occult Science, Theosophy and the Catholic Faith*, Temple Lodge, London 1993. See particularly the second lecture in which we read about the people of Russia: 'The Russian empire must die that the Russian people may live (...) We need not pursue the subject further than to say that the national character will enable them to carry out *experiments in Socialism, political and economical*, which would present innumerable difficulties in Western Europe.' Harrison also speaks of *'the next great European war'*. (Italics T.H.M.)
8. George Brandes, see R. Steiner, *The Karma of Untruthfulness*, Vol. I, London 1988, lecture of 4th December 1916.
9. In the German volume I of this book parts of notes by Lieutenant-Colonel Hans von Haeften (1870–1937), who was Moltke's adjutant at the outbreak of the war, were published. These notes with the title 'Meine Erlebnisse aus den Mobilmachungstagen 1914' (My experi-

ences during the days of mobilization, typescript, 38 pages.) have never been published in full. For future historians they will be another key document in connection with the question of war guilt. Already the following passage with a verbatim quotation of Moltke's own words gives the lie to all false statements about an absolute long-term determination on the part of Germany to provoke the war: 'Tomorrow noon [31 July 1914] the decision about war or peace will be taken. The Chancellor [Bethmann-Hollweg], the Minister of War [Falkenhayn] have to report jointly to His Majesty. But before I will advise His Majesty to proclaim general mobilization I want to *await* a third confirmation of the Russian mobilization. I expect it tomorrow morning, at the same time as information from Vienna as to whether the Austrian-Hungarian Army is going to be mobilized or not. As things are, there is hardly a flicker of hope that peace can be maintained.' (Haeften, p. 28, italics by the editor. The document is to be found in the Bundesarchiv/Militärarchiv, Freiburg im Breisgau, Sign N 35/1.)

10. See, e.g., R. Lissau's Introduction to Steiner's lectures *The Karma of Untruthfulness*, Vol. II, London 1992.
11. See the essay by Johannes Tautz, p. 9, and note 16.
12. See page 9, note 17.
13. See also Foreword to this book.
14. Rudolf Steiner, *Knowledge of the Higher Worlds—How it is Achieved*, chapter 'Control of Thoughts and Feelings'.
15. Friedrich, op. cit. p. 283ff.
16. The corruption of the East has to do with what was outlined in the so-called 'Testament of Peter the Great'. See R. Steiner, *The Karma of Untruthfulness*, Vol. I; L. Polzer-Hoditz, *Das Testament Peters des Großen. Der Kampf gegen den Geist*, Dornach 1989. T. Meyer, *Ludwig Polzer-Hoditz—Ein Europäer*, Basel 1994. A representative of the true Slav nature is Demetrius.
17. A similar distinction should be made for the 'materalistic' West. One might speak of the Rhodes or Wilson layer in contrast to the Wycliffe or Shakespeare or Emerson layer. What is said in these documents about the western people should be looked at from the point of view of such a distinction. Clearly, in a man like Emerson, we meet a representative of the highest and most significant spirituality in the West. But just as in Central Europe the impulses of Goethe or Steiner have not to date become really relevant for the external social-political structure, the same has to be said of the impulses of an individuality like Emerson in connection with the American West.
18. See Samuel Huntington, *The Clash of Civilizations and the Remaking of World Order*, New York 1996.

19. This natural tendency for a threefold inner life of man with a relative separation between the three main soul powers is marked most clearly by certain increasing *pathological* phenomena of today: murders without rational or emotional motive; the widespread difficulty in connecting thoughts with real willpower in order to produce concrete actions; or religious feelings unguided by the intellect.

20. See R. Steiner, *Towards Social Renewal*, London 1997.

Bibliographical Note: See references on p. 294 and notes 77ff. on p. 301ff.

Helmuth von Moltke and Rudolf Steiner

1. Lecture of 20 June 1916 in GA 169. See page 169.
2. As above.
3. As above.
4. See page 54. (5 March 1904).
5. See page 101, 'Reflections and Memories'.
6. In *Aufsätze über die Dreigliederung des sozialen Organismus und zur Zeitlage 1915–21*, GA 24.
7. Jürgen von Grone, *Rudolf Steiner und Helmuth von Moltke. Authentische Aussagen*. Private printing, Stuttgart 1972.
8. Rudolf Steiner, *Anthroposophische Leitsätze*, No. 44 ff., GA 26.
9. Albert Steffen, *Der Chef des Generalstabs*, Dornach 1927. Emil Bock, *Rudolf Steiner, Studien zu seinem Lebensgang und Lebenswerk*, Stuttgart 1990.
10. See note 8, Leading Thought 51.
11. Compare also lecture of 14 January 1915 in GA 64.
12. Lecture of 17 January 1915, GA 157.
13. Lecture of 19 October 1914, GA 287.
14. See GA 287.
15. Lecture of 16 March 1915, GA 157.
16. Lecture of 22 June 1919, GA 192.
17. *Die geistige Signatur der Gegenwart*, in GA 30.
18. See page 160.
19. *Mitteilungen aus der anthroposophischen Arbeit in Deutschland* No. 47, Easter 1959. With reference to this drawing Rudolf Steiner wrote: 'Spiritual science which is independent of anything national takes up Goetheanism and transforms it (1) into a spiritual understanding of the world, (2) into the social threefolding of the world.'
20. *An das deutsche Volk und die Kulturwelt*, March 1919, in GA 23.
21. See Herbert Witzenmann, *Über Trümmern Vertrauen*, Dornach 1979.

22. Lecture of 4 July 1924, GA 237.
23. See note 8, Leading Thoughts 53–55, of 22 June 1924.
24. See page 30, 1 November 1877.
25. Rudolf Steiner's prefatory remarks to *Die Schuld am Kriege, Betrachtungen und Erinnerungen des Generalstabschefs H. v. Moltke über die Vorgänge von Juli bis November 1914*, in GA 24. See also R. Steiner, *Die Kernpunkte der sozialen Frage*, chapter 4, GA 23. See also page 93 of this volume.
26. Compare also R. Steiner's letter to Eliza von Moltke of 6 August 1919, page 252. See also Hans Kühn, *Dreigliederungszeit—Rudolf Steiners Kampf für die Gesellschaftsordnung der Zukunft*. Dornach 1978.
27. Letter of 19 June 1911, page 73.
28. First published in Walter Johannes Stein, *The Ninth Century, World History in the Light of the Holy Grail*, London 1992.
29. Letter of 2 October 1895, page 41.
30. See note 8, Leading Thoughts 50 and 51 of 15 June 1924.
31. R. Steiner, *Die Grundimpulse des weltgeschichtlichen Werdens der Menschheit*, lecture of 1 October 1922, GA 216.
32. Message of 28 July 1918, page 216.
33. Message of 17 June 1924, page 288.
34. Message of 3 May 1919, page 246.

Further references

Gräfin Johanna Keyserlingk, *Zwölf Tage um Rudolf Steiner*, Stuttgart 1948.
Adalbert Graf von Keyserlingk (ed.), *Koberwitz 1924, Geburtsstunde einer neuen Landwirtschaft*, Stuttgart 1974.
Michael Kirn, *Der deutsche Staat in Europa*, Aufgaben und Ziele des Vereinigten Deutschland, Stuttgart 1991.
Christoph Lindenberg, *Vom geistigen Ursprung der Gegenwart*. Studien zur Bewußtseinsgeschichte Mitteleuropas, Stuttgart 1984.
Hermann Poppelbaum, *Studien über das Schicksal auf Grund der Leitsätze Rudolf Steiners*, Dornach 1957.
Sergei O. Prokofieff, *The Spiritual Origins of Eastern Europe and the Future Mysteries of the Holy Grail*, London 1983.
Heinz Herbert Schöffler (Hrsg.), *Der Kampf um das Menschenbild, Das achte ökumenische Konzil von 869 und seine Folgen*, Dornach 1986.
Generaloberst Helmuth von Moltke, *Erinnerungen, Briefe, Dokumente 1877–1916*, Hrsg. von Eliza von Moltke, Stuttgart 1922.
T.H. Meyer (Hrsg.), *Helmuth von Moltke (1848–1916), Dokumente zu seinem Leben und Wirken*, Vol. 1, Basel 1993.

Part One

1. On 1 September 1870 Sedan was encircled and Emperor Napoleon III, who capitulated on 2 September, was captured.
2. According to Rudolf Steiner this letter contains the first 'germ of anthroposophical thoughts'. See Part Two, page 222.
3. On 16 June the funeral service took place following the early death of Kaiser Friedrich on the day before.
4. Wilhelm I had died on 9 March 1888.
5. On 15 November 1894 Eliza von Moltke's father Vladimir von Moltke-Huitfeld died in Quesarum (Sweden). He was born on 4 September 1834 in Rome.
6. Following the death of Tsar Alexander III in November 1894 his son Nicholas (II), who was born in 1868 and was murdered by the Bolsheviks in 1918, ascended the Tsarist throne as the last of the Romanovs.
7. This letter, especially the real-symbolic 'glove scene' described therein, plays an important part in the letters in Part Two. See messages 44 and 79. The picture by Professor Knackfuß is reproduced in the plate section.
8. Humbert = Umberto.
9. The fear about the future expressed here in thought was to become sad reality on 1 August 1914, in consequence of the Kaiser's high-handed interference with minutely-detailed military planning.
10. On 4 August 1903 Pius X (Guiseppe Sarto) was elected to succeed Leo XIII.
11. At the Vatican I Council of Rome the Dogma of Papal Infallibility (for pronouncements ex cathedra) was proclaimed by Pope Pius IX on 18 July 1870; to Moltke this was unacceptable.
12. *Friedrich Nietzsche—Ein Kämpfer gegen seine Zeit*, Weimar 1895. This is the first mention of Rudolf Steiner in Moltke's letters. It is clear from the letter of 8 March that he had already met Steiner once at that time. The meeting had been initiated by Eliza von Moltke and probably took place at the end of February/beginning of March 1904 in Berlin.
13. *Haeckel und seine Gegner*, Minden, 1900.
14. Thomas Carlyle (1795–1881), English writer and historian. His work *The French Revolution, A History* had been published in German translation in 1897.
15. The book *Theosophie—Einführung in übersinnliche Welterkenntnis und Menschenbestimmung* had only been published at the beginning of May. Hence Moltke was among the first to read this fundamental work of Rudolf Steiner.

16. Annie Besant (1847–1933), leading personality of the Theosophical Society. Her book *The Four World Religions* was published in German in 1904.

17. This letter bears testimony to Moltke's honest and open approach and his willingness to be very frank with the Kaiser. The conversation described here—it served to *strengthen the bond of trust* between Moltke and the Kaiser—forms the backdrop to that fatal scene on 1 August. See page101 ff.

18. *The Kaiser always brings with him something of the Middle Ages*: from the symptomatic point of view a very interesting observation; see Part Two.

19. Cf. Rudolf Steiner's remarks in his lecture of 4 December 1916, in GA 173, Dornach, 2nd ed. 1978.

20. Today Obernai.

21. The convent on St Odilie's Mount was established at the end of the seventh century; its first abbess was Saint Odilie (died 720), the daughter of the Alemannic Duke Eticho. An important Christan spiritual stream emanated from this convent. See Part Two, pages 185 and 277.

22. Today Haute Koenigsbourg. Wilhelm II had the medieval castle refurbished to his taste between 1900 and 1908.

23. Saverne.

24. The words of Helmuth von Moltke about the Kaiser's trust in him as '*source of my strength*' are well worth pondering. The devastating effects on Moltke of the *breach* of trust on 1 August 1914 can only be fully appreciated against the background of Moltke's deep-seated trust in the Kaiser.

25. On 28 June 1914 the Austrian Heir to the Throne, Franz Ferdinand, was murdered in Sarajevo by the Bosnian student Gavrilo Princip on behalf of the secret organisation 'the Black Hand', with the indirect involvement of the Serbian government.

    In response Austria-Hungary made an ultimatum limited to 48 hours to Serbia, requesting the government to take steps against anti-monarchist subversive activities. Serbia initiated a partial mobilization on 25 July.

    Without Russia's intervention the conflict would have remained limited to Austria-Hungary and Serbia.

    Already *before* the ultimatum to Serbia, Russia had been assured of France's loyalty to the alliance by the French President Poincaré as well as his Minister, President Vivani, in Petersburg.

26. These words of Moltke, besides many other of his comments with respect to this, may be taken as proof of the fact that Germany's real military leadership in no way consciously brought about the outbreak of war.

27. Alexander I (born 1876), son of King Milan of Serbia, himself Serbian King since 1889, was murdered in Belgrade on 10 June 1903, together with his wife Draga Maschin.

28. The Austrian heir to the throne, Franz Ferdinand, was murdered in Sarajevo on 28 June 1914. See note 25.

29. Moltke's note on the margin: '*Has happened in the meantime.*'

30. With regard to the role of Hentsch, see notes on messages 72 and 76 in Part Two.

31. Compare this report with what is expressed in November 1914 on page 101 ff.

32. The brochure produced in May 1919 was entitled: 'The Question of War-"Guilt"—Reflections and Memories of Chief of the General Staff H. v. Moltke about the events from July 1914 to November 1914.' It was published by the 'Bund der Dreigliederung des sozialen Organismus', 'introduced in agreement with Frau Eliza v. Moltke by Rudolf Steiner'. Rudolf Steiner's preface is dated May 1919. With regard to the genesis of Rudolf Steiner's decision to publish these notes of Moltke, please refer to Part Two, notes on letters 62 and 66. Compare also Hans Kühn, *Dreigliederungszeit*, Dornach 1978.

33. Note of Rudolf Steiner: 'Refer to the author's *Kernpunkte der sozialen Frage*, Verlag Greiner & Pfeiffer, Stuttgart 1919.' (Today GA 23 in Rudolf Steiner Gesamtausgabe.)

34. Cf. Rudolf Steiner's characterization of the war aims of the various European nations on 31 October 1914 (GA 157). With regard to the way in which the German strives and fights, the following is stated: 'One fights for *existence* or something connected with *existence.*'

35. Friedrich von Bernhardi (1849–1930), Prussian General and military author, wrote in 1912 *Deutschland und der nächste Krieg*.

36. Refer to the real spiritual background to Moltke's after-death agreement with this publication as described in Part Two.

37. Cf. Renate Riemeck, *Mitteleuropa—Bilanz eines Jahrhunderts*, 3rd edition, Potsdam 1990. Chapter 'Ein lange und gut vorbereiteter Krieg'.

38. Today this statement must be taken to encompass the American policy of the 'New World Order'.

39. On 3/4 August German troops invaded Belgium in accordance with the 'Schlieffen plan' as modified by von Moltke; subsequent to that Great Britain, after an ultimatum to Germany requesting Germany to respect Belgian neutrality—de facto a declaration of war—officially declared war on Germany on 5 August, and on 12 August also on Austria–Hungary.

40. This and the following theory of the different developmental stages of the Latin and Slav peoples was clearly stated in C.G. Harrison's work *The Transcendental Universe*, London 1893. Rudolf Steiner, who knew this work, probably touched on this subject in private conversations with Moltke. What is said here about nations must, of course, not be taken in terms of individual human beings who, in their essential being, are always *above* the element of nation.

41. This refers to the *spiritual* progression of humanity. It is therefore clear that it would be absurd to try and range these and other statements of Moltke among nationalist slogans about the 'German world mission' which, in the Third Reich, had nothing at all to do with the spirit, but a great deal indeed with blood, earth and irrational instincts.

42. Cf. Rudolf Steiner's statements on 31 October 1914 in Berlin (GA 157) as well as note 34.

43. Vladimir Sukhmolinov, Minister of War from 1910.

44. The identity of this 'Military Attaché' could not be established.

45. One of the main points in Moltke's notes to which General von Dommes raised objections, unfoundedly.

46. On 30 July.

47. Erich von Falkenhayn (1861–1922), Minister of War and from autumn 1914 for a certain time also Chief of the General Staff.

48. Karl Max, Prince of Lichnowsky (1860–1928), Ambassador in London from 1912.

49. Edward Grey (1862–1933), British Foreign Minister 1905–16.

50. It should not be overlooked that this sentence is contained in confidential notes intended only for Moltke's wife; those who made it their business to slander Moltke probably drew their own theories' fake confirmations of Moltke's feebleness from this and similar remarks.

51. Gerhard Tappen was Head of the Operations and Railway Division.

52. Max Clemens Freiherr von Hausen (1848–1922), Commander-in-Chief of the 3rd Army.

53. Moritz Freiherr von Lyncker (1853–1932) was Head of the Military Cabinet and due to this position one of the most influential personalities in the Kaiser's political clique.

54. *The publication of Moltke's notes is something that I consider important today so that the truth about important events may be known.* [Note by Eliza von Moltke, from the original 1922 German edition.]

55. These documents are filed in the Federal/military archive in Freiburg im Breisgau (Sign. 512/4). It was extremely difficult to decipher Dommes' manuscript, and the task was greatly supported by Hartwig von Volkmann. The few remaining illegible words were marked [...], uncertain passages (?). Additions in [ ] are the publisher's. Comments

in ( ) are von Dommes'. Passages relating to other contexts were left out and marked (...). See also note 66 to Part Two.

56. This comment shows that Frau von Moltke had told von Dommes about the after-death communications of her husband which had been revealed to her by Rudolf Steiner in numerous messages written down by him. However, the following sentence 'Frau M. read all this out to me' refers to the pamphlet which Rudolf Steiner had sent to her on 28 May.

57. Hans Adolf von Moltke (1884–1943), who was at that time the Prussian Attaché in Stuttgart, had received a copy of the freshly produced pamphlet on 27 May from Emil Molt, whereupon he immediately informed his father Fritz von Moltke in Berlin, who was the head of the family after Helmuth von Moltke's death. Fritz von Moltke then got in touch with the Foreign Office.

58. Astrid (Bethusy-Huc) and Else (Koennecke).

59. Partly reproduced in *Nachrichten der Rudolf Steiner Nachlaßverwaltung*, No. 27/28, page 29. Eliza von Moltke writes to Rudolf Steiner on 30 May: 'The General von Dommes who will bring you this letter came to see me yesterday; he was called here by the General Staff of Insterburg because of the impending publication of the notes (...) My dear Doctor—I am in a terrible state of inner torture, because I am faced with something that I cannot master inwardly (...) I feel as if I had committed an injustice, a betrayal *vis-à-vis* the dear soul.'

60. Bethmann not only believed in England's neutrality until the eleventh hour, but also in that of France. Furthermore he delayed an appeal to Poland which had been requested by Moltke and was to be drafted by von Haeften and in which Poland was addressed as ally of Germany and Austria-Hungary in return for a promise of future national autonomy. This appeal was to be dropped over Poland from a Zeppelin airship in the night of 3/4 August. Bethmann, who had at first given his agreement to this, believed as late as 1 August, 10 p.m., that there was 'still a slight prospect of maintaining peace'.

Only when news of the anti-Russian mood in Warsaw reached the Reichskanzlei through a Polish Member of Parliament did Bethmann approve the release of the appeal which then took place during the night of 5/6 August.

The debates about the Poland appeal, in which also Under-State Secretary Zimmermann as well as the State Secretary of the Foreign Office were involved, are further evidence of the 'nullity' of Germany's political leadership at that time.

61. Von Dommes might have thought of statements of the Kaiser such as 'Well, we will simply deploy the entire army in the East' or 'Now you may do as you wish'.

62. See in this context messages 61 and 70 in Part Two and the notes thereto.

63. See in this context Rudolf Steiner's letter to Eliza von Moltke of 6 August 1919 (Part Two, page 252) in which he once again addresses this question of the subjective 'correctness' of the notes.

64. This condition—the soul's belief in the correctness of the notes—was, however, not waived in reality; see also note 63.

65. This refers to the 'Bund der Dreigliederung des sozialen Organismus' which was to publish the notes.

66. Apart from the notes reproduced here no further notes about his conversation with Rudolf Steiner were found in von Dommes' estate.

67. Jurgen von Grone (1887–1978), active officer in the First World War, was predestined—on account of his career path as well as study of anthroposophically orientated spiritual science—to create a testimony to Helmuth von Moltke's military and life path. After the deaths of Rudolf Steiner and Helmuth von Moltke he became the most important defender of Moltke against the flood of attacks from military-historian and nationalist circles. Cf. his contribution on page 127 of this publication as well as Jens Heisterkamp's commentary on page 130 ff.

    These notes of von Grone were found in his estate. They date from 1965.

68. This letter, which was already referred to in note 63, is contained in Part Two, page 252.

69. This refers to the decision to withdraw the western armies of 11 September 1914.

70. On 5 October 1921 the Paris daily *Le Matin* published an interview by the journalist Jules Sauerwein (1880–1967), a friend and student of Rudolf Steiner, which the former had conducted with the founder of anthroposophically orientated spiritual science on 30 September in Dornach. It was entitled 'Une lueur sur les origines de la guerre' and the subtitle was 'Ce qui contiennent les memoires inédits et interdits en Allemagne du chef d'état-major de Moltke'. The publication of this interview in the *French* press was a feat of journalistic courage. On 12 October a German translation was published under the heading 'New Facts about the Events that led to the World War' in the journal *Dreigliederung des Sozialen Organismus* (Jg. 3, No. 15). This interview triggered various arguments and accusations as a result of which Rudolf Steiner found it necessary to comment anew on the situation. (Cf. in this context Rudolf Steiner, *Über die Dreigliederung des sozialen Organismus und zur Zeitlage—Schriften und Aufsätze 1915–1921*, GA 24, which contains the interview as well as Rudolf Steiner's subsequent commentary, p. 398 ff.)

71. Hans Adolf von Moltke. See also note 57.
72. General von Dommes.
73. See page 80 of this publication.
74. Colonel von Tappen.
75. The conversation in Niederlahnstein near Koblenz took place in the presence of Eliza von Moltke. Jürgen von Grone revealed an important point with regard to how this meeting with Rudolf Steiner, who was en route from Dornach to Berlin, came about: 'Rudolf Steiner later assured me *"that he resolved to make this journey only after three requests from Frau von Moltke."*' (Jürgen von Grone, *Helmuth von Moltke und Rudolf Steiner*, private printing, Stuttgart 1972.)
76. General Alexander von Kluck (1846–1934) was Commander-in-Chief of the 1st Army.
77. For example:
    Eugen Bircher, *Die Schlacht an der Marne*, Bern 1918.
    Hermann von Kuhl, *Der Marnefeldzug*, Berlin 1921.
    W. Müller-Loebniz, *Der Wendepunkt des Krieges; Beiträge zur Marneschlacht*, 1921.
    G. Tappen, *Bis zur Marne 1914*, Oldenburg 1920.
    The extraordinary significance of the Marne Battle for German historical thinking between the World Wars is examined by Karl Lange in his book *Die Marneschlacht und deutsche Öffentlichkeit 1914–39*, Düsseldorf 1974.
78. Erich Ludendorff, *Kriegsführung und Politik*, München 1922.
79. München 1934. Unfortunately the spectres around Ludendorff are by no means a thing of the past, as is borne out by a book published in 1985, *Ludendorff—Studie eines Revolutionärs* (Verlag Hohe Warte, without mention of the editor), which contains serious defamations of the spiritualist activities of Moltke's wife.
80. Edition of 12 January 1933.
81. *Das Goetheanum*, No. 10, 5 March 1933.
82. According to the German historian Goetz, this von Moltke came from the Danish branch of the family.
83. Also published as special imprint: Jürgen von Grone, *Die Marneschlacht*, Stuttgart 1934.
84. In *Walter Johannes Stein—Eine Biographie*, Dornach 1989, p. 170. With regard to the destiny background of the Moltke individuality, see Part Two. This background is touched upon—unfortunately in a very distorted manner—in the publication *The Spear of Destiny* by Trevor Ravenscroft, London 1972. See Introduction.
85. *Biographisches Wörterbuch zur deutschen Geschichte*, 2nd vol., München 1974, p. 1923 f.
86. Hermann von Kuhl was Chief of the General Staff of the army

commanded by General Alexander von Kluck which was positioned at the extreme right wing and whose unauthorized crossing of the Marne made possible the French counter offensive.

87. Walter Görlitz, *Der deutsche Generalstab. Geschichte und Gestalt 1657–1945*, Frankfurt am Main 1950.

88. The younger of Moltke's sons, Adam von Moltke, responded to Görlitz's distortions in 1958 with an article: 'A response to Herr Walter Görlitz referring to the chapter "The War without a General" in his book *Der deutsche Generalstab*.' (Federal archive/military archive, Freiburg im Breisgau, 78/37.)

89. Refer to:
Fritz Fischer, *Der Griff nach der Weltmacht*, Düsseldorf 1961.
Immanuel Geiß, *Julikrise und Kriegsausbruch 1914*, 2 vols., Hannover 1963.
Adolf Gasser, *Preußischer Militärgeist und Kriegsentfesselung 1914*, Basel und Frankfurt am Main 1985.
From the anthroposophical side Christoph Lindenberg, too, considers Moltke an 'unfortunate exponent' of German 'militarism' (*Goetheanum*, Jg. 2, 1970, p.11); he is similarly critical of Moltke in his book *Vom geistigen Ursprung der Gegenwart*, Stuttgart 1984, p. 155.

90. Especially Gerhard Ritter, *Staatskunst und Kriegshandwerk. Zum Problem des Militarismus in Deutschland*, 4 vols., München 1954–68.

91. Yehuda L. Wallach, *Das Dogma der Vernichtungsschlacht. Die Lehren von Clausewitz und Schlieffen und ihre Wirkungen in zwei Weltkriegen*, Frankfurt am Main 1967.

92. Wallach, op. cit., p. 177.

93. Bergisch Gladbach 1982. Co-authored by Wolfgang Venohr.

94. Rolf Hochhuth, *Sommer 1914. Ein Totentanz*, Hamburg 1989.

Part Two (note numbers refer to letter numbers)

Abbreviations:

BT—Bock-typescript of the Moltke documents.

BS—Emil Bock, *Rudolf Steiner, Studien zu seinem Lebensgang und Lebenswerk*, 3rd edition, Stuttgart 1990.

SG—W.J. Stein, *Weltgeschichte im Lichte des Heiligen Gral*, 4th edition, Stuttgart 1986 (*The Ninth Century*, Temple Lodge, London 1991.).

LC—Christoph Lindenberg, *Rudolf Steiner—Eine Chronik*, Stuttgart 1988.

NSN—Nachrichten der Rudolf Steiner Nachlaßverwaltung.

KD—Hans Kühn, *Dreigliederungszeit*, Dornach 1978.

1. Eliza von Moltke was among the first of Rudolf Steiner's pupils to be admitted into the *Esoterische Schule* (ES). It is presumed that this happened as early as 1904, i.e. the year in which Rudolf Steiner first became aquainted with Eliza von Moltke's husband. In that year Rudolf Steiner frequently visited the Moltke household.

    In 1904 Rudolf Steiner did not give lectures. Among other things he was engaged with an extensive ES-correspondence, i.e. he sent meditation instructions to the members of the ES or accepted new members to whom the 'rules' were then sent. See GA 264, pp. 62–77. Steiner expressly invited ES-students to ask questions, hence answers to questions such as that in No. 2 were not at all uncommon.

    On 20 July 1904 Eliza von Moltke wrote the following letter to Rudolf Steiner:

    My dear Dr Steiner
    Have you forgotten me altogether! I know that patience is one of the main assets we human beings must strive for and I would have patiently waited for a longer time if I did not urgently need some spiritual help—you were kind enough to say that you would look after me in this respect and give me hints about how I need to work on myself in order to one day attain the greatly longed-for goal: to help others (...) I am most willing now to work on myself in the manner you consider appropriate and I am keen to succeed—and when you have received the instructions relating to this which you said you would have to ask for from a higher plane, please be so kind and communicate them to me (...)

    Rudolf Steiner's letter of 12 August 1904 is the first of the letters to Eliza and Helmuth von Moltke referred to as 'soul guidance letters' by Emil Bock. Exactly 14 years later this 'soul guidance' reaches a certain conclusion and/or enters into a new phase. See message No. 52.

    The 'enclosed document' mentioned in the letter, probably a meditation instruction, was not retained.

2. In view of the future task to be fulfilled by Eliza von Moltke of developing a totally conscious connection with the 'spiritualized human essence' of her deceased husband, these comments right at the beginning of the 'soul guidance' process about the Bodhisattva and Buddha principle are of symptomatic-prophetic significance. (Regarding the Dalai Lama and the Bodhisattva-Avalokitischvara, see also Eugenie von Bredow's notes from memory relating to an Esoteric Lesson on 13 December 1905 in GA 264.)

4. The first two verses were given to Helmuth von Moltke during a conversation with Rudolf Steiner on 27 August 1914, hence before the

Battle of the Marne in Niederlahnstein near Koblenz. See the '*Matin* interview' in GA 24, p.398, as well as on page 121 in this volume.

The third verse is contained in GA 40.

5. On 14 January 1915 Rudolf Steiner held a lecture in the Architektenhaus, Berlin entitled 'The Germanic Soul and the German Spirit' (GA 64).

6. First 'soul guidance letter' from Rudolf Steiner to Helmuth von Moltke after the latter's dismissal in September 1914.

9. *From that side of the spiritual world known to you:* The older Moltke, who is referred to in the following letter, cannot be meant here. It might be a reference to the individuality later called 'Umi', or else to the individuality of the Folk Spirit.

10. *... from the soul of the personality once so close to...:* The older Helmuth von Moltke (1800–91), the victor of Königgrätz and Sedan. Emil Bock (1895–1959) pointed out that the occasional messages of the old Field Marshal to his nephew, of which this is the first one, form a kind of prelude to the later after-death letters of the younger Moltke to his wife.

... the feelings that 23 March brought to me: On that day Rudolf Steiner held a lecture in Munich about concrete experiences after death, the karma of the European Folk Souls and the background to the catastrophe of the war (contained in GA 174 a).

11. *Regarding your son's injury:* The eldest son Wilhelm von Moltke (called 'Bill') had been shot through the ankle which caused severe ischiatic pain.

13. *The spiritual being of which I have often spoken:* See note referring to letter 9.

14. *From out of the spirit that has often been referred to:* See note referring to letter 9.

18. *Many a thing that appears now to be a gain:* After the victories on the eastern front in 1914 (the Battle of Tannenberg and at the Masurian Lakes was followed by the conquest of eastern Galicia in autumn 1914) the German army's wave of victories in the East continued—albeit with a number of setbacks—into early autumn 1915: on 5 August Warsaw was beaten, Brest-Litovsk on 18 August and Wilna on 18 August. At this time of destiny *spiritual* victories would have been required on the part of influential circles of the German people.

As there were no victories of that nature, the outer victories, from the point of view of the German Folk Spirit, were bound to be of an illusory nature. With regard to the true tasks of the German people, see also Rudolf Steiner's last letter to Helmuth von Moltke of 23 November 1915 (No. 19).

20. Rudolf Steiner wrote this verse for Helmuth von Moltke on the back of a photograph on 11 December 1915.

21c. The memorial services on 19 June (Monday) and 20 June 1916 took place in the Moltke apartments in the General Staff Building in Berlin. About Rudolf Steiner's presence in Berlin at the time of Helmuth von Moltke's death, Emil Bock commented as follows: 'It was not a matter of course that Rudolf Steiner was present in Berlin when Helmuth von Moltke died on 18 June 1916. He had already been waiting some time for an opportunity to depart for Dornach for a longer sojourn there. It was only the delay in finalizing the production of his book *Vom Menschenrätsel* which detained him in Berlin until the end of July.' (BT)

The keyword of this memorial address is the 'deeply significant historical symbol', the fact that Helmuth von Moltke 'served the outer life and nevertheless found the bridge to the life of the spirit which is sought for by this spiritual science'. Bridge is 'pons' and the Roman Pope has been entitled 'Pontifex'—builder of bridges—since the time of Silvester I, if not before. In view of Moltke's 'pontifex-past' Rudolf Steiner's choice of words is significant as it points to the continuity of the metamorphosed pontifex principle in Helmuth von Moltke's life. See comments in note 22.

It is likely that Rudolf Steiner first told Helmuth von Moltke about his karmic connection with Pope Nicholas I (?–867) during Moltke's time of suffering after the Battle of the Marne and his demotion on 14 September 1914. In August 1915 Helmuth von Moltke took extensive notes from the book *Geschichte der Stadt Rom* by Ferdinand Gregorovius (1821–91), a copy of which was later made available to Walter Johannes Stein (1891–1957) by Eliza von Moltke. (Stein was indebted to Eliza von Moltke for supplying important data which he utilized in his Grail book *The Ninth Century*. Cf: Johannes Tautz, *W.J. Stein—A Biography*, London 1990.

Of particular relevance in this context are Emil Bock's observations on the karmic connections between the century of the Holy Grail (ninth century) and the present contained in his book about Rudolf Steiner (BS).

In terms of the symptomatic phenomenology of the karmic connection between Nicholas I and Moltke, the following letters are of interest in that they reveal in one way or another some of the karmic root layer of the ninth century: 1 November 1877 (which contains the 'germ of anthroposophical thoughts' as Rudolf Steiner noted in message 51 (page 222); 24 January 1878; 10 February 1878; 2 October 1895 ('glove-scene'); 9 August 1900; 10 April 1903; 16 April 1903; 4 August 1903 (commentary on Papal Elections); 8 March 1904 (3rd moon node, reading Steiner); 17 July 1904 (Jesus studies); 26 January 1905 (reference to Roman history); 29 January 1905 (talk with Kaiser); 19 June 1911 (excursion to St Odilie's Mount).

22. These words from the Moltke individuality—conceived and translated into earthly language by Rudolf Steiner and written down for Eliza von Moltke—form the starting point to the consciously-developed after-death connection between Helmuth and Eliza von Moltke. They represent, as it were, the bridge Rudolf Steiner constructed to enable the souls to approach one another in order to enter into conscious connection. Hence the title 'Pontifex Meditation'.

23. This letter shows that the 'verse' communicated to Eliza von Moltke (see No. 22) could also serve Rudolf Steiner as a bridge to the departed v. Moltke, in spite of the fact or indeed perhaps by virtue of the fact that he had not built it for his own direct 'use'.

24. *... the words of the meditation given to you:* refers to the 'Pontifex Meditation' (Note 22).
Isidoric Documents (Decrees): Refers to the so-called pseudo-isidoric decrees. The decrees—a compilation of falsified materials—were intended to strengthen the power of the bishops in relation to the king, the aristocracy as well as the metropolites (archbishops), and increased the central power of the Pope for that purpose. 'Nicholas first rejected them but later used them,' Walter Johannes Stein writes in his Grail book (SG, p.386). See also: F. Thaner, 'Zu Pseudoisidor', in *Mitteilungen des Instituts für österreichische Geschichtsforschung*, Bd. XI, Innsbruck 1890.
Struggle with the power known to you: the Kaiser(?).

25. *The matter of your son:* The second younger son Adam was before Verdun.
The fight with the person alluded to earlier: the Kaiser (?).
Your faithful H.R.K. a. Gr.: Helene Röchling, Kundry and Grail.

26. *The change that has taken place (Hindenburg):* Paul Hindenburg (1847–1934) was appointed to the Oberste Heeresleitung (Supreme Command) on 28 August 1916 together with Erich Ludendorff (1865–1937). Ludendorff was loyal to Moltke right up to Moltke's death. Later he became one of his bitterest opponents.
Lehmann: Cover-up name for Kaiser Wilhelm II.

27. *Relationship to Lehmann inc.:* See note 26.
H. event: probably refers to the change in the Supreme Command. See note 26.

28. *because Lehmann is nothing (zero) over there:* Before Moltke's spiritual view—*viewed from over there*—the Kaiser appears as a 'zero'.
He is at the service...: This refers to Helmuth v. Moltke.
The old General Field Marshal: the older Moltke.

29. *At that time my 'I' did not want the separation:* According to this a modifying influence played into Nicholas's church policies in the ninth

century, most probably through the church dignitary described in the following.

Influenced by a high-ranking church dignitary: This might refer to Arsenius; as previous incarnation of the Kaiser, see BS, pp. 342 and 356 ff.

gave the command to pull back the troops to Hausen: Lieutenant-Colonel Max Clemens Freiherr von Hausen (1846–1922) was Supreme Commander of the 3rd Western Army. In 'Reflections and Memories' (see page 111) Moltke says: 'When I came to A.-O.-K. 3 (Army Supreme Command 3) General v. Hausen explained to me that he could not hold the line allocated to him as his troops were no longer operative. Therefore I was forced to give the 3rd Army a shorter line further back while at the same time taking the 4th and 5th Armies further back in order to restore a closed army front (…) It was a hard decision which I had to take without seeking His Majesty's permission beforehand. The hardest decision of my life which cost me my life blood. But I envisaged a catastrophe, had I not taken the army back.' Molte's command to retreat on 11 September led to his dismissal by the Kaiser three days later. See also 'Helmuth von Moltke on the Retreat from the Marne' of summer 1915 on page 85.

Many who held positions in the HQ were in Capua in their previous incarnation: See BS, p.360 ff.

30. *What 'she' is to me now* … Eliza von Moltke. Throughout the after-death communications Moltke's widow is referred to as 'she' and 'her'.

There is still work to be done on the Group: The wooden group at the Goetheanum with the so-called 'Representative of Man'.

31. *The recently departed soul:* Colmar Freiherr von der Goltz (1843–1916).

34. *Living through the first period (…) of theosophical communications:* In a letter from Norway dated 17 July 1904 (see page 56) Helmuth von Moltke wrote to his wife: 'In addition, I am occupied with Steiner's *Theosophy*. Quite by accident yesterday conversation turned to the theosophical conception of the world. There were four or five of us sitting together and as I was the only one who knew anything about these matters it fell to me to lead the discussion. At first some of them laughed, then they became increasingly serious and in the end they were listening to me as if I was a pastor in church.'

35. Emil Bock commented on the peculiar gap in the series of documents in the year 1917. He emphasized that records from that year had once existed as Eliza von Moltke had read or dictated a few passages from those in 1929. Bock considers it likely that 'in 1917 conversations with Rudolf Steiner had taken the place of the letters that were sent before and after', of which Eliza von Moltke had taken her own notes, as was

the case, for example, after the communications about St Odilie (No. 36). Rudolf Steiner was in Germany from the beginning of February to the end of September. But why are there so many recordings by Rudolf Steiner from the year 1918 when he was in Berlin from January until August? 'The actual letters in Rudolf Steiner's handwriting only started (...) in 1918,' Bock states (BT).

Why is this so? It might be assumed that these 'actual' letters of Rudolf Steiner required something specific to happen before the flow could start, as it were. It might further be assumed that this is connected with the communications about St Odilie from the year 1917. As a result of these Rudolf Steiner took Eliza von Moltke on her very first visit to Dornach to the *Eremitage* in order to show her St Odilie's refuge (no. 36, second message). These messages about St Odilie and, above all, the experience of the hermitage must have also been significant to the departed soul who would have accompanied the above; all this may well have contributed to 'loosening his tongue' in the spiritual sense.

'In this context [with the Odilie conversations] Dr Steiner must have also said that Wilhelm II had been, before acting as Pope Nicholas' evil counsellor, the Duke Eticho, the father of Saint Odilie,' Bock states in the conclusion to his notes from 1917. About the personality of Odilie see SG, page 397 ff.; H. Jülich, *Arlesheim und Odilie*, Arlesheim, 5th ed. 1988; Th. Maurer, *Die heilige Odilie*, Dornach, 2nd rev. ed. 1982.

Pseudo-isidoric decretals imposed on him: See message No. 24 and notes.

He was in Hibernia on an expedition: On 18 November 1917 (GA 178) Rudolf Steiner speaks about a colonization of Ireland originating from Greek Mysteries. See also note on 'Laurentius—Field Marshal' below.

Oskar Hertwig: 1849–1922, zoologist.

Now Umi needs him: First direct hint at this individuality who is so significant in the destinies of the Moltke family and appears again and again starting on 1 March 1918 (No. 40).

Umi suggests to Novalis his over-appreciation of the Jesuits: This overappreciation is most tangible in certain passages of Novalis's essay *Die Christenheit und Europa*, which Goethe had advised not to publish, probably for that reason.

Laurentius—Field Marshal: In a letter dated 15 March 1931 to Walter Johannes Stein, Eliza von Moltke answers his request for material for a planned memorial essay on the 40th anniversary of the older Moltke's death with the following: 'The great strategian, battle leader, general has been discussed in many ways (...) what was behind all that no one knows (...) But nothing other than that can be given to people today because the *other* reaches far into the supersensible world. And people do not want to hear or know anything of this world—or do you think one could say to people today that he was the martyr Laurentius, that he was someone who before the time of Christ was an initiate in Greece—who had an inspiring effect on Nicholas in the ninth century? (...) Helmuth von Moltke I is such a book [with seven seals] and will have to continue to be so until the seals fall off in the course of humanity's further evolution (...) He still stands there as the great 'Silent One'—also a sign by which those who have a sense for Mystery wisdom and secrets may recognize him—as a Hibernian initiate he carries this mark.' Concerning Laurentius and Uriel the author is indebted to Hartwig von Volkmann for valuable indications.

In connection with the Uriel note: At the request of Eliza von Moltke, who had shown a remarkable interest in spiritualism ever since her youth, Rudolf Steiner attended nine or ten séances which took place at the Moltke household between 21 March 1904 and 24 May 1905. There a spirit expressed himself through a medium (unknown) who called himself Uriel. According to Christian-Judaic tradition it is one of the tasks of this archangelic being to 'mediate revelations' (*Lexikon für Theologie und Kirche*, Freiburg im Breisgau 1965). Already at the first séance Uriel draws attention to the martyr Laurentius who suffered death by fire on 10 August 258 in Rome. It becomes clear in the Uriel protocols that Rudolf Steiner 'as a positive and tolerant witness to the séance (...) clearly understands what is happening and sometimes also corrects the medium' (Tautz, *W.J. Stein, A Biography*).

There is no doubt that Rudolf Steiner wished to encourage Eliza von Moltke through his objective-critical presence to form clear concepts in a realm where so much charlatanism holds sway. It is probable that Steiner's Berlin lectures on spiritism and mediumism in spring 1904 (see GA 52) were initiated by Eliza von Moltke's request to him to participate in sessions of this nature.

Emil Bock refers to the séances in the Moltke household as the 'prelude in the incipient workings of great destinies'. (BT)

Lecture of 31 July 1917: contained in GA 176.

African Spir: 1837–90, philosopher.

36. Eliza von Moltke sent this message on 26 November 1927 to W.J. Stein who had asked her for permission to incorporate it in his Grail book; the second note was appended to a letter of 27 December in the same year. Stein reproduced both of these in facsimile in his book.

From the window: from the window of Castle Birseck. Ilona Schubert, who was a friend of Helene Röchling, refers to a cave in the 'hollow rock' at Arlesheim as the very place where St Odilie took refuge (with illustration) in her book *Selbsterlebtes mit Rudolf Steiner und Marie Steiner.*

37. The message referring to the location of Dornach must have been written down before 20 January as this was the day when Rudolf Steiner departed for Berlin together with Marie Steiner [and Eliza von Moltke?].

After the 'Odilie walk' of Eliza von Moltke and Rudolf Steiner in autumn 1917 Eliza von Moltke started 'reading' to her deceased husband the letters he had written to her. (To the extent that these were published by Eliza von Moltke in 1922 they have now been reprinted in *Helmuth von Moltke 1848–1916*, Vol. 1, Perseus Verlag Basel, 1993. A selection of these is contained in Part One of this book.) This process is continued over roughly half a year until August. The letter retrospective directed to the Moltke individuality in this manner evidently achieved a great deal in enhancing and freeing the latter's consciousness and advancing his spiritual development. He himself refers to the 'releasing of a very special power'. Many other affirmations of the great value of this letter retrospective to the departed soul may be found throughout the after-death messages. In that sense the 'Odilie walk' may be seen as a 'triggering' event.

The connection of Helmuth von Moltke and his wife with Rudolf Steiner's individuality and his working in the world was a very close one; therefore it will be very difficult to fully grasp the essence of the messages (especially from 1918 onwards) without also considering Rudolf Steiner's lectures held in parallel with these communications. Most relevant to the year 1918 are the members' cycles of 21 lectures held by Steiner between 22 January and 6 August in Berlin (GA 181); furthermore the public Berlin lectures of that time, given from January to the end of April (GA 67). The lecture of 5 February (GA 181), which was followed by the discarnate soul (see message No. 39), might serve as a starting point for a more thorough study of the after-death messages.

Live in all the forms: Forms of the first Goetheanum. Eliza von Moltke was probably still in Dornach at the time when this message was written down in January 1918.

Rudolf Steiner once referred to the forms of the first Goetheanum as 'forms that can engender the perceiving of karma' (27 April 1924, GA 236); so this effect could obviously also be shared by discarnate souls, at least in so far as these had a relationship to this building via a karmically connected person still on earth. What a loss the destruction of the old Goetheanum on New Year's night 1922/1923 represents from this point of view alone!

Cyrillius and Methodius: The two Slav apostles of the ninth century.

Nicholas had asked them to come to Rome but died before their arrival. 'Whence will the Christian Slavs turn, to Rome or Byzantium? (...) They [Cyrillius and Methodius] did not want the East cut off,' Emil Bock writes (BS, p.359). 'There is ill fate over that time when the Slavs wanted to join up with Rome, and in any case, they then go along with the separated East.'

38. *Birthday greetings written in May 1901:* Not among the letters from Helmuth von Moltke to Eliza von Moltke subsequently published by her.

39. *In the 'forms' of Dornach:* see No. 37.

'El' must be supported: 'El' refers to Eliza and Helmuth von Moltke's third child, Else, who was born in 1885.

It has a warming effect on me that 'she' now has 'it' with her again: 'It' refers to Eliza and Helmuth von Moltke's second child Astrid (later Countess Astrid Bethusy), who was born on 6 March 1882. This daughter was very important to the spiritual development of both parents. From early childhood she had a deep connection with the spiritual world. Rudolf Steiner devoted several meditation verses to her which are now contained in *Wahrspruchworte* (GA 40). These are: 'Freuden nehme man...' of 14 June 1905; 'Wer stets zum Geiste strebt...' of 15 May 1906; 'Der eigenen Seele Geheimnisse...' of 25 July 1915.

This has to do with the fact that 'it' was also an intermediary to the spiritual world for my soul: Astrid Bethusy had numerous spiritual experiences in her youth, about which she writes: 'When I had recovered (...) from a severe attack of unconsciousness which left me sick for a long time after and during which I experienced a most intimate connection with the spritual world (...) my mother, too, who accompanied me throughout, found a new bridge to the realms she was seeking for, and finally (...) her way to Rudolf Steiner in whom she instantly recognized the great initiate. I followed her soon after.' These incisive experiences took place around the turn of the century. *Lecture on Tuesday:* This refers to a lecture Rudolf Steiner gave on 5 February 1918, with the title 'The Dead and the Living', as part of a cycle of lectures in Berlin. (See *Erdensterben und Weltenleben*, GA 181). This lecture contains several motifs which appear to be echoing in subsequent messages:

1. The motif of 'dreaming or sleeping through' the 'real impulses' of historical evolution, as experienced by the ordinary, uninitiated consciousness.

2. The hint at the Vienna cycle of lectures *Inneres Wesen des Menschen zwischen Tod und neuer Geburt* from the year 1924 (GA 153).

3. A brief characterization of the Council of Constantinople of 869, at

which the spirit was 'abolished'. The discarnate Moltke individuality must have connected itself strongly with the motifs of this lecture, which is not only suggested by the formulation 'the lecture (...) came to me almost in its entirety', but also by: 'I could already read the contents of the lecture beforehand, as if they had been written in the Akashic Record (...)'

Lecture cycle on the Folk Souls: This refers to the cycle *Die Mission einzelner Volksseelen im Zusammenhang mit der nordisch-germanischen Mythologie*, held in Oslo between 7 and 17 June 1910. Rudolf Steiner wrote or dated a preface to the new edition of this cycle *on the same day* that he noted down this after-death message (8 February 1918). He sent the former to Max von Baden (1866–1929). On his return from Dornach to Berlin in January 1918 Steiner had conducted his first talk with the prince who was to become the last Imperial German Chancellor. Although the latter was open to the idea of the threefold social order and national psychology, he did not give expression to that in his inaugural address in October—the last opportunity for the official Germany to put up an alternative to Wilson's Fourteen Points (KD, p.18ff). Exceptionally, Rudolf Steiner's disappointment was almost beyond measure. Now 'the German military capitulation had been followed by a capitulation of the spirit, the capitulation before Wilson's utopia (...) through that individual (...) in whom the German people had invested something of their last hopes in that destiny-laden time' (31 May 1919, GA 330). 'Never again did I witness Rudolf Steiner more deeply shattered than on the occasion of this terrible disappointment, which to him marked the beginning of the German people's path of decline and suffering,' Hans Kühn said (KD, p.20). In this context the last sentence of message No. 39 is especially interesting: 'In its present form it [the cycle on the Folk Souls] can only be understood by very few.'

41. *The bora which (...) took hold of the ship:* This is obviously a reference to an event during a Dalmatian trip in 1914 which Eliza von Moltke would have known about but is not mentioned in the published letters.

Now the matter of L. is coming up: It is not entirely clear what is meant by this 'matter'. It appears to be related to happenings during the first weeks of war in the year 1914—a period already referred to at the beginning of this message. L. might mean Lehmann=Kaiser, in which case this would refer to his conduct on 1 August as well as during the period leading to Moltke's dismissal on 14 September. However, it might refer—and this is more likely—to General Moritz Freiherr von Lyncker (1853–1932), head of the Military Cabinet. This institution was independent of the War Ministry and the General Staff, and von Lyncker was responsible for postings, promotions and awarding of honours. His influence over Wilhelm II was considerable and within the 'political clique around the Kaiser' he was a leading figure. Von Lyncker communicated to von Moltke on 14 September 1914 that the Kaiser requested von Moltke to resign on the grounds of sickness 'as General von Falkenhayn was to lead operations now'. 'This cruel blow,' Moltke writes in his draft letter to General von Plessen on 2 May 1915, 'then led to my collapse (...) After this [Antwerpen] had fallen I was deprived of any further opportunity to act and I finally became what General von Lyncker had been wishing for me for a long time, namely, ill.' (Quoted from Jürgen v. Grone, 'Marneschlacht' in *Die Drei*, 1964, No. 5, p. 372.) In July 1918 von Lyncker, who had had a disagreement with Ludendorff, was forced to resign; the public was told that he had to resign 'for health reasons'.

We may not approach the East with purely economic thinking: What follows is a clear differentiation between the true nature of the eastern people and that which is corrupted by western impulses. This corruption has been pursued for centuries along the lines described in the so-called Testament of Peter the Great, and its effects reach up to the present time. See also Ludwig Polzer Hoditz (1869–1945): *Der Kampf gegen den Geist und das Testament Peters des Großen*, Dornach, 2nd ed. 1989. See also Introduction, note 16.

42. *The soul without the spirit:* At the 8th Ecumenical Council of Constantinople in 869 'the spirit was abolished', as Rudolf Steiner expressed it. In formal terms the Council Elders condemned Photius's (appr. 810 to appr. 897) teaching of the soul's duality in the eleventh canon. We owe our knowledge about this Council which changed world history to the protocols of Anastasius Bibliothecarius. See also notes on No. 39. On the subject of the Council of Constantinople, see also: H.H. Schoffler, *Der Kampf um das Menschenbild—Das achte ökumenische Konzil von 869 und seine Folgen*, Dornach 1986; on page 112 there is a reference to Rudolf Steiner's comments pertaining to this Council.

Not before 867: The year in which Pope Nicholas I died.

Natural beauty of the North: See letters of 20 and 23 July 1897 in Part One.

In the pictures of Sicily: Another reference to impressions decribed in letters to Eliza von Moltke; not contained in this volume.

The image of the coast of Dalmatia: The same real-symbolic picture of the swaying ship referred to in message 41.

History is being dreamt through: An expression often used by Rudolf Steiner from the year 1917 onwards to denote that the degree of consciousness usually applied to grasping real historical processes is no higher than ordinary dream consciousness. He added to this characterization that historical processes can only be adequately understood by means of a cognition that arises out of Imagination and Inspiration. See Rudolf Steiner, *Die Ergänzung heutiger Wissenschaften durch Anthroposophie* (GA 73), lecture of 7 November 1917. See also notes No. 39.

43. *Rasputin:* Grigorij Jefimowitsch Rasputin (1872–1916) worked as a faith-healer at the Tsarist Court, providing a counterweight to the influence of the Catholic occultist Papus on Nicholas II. Rasputin was opposed to Russia's general mobilization in summer 1914. He was murdered on 30 December 1916.

Re. Rasputin, see Sergei Prokoffieff, *Die geistigen Quellen Osteuropas und die künftigen Mysterien des heiligen Gral*, Dornach 1989, p. 231; also there Rudolf Steiner's comment on Rasputin, 'that despite all the dubious (...) traits of his personality, the Russian Folk Spirit may now work in Russia through him alone'.

44. *I stood before the Tsar:* Nicholas II Alexandrovich (1868–1919). See Moltke's letter of 2 October 1895 in Part One. The 'picture' mentioned later on was a drawing by Professor Knackfuss commissioned and based on a draft by Wilhelm II who entitled the picture 'Peoples of Europe, guard all that you hold most holy'. See also message 79 of 8 December 1922.

Cycle on the Folk Souls: See note No. 39.

Lectures about death and rebirth: Inneres Wesen des Menschen zwischen Tod und neuer Geburt, GA 153. This cycle of lectures was explicitly referred to by Rudolf Steiner in the lecture of 5 February 1918 which Helmuth von Moltke perceived. Hence the individuality most probably had *this* cycle in mind, and not the Berlin cycle of 1912/13 (GA 141) although this cycle, too, might have been known to the surviving family. See also notes No. 39.

Michael forces: First mention of the Being of Michael.

46. *Now the name and the words of the 'old man' have been uttered to the German people:* This has to be viewed together with the reference to the 'old man' in message 76 ('Sometimes he gets right through to people on earth'). What is expressed in these references is born out by what Rudolf Steiner himself said to two different people. Friedrich Rittelmeyer (1872–1938) writes in his book *Meine Lebensbegegnung mit Rudolf Steiner*, Stuttgart 1983: 'A singularly interesting experience during those months shall be recorded here for historical reasons. It was at midsummer, 1917. Kühlmann had resigned. So Dr Steiner started out one day: "You are always keen on knowing things that are confirmed afterwards. Now I will tell you something. I have dis-

covered that Moltke (not the Chief of the General Staff, but his uncle, the Field Marshal) is trying to work for peace from the spiritual world. And now read Kühlmann's speech. Again and again he quotes the old Moltke. The others—I will not mention names—went to Kühlmann afterwards and reproached him for having broken his agreement. Kühlmann told them that he did not know himself what made him do such a thing." And then Dr Steiner gave a poignant description of Kühlmann's bodily condition that particular morning which resulted in a somewhat lowered consciousness. This made him particularly susceptible to supersensible influences, and they flowed into him under the most unfortunate conditions.'

In summer 1917 Richard von Kühlmann (1873–1948), through Otto Count Lerchenfeld, came into possession of a memorandum by Rudolf Steiner which was intended for German government circles and dealt with the need for a new social order in terms of the threefold principle (GA 24). In August of the same year Kühlmann was appointed State Secretary of the Foreign Office. Around that time he had a personal conversation with Rudolf Steiner during which the latter said to him: 'You have a choice, either you follow the voice of reason now and pay attention to what is called for in humanity's development, or you prepare for revolution and cataclysms' (LC, p.386). In 1918 Kühlmann made peace treaties with the Soviets in Brest-Litovsk (5 March) and the Romanians in Bucharest (7 May) without making use of the ideas known to him, which was a great disappointment to Rudolf Steiner. Rittelmeyer's report is not quite accurate with regard to the date stated. His conversation with Rudolf Steiner must have taken place in summer 1918 (not 1917), after Kühlmann's resignation in August 1918. This is also indicated by the remarks of the *second* crown witness to this symptomatic occurrence that forms such a vital clue to understanding the older Moltke's after-death development. Hans Kühn describes the event in the annexe of his book on the threefold social order like this: 'After Moltke's death Rudolf Steiner had tried to keep in touch with him. He once talked about how Moltke's soul tried to influence the Foreign Minister von Kühlmann when he was expected to make clear the war aims of the German Reich in an important foreign policy speech before the Reichstag. Instead he delivered what was practically a peace address which was so badly received that he was then forced to resign. It was a speech before the Reichstag during which it was inferred that the war could not be won by military means alone, without any diplomatic efforts.' (KD, p.363.) Kühn obviously took the view that it was the younger Moltke who influenced Kühlmann, whereas it was in fact the older Moltke.

47. *In the ninth century 'she' is by my side:* Eliza von Moltke made the ensuing passage of this message available to W.J. Stein for his Grail book (SG, following p.388).

    Marcher's soul: Friend from Eliza von Moltke's youth; he owned estates in Sweden.

48. *Odilie's stream:* First mention of 'Odilie' by name in these after-death messages. Further important remarks about Odilie are contained in messages 36, 71 and 82.

    'Dream in Ragaz': The actual dream is not referred to in the published letters from Moltke's earthly life. One can glean how the individuality living in its spirit form is developing an organ, as it were, for the real-symbolic content of images experienced on earth; here these are images from a dream.

50. *The thought structure of the world's spiritual evolution:* Refers to the letter of 1 November 1877 in Part One. See also note No. 51.

    Whether people's superficiality was not deeply unsatisfying. See letter of 28 November 1877, in which Helmuth von Moltke addresses a question of this nature.

51. *1 November 1877: Germ of anthroposophical thinking:* On 1 November 1877 Helmuth von Moltke wrote a significant letter to his bride and future wife (see Part One). She probably provided Rudolf Steiner with excerpts of this letter in 1918 (it was first published in 1922) and this note must be based on those. 'I have often thought that a human spirit's thoughts are a model of how he will later develop,' Moltke begins his profound thoughts about life after death and he closes with this exclamation: 'We sleep a lot down here on earth already without needing to get down to it properly after death!'

    Moltke's earlier letter to his bride of 10 August 1877 which Rudolf Steiner considered to be the 'announcement' of the anthroposophical 'germ' was not published by Eliza von Moltke. See note No. 50.

52. This letter is final in several respects. It was written immediately before Rudolf Steiner's departure for Dornach where he was to remain until 20 April 1920. It also shows Rudolf Steiner's satisfaction 'that the cycle of time devoted to reading the letters [to the discarnate soul] could be drawn to a close' and gives expression to his hope that it would be followed 'by a momentous development' on the part of the discarnate individuality. It was written, after all, exactly 14 years to the day after that first letter which the spiritual teacher had written to Eliza von Moltke on 12 August 1904: two seven-year cycles of spiritual schooling thus came to a conclusion; in an unusually specific manner they served the elaboration of spiritual methods of living and working together between incarnate and discarnate individualities; at the same time a cycle of Eliza von Moltke's spiritual pupilship is completed.

The events she experienced and the knowledge she acquired enter into a kind of *pralaya* state—in order that she, too, may bring forth and develop something new in the third seven-year cycle. Also, the sensible/supersensible presence of the two Moltkes during Rudolf Steiner's lectures is interrupted for a while now. As we learn from message No. 53 of 30 August 1918, which was conveyed by Helene Röchling: 'At present I am not to share in other endeavours of spiritual science on earth but solely in what "she" is involved in.' Of course this would not hinder the discarnate soul from participating in spiritual-scientific work conducted by Eliza von Moltke alone or within her circle.

54. *End of the seventies:* In 1877 Helmuth von Moltke and Eliza Countess Huitfeld became engaged, and in 1878 they were married.

55. *A new order without the spirit:* On 3/4 October the German government had submitted to the American President Woodrow Wilson a ceasefire proposal which was based on his Fourteen Points. On 3 October 1918 the German Chancellor of the Reich, Max von Baden, had failed to use the last possible chance of proposing, in his inaugural address, a plan for the reconstruction of the country which incorporated the dimension of the spirit. See also notes No. 39.

57. *Germany is to blame for this world war:* This is the first of several messages in which the question of Germany's war-guilt is raised in different ways. On 18 January 1919 the so-called Peace Conference was opened in Paris. The date of its opening alone shows that from the outset this peace was to be directed *against* Germany: on 18 January 1871 the German Reich had been proclaimed in the Hall of Mirrors of Versailles. In the Hall of Mirrors of Versailles the German Delegation was to acknowledge the sole guilt paragraph 231 by signing the appropriate document on 28 June (the commemorative day of the Austrian heir apparent Franz Ferdinand's murder which had triggered the outbreak of war). However, what are the victors gaining, in spiritual terms, from this 'peaceful' act?
Central Europe has betrayed the spirit (...) Western Europe and America will experience through their victories what Central Europe is experiencing through its defeats, is conveyed in the message before 27 January 1919 (No. 58). In the terms of this message, Germany-Austria's only guilt to speak of would consist in this betrayal of the spirit.
Bismarck: Otto Fürst von (1815–98), German Chancellor of the Reich from 1871–90.

58. *The sons:* Wilhelm and Adam.
The German Folk Spirit has not failed: It is instructive to consider the views of the discarnate soul about the Folk Spirit conveyed in this

message in context with those contained in 29, 31 and 33, for example. The soul's perception of the Folk Spirit is deepened and expanded over time—a clear indication of the *evolving* nature of certain recurrent 'after-death motifs'.

60. *So Ahriman achieved for once what he was after:* See the Dornach lecture of 6 April 1919 (GA 190). On this occasion Rudolf Steiner speaks about an incisive experience of a person whose name he does not mention, but who was Wilhelm II: 'And so there was until a short time ago a personality who was considered a very leading personality—although he did not lead a great deal—a highly esteemed personality (...) This personality was once incarnated in the ninth century (...) and was in this ninth century a kind of black magician, in a more southern region of Europe. This worked into the present incarnation of this person in such a way that, when this decision was taken, this decisive event, the body was left by the soul which had incarnated into that body. However, the person carried on living, in an outer sense; he continued to exist in spite of that. Now imagine what an opportunity this would have offered for all sorts of ahrimanic spirits and individualities to live on in a human being who had thus died! (...) It will not be possible to judge the so-called background of this world war in the usual terms of history-making, because everywhere windows were opened for ahrimanic beings who were entering in. And because the most dubious and peculiar kind of spiritual causes played into the events of July 1914 it will not be possible to speak about that which led to this world war catastrophe without taking spiritual factors into account.' The 'important decision' in the life of Wilhelm II is doubtlessly connected with the happenings at the outbreak of war, especially the events on 1 August. However, in the context of the psycho-pathological genesis of this personality who 'died' in 1914, it is also worth considering the *Daily Telegraph* affair six years previously—an interview with this English newspaper in which the Kaiser made himself out to be a great friend of England and lost credibility all over Germany. See the chapter 'Rudolf Steiner über Wilhelm II' in Karl Heyer, *Aus meinem Leben*, Basel, 1990, p.113 ff.

People will have to believe: First reference to the Etheric Christ.

61. *Black magic in Rome:* See lecture of 6 April 1919 (GA 190) and notes No. 60.

Falkenhayn was the tempter of the Kaiser as early as 856: As official Minister of War, Erich von Falkenhayn (1861–1922) also became Moltke's successor. Moltke had formally covered operations with his name between 14 September, the day of his demotion, until 3 November—an experience to which he later referred as 'martyrdom'.

Falkenhayn was soon to initiate exactly that which Moltke, who pursued the strategy of a movement war, had tried to prevent at all events: the protracted war of position at entrenched fronts.

'For my wife only': At the end of Moltke's 'Reflections and Memories' from 1914 (see Part One) he wrote: 'They [these records] are intended for my wife only and must never become known to the public.'

It was probably this after-death message which caused Rudolf Steiner, in a letter sent two days later, to ask Eliza von Moltke for a copy of the records referred to (No. 62). This put in motion all that led to the intended publication of the pamphlet *Die 'Schuld' am Kriege—Betrachtungen und Erinnerungen des Generalstabschefs H.v. Moltke über die Vorgänge vom Juli 1914 bis November 1914* (see page 93 ff). The publication of this was, however, prevented at the eleventh hour. A symptomatically significant example of how it can be necessary, against the background of spiritual cognition and with regard to the actual progress of events in the world, to disregard a discarnate individuality's earlier request in order to be able to act in accordance with that individuality's remit. The plan to publish Helmuth von Moltke's memoirs, in addition to founding the Waldorf school and publishing an appeal to the German people, was already conceived during a Dornach meeting between Rudolf Steiner, Emil Molt (1876–1936), Hans Kühn (1889–1979) and Roman Boos (1889–1952) on 27 January 1919. This was considered to be a 'necessary account of the causes of war with a view to the impending peace negotiations'.

However, at that time Rudolf Steiner was still obliged to emphasize that 'it is not certain, whether she [Frau von Moltke] will give her agreement. The records are appended with an instruction that they were written for Frau von Moltke only. But I can speak about nearly everything, because Moltke has told me personally' (NSN, No. 24/25, p.21f).

Schlieffen was a great strategist: Alfred Count von Schlieffen (1833–1923) was Moltke's predecessor and held the post of Chief of the General Staff from 1891 to 1 January 1906. Shortly before he stepped down he submitted, for the event of a war, a written campaign plan. In 1905—Russia had just lost the war against Japan—Schlieffen did not yet envisage a simultaneous war on two fronts and conveived the plan of an indirect offensive advance against France that was to bring about a quick decision in the West. Leaving out the French fortified belt the troops were to march through Belgium (and southern Holland) into France in order to then take France from the rear by means of a very strong right wing of the army. This was conditional upon violating Belgian (and Dutch) neutrality which, as Schlieffen knew, might call England to the scene. After Schlieffen's retirement the political landscape changed fast: due to enormous financial help from France, Russia recovered quickly and reorganized its army. Moltke had to modify the plan; having first considered an offensive in the East, he increased the number of troop formations in the East to attain immunity against the newly strengthened Russia. Furthermore he abandoned the plan of also passing through southern Holland with part of the army and planned the surprise coup on Lüttich according to which the most important railway lines leading to France were to be occupied without violating Dutch neutrality.

With regard to the Schlieffen plan and its modification by Moltke see: Jürgen von Grone, *Die Marneschlacht*, Stuttgart 1934; also Walter Görlitz, *Kleine Geschichte des Generalstabs*, 2nd ed., Berlin 1977. See also Steiner's indications in the interview with Jules Sauerwein for *Le Matin* (page 121). The coup on the fortress of Lüttich, which was decisive for the course of the war in the West, was carried out by Ludendorff in an abnormal state of consciousness. See with regard to this Gundhild Kacer, 'Zu einer Äußerung Rudolf Steiners über General Ludendorff', *Mitteilungen aus der anthroposophischen Arbeit in Deutschland*, No. 144, Johanni 1983.

Peoples of Europe, guard what you hold most holy: See notes 44 (message of 24 May 1918).

'There will also be setbacks': Possibly something Eliza von Moltke had said to Helmuth von Moltke.

Bethmann: Theodor von Bethmann Hollweg (1856–1921), Chancellor of the Reich from 1909–17.

Jagow: Gottfried von Jagow (1863–1935), occupied the post of permanent Secretary in the German Foreign Office from 1913–16.

Pourtalès: Friedrich Pourtalès, German Ambassador in Petersburg.

62. *Copy of the notes:* Refers to Moltke's 'Reflections and Memories' (page 101) which were now to be published with a foreword by Rudolf Steiner by the 'Bund der Dreigliederung des sozialen Organismus'.

And we may be certain of the dear soul's agreement: See notes No. 61.

Die Kernpunkte der sozialen Frage: Rudolf Steiner's fundamental work on the Threefold Social Order from 1919 (GA 23).

The horrors of Munich: Due to violent clashes between members of the *Räterepublik* and Noske troops in Munich, a State of Emergency had been declared on 2 May.

To the Minister of Labour here: Ferdinand Lindemann.

The present preliminary peace: On 7 May the peace conditions of the *Entente* were submitted to the German delegation.

When you (…) wanted to authorize H.: According to Jürgen von Grone this refers to Colonel Hans von Haeften (1870–1937), Head of the Foreign Affairs Department in Berlin. He was probably introduced to

Rudolf Steiner by Eliza von Moltke in June or July 1916. At the end of 1914 he was allocated to Helmuth von Moltke and entrusted with heading the War Intelligence Service East in Posen. In January 1915 he undertook an intervention with the Kaiser with the aim of bringing about Falkenhayn's substitution with Helmuth von Moltke (which also accorded with the wishes of Ludendorff and Hindenburg) as well as supporting Hindenburg's request to release all available forces to the East. The Kaiser totally refused to reinstate Moltke and threatened to bring von Haeften before the War Tribunal. From 1916 von Haeften was military adviser to the German Foreign Office.

Von Grone writes as follows about the initiative in question: 'After the Battle of Verdun and the subsequent Battle of the Somme, in spring and summer 1916, a military stalemate was reached on the Western Front. None of the opponents had managed to achieve military superiority. In addition, the USA had not yet entered the war (...) In autumn 1916, some months after Moltke's death, the government envisaged establishing a central intelligence service in Zürich which was to inform the world public about the war and peace aims of the Central Powers. In one official quarter it was planned to approach Rudolf Steiner with the request to head this institution. The Chief of the General Staff von Moltke in his later position as Chief of the Acting General Staff had been allocated Colonel-in-Chief von Haeften. He had official contact with the army's leadership as well as with the government. This personality enjoyed von Moltke's absolute confidence, as is borne out by these memorable words which Haeften addressed to his superior one year after the outbreak of war: "In a few days' time it will be a year ago that the war broke out and along with it— so one may say with inside knowledge—the time of suffering for Your Excellency. After all it is since that crisis on 1 August that the relationship of trust between the Supreme Commander and his Chief of the General Staff, which was the prerequisite to any successful working together in war, has been shattered." It can be assumed that it is this personality who supported the idea of offering Rudolf Steiner the post in the institution referred to.' (*Rudolf Steiner und Helmuth von Moltke—authentische Aussagen*, private printing, Stuttgart 1972, p.16.)

Christoph Lindenberg states in his *Chronik*: 'In those days von Haeften was preparing the establishment of the "Military Office" within the German Foreign Office. Rudolf Steiner must have discussed with him Germany's fateful self-representation in connection with the war aims debate. He considers that a different kind of spiritual representation of German policy to the outside world is necessary.' (LC, p.373.)

Rudolf Steiner in turn speaks about this initiative on 2 January

1921 in Stuttgart (GA 338) as follows: 'You see, I have, after all, against the background of the threefold social order, managed to bring it about during the so-called world war, that someone [Colonel-in-Chief von Haeften] undertook extraordinary efforts to establish a proper intelligence service in Zürich during the world war. I succeeded in making clear to someone that nothing at all can be achieved with the old system of news proliferation. The matter had progressed so far that I was told (...) that the prospects were good for me to go to Zürich in the next few days in order to establish the intelligence service there. On the next day this was cancelled by headquarters (...) with the information that, after all, so many people in Germany were waiting for such a post that one could not choose an Austrian to occupy it.'

However, as early as 27 January 1919, on the very day Helene von Röchling wrote down an after-death message which touched on the question of guilt for this war (No. 58), Rudolf Steiner had commented on this refusal at a meeting in Dornach: 'In 1916 I said to Ludendorff's right-hand man [Hans von Haeften] that he should make it possible to speak up for the official Germany in Switzerland. This was ruined at the last minute *by Ludendorff* on account of the fact that I am not a national of the German Reich.' (NSN, No. 24/25, p.13.) He also briefly referred to this aborted initiative during a public evening lecture at the Gustav-Siegle-Haus in Berlin (GA 330) on 3 May itself, the day he wrote down an after-death message for Eliza von Moltke which accompanied his letter to her (No. 63).

This act of preventing the establishment of a free intelligence service in Zürich can be viewed as something of a fatal prelude to the even more fatal prevention of the publication of the Moltke memoirs which was to unfold in the ensuing days. Both initiatives were primarily designed to save Germany from becoming a helpless victim of the *Entente's* 'peace-war policy' on the pretext of Germany's alleged sole guilt for the war. (With regard to the 'war-guilt' question in connection with von Moltke, see also Rudolf Steiner's Stuttgart lecture of 21 March 1921 which he held in the presence of Eliza von Moltke (GA 174b); also Hellmut Blume's comments in NSN, No. 13). *Herr v. Moltke, your nephew:* This refers to Adolf von Moltke, a nephew of Helmuth von Moltke, who was a Prussian attaché in Stuttgart at that time. Adolf von Moltke's mother, Julie v. Moltke, was the wife of Fritz von Moltke who was head of the family after Helmuth von Moltke's death.

64. *Harden's article:* Maximilian Harden (1861–1927), writer and journalist, was the editor of the weekly *Die Zukunft*. He was opposed to the Kaiser.

The second appeal: This does not refer to the 'Appeal to the German People and the Civilized World' of February 1919 (in GA 24) but to the appeal 'To the German People and the German Government' which was sent out by Hans Kühn, the Managing Director of the 'Bund für Dreigliederung' together with the announcement of the Moltke pamphlet. *This* appeal essentially calls for a truthful representation of the causes of the war in order to create a proper foundation for the war guilt discussion. (NSN, No. 27/28, p.25f.; also KD, p.196.) The version used here corresponds with Helene Röchling's protocol which she sent to Eliza v. Moltke; this was changed in some places by Hans Kühn before he sent it out.

66. *The brochure is due to be published in the next few days:* On 27 May Emil Molt (LC, page 411) who 'was involved with preparatory work for the submission of the brochure in Versailles' (KD, p.62) picked up a few copies from the printer. 'However, instead of taking the first copy to Rudolf Steiner the person concerned, bursting with enthusiasm, took it straight to the Prussian Embassy, where a nephew of Helmuth von Moltke, Hans Adolf von Moltke, held the post of attaché. He objected that Eliza von Moltke was not entitled to authorize the publication of such a Memorandum without the agreement of his father, the head of the family. In addition, he felt obliged to submit the Memorandum to the Foreign Office, which immediately contacted Eliza von Moltke' (KD, p.62). Hans Kühn as chief witness of these events continues: 'But the General Staff also became involved. The Memorandum was confiscated by the head of the family, Fritz von Moltke.'

On 29 May General Wilhelm von Dommes (1867–1959) paid a visit to Eliza von Moltke and put pressure on her with 'his own reservations and the reservations of the General Staff and the Foreign Office' as Frau von Moltke, herself now in a state of deepest uncertainty, wrote to Rudolf Steiner on 30 May. (NSN, No. 26/27, p.29f.) For a short while she is in doubt as to whether the plan to publish the Memorandum had really been made with the interests of the deceased in mind! In the midst of this world-historical 'suppression tragedy' we are witnessing the highly individual soul drama of one of Rudolf Steiner's esoteric pupils! 'Now it is necessary to stand firm whatever may come to pass,' Rudolf Steiner had written to Eliza von Moltke on 28 May as a communication from the 'soul'. Now—two days later—she is faced with a most severe and unexpected trial in connection with this matter... With Eliza von Moltke's help von Dommes then initiates a meeting with Rudolf Steiner in Stuttgart on 1 June and claims in the course of several hours of conversation that Moltke's notes contain three factual errors and could not be published for that reason.

'Rudolf Steiner is unable to refute the General's false assertions which refer to the German war strategy and its development. So the brochure is withdrawn and pulped.' (LC, p.412.)

It was this intervention by General Dommes, who agreed to testify on oath to the falsity of the three points (see NSN, No. 27/28, p.31f), which persuaded Rudolf Steiner to resign himself to the withdrawal of the publication. For further details see Steiner's letter to Eliza v. Moltke of 6 August (No. 67). 'The deeper reason for the confiscation,' Hans Kühn writes, 'was none other than the fact that the Moltke family and the high-ranking officers found it unbearable that the Kaiser who was then living in exile in Holland should be exposed in all his weakness in this memorandum. Therefore its very much more important purpose was thwarted—that of saving the German people from the accusation of sole guilt for the war.'

One important detail for the symptomatological research of history aptly illustrates the world-historical dimension of this 'deed of suppression': the Moltke family, who had agreed to pay for the printing costs of the pulped material, received the invoice for this, made out by the Goetheanum Trust Company in Stuttgart, on the very day that the so-called Peace Treaty was signed in Versailles—on 28 June 1918. See also notes 55–59 to Part One.

(...) for which I have severely reprimanded the Managing Director...: Fifty years after this event Hans Kühn commented on it as follows: 'In my capacity as Managing Director I was acutely aware of the importance of the Moltke brochure and knew how important its publication was to Rudolf Steiner—he accompanied me personally to the printer, Greiner u. Pfeiffer, in order to select the typeface for it—hence I considered it my absolute duty to take the first copies released by the printer to him myself. I had no idea whatsoever that one (or even several) copies had already been collected the day before. Initially, Dr Steiner held me personally responsible for this mishap until it became clear what had really happened. He was incensed. (NSN, No. 27/28, p.27.) See also previous reference. For the rest of his life Kühn had to live with the inner picture of this world-historical mishap for which he was severely reprimanded on 28 May 1919 and for which he felt partly responsible in spite of the fact that he had not caused it directly. In view of the catastrophic consequences, Rudolf Steiner's strong reaction to the 'mishap' must have affected him deeply. From the symptomatological point of view it is interesting that his earthly existence ended on 28 May 1979.

67. The tender earthly-spiritual communication between the Moltke soul and Rudolf Steiner was about to culminate in an important historical

deed; this was made impossible all of a sudden by General von Dommes' destructive intervention.

Three points in the notes: See Jürgen von Grone's comments in Part One, chapter 5 (iv) of this publication.

There is no indication that the soul does not wish for the publication to go ahead: See notes 66 referring to Eliza von Moltke's sudden (and understandable) doubts in relation to this question.

Ludendorff's words: Could not be found.

68. *Koennecke:* First husband of Else von Moltke.

69. *With young Herr Bartsch:* Hellmuth Bartsch (1898–1982) took part in the agricultural course at Koberwitz in 1924 and later managed the farm at the country estate Marienhöhe near Bad Saarow.

70. *'My notes'—they must be known:* It seems remarkable that the soul only becomes aware of the fact that there have been complications in relation to this publication some five months after its suppression. Without any doubt this may be attributed to Rudolf Steiner's spiritual conduct, who took great pains not do do anything that might cause unrest on the other side (see his letter of 6 August 1919, No. 67). On the other hand there are also instances of after-death experiences of Helmuth von Moltke which are related relatively closely in time to certain events and circumstances in the physical world, such as happenings within the family circle or the experiencing of certain lectures of Rudolf Steiner (see for example message 39 of 8 February 1918). This suggests that earthly events for which there is a very strong interest are experienced more or less at the same time or very shortly after, whereas matters that are not of special interest to the soul are experienced with a certain time-lag.

71. *The time when so many Europeans moved to the Orient:* era of the Crusades. See Rudolf Steiner's lecture of 1 October 1922 (GA 216).

The false magician: Wilhelm II.

With the one who took my place: Falkenhayn.

Princes of Andlau: See with regard to this BS, p.361f.

72. *12 September 1914:* On 9 September, due to the dissemination of false information by Lieutenant-Colonel Richard Hentsch (1869–1918), the head of the intelligence department whom Moltke had sent to the Western Front, the retreat of the 2nd and 1st Armies was ordered. Moltke later said about this sudden retreat to which the French referred as the 'miracle of the Marne': 'Two hours of waiting, and the victory would have been ours (...) The French would have already had the order for retreat in their pockets.' (Compare in this context the after-death comment of May 1921, for example (No. 73): 'In Central Europe no forces of sufficient spiritual strength existed which could have used such a victory in the cause of progress.') This partial

retreat of the Western Armies caused Moltke on 11 and 12 September to 'also call back the 3rd, 4th and 5th Armies in order to restore a closed front', as he writes in his 'Reflections and Memories'. See also notes No. 29.

A being which comes from the darkest depths of the earth (...) Cahnheim: Dr Otto Cahnheim was the Imperial Medical Staff Officer of Wilhelm II. Nothing is known about his relations to Moltke.

73. *Digitalis:* Rudolf Steiner appears to have recommended a Digitalis treatment to Helmuth von Moltke.

To use such a victory in the cause of progress: See notes No. 72.

My worst day was 16 May 1916: Exact reference not clear.

Bethmann's soul: Theodor Bethmann died on 2 January 1921.

75. *The thoughts of the 'other':* Probably refers to Else's first husband (Koennecke). See message of 20 September 1919 (No. 68).

What I have written down for 'her': This refers to Moltke's 'Reflections and Memories'. This statement is noteworthy: 'There is nothing in there which could be impugned.' From this remark it is clear that the soul's relationship after-death *vis-à-vis* these 'Reflections and Memories' essentially passes three stages: 1. It affirms their publication (message of 1 May 1919, No. 61); 2. It becomes aware that these statements are impugned (message of 26 October 1920, No. 70); 3. It confirms, after an after-death 'check', their absolute truthfulness (this message).

76. *The truth about my position must be revealed:* In the period between October and December 1921 Rudolf Steiner fought hard for this, for instance in the *Matin* interview with Jules Sauerwein, which was followed by a controversy, during which also Hans von Haeften came out in opposition (GA 24, p.398ff. and Part One, chapter V of this volume).

Simons has made awful mistakes: Walter Simons (1861–1937) was Germany's Foreign Minister from June 1920 to May 1921 and represented Germany in March 1921 in London at the negotiations about the reparation payments imposed on Germany due to the sole guilt paragraph of the 'peace treaty' of Versailles. See also notes No. 78.

There was a man who played a very evil part: Lieutenant-Colonel Richard Hentsch. See also notes on the message of 16 February 1921 (No. 72)—Jürgen von Grone extensively researched Hentsch's role; see his essay 'Das Eingreifen des Abgesandten der Obersten Heeresleitung in die Operationen' (in *Korrespondenz der Anthroposophischen Arbeitsgemeinschaft*, 1 December 1931). Jürgen von Grone writes: 'At the very most the head of the intelligence service would have been expected to *advise* the army leaders in charge. No more than that. He was, however, driven by his own unconscious will to undermine the objectives of the General. He issued wrong instructions in his name and overlooked the reality of the victory when he initiated the ending of the battle. This man, who thus destroyed the first campaign plan, was like another 'ego' that joined up with the General as one of his leading officials and then placed himself in the leading position through his deed which stands unique in the history of war. He became Moltke's *alter ego* which had become an instrument of the guidance of nations from some dark destiny.' Jürgen von Grone, who was probably the man with the greatest knowledge about the exact outer course of this 'greatest battle of recent history', at the same time familiarized himself intimately with the Moltke documents; this enabled him to gain a perspective of the individual karmic background of this battle. He writes: 'The Battle of the Marne is a problem of individualities. Its outcome cannot be attributed, as is often done so lightly, to a weakness in the will of the then Chief of the General Staff. In these leading and significant personalities—the Kaiser, Moltke, Hentsch—and in their mutual relationships destiny was working.'

Sometimes he gets right through to the people on earth: See note 46.

When 'she' was in the regions: this might refer to a visit of Eliza von Moltke in Dornach or Arlesheim.

The spirit of Peter: First mention of St Peter.

77. *He who gave me so much cause for worry:* Wilhelm II.

78. *Rathenau's soul:* Walter Rathenau (1867–1922) was German Foreign Minister from 1 February 1922 until his assassination in June 1922 and negotiated a partial moratorium on the German reparation payments. Rathenau was murdered on 24 June 1922 by two anti-Semitic officers.

   But others are not writing the complete truth in this matter: By the year 1922 memoirs had already been published by Wilhelm II, Ludendorff, Hindenburg, von Kluck and von Hausen, among others.

   When 'she' listens to lectures in the wooden building: In the lecture room of the first Goetheanum.

79. *He has remarried:* Two years after the death of his first wife Wilhelm II married Hermine Prinzessin Schonaich-Carolath on 5 November 1922.

   My memoirs will be published: already in the morning and afternoon of 22 November Rudolf Steiner had held discussions with Eliza von Moltke about the book: Helmuth von Moltke, *Erinnerungen, Briefe, Dokumente 1878–1916*, due to be published by her. She had written a foreword, at the end of which Rudolf Steiner inserted various formulations. This work also contains the 'Reflections and Memories' suppressed in 1919, however without Rudolf Steiner's introduction.

The book was published in the middle of December. (LC, p.499.)

The picture 'Peoples of Europe...': See letter of 2 October 1895 in Part One. See also message of 24 May 1918 (No. 44).

80. It appears that the Moltke individuality shared deeply in the way the book *Erinnerungen, Briefe und Dokumente* was received; a second edition came out in the year of its first publication. The statement 'Hence the enlightenment which this book could have brought about is not happening, unfortunately' indicates that in the eyes of the Moltke soul it could have had a more significant effect in 1923, too.

82. *In the mountains of Alsace and Switzerland:* It is very probable that Eliza von Moltke visited Odilie's Mount in the Vosges during her summer sojourn at Dornach/Arlesheim. The individual karmic connection with the stream of St Odilie is subtly hinted at in this message, as also in the message of 28 July 1918 (No. 48): 'Then the centuries in which materialism spread more and more came over Europe. The spiritual essence of Odilie's stream survived only in a few individuals then. By then "she" was in the realm of the spirit together with my soul.' And in this message: 'Odilie is the name of a light that shone in the darkness from the Vosges mountain towards the German East. What we had to inaugurate in the ninth century in Rome penetrated to that place.'

83. *With the oriental demons:* See in this context Rudolf Steiner's lecture of 15 July 1923 (GA 225).

'Practise Spirit Remembrance...': See the 'Foundation Stone Verse' in: *Die Weihnachtstagung zur Begründung der Allgemeinen Anthroposophischen Gesellschaft,* GA 260.

84. This last surviving record was written down in Koberwitz where Rudolf Steiner was holding the 'Agricultural Course' (GA 327) between 7 and 16 June. After an early-morning address to a group of young people, Rudolf Steiner travelled on to Jena together with Elisabeth Vreede (1879–1943) and Guenther Wachsmuth (1893–1963).

Countess Johanna Keyserlingk (1879–1966) reports that in Koberwitz after-death messages of Helmuth von Moltke were given. 'On the morning of his departure from Koberwitz, Dr Steiner came out from his living room with a request to Carl to pass the letter on to Frau von Moltke' (*Zwölf Tage um Rudolf Steiner,* Stuttgart 1949, p.33). Countess Keyserlingk had first met Rudolf Steiner in the summer of 1918 through Eliza von Moltke; now the Kaiserlingks convey Helmuth von Moltke's last message to Eliza von Moltke. Rudolf Steiner wrote to Eliza von Moltke in the first surviving letter: 'What I experience spiritually is (...) free from any imagination, any deception, any superstition.' And now—in the last message conveyed by Rudolf Steiner—these words resound from 'her' earlier incarnation:

'There can only be certainty where the higher spirits speak'.

Yet there is Conrad: Conrad von Hötzendorf (1852–1925), Head of the Austro-Hungarian General Staff, wrote the five-volume memoir *Aus meiner Dienstzeit 1906–18*, which was published between 1921 and 1925.

English Translations of Works by Rudolf Steiner
(referred to in this book)

GA = Gesamtausgabe, the collected works of Rudolf Steiner in the original German (published by Rudolf Steiner Verlag, Dornach, Switzerland)

RSP = Rudolf Steiner Press, London

AP = Anthroposophic Press, New York

GA

23   *Towards Social Renewal* (RSP, 1977)

24   *The Renewal of the Social Organism* (AP, 1985)

26   *Anthroposophical Leading Thoughts* (RSP, 1973)

30   *Individualism in Philosophy*, (Mercury Press, New York, 1989)

40   Partly translated in English as *Calendar of the Soul* (AP, 1988) and *Prayers for Parents and Children* (RSP, 1995). The verse referred to in the text is in neither of these, but appears in the German edition: *Wahrspruchworte*

52   *The History of Spiritism and The History of Hypnotism and Somnambulism* (AP, 1943)

64   Not translated. German edition: *Aus schicksaltragender Zeit*

67   Not translated. German edition: *Das Ewige in der Menschenseele. Unsterblichkeit und Freiheit*

73   Not translated. German edition: *Die Ergänzung heutiger Wissenschaften durch Anthroposophie*

141   *Between Death and Rebirth* (RSP, 1975)

153   *The Inner Nature of Man and Our Life Between Death and Rebirth* (RSP, 1994)

157   *The Destinies of Individuals and of Nations* (RSP, 1987)

169   *Toward Imagination* (AP, 1990)

173   *The Karma of Untruthfulness*, Vol. 1 (RSP, 1988)

174a   Not translated. German edition: *Mitteleuropa zwischen Ost und West*

174b   Not translated. German edition: *Die geistigen Hintergründe des Ersten Weltkrieges*

176   Lecture of 31 July 1917 published in *The Karma of Materialism* (AP, 1985)

178   Lecture of 18 November 1917 appears in *The Reappearance of Christ in the Etheric* (AP, 1983)

181   *Earthly Death and Cosmic Life* (RSP, 1964)
190   Not translated. German edition: *Vergangenheits- und Zukunft-simpulse im sozialen Geschehen*
192   Not translated. German edition: *Geisteswissenschaftliche Behandlung sozialer und pädagogischer Fragen*
216   *Supersensible Influences in the History of Mankind* (RSP, 1956)
225   Not translated. German edition: *Drei Perspektiven der Anthroposophie*
236   *Karmic Relationships* Vol. II (RSP, 1974)
237   *Karmic Relationships* Vol. III (RSP, 1977)
260   *The Christmas Conference for the Foundation of the General Anthroposophical Society* (AP, 1990)
264   *From the History and Contents of the First Section of the Esoteric School* (AP, 1997)
287   Not translated.
327   *Agriculture* (B.D. Farming & Gardening Assoc. Inc., Kimberton, 1993)
330   Not translated. German edition: *Neugestaltung des sozialen Organismus*
338   Not translated. German edition: *Wie wirkt man für den Impuls der Dreigliederung des sozialen Organismus?*

Index